CLASSISM

This book is the first in-depth analysis of classism and the law.

Why doesn't the law protect class? Why do people often ignore classism as a form of discrimination? Why does legal scholarship sideline class and classism?

Arguing that class and classism have been ignored in much legal analysis, this book presents a new framework for approaching classism as a form of discrimination. Its examination of a much-overlooked topic combines theoretical argument with detailed analysis of the law. While accepting the dangers of using the law to protect against classism, this book suggests that reform in this area is long overdue.

This is a thoughtful, nuanced and important work on a crucial question.

Classism

Discrimination the Law Ignores

Alex Benn

• HART •
OXFORD • LONDON • NEW YORK • NEW DELHI • SYDNEY

HART PUBLISHING
Bloomsbury Publishing Plc
Kemp House, Chawley Park, Cumnor Hill, Oxford, OX2 9PH, UK
1385 Broadway, New York, NY 10018, USA
Bloomsbury Publishing Ireland Limited, 29 Earlsfort Terrace, Dublin 2, D02 AY28, Ireland

HART PUBLISHING, the Hart/Stag logo, BLOOMSBURY and the Diana logo are trademarks of Bloomsbury Publishing Plc

First published in Great Britain 2026

1

A catalogue record for this book is available from the British Library.

A catalogue record for this book is available from the Library of Congress.

Library of Congress Control Number: 2026944583

ISBN: HB: 978-1-50998-664-4
ePDF: 978-1-50998-666-8
ePub: 978-1-50998-665-1

Typeset by Amnet

For product safety related questions contact productsafety@bloomsbury.com

To find out more about our authors and books visit www.hartpublishing.co.uk. Here you will find extracts, author information, details of forthcoming events and the option to sign up for our newsletters.

To Sheila and Mary, who were many things

And to Angela, who still is

Acknowledgments

My thanks go to:

my editors;

Rebecca Durkin for her thoughts on draft chapters, particularly on Marx;

Tilly Nevin and Priya Khaira-Hanks for their comments on draft chapters, incisive as ever;

Meghan Campbell for first giving me the opportunity to write about these issues and for many comments over the years;

Jacob Rowbottom for first offering me the chance to teach;

Andrew Dickinson, Justine Pila and Tom Adams for their guidance, both when I was a student and in the years since;

Jordan Scott for his time discussing the meaning of discrimination;

Clare Hills-Nova for her help in the Bodleian Law Library;

Elizabeth Adams for always finding time to talk and helping me to find the books I needed to write this one;

Alex Kent for teaching me much of what I know;

Roman for many comments and much support, and for keeping the world in view;

my friends, lawyers and all;

my mum for already reading the whole of this book (possibly under emotional duress);

my dad for his support (and his promise that he will, really, read this book); and

my sister for many wise words.

Contents

Table of Cases and Legislation

DOMESTIC CASES

INTERNATIONAL CASES

DOMESTIC LEGISLATION

INTERNATIONAL LEGISLATION

Introduction

IT SEEMS USEFUL to start a book about classism with some examples, concentrating for now on the UK.

A person is refused a job, treated unfairly by the police or denied entry to a place because that person:

- *speaks with an accent or dialect considered to be 'common' or that does not make them sound 'polished';*
- *lives or grew up in an area considered to be 'dodgy' or 'rough';*
- *attended a state school, rather than a school that requires its students to pay fees (or obtain fees-based scholarships);*
- *at one time received state benefit payments;*
- *does not have an aristocratic family;*
- *has a name considered to be 'chavvy' or 'trashy'.*

These examples involve features that we associate with class. Although they refer to specific instances of one person mistreating another, they link to more general issues in a society. The connection between specific instances of mistreatment and broader structural problems is well-recognised in the literature on forms of discrimination, such as racism, and the law. It therefore also seems useful to give another list of examples of bigger issues associated with class, again with a focus on the UK.

Some people:

- *enjoy huge wealth while some people have very little;*
- *benefit from high-quality education while some people have little access to education or receive low-quality education;*
- *expect much better health outcomes because of their region and wealth while some people have no such expectations;*
- *benefit from connections with influential people in positions of power while some people have no such connections;*
- *live in areas typically regarded as 'nice' and 'posh' while some people live in areas derided as 'rough' and 'dodgy';*
- *enjoy culture and entertainment regarded by some as intellectual and valuable, while others enjoy culture and entertainment regarded by some as unworthwhile and 'tacky'.*

Taken together, these two lists should make us think of something beyond *merely* a collection of examples of inequalities or sad realities in the UK today, one list dealing with specific treatment and the other with the broader issues across society. There is more to them. These lists should lead us to describe a form of discrimination. Why, then, does the word 'classism' tend to escape us?

PART I: CLASSISM

In Part I of this book, I explore that question. My main argument is that we should not be afraid of class because it has different meanings or a complicated history. Despite its political and intellectual baggage, for many of us class remains a familiar idea. Class has a distinguished existence in the United Kingdom (implied even in the country's name). Although class has various definitions, it is commonly viewed as a situation in which some people have less power in a society than others because of their place in a hierarchy, typically one based on wealth. Class is also highly developed: its meanings pervade our rules, jobs, tastes, interests, relationships, money and voices. It has helped to define our legal ideas and institutions. Class is something we speak and think about every day, whether or not we realise it. Yet, despite how much it shapes lives, class has not been mentioned so much in the context of discrimination. Gender, race, disability, sexuality, religion, belief: these ideas have featured prominently, while class has often been sidelined. A lot of scholars seem to have ignored class and, importantly, the possibility of classism.

Some people, including scholars, claim that class no longer exists. This claim sometimes seems to be self-serving: to acknowledge class is to concede a problem or an opponent's political standpoint. If class does not exist, it is not an issue that we must confront. Others suggest that class is too vague to do anything with. Still others avoid talking about class at all – at least not in a plain and obvious way. It is not 'classy' to talk about class. Some people, notably certain politicians, have even started to realise that class has been ignored. They now try to use class to guard their own interests.

In response to these points of view, I develop an understanding of classism as a form of discrimination. I do so by concentrating on the UK, since it is the place I know best, while referring to material I find helpful from other countries. Since class has a complex history in life and scholarship, that history deserves attention before class is ready for use in legal analysis. To that end, I consider political and sociological theory. The debates in some fields have been extensive and, frequently, technical. Karl Marx, Max Weber and Pierre Bourdieu appear time and again. I do not try to resolve the debates, but I aim to draw on them to give legal analysis a working knowledge of key issues surrounding class.

Chapter 1 addresses the sense that class has, somehow, gone away. Although this appears to be a single claim, it in fact refers to a range of different processes. Chapter 2 considers approaches to class, with characteristic features of legal analysis in mind. In Chapters 3 and 4, I argue that class has a discriminatory character. I suggest that we need the language and idea of classism, both in general thought and in legal analysis. This is so even if classism blends with other forms of discrimination. Only once we have a deeper understanding of both class and classism, led by examples, should we try to use them in the law. This book is firm about the benefits of that approach: we should know a subject well before we make law about it.

PART II: LAW

This book is also about the law. The law and much of legal scholarship have paid little attention to class and almost none to classism. Although class sometimes appears in work that connects sociological analysis with legal issues, it has been absent from much of the work surrounding discrimination law and other areas of the law. When it does appear, it is wrapped in euphemism. Class, unlike an idea such as race, has tended not to get its own label in legal analysis. 'Socio-economic background' and 'socio-economic status' – these phrases seem to multiply. Yet they are unhelpful. They include too much, make the 'socio-' hollow or subtly remove the '-economic' from other forms of discrimination. Class is left to compete with many ideas under a swelling banner of the 'socio-economic'.

In Part II, then, my focus turns to the law. The discussion becomes more doctrinal. Since the law has overlooked classism, it seems to be a good idea to explore how we might use the law to address classism. Chapters 5, 6 and 7 each take an area of the law – the UK Equality Act 2010, the law concerning hate crime, and administrative law principles – and consider how we might craft protections against classism. Some possibilities are closer to being realised than others. Administrative law could be the most transformative, for example, but finding class a place in it would require a lot of effort and ambition. There is definite potential. The challenge, however, is to keep an eye on the detail while recognising that the law needs more widespread changes. In Chapter 8, I move beyond proposals specific to one area of the law alone and think more generally about what aspects of the current law we might use – or remove – to address classism.

PART III: LIMITS

In a book like this, it could be tempting to find a slogan for a new banner: protect class in law now!

However, excitable exclamation marks aside, a book about classism and the law needs to be realistic about certain big challenges. This is my task in Part III. Chapter 9 addresses one challenge: the possibility that the law, even with my proposed reforms, would do more harm than good. Especially in recent years, the law concerning discrimination has been the subject of criticism and attack from various places. What if legal protections against classism cause more resentment and ridicule towards lower-class people? The law is also vulnerable to misuse and distortion. How might upper-class people use new legal principles about class for their own benefit? Sometimes, the negative consequences are hard to predict. Wealth and connections may do a lot of damage through law that means well. Although classism is a form of discrimination and should be understood as one, we should think carefully about whether the law is an appropriate tool to combat it.

Some limits of the law feature in Chapter 10. From the roles that money has in the law to the way that the law tends to view the world, I consider the parts that the law may not be able to play. To address classism effectively, there may even be scope for breaking the law.

The final picture will be mixed. I will argue that the law does have an important part to play in the struggle against classism. However, to end classism, the law must go through deeper changes alongside many parts of societies. Only bigger transformations will end classism. But we should not give up hope on the law. Without recognising classism and introducing protections against it, the law will remain both incoherent and a contributor to the problem. Even recognising the challenges, the law must be part of the transformations we make. Lawyers – and anyone who wants to end discrimination in all forms – should stop ignoring classism and the law's place in the struggle against it.

Part I

1

Where Did 'Class' Go?

GIVEN THE FOCUS of this book, it might be logical to begin by defining 'class'. I will do that, but not yet. This is not (at least not primarily) because I am trying to be difficult. I started writing about classism as I thought that class had been ignored in discussions of discrimination. In thinking about the topic, I came across the sense that class had, somehow, gone away. This is a sense I want to begin by exploring. To do so, I consider some examples of 'class' – understood, for now, loosely and in different ways – across contexts. The contexts vary: popular culture, party politics, political theory, sociology, legal scholarship. The meaning across those contexts also varies. Class may be simply another word for wealth or employment, for example, or it may refer to a specific sociological model found in the academic literature.

Surveying class at its loosest allows me to focus on the general idea that it has disappeared before I delve into technical debates about definitions. My survey will not be exhaustive or strictly methodological, but it should reveal the backdrop of a more specific issue: why class has often been absent in the law and in legal scholarship.

1. IN GENERAL: THE 'DISAPPEARANCE' OF CLASS

The past tense has become a close friend of class. Terry Nichols Clark laments: 'Once upon a time, class was everything, or so it seemed . . . Arthur Stinchcombe even suggested that class was sociology's only concept.'[1] John Curtice offers his own summary:

> Britain has witnessed a great deal of social change . . . Reflecting these changes, debates about equality are no longer primarily focused on differences between classes, and more often are about how fairly a variety of other groups are being treated, including women, those from a minority ethnic background, and those who identify as LGBTQ+.[2]

[1] TN Clark, 'The Debate over "Are Social Classes Dying?"' in TN Clark and SM Lipset (eds), *The Breakdown of Class Politics: A Debate on Post-Industrial Stratification* (London, Johns Hopkins University Press, 2001) 237.

[2] J Curtice, *British Social Attitudes 40 Overview – Secular or Cyclical? 40 Years of Tracking Public Opinion* (London, National Centre for Social Research, 2023) 4.

If these views are right, we might ask where class went. The assumption underneath that question is misleading, though. In truth, I suggest, class has never *gone* anywhere. It remains an important way in which people think of themselves, others around them and their lives in general. Especially in the UK, class shapes experiences of education, employment, lifestyle, relationships of many kinds, and culture.[3] Some things are 'fancy' and 'posh'. Some are 'rough'.[4] Some are 'common' or, to use a newer euphemism, 'accessible'.[5] Others are even 'classy'.[6] Much of the meaning of these words depends on their associations with class. Not only does this language persist, but research suggests that people still describe themselves in terms of class.[7]

However, we should not ignore the question because of its assumption. The assumption helps to tap into important themes. At least in some contexts, there *is* a reasonable argument to support a claim that the language and ideas of class have faded or all but disappeared.[8] To be clear, there are several claims being made, which are related to each other. I will identify three of these claims and go through them in more detail.

1.1. Three Claims

A. *Class no longer exists.*

The first claim is that class no longer exists.

At the outset, this claim should not be confused with a general hostility to the idea of class or with simplistic declarations that class has *never* existed. Some politicians have promoted that much less nuanced view. For example, when Margaret Thatcher mentions class in her later writing, she does so only to deprecate it as a 'Communist concept' that 'groups people as bundles and sets them against one another'.[9] On this view, class could not be dead because it had never lived. It had always been a left-wing invention. Denying class was plainly in Thatcher's political interests, both in her view of the world and in her belief

[3] See, concentrating on the impact of class in the context of employment, S Friedman and D Laurison, *The Class Ceiling: Why it Pays to Be Privileged* (Bristol, Policy Press, 2019).

[4] See, eg, 'Ten Words that Prove You Aren't Posh', *BBC Radio 4* (undated): www.bbc.co.uk/programmes/articles/3qF356d7d2D6h98CdCWxf8z/ten-words-that-prove-you-arent-posh; O Keens, 'I Will Never Stop Admiring the Ways Posh People Pretend They're Not Posh', *Independent* (3 May 2023): www.independent.co.uk/life-style/fake-posh-accent-celebrities-class-b2330870.html.

[5] One that seems, depending on the context, to hint towards class or disability.

[6] See, eg, A Dean, 'Shake that Class', *Town and Country Magazine* (6 September 2023): www.townandcountrymag.com/society/money-and-power/a1166/classy.

[7] See, eg, D Difford, 'How Do Britons Define Social Class?' (YouGov, 12 December 2024).

[8] UK Equality Act 2010, s 4 (to which this book returns). See also, concerning diversity initiatives in employment contexts, E Jacobs, 'Class Is the Missing Link in Employers' Diversity Drives', *Financial Times UK* (2 June 2025): www.ft.pressreader.com/article/281741275355258.

[9] M Thatcher, 'Don't Undo My Work', *Newsweek* (27 April 1992). For criticism of the dismissal of the existence of class entirely, see generally D Eribon, *Returning to Reims* (M Lucey trans, London, Penguin, 2019) 122–25.

that to acknowledge a problem was to bow to it. But this kind of self-interested denial does a disservice to the more sophisticated arguments that underpin the first claim.

Those arguments fill the academic literature. Some scholars have concluded that class is indeed 'dead'. Jan Pakulski and Malcolm Waters put forward one of the most comprehensive sets of arguments in support of this view. In outline, they argue that class 'no longer exists as a meaningful social entity'.[10] They suggest that societies have changed to the point that it is no longer analytically useful to try to identify patterns or frameworks based on a notion of 'class'.[11] Similarly, Terry Nichols Clark and Seymour Martin Lipset argue that '[c]lass analysis has grown increasingly inadequate in recent decades as traditional hierarchies have declined and new social differences have emerged'. This, in turn, shows 'the decline of social classes and the fragmentation of social stratification'.[12]

Other scholars have criticised the claim that class has somehow died. While they accept that there may have been changes in class arrangements (such as the shrinking of the manual working class),[13] they argue that the evidence supports the conclusion that class remains, even if other forms of inequality have become more pronounced.[14] In response to Pakulski and Waters, Erik Olin Wright argues that changes in the structure of class should not be confused with the assertion that class has 'disappeared' entirely.[15] Change does not necessarily mean disappearance. Wright proposes that we should update traditional Marxist ideas of a broadly two-class division between the bourgeoisie and the proletariat to reflect the changes in societies, at least when analysing the 'mode of production'.[16] To this end, Wright outlines more diverse categories of class and other concepts to address perceived inadequacies, especially the difficulty of fitting 'the middle classes' within Marxist explanations of class structure.[17]

Clark and Lipset reject these attempts to re-formulate class and are optimistic about the progress of 'social mobility'. They observe that the theories of

[10] J Pakulski and M Waters, 'The Reshaping and Dissolution of Social Class in Advanced Society' (1996) 25(5) *Theory and Society* 667. In their later work, Pakulski and Waters warn against oversimplifying their arguments: I deal with their elaborations later in this chapter.

[11] J Pakulski and M Waters, *The Death of Class* (London, Sage, 1995) 3–4.

[12] TN Clark and SM Lipset, 'Are Social Classes Dying?' (1991) 4(6) *International Sociology*, 397–410; reprinted in TN Clark and SM Lipset, *The Breakdown of Class Politics* (London, Johns Hopkins University Press, 2001) 39, 40.

[13] M Hout, C Brooks and J Manza, 'The Persistence of Classes in Post-Industrial Societies' 8(3) *International Sociology* 259–77; reprinted in Clark and Lipset, *The Breakdown of Class Politics* (n 12) 55, 69.

[14] Hout, Brooks and Manza (n 13) 59–60.

[15] EO Wright, *Understanding Class* (London, Verso, 2015) 140.

[16] Rather than at the level of the 'conjunctural political analyses' in Marx, which are much more complex: EO Wright, *Classes* (London, Verso, 2023) 7. For Wright's consideration of some of the societal changes, see his discussion of the role of the state in the expansion of 'middle-class' positions: *Classes* 207.

[17] Wright (n 16) 13. See also Wright's idea of 'contradictory class locations' with 'a multiple class character' (such as managers): 43–45.

class available (at least in the 1990s) lagged behind '[m]ajor social changes'.[18] They note the effect of technology on manual labour and the relative decline of big firms in some industries. They refer to more egalitarian personal relationships and a form of 'social mobility' less reliant on family structure. They also rely on evidence such as changes in the connections between class and voting patterns in a variety of countries between the 1940s and 1980s, as well as significant changes in the organisation of the economy.[19] Like Clark and Lipset, others supporting this claim tend to rely on evidence of voting patterns. Complications in the connections between class and voting patterns have certainly persisted in a number of countries.[20] However, it depends how we draw the lines of class as well as whether we trace political parties or particular topics (such as changes in parties' economic policies).[21]

In general, Clark and Lipset's optimism seems naïve when assessed with the benefit of hindsight. They were writing on this topic in the 1990s. The legacy of the global financial crisis of 2007 to 2009, originating largely from bad credit arrangements, is just one reason to doubt their idea of an increase in some form of merit-based 'social mobility'.[22] In recent years, too, numerous industries have recorded worse rates of lower-class people rising through the hierarchies.[23] Family, meanwhile, is still a big predictor of conventional badges of success, such as the type of employment and income a person obtains.[24] There is also heightened inequality between a small, incredibly rich group and the poorest groups in societies.[25] The claim that class no longer exists seems unconvincing in the face of evidence of such entrenched divisions linked to work, family and wealth.

[18] Clark and Lipset, *The Breakdown of Class Politics* (n 12) 45. Note, though, that Wright's later re-formulations were published much later.

[19] Clark and Lipset, *The Breakdown of Class Politics* (n 12) 45–52.

[20] See, eg, A Marchesi, 'Voting Patterns in Western European Countries (2022) 4 *Frontiers in Political Science* 1.

[21] G Evans, 'Class Voting: From Premature Obituary to Reasoned Appraisal' in G Evans (ed), *The End of Class Politics? Class Voting in Comparative Context* (Oxford, Oxford University Press, 1999) 1, 12; Marchesi (n 20) 2–4.

[22] Social Mobility Commission, *Innovation Generation: Next Steps for Social Mobility* (2024) 31.

[23] See, eg, Rise Associates, *Class Ceiling: A Review of Working Class Participation in the Arts Across Greater Manchester* (January 2026); Creative Industries Policy and Evidence Centre: H Carey and others, *Getting In and Getting On: Class, Participation and Job Quality in the UK Creative Industries* (August 2020); O Brook and others, 'Social Mobility and "Openness" in Creative Occupations since the 1970s' (2022) 57(4) *Sociology* 789.

[24] M Wolf, *The Crisis of Democratic Capitalism* (London, Penguin Random House UK, 2023) 92–93. In the context of a broader and unpersuasive argument about 'the metropolitan elite', M Lind identifies the findings that surnames from William the Conqueror's aristocracy still sit atop the UK's class hierarchy: *The New Class War* (London, Penguin, 2020) 8, citing G Clark and N Cummins, *The Son Also Rises: Surnames and the History of Social Mobility* (Princeton, Princeton University Press, 2014).

[25] See, eg, M Savage, *Social Class in the 21st Century* (London, Pelican, 2015) 52–53; Wolf (n 24) 88–99.

B. Class, though it may exist, is no longer meaningful in the way people understand their lives.

The second claim is, in a sense, a softer version of the first: though class might still exist, it has lost its explanatory and symbolic power in people's perceptions of themselves, those around them and their lives in general.[26]

While earlier generations might have held a firm idea of their own class and their communities, changes in societies have significantly weakened the idea. This claim suggests that class no longer features so much in people's lives and in their language. People no longer use class to identify with, or separate from, others. Rather than concentrating on the more extreme view that class has entirely gone away, Wright summarises the core of Pakulski and Waters's arguments to be that 'class is no longer a powerful or salient explanatory category'.[27] This argument also comes in the slightly later work of Clark and Lipset. Alongside Michael Rempel, they clarify that class 'may not have died' but its 'political significance has declined substantially'.[28]

They point to causes including the rise of the welfare state, increased diversity in what work people do, the rise of local identities in party politics, and apparent increases in general affluence.[29] They also rely on various effects, such as the lack of predictable class-based voting in elections, changes in which political issues get priority (eg the 'social' and not the 'fiscal'), and the prominence of the 'middle class'.[30] While Clark, Lipset and Rempel do not wholly reject class analysis in this revised argument, they conclude that class membership is 'less subjectively salient and less politically influential'.[31]

Although these debates become complex, there is some common ground. Even if they use different definitions of class, all involved accept that it has changed.[32] For example, John Goldthorpe rightly notes that many who suggest the 'decline' of class attack an old Marxist version of class which has had little updating or refinement.[33] Even accepting that definitions vary, the view that class has changed is a sensible one in the light of the evidence.[34] Alongside trends

[26] J Goldthorpe identifies three versions of this proposition in his setting out of three of his 'four different positions' underlying arguments about the 'decline of class', specifically (1) the re-drawing of the main social divisions, (3) the decline of the impact of class on politics due to changes in political action, and (4) a general decline of class itself in determining features of our lives: 'Class and Politics in Advanced Industrial Societies' in Clark and Lipset, *The Breakdown of Class Politics* (n 12) 105, 105–08.

[27] Wright (n 15) 141.

[28] TN Clark, SM Lipset and M Rempel, 'The Declining Political Significance of Social Class' (1993) 8(3) *International Sociology* 293; reprinted in Clark and Lipset, *The Breakdown of Class Politics* (n 12) 77, 78.

[29] Clark, Lipset and Rempel (n 28) 82–90.

[30] Clark, Lipset and Rempel (n 28) 90–100.

[31] Clark, Lipset and Rempel (n 28) 101.

[32] Clark, Lipset and Rempel (n 28) 79.

[33] Goldthorpe (n 26) 112.

[34] See, eg, D Grusky and K Weeden, 'Decomposition without Death: A Research Agenda for a New Class Analysis' (2001) 44(3) *Acta Sociologica* 203.

in scholarship and party politics, broader changes in societies explain why there is a sense that class has faded in significance. The familiar argument is that lower-class communities used to be identifiable by common cultural and political beliefs, types of work, and geographical centres.[35] The easiest image here may be that of a working men's club in an industrial town in Lancashire, with most people working in manual trades and factories. After the increase of people moving elsewhere and general migration, the decline of many forms of traditional manual work, the rise of new and precarious forms of work, wider access to formal education at higher levels, and changes in patterns of support for political parties, 'class' seemed to lose its usefulness as a tool for analysis. Against this background, it is not difficult to understand why arguments such as those of Pakulski and Waters emerged.[36]

However, once more, change does not necessarily mean loss. It may be that changes in societies have brought complexity to class but not actually weakened its power. Wright, for example, uses evidence from the United States, Canada, Sweden and Norway to show that, in fact, there are still divisions between people in terms of property, income and their sense of their own class.[37] In another academic context, in order to reflect changes while retaining the concept of class, Guy Standing proposes a new class, the 'precariat', centred not only on insecure jobs of limited duration and with minimal protection of their labour, but also on those with 'no sense of career, no sense of secure occupational identity and few, if any, entitlements to the state and enterprise benefits' of generations before.[38] Even if markers of class have changed or become more complex, then, these facts alone do not tell us that 'class' itself has lost power.

The UK is a prime example. Although the National Centre for Social Research's report in 2023 found that class had lost priority in 'debates about equality', participants' tendency to describe themselves as working-class or middle-class was much the same as it had been in the 1980s, as was their perception of the difficulty of moving between classes.[39] In addition to the academic studies that support this view and retain the idea of class, there are examples from more general contexts which suggest that class remains an important part of people's perception and expression. Akala, the rapper and writer, relies on a popular idea of class in his book, *Natives: Race & Class in the Ruins of Empire*, which emphasises the lives of lower-class black people in London.[40] In his speech accepting an Emmy award in 2025 for his performance in *Adolescence*,

[35] See also, for discussion of the shrinking of, and divisions within, the modern working class, D Evans, 'Is the Working Class Back?' (2024) *New Socialist*, www.newsocialist.org.uk/is-the-working-class-back.

[36] Pakulski and Waters (n 11).

[37] Wright (n 15) 146–55.

[38] G Standing, *The Precariat: The New Dangerous Class* (London, Bloomsbury, 2011 and 2014) 41, though see criticism of understanding the precariat as a class in Wright (n 15) 157.

[39] Curtice (n 2) 4, 15.

[40] Akala, *Natives: Race & Class in the Ruins of Empire* (London, Two Roads, 2018).

Stephen Graham said, 'This kind of thing doesn't normally happen to a kid like me. I'm just a mixed-race kid from a block of flats in a place called Kirkby.'[41] The criticism 'classist' has also begun to appear when some need to articulate injustice relating to class. In 2022, when the Tory and former Prime Minister, Boris Johnson, mocked Labour's Angela Rayner in Parliament, she called his remarks misogynist and 'steeped in classism'.[42] In 2023, the English singer-songwriter, Raye, used 'Environmental Anxiety' to describe country leaders as 'classist' among other wrongs.[43] While it is difficult to tell if this reflects a consistent pattern or a re-emerging willingness to talk about class more generally, this small selection of examples indicates that class (in its various senses) may not have faded. This may be especially so when combined with the earlier academic research on lingering divisions connected with work, family and wealth. Even if the structures and markers of class have changed, it seems still to be meaningful to many people.[44]

C. *Class exists, but it is less common to hear it discussed expressly.*

Instead of rejecting the existence of class entirely or suggesting that it has lost meaningfulness, as the first and second claims do, the third takes a different approach. This claim accepts that class exists and remains meaningful but suggests that it is less common today to hear class discussed in express terms.

Michael Ignatieff's work offers an example of this perspective. Ignatieff argues that, 'while inequalities of gender, race, and sexual orientation have been made visible in the last forty years, older inequalities of class and income have dropped out of the registers of indignation'.[45] In examples from popular discussion and party politics, there is support for this point of view. Labour's manifesto in 2024 made only one mention of 'class' in the form of a 'class ceiling on the ambition of young people in Britain'.[46] Rather than speaking of 'working-class people', politicians have often chosen to saw off the hyphen and get rid of the middle. The result is an anodyne phrase: 'working people'. This appears to have been the Labour government's approach when announcing its budget in the autumn of 2024. Ministers did contortions to avoid using the word 'class'

[41] S Graham, 'I'm Just a Mixed-Race Kid from Flats in Kirkby', *BBC News* (15 September 2025): www.bbc.co.uk/news/articles/cx2rjgdwweyo.

[42] A Woodcock, 'Angela Rayner: "Basic Instinct" Slur Was not only Sexist but Classist', *Independent* (26 April 2022): www.independent.co.uk/news/uk/politics/angela-rayner-misogyny-sexism-labour-b2065564.html.

[43] Raye, 'Environmental Anxiety' from *My 21st Century Blues* (London, Human Re Sources, 2023). See also, for another example of express discussion of class alongside race by a musician, M Carey, with MA Davis, *The Meaning of Mariah Carey* (London, Macmillan, 2020) 10.

[44] See also, applying Bourdieu's framework of class to black school students in London, D Wallace, 'Reading "Race" in Bourdieu? Examining Black Cultural Capital among Black Caribbean Youth in South London' (2016) 51(5) *Sociology* 907.

[45] M Ignatieff, *The Rights Revolution* (Toronto, Anansi Press, 2000) 92.

[46] Labour Party, *Change: Labour Party Manifesto 2024* 13.

when claiming that 'working people' would not pay more tax as a result of the budget.[47] They tied themselves in knots attempting to define 'working people', a phrase that, on its face, includes billionaires and bankers as easily as bartenders and bus drivers.

Granted, class is not unique in this respect. Euphemisms and misphrasing exist elsewhere. The imprecise acronym of 'BAME people' is one illustration in the context of race, criticised for the way in which it avoids naming black and brown people and for conflating all forms of racism (especially in settings where only some groups in the category of 'BAME' are well-represented).[48] However, ideas like race and racism are found in express terms in various influential contexts. The law is a clear example that will take up much of this book. The UK Equality Act 2010, supposed to be the centrepiece of a modern and egalitarian framework, entirely omits 'class'. Section 4 sets out the 'protected characteristics', which help to determine when it is illegal to discriminate against someone in particular contexts. 'Race', 'sexual orientation', 'sex', 'religion', 'belief', 'disability' and others – these characteristics are all present. Class, by contrast, is absent. Other significant pieces of legislation also omit class, including those providing for hostility-based crimes like the Public Order Act 1986.[49] In popular movements, too, we see Pride marches alongside the Black Lives Matter and 'Me Too' movements without an expressly class-based equivalent.[50] There have been some examples of anti-austerity protests, which address issues relating to class: poverty, the deterioration and reduction of publicly funded services, the targeting of the poorest parts of society, increases in inequality.[51] But they do not emphasise classism as Black Lives Matter emphasises racism or the 'Me Too' movement emphasises misogyny.

The strength of this claim depends, of course, on how we interpret it. One variation is about the meaning of 'expressly'. If 'expressly' includes language broader than 'class' and 'classist', people still discuss class regularly. I have noted that, in the UK, everyday language like 'posh', 'fancy', 'common' and 'rough' habitually describes other people, culture, habits and areas.[52] These are words closely associated with understandings of class; they form the vocabulary of class and classism, even if people do not necessarily speak the word 'class'.

The strength of the claim also depends on where we look when testing it. The picture in scholarship is more mixed than daily language. In the literature

[47] F Masud, 'What Is a "Working Person" according to Labour', *BBC News* (28 October 2024): www.bbc.co.uk/news/articles/cwyg44lwjydo.

[48] See, eg, A Brandon and G Dingwall, *Minority Ethnic Prisons and the COVID-19 Lockdown* (Bristol, Bristol University Press, 2022) 28.

[49] Public Order Act 1986, Pts III and 3A.

[50] Protests about austerity, for example, may emphasise poverty and disability, but they do not usually give the same emphasis to class.

[51] See, eg, P Krugman, 'How the "Unforced Error" of Austerity Wrecked Britain', *The Guardian* (28 June 2025): www.theguardian.com/politics/ng-interactive/2024/jun/28/how-the-unforced-error-of-tory-austerity-wrecked-britain.

[52] nn 4–6 (above).

exploring 'identities', Sherry Ortner notes that class is often missing or truly peripheral.[53] In the context of the law and legal scholarship, class has rarely been discussed in express terms. In other contexts, though, there has continued to be express discussion of class. If you were to research Marxist theory in the last few decades, for example, you would find references to class on almost every page. In certain areas of academia, scholars have never avoided the language of class. It is still a 'master concept' in some areas of study.[54] Erik Olin Wright wrote prolifically about class from the 1970s until his death in 2019. Rosemary Crompton resisted the rising chants of 'class is dead' by spending her career writing about analysis of class, offering insightful overviews of the debates in her *Class and Stratification* series.[55]

In addition to the academic context, there are some indications that express language of 'class' retains a place in public consciousness. There is the example of Angela Rayner, above, in her use of 'classism'. Some people also seem to be more comfortable with the language of the 'middle class'.[56] This is perhaps because the middle class is perceived as less threatening or, even, as hopeful.[57] Tony Blair's government exemplified this pattern when it came to power in 1997, with his deputy, John Prescott, declaring that 'we're all middle-class now'.[58] Later, Eton-educated David Cameron (the child of a London stockbroker) described himself and Samantha Cameron (the child of a baronet) as part of the 'sharp-elbowed middle classes'.[59] Hillary Rodham Clinton was comfortable making 'the middle class' a central part of her campaign in the US election in 2016, but not so much the classes either side of that – unlike her party rival, Bernie Sanders, who spent much of his campaign criticising 'the billionaire class'.[60] There is also comfort in the idea of the middle class as a topic of intrigue or the subject of an opinion piece. Articles about tracking your middle-class

[53] S Ortner, 'Identities: the Hidden Life of Class' (1998) 54(1) *Journal of Anthropological Research* 1.

[54] As quoted above at n 1: 'The Debate over "Are Social Classes Dying?"' in Clark and Lipset, *The Breakdown of Class Politics* 237.

[55] R Crompton, *Class and Stratification* (London, Polity, 2008). See generally for a more recent express analysis of class alongside race, the Runnymede Trust and the Centre for Labour and Social Studies, *We Are Ghosts: Race, Class and Institutional Prejudice* (2019): www.runnymedetrust.org/publications/we-are-ghosts-race-class-and-institutional-prejudice.

[56] See also, on the widely held perception in Alberta, Canada, that most people fall (or at least the average person falls) within the middle class, M Maroto, D Brown and G Durou, 'Is Everyone Really Middle Class? Social Class Position and Identification in Alberta' (2023) 60(3) *Canadian Review of Sociology* 336.

[57] See also the discussion of a 'parochial' idea of class that actually serves to uphold existing institutions, such as the UK's monarchy: T Nairn, *Enchanted Glass* (London, Verso, 2011) 188.

[58] T de Castella, 'The Evolution of the Middle Class', *BBC News* (16 January 2014): www.bbc.co.uk/news/magazine-25744526.

[59] N Cohen, 'The Middle Class Will Get You, Mr Cameron', *The Guardian* (15 August 2010): www.theguardian.com/commentisfree/2010/aug/15/david-cameron-middle-class-wealth.

[60] 'Clinton Links Campaign to Middle Class Fight', *CBS News* (12 June 2015): www.cbsnews.com/texas/news/clinton-links-campaign-to-middle-class-fight.

'status' remain a frequent feature in certain publications.[61] While the analytical value of this language is minimal, it offers a limited exception to the claim that class is rarely discussed in express terms. At least in popular contexts, it seems more accurate to claim that it is less common today to see *some* types of class discussed expressly. The middle class – perhaps because it is perceived as a harmless topic or an optimistic catch-all – is an exception.

Although this third claim is persuasive, it needs careful interpretation. There are contexts in which the language of class remains express, including some academic fields and media pieces. However, there are many contexts in which class is either ignored or, when it appears, it is less express than other ideas relating to inequality and discrimination, such as race and gender.

1.2. Taking Stock

Taking stock of these three claims, we can put ourselves in a better place to assess the supposed death or disappearance of class.

(a) Class – in whichever definition – has changed and may be more complex than it used to be.
(b) Even though it has changed and may be more complex, class still has significant explanatory and symbolic power in people's lives and their societies (as seen in academic research and popular examples). If class is dead, its grave certainly has a high number of visitors.
(c) The extent of the supposed death or disappearance of class depends significantly on the context. In some contexts, such as academic sociology, it continues to be discussed expressly. In other areas, such as party politics, class used to be discussed in express terms more than it is now (with the apparent exception of the middle class). In yet others, such as the law, it is rare to find class discussed expressly at any time.

With these observations in mind, it is incorrect to conclude that class is dead or has lost its importance. Instead, class has often been ignored or euphemised in important contexts. This provides a useful, yet concerning, backdrop. For the rest of this chapter, I turn to the law and legal scholarship in more detail.

2. THE 'DEATH' OF CLASS IN THE LAW AND LEGAL SCHOLARSHIP?

In my discussion so far, I have suggested that the law and legal scholarship have paid little attention to class. The question now is why. It is possible to find the

[61] See, eg, L Craik, 'So long, Aesop hand wash – these are the new middle-class status symbols to know about', *Telegraph* (20 February 2025): www.telegraph.co.uk/family/life/new-middle-class-status-symbols; S Gugliara, 'Revealed: The Enormous Amount of Money You Now Have to Earn to Be Considered Middle Class', *Mail Online* (2 March 2025): www.dailymail.co.uk/news/article-14452671/enormous-money-earn-considered-middle-class.html.

answer by considering two main themes in this area: (i) over-correction in the scholarship surrounding discrimination; and (ii) the role of party politics.[62]

2.1. Over-Correction: Anti-Discrimination Scholarship

There has been no developed analysis of class or classism in the context of the law. While there have been analyses of the law in which class plays an important role (such as Marxist approaches to the law), it has not been subject to the elaboration in legal scholarship and the law that race, gender, sexuality and other issues of discrimination have.[63] This seems to be, in part, a product of the influences on the development of the law and legal scholarship.

At least until the 1980s, class was a leading concept in general sociology when seeking to understand inequality, as I have noted. Crompton describes the development of sociology in Britain from the late 1950s until the 1970s, with intense debate about the meaning and theory of class structure.[64] Different countries have seen varying levels of intensity towards the issue of class. In France, the work of Pierre Bourdieu in the 1970s and 1980s was hugely influential in furthering analysis of class, using concepts including 'capital', 'field' and 'habitus'.[65] In the UK and US, new interpretations and analyses of Bourdieu's work continue to be published.[66] For instance, Derron Wallace uses Bourdieu's idea of 'cultural capital' in an article published in 2016 to explore themes of race and class among black Caribbean young people at a state school in south London.[67] In these areas, as I have argued, it is wrong to say that class has died or disappeared.

Yet, beginning noticeably in the early 1980s, feminist and anti-racist scholars in a variety of areas put forward compelling criticisms of class. They argued that class presumed a white, straight and masculine norm.[68] Class was a concept that tended to exclude people of colour (whether queer or not), white queer people and white straight women.[69] Rather than using a concept wrapped in

[62] I accept that broader changes in societies have added to this lack of attention. However, as I have already discussed them and consider that they are not specific to the issue of the law and legal scholarship, I do not repeat them.

[63] See, eg, Hugh Collins, *Marxism and Law* (Oxford, Oxford University Press, 1984).

[64] Crompton, *Class and Stratification* (n 55) 35–37.

[65] P Bourdieu, *Distinction: A Social Critique of the Judgement of Taste* (Richard Nice trans, Abingdon, Routledge, 2010). See generally M Grenfell (ed), *Pierre Bourdieu: Key Concepts* (Abingdon, Routledge, 2014).

[66] See, eg, Grenfell (n 65); J Thatcher and others (eds), *Bourdieu: the Next Generation* (London, Routledge, 2016).

[67] Wallace (n 44).

[68] See, eg, B Campbell, 'Women: Not What They Bargained For' (1982) *Marxism Today* 20; L Robinson, 'The Bermondsey By-Election and Leftist Attitudes to Homosexuality' in M McCormack (ed), *Public Men: Masculinity and Politics in Modern Britain* (London, Palgrave, 2007) 168.

[69] Robinson (n 68); D Payling, '"Socialist Republic of South Yorkshire": Grassroots Activism and Left-Wing Solidarity in 1980s Sheffield' (2014) 25(4) *Twentieth Century British History* 607.

technical debates and which catered to a limited set of people, scholars sought to focus on race, gender and sexuality. These approaches have sometimes been called, simplistically, 'identity politics'.[70] Despite the label, they are often deeply concerned with systemic issues, hardly deserving the individualistic and inward-looking connotations of that label.[71] Nevertheless, in their various forms, the influence of these scholars' criticisms and change in focus contributed to class losing prominence in analysis.

The emergence of Critical Legal Studies in the US in the late 1970s is probably – for better or worse – one of the more famous developments in the scholarship surrounding the law and discrimination. Although specialisms like Critical Race Theory have been derided (and distorted) by some, the core of this scholarship draws on ideas such as race and racism, understood without essentialising and with some scepticism, in order to offer new and incisive analysis of the law. It was within this intellectual context that Kimberlé Crenshaw published her article on discrimination law and 'intersectional' cases in 1989, though the substance of the idea of intersectionality was present in other scholars' work.[72] There was renewed and sophisticated analysis of race, gender and other 'identities' – but not, on the whole, class. Sherry Ortner makes the point when considering Kwame Appiah and Henry Gates's book, *Identities*, a collection of articles about identities including race, gender, sexuality, nationality and religion. Ortner notes that, apart from a reference to 'class' on page 1 (and then a reference back to the same page in the index), there is no other reference to class in the book.[73] Ortner's example is just one that indicates how stark the absence of class has sometimes been. There is no recognisable 'Critical Class Theory'.

It may be that there were bigger societal factors in this rejection of class as a leading concept, rather than (esoteric) academic criticisms. For instance, Cedric Robinson identifies '[t]he absence of . . . a class consciousness' among black people in the US and 'in its stead the presence of a racial consciousness'.[74] That said, even if there are other causes, it is difficult to deny the role of discrimination studies in the sidelining of class and classism. This observation is especially pressing in the law and legal scholarship. While some academic work has sought to introduce class as a key concept, it has been both recent and limited to a

[70] E Hobsbawm, 'Identity Politics and the Left' (1996) I/217 *New Left Review* 13.

[71] See also, on the appropriation of identity politics by those in power, OO Táíwò, *Elite Capture* (London, Pluto Press, 2022) 32.

[72] See, eg, C Robinson, *Black Marxism* (London, Penguin, 2021) 181, 195; A Lorde, 'Scratching the Surface: Some Notes on Barriers to Women and Loving' in A Lorde (ed), *Sister Outsider* (London, Penguin, 2007) 35, 42; AY Davis, *Gender, Race and Class* (London, Penguin, 2019) 179. See generally Ange-Marie Hancock, *An Intellectual History of Intersectionality* (Oxford, Oxford University Press, 2016), tracing the idea to work including by William Du Bois in the late 1800s.

[73] Ortner (n 53).

[74] Robinson (n 72) 218.

handful of writers.[75] Note the omission of analysis of class as a category like race and gender from major titles on the theory of discrimination (especially those that interact with the law) published in the last 15 years: Deborah Hellman's *When Is Discrimination Wrong*? does not consider classism, nor does Tarunabh Khaitan's *A Theory of Anti-Discrimination Law*, nor Benjamin Eidelson's *Discrimination as Disrespect*, nor Sophia Moreau's *Faces of Inequality*.[76]

As the main aim of these works is to develop an overarching theory of discrimination (and when it should be said to occur), it may be that their focus is elsewhere. Class and classism could slot into their frameworks. That said, they naturally use examples throughout to interrogate the issues. Even in those examples, class and classism do not feature. None of the books proposes classism as a form of discrimination or considers it on the assumption that it is. When there is reference to class, it is either peripheral or a background issue. It may be true that many legal academics overlook the role of classism because those academics have been (or have become) advantaged by class, as Angela Harris suggests in the context of feminist legal theory.[77] Whatever the exact explanation, when scholars have drawn on discrimination theory to inform their analysis of the law, they have done so by considering forms of discrimination apart from one based on class. This has led to marked neglect of both class and classism in theories of discrimination and, particularly, the law relating to it.

At least in the UK, the background to the Equality Act 2010 offers an example of the legislative consequences of this academic inattention, an issue I return to later in this book. As commonly cited, the Cambridge Review by Bob Hepple, Mary Coussey and Tufyal Choudhury is perhaps the academic work that most directly influenced the drafting of the Equality Act. The Labour government favourably received their report, and the report's main supporter, Anthony Lester, introduced a Private Member's Bill in 2003. Yet there is only one reference to 'social classes' in the report's 147 pages.[78] Despite recommending the inclusion of all grounds in a single piece of legislation that brings 'consistency' with the Human Rights Act 1998 and future European Community directives, 'social origin' (which appears in the European Convention on Human Rights and Fundamental Freedoms) and class are omitted.[79] While especially obvious in

[75] D Elson and M Sharples, 'Addressing Intersecting Inequalities through Alternative Economic Strategies' in S Atrey and S Fredman (eds), *Exponential Inequalities* (Oxford, Oxford University Press, 2023) 43–60. See also, for another example of some consideration of class (though euphemised as 'socio-economic status'), Trades Union Congress, 'Building Working Class Power' (2019).

[76] D Hellman, *When Is Discrimination Wrong?* (Cambridge, Massachusetts, Harvard University Press, 2008); T Khaitan, *A Theory of Anti-Discrimination Law* (Oxford, Oxford University Press, 2015); B Eidelson, *Discrimination as Disrespect* (Oxford, Oxford University Press, 2015); S Moreau, *Faces of Inequality: A Theory of Wrongful Discrimination* (Oxford, Oxford University Press, 2020).

[77] A Harris, 'Race and Essentialism in Feminist Legal Theory' (1990) 42(3) *Stanford Law Review* 581, 588–91.

[78] B Hepple, M Coussey and T Choudhury, 'Equality: A New Framework. Report of the Independent Review of the Enforcement of UK Anti-Discrimination Legislation' (2000) 12.

[79] Hepple, Coussey and Choudhury (n 78) 42–43.

the UK, the problem is not isolated to that country. The US, the European Union regime, the ECHR regime and many other jurisdictions do not have express legal protections concerning class or classism. Jurisdictions that offer some such protections (such as Cyprus and Türkiye) are exceptions to a general rule.[80]

It is right to summarise the reaction against class by scholars working in discrimination studies as one of 'over-correction'. Criticism of the prevailing approach to class led them to emphasise other concepts and, in doing so, they pushed class aside. By the time that such theory had considerable influence over some areas of legal scholarship, including 'critical' analyses of the law, scholars tended to focus on race, gender and other categories – but not class. Rather than fully integrated approaches that understood class alongside those other categories, scholars moved to euphemise class as 'socio-economic disadvantage' or similar.[81] In short, good intentions to correct biased norms stopped class from flourishing as an idea in legal analysis.

2.2. Party Politics

Earlier in this chapter, my discussion of the supposed disappearance of class considered examples from party politics in the UK, from Thatcher to Blair to Cameron to Starmer and Rayner. Although party politics and scholarship influence each other, the aims and techniques of party politics are distinctive. For example, Thatcher's motive when denying class was very different from the reasons for Pakulski and Waters's claim about its death. Once again, it is difficult to synthesise all parties, policies and eras of political life. Nevertheless, it is possible to give an overview of how the attitudes of politicians in the UK had an impact on the law.

By contrast with the Labour government's approach around the time of its budget in 2024, there seems to have been a time in which the major political parties were more comfortable with the language of 'class'. It may also have been that they were more used to the language and, at the time, saw little problem with using it to communicate. The general trends of the modern landscape are quite different. In the tradition of Margaret Thatcher, Tory politicians tend to avoid the language of class, apart from to assert that left-wing policies are forms of 'class war'.[82] As mentioned above, the Labour government ended up

[80] The Constitution of the Republic of Cyprus, Art 28(2); Turkish Penal Code, Art 216.

[81] See, eg, JC Benito Sanchez, 'Towering Grenfell: Reflections around Socioeconomic Disadvantage in Antidiscrimination Law' (2019) 5(2) *Queen Mary Human Rights Review* 1.

[82] See, eg, J Wright, 'The Radical Labour Council Waging Class Warfare on the South Coast', *Telegraph* (5 February 2025): www.telegraph.co.uk/money/jobs/schools-universities/radical-labour-council-class-warfare-south-coast/; D Churchill, 'Angela Rayner Accused of Waging "Class War" over Her Plans to Cut Funding for Wealthier Southern Areas So More Can Be Spent in the North', *Mail Online* (21 June 2025): www.dailymail.co.uk/news/article-14833797/Angela-Rayner-accused-waging-class-war.html.

in a conceptual maze with its use of the phrase 'working people' when discussing tax in 2024. Has it really become so undesirable to recognise class in order to explain imposing tax on some people but not others? If politicians consider class too vague, how is the replacement – 'working people' – any better? Reading between the lines, I suspect that the Labour government was aware of the accusations of 'class war' that would have come if it had used the language of class *in addition to* making changes to taxation in its first budget.[83] Unfortunately, such fears led the government to language that was easy to ridicule. It was also a bad euphemism for a justifiable political position: progressive taxation.[84]

It is not solely the problem of 'working people' without '-class'. Published in 2007, the report of the Equalities Review analyses inequality due to 'socio-economic status and social class' alongside gender, race and disability (though it restricts the idea of 'discrimination' to the last three).[85] But the Discrimination Law Review's proposals published later that same year omit class.[86] A 2009 policy paper makes some reference to 'social class', but then politicians seem to have forgotten it.[87] In its place, some politicians have moved to different ideas. Jo Littler observes that politicians regularly rely on ideas of 'equal opportunity' and 'social mobility' in their speeches among an overarching rhetoric of 'meritocracy'.[88] Most obviously, there seems to be a reluctance to use the language of class because of the political consequences and predictable attacks from opposing parties as well as certain parts of the press. There may also be a genuine belief, which is less self-conscious, that class is too fixed an idea in British society. This may be wrapped up with conceptions of the role of politics in inspiring change and a view that individualistic notions of 'opportunity', 'social mobility' and 'merit' represent better slogans than the baggage of 'class'.[89] Perhaps there is a concern, too, that relying on the categories of class will entrench class-based inequality rather than eliminate it. This all means that politicians have not pushed for class to be included in legislation concerning inequality and discrimination.

Here, the influence on the law does not come from honourable intentions of feminist and anti-racist scholars making genuine criticisms of the biased norms of class. For some politicians, there is a deeper hostility to the power of class. One technique is to inflame fears of 'class warfare'. Another technique more

[83] See, eg, T Baker, 'Labour is "Absolutely Not" Engaged in Class War, Prime Minister Keir Starmer Insists', *Sky News* (19 November 2024): www.news.sky.com/story/labour-is-absolutely-not-engaged-in-class-war-prime-minister-sir-keir-starmer-insists-13256630.

[84] See also, for analysis of the evidence to support the effectiveness of progressive taxation to reduce overall inequality, T Piketty, *A Brief History of Equality* (Cambridge, Massachusetts, Harvard University Press, 2021).

[85] The Equalities Review, 'Fairness and Freedom: The Final Report of the Equalities Review' (2007) 1, 26.

[86] Communities and Local Government, 'Discrimination Law Review: A Framework for Fairness' (2007).

[87] UK Government, *New Opportunities: Fair Chances for the Future* (2009) Cm 7533.

[88] J Littler, *Against Meritocracy* (Abingdon, Routledge, 2017) 27–28.

[89] See also, on the increased prominence of 'social mobility' on politicians' agendas, G Payne, *The New Social Mobility* (Cambridge, Polity Press, 2017) vi.

insidiously encourages class to fall into disuse.[90] Sometimes, those techniques combine. At the mention of class or related issues, melodramatic retorts of 'class warfare' shun debate and discourage politicians from talking expressly of class and classism. Faced with those retorts, politicians have tended to move towards other language and ideas, leaving class to gather dust.

It is not merely by coincidence or the combination of 'neutral' patterns that class tends to be sidelined or discussed in euphemism. There have been deliberate efforts to destroy its rhetorical and mobilising power. As Mike Hout, Clem Brooks and Jeff Manza argue in the context of the debate surrounding the supposed death of class, class has a clear dependence on politics rather than necessarily *determining* those politics.[91] We should not forget this insight: politicians' strategies affect, and even form a part of, the existence of class, including by shaping popular ideas of class. Not mentioning class in political debate and legislation contributes to the loss of it. Together with academic over-correction, this technique has fed into the minimising of class in the law and legal scholarship.

3. WHERE IS CLASS NOW?

Appraising the 'untimely prediction' of the end of class in the third edition of *Class and Stratification*, Rosemary Crompton quotes Mark Twain: 'The report of my death was an exaggeration.'[92] Crompton does not deny that class has changed or that the idea of class has 'lost its importance as a central discourse, or political organising principle, in contemporary societies'.[93] Crompton gives her own example of Blair's Labour government and its focus on developing an individual's capacity for 'inclusion' in society, rather than on transforming society in order to reduce inequality. Yet Crompton does not abandon class altogether. She recognises that the changes in political ideology and culture mean that we should revisit our approaches to class and refine (and, perhaps, reinvent) them to ensure they remain useful.[94]

Here, Crompton reflects one of my purposes in the rest of this book, though I focus on legal analysis rather than sociological method. I accept that class is complex. I accept that, certainly in public discourse and in some areas of scholarship, discussion of class has been less express than that of race, gender and other categories. I also accept that class has often been understood using biased norms. Nonetheless, I maintain the view that class is a meaningful category within societies and a crucial idea. Class now needs precise analysis to understand *what* it means and *how* it shapes people's lives.

[90] 'The Guardian View on Class Politics: It Has Faded as Culture Wars Have Risen', *The Guardian* (5 February 2025): www.theguardian.com/commentisfree/2025/feb/05/the-guardian-view-on-class-politics-it-has-faded-as-culture-wars-have-risen.
[91] Hout, Brooks and Manza (n 13) 69.
[92] Crompton (n 55) 71.
[93] Crompton (n 55) 3.
[94] Crompton (n 55) 150.

2

Choosing the Best Approach to Class

As I HAVE written, one purpose of this book is to understand classism as a form of discrimination and then use that idea in legal analysis. Therefore, it is necessary to understand what 'class' is. Since my focus is on the law, however, you might ask if it is also necessary to have a chapter unpicking abstract, technical debates about the meaning of class in political theory and sociology. The debates are vast. Their intricacies may be unlikely to matter for the purposes of legal analysis. But you could also ask: well, if class is going to be at the centre of this book, can we really avoid the difficult question of what it means, including in technical debates?

In his memoirs about the Wolfenden Report, John Wolfenden describes his committee's approach to legal analysis and the topic of being gay:

> We were concerned with the law. We were not concerned with homosexuality as a state or condition, except in so far as that was relevant to the treatment of those who had already been convicted by the courts. We were not there to write a sociological treatise or a handbook of moral theology or a textbook for medical students.[1]

Like Wolfenden, I am not writing 'a sociological treatise'. Unlike Wolfenden, though, I reject the idea that legal analysis of ideas in societies – like class and sexuality – should pretend to be concerned with the law *in isolation from* those underlying ideas. Wolfenden's distinction seems artificial. Those embarking on legal analysis should understand such ideas in a detailed and sophisticated way, even if the overall focus is on the law and some issues must be left unresolved.

This chapter's approach aims to find a middle ground. It is unnecessary to recite all the detail of debates about class. I do not try to resolve or summarise each debate. Instead, I will sketch major approaches to class in political, sociological and historical literature, considering how they relate to certain features of legal analysis. To make law well, we should find an approach to class from which we can take inspiration.

[1] J Wolfenden, *Turning Points: The Memoirs of Lord Wolfenden* (London, Bodley Head, 1976), cited in J Joyce, *Odd Men Out* (Manchester, Manchester University Press, 2022) 50.

1. THE 'WHAT' OBJECTION

To begin, there is the 'what' objection. In the process of writing a book about class and classism, I have found this to be the most common reaction: 'What is class, though? How do you define it? Isn't it much harder to define than, say, race or gender?'

This reaction makes sense. Class seems difficult to pin down. Is it about money? Power? Parents and education? Is it to do with aristocratic heritage? Is it wrapped up in theories of capitalism and Marxism? That is not to say there is no general understanding of class. Class often describes a situation in which some people have power in a society because of their place in a hierarchy, a system of ranking based on wealth and labour. But other ideas – like race and gender – seem more concrete. To some people, those ideas are much simpler. We tend to reduce race to skin colour and gender to genitals. The 'what' objection has an instinctive appeal.

But the objection is still false. First, it **rests on a simplistic understanding of other categories** in societies, like race, gender and disability. It presumes they are easier to define because they are somehow obvious or innate, creating few difficulties of definition. Yet a quick scan of both academic literature and courts' decisions tells us otherwise. Academics across topics have long argued that race and racism are 'dynamics', which 'emerge from a messy configuration of physical marks, social characteristics and cultural symbols' shaped by 'changes in political economy and geopolitics'.[2] A well-known example is the racialising of Irish people at certain times and in certain places, despite their 'white' skin. Meanwhile, courts in the UK have had to deal with the meaning of race in the Equality Act 2010. It includes 'colour', 'nationality' and 'ethnic or national origin'. Courts have also grappled with the meaning of 'religion' and 'philosophical belief' in decisions about democratic socialism and ethical veganism.[3] Despite these challenges, there seems to be an overriding commitment to stop racism, misogyny and certain other forms of discrimination. We persevere through difficulties of definition. When it comes to class, however, the 'what' objection tells us to give up.

Second, the objection **presumes that a definition must take the form of a short statement with minimal context**. It seeks a neat sentence in which an 'upper-class' person, for instance, is made up of one or two ingredients: 'an upper-class person is someone who went to private school and now earns more than £200,000 per year after tax'. Yet this is not how these ideas work. Like race, class is a 'messy configuration' of physical, social, cultural and economic features. Sometimes, it boils down to one indicator. Sometimes,

[2] See, eg, A Shafi and I Nagdee, *Race to the Bottom: Reclaiming Antiracism* (London, Pluto Press, 2022) 10.

[3] *The General Municipal and Boilermakers Union v Henderson* (2015) UKEAT/0073/14/DM; *Casamitjana Costa v The League Against Cruel Sports* (2020) ET (Case No 3331129/2018), [33]–[39].

it does not. To understand ideas like class, our approach should be led by examples from societies while being informed by theoretical guidance. We should find an approach that helps to explain the two lists of examples I gave in the Introduction, which span housing, education, income, assets, connections, accents and regions.

This method might worry some readers, especially lawyers who are used to certain ways of defining concepts. However, as Geoffrey MacCormack has explained in the context of Roman law, legal definitions may be less like *definitive* statements (in the modern sense of a sentence with minimal context) and more like useful guidelines or convenient summaries.[4] In this tradition, I do not accept that it weakens my arguments if class cannot be reduced to pithy definitions, as if it were a neat rule of science. Defining class is, I suspect, more like trying to define a colour. If I see it, I know it. But coming up with a written definitive statement of it is hard. The difficulty of that task does not make colour meaningless. It just tells us that colour requires a different approach to the definition, which recognises that colour is still something we can speak of meaningfully. That is my approach: to find a way of understanding class that guides us when considering examples without over-simplifying or misunderstanding class. Such an approach, in fact, may be a strength of class. It falls into the category of 'essentially contested concepts'.[5] As Judith Butler and William Scheuerman argue in another context, this quality can open up opportunities for intellectual progress rather than close them.[6] This is where the literature in sociology, politics and history can help.

2. SKETCHING APPROACHES TO CLASS

2.1. The Class Trap

That deals with the 'what' objection. When turning to consider the literature, the key is not to fall into **the class trap**. It is tempting to treat each approach to class as if it were diametrically opposed to all others. Rosemary Crompton makes the point well: disputes about understanding class are often due to 'fundamental (and probably non-resolvable) differences in methodological approaches to sociology as a discipline', rather than specific disagreements about a fixed meaning.[7]

[4] G MacCormack, '*Dolus, Culpa, Custodia* and *Diligentia*: Criteria of Liability or Content of *Obligatio*' (1994) 22 *Index* 189.

[5] WB Gallie, 'Essentially Contested Concepts' (1955–1956) 56(1) *Proceedings of the Aristotelian Society* 167.

[6] J Butler, *The Force of Nonviolence: An Ethico-Political Bind* (London, Verso, 2020) 6–7; W Scheuerman, 'Introduction: Why, Once Again, Civil Disobedience?' in W Scheuerman (ed), *The Cambridge Companion to Civil Disobedience* (Cambridge, Cambridge University Press, 2021) 1, 5.

[7] R Crompton, *Class & Stratification* (London, Polity Press, 2008) 9.

Take an example from the previous chapter and the debate about the supposed 'death' of class. In the exchange following Terry Nichols Clark and Seymour Martin Lipset's initial article, they and Michael Rempel argue that their opponents use a different idea of class. For example, noting that Michael Hout, Clem Brooks and Jeff Manza rely on evidence that class exists in distinctions between small- and large-firm employees or managers and supervisees, Clark, Lipset and Rempel argue that this entails 'a quite different conception of class'.[8] They conclude that their opponents confuse the existence of those distinctions with the more complex question of the 'political significance' of class. The question depends on 'the *strength* of the *relationship* between those stratification patterns and political outcomes', not just the existence of the distinctions themselves. Whoever wins this debate, Crompton's point remains. We need to be aware that people may be using different senses of 'class'. Otherwise, we will argue past each other.

An approach to class depends, therefore, on what it aims to achieve. Some approaches to class seek to explain how we interact with other people in our daily lives, how we navigate and influence our environments, and how we understand culture. Pierre Bourdieu, for instance, gives us ideas such as 'field', 'habitus' and 'capital' in order to make sense of class in contexts ranging from art to dietary habits.[9] Others strive to explain, and perhaps in doing so create, transformations through the conflict of forces in societies. For those like Erik Olin Wright, class is 'not necessarily meant to explain dietary preferences' but rather to articulate the kind of exploitation that Karl Marx identified.[10] Still others wish to collect data to observe how patterns in money, education and work affect other aspects of our lives.

Is class whatever we want it to be, then? If the idea shifts depending on our aims, how can it have some independent meaning? These concerns, however, tempt us into vacuity. At their extreme, they reduce us to statements like 'class is whatever we make it' or, worse, 'class has no real meaning'. In truth, class is an idea that people in societies have made. EP Thompson put it one way decades ago: class is defined by people as they 'live their own history, and, in the end, this

[8] TN Clark, SM Lipset and M Rempel, 'The Declining Political Significance of Social Class' in TN Clark and SM Lipset, *The Breakdown of Class Politics: A Debate on Post-Industrial Stratification* (Baltimore, Maryland, Johns Hopkins University Press, 2001) 77, 78–79, originally published under the same title: (1993) 8(3) *International Sociology* 293–316. Related to this, there is also the problem of describing the 'relationship between flesh-and-blood human individuals and social relations' (eg class as an interpersonal phenomenon versus class as a structure in societies): EO Wright, *Classes* (London, Verso, 2023) 10 n 4.

[9] P Bourdieu, *Distinction: A Social Critique of the Judgement of Taste* (R Nice trans, Abingdon, Routledge, 2010) 397. See also, for discussion of Bourdieu's framework in this respect, J Lane, *Pierre Bourdieu: A Critical Introduction* (London, Pluto Press, 2000) 141–48; N Crossley, 'Social Class' in M Grenfell (ed), *Pierre Bourdieu: Key Concepts* (Abingdon, Routledge, 2012) 85, 86.

[10] Wright (n 8) 137.

is its only definition'.[11] In this vein, class has a close relationship with perceptions that people have, though it is not entirely a question of self-identification. Note that these facts do not force us to accept vacuous statements. The variety of approaches to class does *not* mean that the idea is so fragmented that it hardly exists until a writer conjures its content. As I suggested in Chapter 1, class remains an important way in which we understand each other and the world around us. We may use 'class' imprecisely, sometimes even in contradiction, and yet it persists.

The challenge is to recognise all this and still find a clear and coherent understanding of class, accepting that the approach that we decide to take inspiration from will likely reflect what we want to achieve.

2.2. Three Heuristics from Legal Reasoning

This brings us to the point of view of legal analysis. I need an approach that allows me to *use* the idea of class in such analysis. The approach must be sensitive to different situations, as the law must be when considering different cases, while providing some guidance at the more general level, as the law must be when drafting legislation or developing principles. These features are significant so that the approach is effective, both in terms of general guidance and in specific applications of it, when combatting classism. Wright makes a similar point in a non-legal context: good theory is essential to understand properly the place of real people in 'class' and the impact of 'class' on them.[12]

Within that framework of guidance and specific applications, it is possible to identify some characteristic features of legal reasoning. I do not suggest that all legal reasoning has these features. But I do suggest that these features often exist in good legal reasoning. For the purpose of evaluating different approaches to class, three features of legal reasoning are especially important. One is **precision**. Legal reasoning should be precise. Think of barristers quibbling in court over a comma in an Act of Parliament or solicitors exchanging heated emails about a sub-clause in a contract. Although precise reasoning is often confused with pedantry (even, sometimes, by lawyers), it is justifiable. It partly reflects the practical point that lawyers should be able to understand the law and use it in their own cases. It is also rooted in the belief that people should be able to follow the law with a fair degree of certainty, as otherwise the law becomes vague and tyrannical.[13]

[11] EP Thompson, *The Making of the English Working Class* (London, Penguin, 1968) 11. I have sidestepped the use of 'men' in the original quotation given the good criticisms of the idea of 'class' for its presumption of a masculine norm, discussed in the previous chapter.

[12] Wright (n 8) 182.

[13] See, for a well-known statement of this aspect of the (much contested and often unwieldy) 'rule of law', J Raz, *The Authority of Law* (Oxford, Oxford University Press, 1979) 210–29. See also, for

A second feature is **accuracy**. When the law is concerned with understanding something, the law should do so in an accurate way. This includes ideas made in societies, such as race.[14] A legal approach to 'class' should reflect what class *is*, at least as far as the law can do so without sacrificing other, sometimes more important aims. This feature taps into claims about the law's expressive qualities, such as 'sending a message' or conveying 'meaning'.[15] It also reminds us of the law's role in increasing understanding and shaping perceptions in societies. As well as general dangers like stereotyping and distraction when the law adopts inaccurate understandings (such as the portrayals of lower-class people as 'ill, violent, drunken, stupid, lazy and so on' that Lennard Davis criticises in the literary context), inaccuracy in the law can lead to specific applications of it being misguided and harmful.[16]

Note how accuracy links with precision. We are often precise because we want to be accurate. We distinguish things, or push for further detail about them, in order to make sure that we understand them correctly. That said, though lawyers are often uncomfortable with this fact, sometimes to be accurate requires us to be imprecise. An illustration comes from John-Pierre Joyce's research about the Wolfenden Report and gay men's lives in the 1950s and 1960s. Joyce explains that there used to be various technical scales and frameworks for 'homosexuality', with neatly defined categories. Alfred Kinsey contrived seven categories, proceeding from the 'exclusively heterosexual' to the 'predominantly heterosexual' to the 'incidentally homosexual' and, stage by stage, to the 'exclusively homosexual'.[17] A family doctors' journal published a three-fold classification painstakingly distinguishing between 'puppy prurients', the 'emotionally immature' and 'regressors'; the British Medical Association gave 'evidence' about categories of such men with 'scientific' criteria.[18] These categories – with their tidy stages and systems – gave the appearance of precision. They were precise in their drawing of distinctions. Yet, *because of* their precision, they were inaccurate to the point of stupidity. They fundamentally misunderstood gay men.

Of course, these examples are easy to deride today. Nevertheless, they are useful reminders of the danger that clinging to precision may cause near-total inaccuracy. This is crucial for legal analysis, especially when considering a concept like class. As Wright observes, 'it is rare that social scientific theories are so well integrated and internally coherent that it is clear precisely which requirements apply to a given concept'.[19] In other words, an accurate approach to class may have to be a bit messy.

---

a fictional but similarly instructive illustration of the effects of vague and unknown law, F Kafka, *The Trial* (I Perry trans, London, Penguin, 2000).

[14] On the topic of race as 'a politically and socially constructed category', see especially S Hall, 'New Ethnicities' in D Morley and K Chen (eds), *Stuart Hall: Critical Dialogues in Cultural Studies* (Abingdon, Routledge, 1996) 442, 444.

[15] See, discussing claims about these expressive qualities of law, R McAdams, *The Expressive Powers of Law: Theories and Limits* (Cambridge, Massachusetts, Harvard University Press, 2015) 11–21.

[16] L Davis, *Poor Things* (Durham, North Carolina, Duke University Press 2024) 152.

[17] Joyce (n 1) 9–10.

[18] Joyce (n 1) 11.

[19] Wright (n 8) 22.

A third feature is less descriptive (though it may describe some legal reasoning) and is more about what I find desirable in legal reasoning. It may be controversial, but it is necessary to consider this when thinking about the law in the context of discrimination. Legal reasoning should strive for the **transformation of societies for the better**. This suggestion is rooted partly in the tradition of common law jurisdictions and the ability of the law to evolve: the ways in which the law can interrogate a set of facts by the application of recognised principles, accept or distinguish other sets of facts, and adjust so that it applies justifiably to sets of facts not envisaged by earlier decision-makers.[20] This capacity, though, is not just about adaptation. It also reflects a moral commitment by scholars and practitioners. Our forms of reasoning should reflect what we want the law to do, including in making societies better.[21]

This last feature might sound vague. It will depend on what 'better' means. It might sound naïve, too. The law has been the source of so much wrongdoing. It can therefore be difficult to believe that the law may also be a tool for good. In the context of political philosophy in *Left ≠ Woke*, Susan Neiman takes up the issue of criticisms of naïve sentimentality about long-held ideals. Neiman argues that we must push past our inhibitions about this sentimentality in order to build something, rather than limit ourselves to disparaging what already exists.[22] While some of her criticisms of 'wokeness' are too negative, Neiman's point translates well to the legal context.[23] In addition to identifying what the law has done wrong, we should also set out what the law can do right. Although the law frequently makes things worse, my task in this book would have little purpose if I rejected from the outset the *possibility* that the law could be a force for good. I would struggle to contemplate the law's potential to address discrimination and improve the conditions of people's lives. Much rests on the content of the law, who makes it and how those in power enforce it. Putting aside naïve sentiment, I accept that the law can make positive changes.

So, I have three features: (i) **precision**; (ii) **accuracy**; and (iii) **transformation of societies for the better**. I can now take existing approaches to class in political and sociological literature and apply these features like heuristics: a simplified but useful way to consider how legal analysis might take inspiration from each approach.

[20] Although it may be the case that the common law is not actually engaged in analogical reasoning, rather than a combination of other types of reasoning: L Alexander and E Sherwin, *Demystifying Legal Reasoning* (Cambridge, Cambridge University Press, 2012).

[21] See generally, for a classic example of a discussion about the relationship between the law and morality, the Hart–Devlin debate: HLA Hart, *Law, Liberty and Morality* (Oxford, Oxford University Press, 1963); P Devlin, *The Enforcement of Morals* (Oxford, Oxford University Press, 1965).

[22] S Neiman, *Left ≠ Woke* (Cambridge, Polity Press, 2023) 140–41.

[23] Neiman calls for a return to 'a model in which your claims to authority are focused on what you've done to the world, not what the world did to you', she over-simplifies what vulnerable groups are suggesting when they rely on their knowledge and experience to claim standing: 25.

3. MARX

3.1. Traditional Marxism and Modified Approaches

Writing about a 'Marxist' approach to class may imply that there is a single, coherent brand of analysis. In reality, there have been many interpretations and modifications of Karl Marx's work over the past two centuries. I have already referred in Chapter 1 to the significant revisions that Wright's work proposes, for example. That said, it is still possible to summarise the qualities that tend to make Marxist approaches to class distinctive.

First, an overview of Marx's framework goes as follows.[24] Marx is primarily concerned with the relations of production that constitute classes. The bourgeoisie own and control the means of production. The proletariat – the workers – own only their ability to work, their labour, which they must sell to the bourgeoisie to live, though they are not always deceived or defrauded into doing so. As a commodity, labour creates value: the workers receive wages for their labour, but the bourgeoisie retains the surplus value generated by labour.[25] In capitalism, the dominant relation of production is the exploitation of (legally free) workers or producers by those who appropriate their surplus labour and make profit.[26] The primacy of market imperatives – to compete, accumulate and maximise profit – defines how people relate to each other. This makes capitalism distinctive from other types of societies, such as feudalism, absolutism and those in which the market is simply for exchange or dissemination.

Second, Marxism typically understands classes as *forces*. In addition to the emphasis on exploitation in relations of production, Marxist approaches view class as *relational* rather than a 'characteristic' inherent to us or 'thing' that exists out in the world.[27] Wright emphasises that Marxist approaches do not rely on 'gradational' norms of class, such as the 'upper', 'middle' and 'lower' classes. Instead, the norms are 'relational': worker versus capitalist, for example. Although 'relational' norms can have a 'gradational' quality (such as workers being poorer, capitalists being richer), they are not defined by this aspect.[28] Here, we must understand what Marx was probably aiming to do. He was not, at least not in most of his work, attempting to complete an empirical study of all systems of differentiation within societies, as sociological research about 'social stratification' might try to do. Instead, Marx set out a framework of ideas to

[24] See, eg, K Marx, *Capital: A Critique of Political Economy, Volume I* (B Fowkes trans, Penguin, 1990).

[25] See especially K Marx, 'The General Formula for Capital' in D McLellan (ed), *Capital: An Abridged Edition* (Oxford, Oxford University Press, 2008) 93–100.

[26] See generally, for a useful distillation of a Marxist understanding of the distinctiveness of capitalism, E Meiksins Wood, *The Origin of Capitalism: A Longer View* (London, Verso, 2017) 94, 96–98.

[27] Wright (n 8) 34–35.

[28] Wright (n 8) 34–35.

analyse the overall structures of capitalist society in order to develop a political movement and, in turn, describe (and drive) the transformation of societies in order to end the exploitation of workers.[29] In Marxist literature, 'class' tends to be less a status, trait or cultural characteristic and more a 'force' that typifies the major conflict in societies, which will, in turn, revolutionise those societies.[30] Marx does not prioritise understanding class at the level of a 'feature' of a person or a factor that might inform a person's identity, a nuance of their daily interactions or (as Wright notes) their 'dietary preferences'.[31] In Marxism, class is usually much bigger.

Third, it is sometimes said that Marx never really develops a specific portrait of classes, preferring broadly drawn groups of 'capitalists' and 'workers'. It is true that Marx never settles on a rigorous theory of class that bears accurately on the complexity of class 'groups' within societies. However, in some of his work, Marx does recognise a more granular picture of class.[32] For example, in *The Communist Manifesto*, Marx and Friedrich Engels refer to earlier times in history and the 'complicated arrangement of society into various orders, a manifold gradation of social rank'. They note the 'patricians, knights, plebeians, slaves' of ancient Rome and the 'feudal lords, vassals, guild masters, journeyman, apprentices, serfs' of the Middle Ages.[33] They call them 'classes' (*Klassen*) and use that history to argue that modern society has 'not done away with class antagonisms' but has rather 'established new classes, new conditions of oppression, new forms of struggle in place of the old ones'.[34] Marx and Engels rely on this view to warn contemporary audiences of the assumption that the 'end' of feudalism created a freer, better society. They argue that '[t]he weapons with which the bourgeoisie felled feudalism to the ground are now turned against the bourgeoisie itself'.[35] By connecting this criticism of earlier hierarchies with their explanation of the new form of wrongdoing under capitalism, Marx and Engels seek to persuade their audience that this new capitalist society must also be transformed for the better.

From passages like this, it seems incorrect to suggest that Marxist thought recognises 'class' *only* in terms of relations of production or forces, at least when we look across Marx's writing. As Wright notes, Marx does refer, at his most abstract, to a more complex picture, though he gives the more diverse groups

[29] See, eg, for rejection of the criticism that Marx deployed 'crude technological determinism': E Meiksins Wood, *The Retreat from Class: A New True Socialism* (London, Verso, 1986) 186–90. See also, for discussion of the more metaphorical approach to determinism in 'humanist' Marxism in the tradition of Antonio Gramsci, R Simon, *Gramsci's Political Thought* (London, Lawrence & Wishart, 2015).

[30] Crompton (n 7) 27.

[31] Wright (n 8) 137.

[32] See generally Crompton (n 7) 29.

[33] K Marx and F Engels, *The Communist Manifesto* (D McLellan trans, Oxford, Oxford University Press, 2008) 3.

[34] Marx and Engels (n 33) 3.

[35] Marx and Engels (n 33) 9.

(such as lords and serfs) 'strictly peripheral importance' rather than 'rigorous theoretical status'.[36] In short, Marx does not offer thorough theoretical analysis of the connection between the struggles of 'actors' in societies and the more abstract picture he paints of class relations or 'forces'.[37] To Marx, what fundamentally makes capitalism distinctive are the relations of production that exploit workers.

Marx accepted this in a letter to Joseph Wedemeyer in 1852: 'no credit is due to me for discovering the existence of classes in modern society . . . [w]hat I did that was new was to prove . . . that the existence of classes is bound up with particular, historic phases in the development of production'.[38] Therefore, while it is not *the* distinctive concept of class in Marxism, Marx accepts the overarching sense in which 'class' refers to an ordering of people within society, a 'gradation of social rank' as in *The Communist Manifesto*. Crompton is correct to suggest that Marx uses class 'both as an analytical concept in the development of his theory of society, and as a descriptive, historical concept'.[39] This discussion gives us some basic qualities that help to identify a Marxist approach to class: exploitation in relations of production; classes mainly as forces; but also an ambiguity of different senses of class, seemingly leaving open a broader sense of class alongside the distinctively 'Marxist' one based on exploitation.

As I foreshadowed, there have been many developments in Marxism since the time of Marx and Engels.[40] Some scholars have tried to remedy perceived shortcomings in Marx's work by modifying it. Rejecting the barer two-tier class structure, Wright offers a more complex framework of class and employment, with the concept of 'contradictory locations within class relations' catering to the sense that the middle class has posed a significant challenge to Marx's approach.[41] Others put forward more nuanced portrayals of class within labour structures as in the middle and late twentieth century.[42] One main concern is that Marxism is reconsidered in the light of changes in societies, especially in workplaces. Going back to the question of what an approach aims to do, such approaches attempt to *explain* the precise position of class in a society's structures more than Marx ever did. These revisions retain the basic qualities of Marxist approaches to class while refining them in the light of criticisms and changes in societies.

[36] Wright (n 8) 7.

[37] Wright (n 8) 7.

[38] Reproduced in G Steenson, *After Marx, Before Lenin* (London, University of Pittsburgh Press, 1991) vii.

[39] Crompton (n 7) 29.

[40] See also, addressing race within Marxist frameworks and discussing the history of black intellectualism in the United States, C Robinson, *Black Marxism* (Chapel Hill, North Carolina, University of North Carolina Press, 2000) 191.

[41] See, eg, EO Wright, *Understanding Class* (London, Verso, 2015) 155. See also, for Wright's distinction between Marx's complexity at the 'conjunctural' level when it comes to his acceptance of more class actors, Wright (n 8) 7.

[42] D Lockwood, *The Blackcoated Worker* (London, Allen & Unwin, 1958).

3.2. Legal Analysis

Applying the three heuristics of (i) precision, (ii) accuracy and (iii) transformation of societies for the better, Marxist approaches have some significant advantages in relation to the first and third.

For **precision**, modified approaches (such as that of Wright) help Marx overcome the imprecision of a two-tier picture, even with the broader understanding of classes as 'forces'. Without those modifications, Marx's writing alone struggles to satisfy the heuristic of precision. Although he refers to the more granular idea of class as a ranking, his distinctive concept involves two tiers or two 'forces'. By comparison, more granular approaches like that of Wright offer an array of precise categories. Wright evaluates different proposals of detailed classifications for members of a society according to occupation.[43] Rather than a simplistic division between 'capitalists' and 'workers', an approach like Wright's offers plenty of specific categories into which to place each person. While the law does not necessarily have to categorise everyone in this way, Marxism's focus on labour and work would give legal analysis a relatively clear metric by which to determine class.

Marxist approaches are perhaps most successful, though, in offering the opportunity for legal analysis to strive for the **transformation of societies for the better**. This is, in part, because it is what Marxist reasoning intends to do: to identify how capitalist societies work at the time of writing, articulate how and why they should change, and encourage people to bring about those changes in doing so. If the law were to commit to eradicating exploitation in the Marxist sense, it would require fundamental changes to societies (as Marx envisaged). One view of the law's role here is that, while the law alone could not bring this about, the use of a Marxist approach to class in the law would encourage it to play a part in that longer and complex process. (A different view based on Marxism, which I address in Chapter 10, is that the law should step aside – or else be pushed – to enable that process to occur.)

It is the heuristic of **accuracy** that poses the main problem when using Marxism alone as an approach to class in legal analysis. On the one hand, there is a great deal of evidence to suggest that Marxist understandings of class – rooted in the exploitation of workers – continue to reflect the world. Again, this issue arose during the debate about the supposed death of class. To rebut Pakulski and Waters's arguments, Wright relied on evidence from a range of sources, which supported conclusions including that class boundaries persisted (especially in terms of divisions in property and mobility between classes) and that inequality in assets remained significant.[44] Even accepting Wright's arguments, though, the main reason why Marxist approaches do not satisfy the

[43] See also, for discussion of D Grusky and K Weeden's 'micro-classes', Wright (n 41) 113.
[44] Wright (n 41) 146–50.

heuristic of accuracy is because of how heavily they put relations of production at their centre.

Marxists might say: but putting relations of production at the centre is the *only* accurate understanding of class. There are two main responses to this. First, widely held understandings of class are about more than relations of production. Class concerns social interactions, prestige, cultural rankings and hierarchies within societies. Marx and Engels acknowledge this much when they use a more general sense of 'class' (as found in its earlier forms in feudalism and ancient Rome) in *The Communist Manifesto*. While Marxist approaches allow for these dimensions of class, they are at most peripheral in the literature. Marx's focus is on his sense of class in relations of production.[45] Marxist approaches do not tend to offer a great deal of nuance when examining why certain forms of culture, for example, are devalued because of their association with lower-class people. This is because of Marxists' typical aims, as Crompton notes. However, if the law is to attempt to address specific instances of how class affects people (and features in discrimination against them), it should be able to explain these aspects of how class works.

Second, even accepting modifications of Marxism to account for gender and race in the understanding of 'labour' and 'production' without formal wages (such as domestic labour that is not usually paid for by transfers of money), labour is only one part of discrimination.[46] In some cases of maltreatment based on class, many other aspects are important. Take the instance of dialects and accents in England. Certain dialects and accents are often associated with class: types of work, yes, and money, but also education, cultural prestige, personal and communal identity, and assumptions of historical backwardness, little worldliness and few worthy social connections.[47] A Marxist approach can be extended to explain how relations of production create and sustain forms of associations of these kinds. However, these issues have not been the Marxist focus. To attempt to analyse these aspects, it becomes necessary to rely on the more general sense of 'class' to which Marx and Engels refer in *The Communist Manifesto*. However, as I have already suggested, this is not the distinctive concept of class in relations of production firmly at the heart of Marxism. The general sense remains under-developed in the Marxist literature. As a result, to be wholly accurate about the aspects of class, we need a more general notion of class that bears in mind the different contexts in which the law may need to consider issues relating to class and analyse them accurately. Marxism struggles

[45] See also, for more detailed criticism of the priority Marx gives to the identification of class with the economic relation between waged labour and capital at the expense of (eg) political and other parts of social hierarchies, J Cohen, *Class and Civil Society: The Limits of Marxian Critical Theory* (Amherst, Massachusetts, University of Massachusetts Press, 1982) 24, 108.

[46] See, eg, for recognition of this revision to Marx albeit in a limited way, Wright (n 8) 197–201.

[47] See generally J Roessel, C Schoel and D Stahlberg, 'Modern Notions of Accent-ism: Findings, Conceptualizations, and Implications for Interventions and Research on Nonnative Accents' (2019) 39(1) *Journal of Language and Social Psychology* 87.

to overcome these two criticisms unless it takes a broader approach to class that is not distinctively 'Marxist'.

4. WEBER

4.1. Weberian Approaches

Like Marx, Max Weber had his own understanding of what his work was trying to achieve. Crompton observes that Marx and Weber's 'approaches to social science were very different'.[48] The point might be made in stronger terms: Marx would likely not have thought that he was writing 'social science' at all. Weber's work, in contrast, understands class in the context of his aspiration for so-called 'value-free' social science. His work seeks to be empirical, concentrating on what we can learn about the structures in societies that is then reducible to each individual's behaviour. Marx and Weber have some points in common. Weber accepts that having property and lacking property is a basic class division. For him, classes are 'not communities' but 'possible, and frequent, bases for social action'. Weber also shares the Marxist focus on the 'economic': the possession of goods and the opportunities for earning money.[49] He maps a working class, a petty bourgeoisie, a kind of managerial and technical layer, and then the most privileged classes.

However, importantly, Weber understands class as referring to the life chances that a person has, as determined entirely by their 'economic interests in the possession of goods and opportunities for income' under the conditions of 'commodity or labour markets', rather than exploitation in relations of production.[50] Overall, '[c]lass situation is . . . ultimately market situation'.[51] In Weber's writing, then, 'class' refers to the life chances that a person has, as determined by the market, rather than exploitation through relations of production.

There are various other distinctions between Weberian and Marxist approaches. One lesser noticed distinction is that Weber, unlike Marx, seems to conceive class as *only* existing when a market exists. For example, Weber refers to the relationship of power between the cattle owner and serf as 'only a fore-runner of real "class" formation'. It is only later, when a market exists, that 'class struggles' can really be said to begin.[52] While Weber seems to recognise a quality, perhaps embryonic, that links class to earlier relationships of power, he stops short of characterising them as 'class' relationships. By comparison, Marx and Engels still characterise earlier forms of societies and their rankings

[48] Crompton (n 7) 33.

[49] M Weber, *Economy and Society: An Outline of Interpretive Sociology* (G Roth and C Wittich trans, Berkeley, California, University of California Press, 1978) vol 2, 304.

[50] Weber (n 49) 302.

[51] Weber (n 49) 303.

[52] Weber (n 49) 303–06.

as involving a type of class, albeit different from the distinctive idea of class as a force in the Marxist theory of capitalism.

In his framework, Weber refuses to characterise enslavement as a form of class in his sense of the word. Those enslaved are, instead, 'a status group'.[53] Status groups do not occupy 'the purely economically determined "class situation"'. Rather, they rest on estimations of social 'honour'. Here, Weber does not divorce status from class. He recognises that 'class distinctions are linked in the most varied ways with status distinctions'. However, he ultimately argues that 'status honour need not necessarily be linked with a class situation'.[54] Like Marx, Weber's work has been modified and applied in various ways. Hira Singh applies Weber's framework to the issue of caste in India, for instance. Singh notes that Weberian analyses have traditionally understood caste as about 'cultural power' and, therefore, a form of 'status' and not 'class'. Singh emphasises the economic aspects of caste and stresses the importance of understanding class relations as 'the very foundation of caste hierarchy'.[55] Singh notes how Weber's distinction between class and status becomes difficult, especially in times when property-based status is precarious and given that the status-giving lifestyle of certain groups is so closely connected with 'relations of production and acquisition of goods'.[56]

4.2. Legal Analysis

On the surface, a Weberian approach seems to be both precise and accurate in understanding class, satisfying the first two of our heuristics: (i) **precision** and (ii) **accuracy**. Weber's emphasis on the market, for instance, reflects the prominence of it in modern societies.[57] In his separation of class from status, Weber also seems to tap into something familiar in widely held understandings of the word 'class'. He suggests that status often 'stands in sharp opposition to the pretensions of sheer property [that may determine class]'.[58] Indeed, particularly in England, there is a long tradition of greater social prestige attaching to the aristocracy rather than people who are simply wealthy or who have vast property.[59]

However, the line between class and status is where a Weberian approach falters in terms of both precision and accuracy. In England, the distinction set out a moment ago would not typically be understood as one between 'class' and

[53] Weber (n 49) 303.

[54] Weber (n 49) 306.

[55] H Singh, 'Class, Caste, and Social Stratification in India: Weberian Legacy' in E Hank and others (eds), *The Oxford Handbook of Max Weber* (Oxford, Oxford University Press, 2019) 393, 408.

[56] Singh (n 55) 397.

[57] See, eg, M Wolf, *A Crisis of Democratic Capitalism* (London, Penguin, 2024) 217.

[58] Weber (n 49) 302–05.

[59] D Weldon, *Two Hundred Years of Muddling Through* (London, Abacus, 2022) 43.

'status': it would be understood by using the traditional definition of the upper class as those who hold aristocratic title and inherited estates, which in turn excludes those who have 'new' money or property.[60] Even accepting this ordinary meaning, Weber's restriction of class to the economic situation of market relations could provide a more precise way to analyse it. Rather than expand class to broader social and cultural questions that seem to make up ideas of 'status' or 'honour', Weber's approach could allow us to focus on the most measurable features of class. By restricting analysis to the market (and goods and money), he retains what makes 'class' distinct from more general ideas like 'status', 'prestige', 'hierarchy' and 'power'. To legal analysis, this perspective might be attractive. Weber's approach could direct attention to features that seem easier to count, which would allow the law to set precise tests. How much money does this person have? How much are they earning? How much property does she have? What does he own?

Yet it suffers from a major weakness when we consider precision *in the light of* accuracy. Weber's approach does not accord with commonly held ideas of class. As I have set out, certainly in England, the traditional upper class has not always been the wealthiest (though it was markedly until the industrial revolution) or with the best chances in the conditions of the markets.[61] But we should still articulate what it is about the distinctive position of those in the traditional upper class that allows them to have high chances of hoarding social prestige and of harnessing education, work and healthcare. That is often partly a question of goods and income, yes, but they are inextricably connected with social and cultural advantage. In such a situation, Weber's approach creates a hard line between 'class' as market-based advantage and 'class' as the full range of social, cultural and economic advantage, despite this range also involving market-based advantage. It is not clear why class should become 'status' simply because the issues are primarily social or cultural.

That weakness may not be fatal. We might add the following lines. 'Fine, we have been thinking of class in the wrong way in England and, as a result, our use of its language is suffering. We should employ the Weberian separation between "class" and "status" to solve this problem.' The difficulty with that response, though, is that it does not offer the quality of analysis that the more encompassing idea of class does. If we restrict class to the market-determined 'economic', we must rely on a narrow concept of the 'economic'. Especially in a world that understands the 'economic' in a much more layered and abstract way than perhaps Weber would have done, markets of 'goods' and 'incomes' can include a huge variety of ways to earn, to acquire and to monopolise. The interplay and overlap between social, cultural and economic advantages suggest

[60] See also, discussing perspectives on the distinction between a new 'wealth-elite' and the traditional landed upper class, D Smith, *The Fall and Rise of the English Upper Class* (Manchester, Manchester University Press, 2023) 18.

[61] Weldon (n 59) 60.

why it is unhelpful to view the 'economic' as if it can be hermetically sealed from the rest of life.[62] While Weber recognises this interplay, he ultimately clings to his division: if there are social and cultural aspects of class, they are separate 'status' issues and not rooted in 'class' as 'a market situation'.[63] By contrast from Weber, understanding class as something not confined to 'economic' market situations emphasises the connections between the different aspects of our lives.

For legal analysis, the crucial benefit would be to give the law an understanding of the ways in which inequalities of goods and income are difficult to separate from inequalities of prestige, status and honour. If we consider how snobbery towards lower-class people might operate in an educational institution, for instance, it may not be best explained through a difference in goods or money. It may be better understood as the social and cultural stigma attached to one group who may often, but not always, be worse off in terms of money. The use of 'class' here, rather than a jump to 'status', would allow legal analysis to identify less traditionally 'economic' features that still entail stigma and inequality.

This point also indicates why a Weberian approach fails to satisfy the third heuristic, which strives for legal analysis to realise its role in the **transformation of societies for the better**. Although Weber rightly identifies how decisive the market can be in determining a person's quality of life, he (unlike Marx) does not develop this diagnosis into a proposed cure. This makes sense if we remember that Weber's ambition, as a 'value-free' social scientist, was empirical. His focus on the market may give the appearance of precision, but his narrowing of class is artificial and (I have argued) leads to inaccuracy. For the purposes of transformation, it risks encouraging the law to sever the economic from the social and the cultural. In the example of an educational institution that I have given, using Weber's approach would prevent the law from finding maltreatment based on class because it would not be considered a class-related issue. This would limit the scope of the idea of class and reduce the extent to which the law could intervene to stop maltreatment, unless it were to develop, alongside class, a ground of Weberian 'status' (which I have already rejected).

5. BOURDIEU

5.1. Bourdieusian Approaches

With the issue of the relationship between the economic, social and cultural fresh in mind, it is time to turn to the work of Pierre Bourdieu.[64] His approach is

[62] See also, for criticism of the separation between culture and economy, J Kaplan, 'Against Economy-Culture Dualism: An Argument from Raced Economies' (2021) 22(3) 381. M Savage makes a similar point as part of his argument in favour of Bourdieu's approach to class: *Social Class in the 21st Century* (London, Pelican, 2015) 48–50.

[63] Weber (n 49) 303.

[64] Bourdieu (n 9).

often reduced to his well-known idea of 'cultural capital'.[65] In a way, this reduction is a self-interested tendency as well as an error by scholars. For many people, it is easier to digest a theory if it seems to move us away from the hard edges of class inequality, with its poverty and deprivations, towards a more detached discussion about the 'values' we attach to different forms of culture. However, Bourdieu's scheme is more complex than this.

First, unlike Marx and Weber, Bourdieu is less concerned with 'class' as a social force or a cause of changes in societies. Bourdieu's eyes rest on understanding class within the context of social relations, whether of power or capital. In this sense, he does not share Marx and Weber's emphasis on the 'economic' quality of class or the centrality of an idea like 'production' (for Marx) or the 'market' (for Weber). Instead of being exclusively or mainly 'economic', class is a form of relation that involves symbols or claims to status. Although it is important not to lose sight of the role of bigger structures in Bourdieu's work, his approach operates much closer to people's everyday practices. To this end, Bourdieu shares with Marx the absence of 'a typology of classes', with his approach to class often being 'implicit' in his other ideas.[66]

Second, Bourdieu's approach is highly distinctive because of the concepts he uses to analyse 'social space'. For Bourdieu, it is possible to view everyone in a society in terms of their place in the 'field', which involves using the concept of 'capital' among others, such as 'habitus' (principles of people's underlying practices) and 'doxa' (internalised rules and understandings). Bourdieu uses 'capital' to explore the ways in which people gain and lose advantage in their relations with others. Economic capital refers to material resources, such as money and property. Social capital refers to the connections we have with other people and the contacts we establish. Cultural capital refers to our interaction with ideas and customs around us, so that we acquire prestige and credentials.[67] Combinations of these (overlapping) forms of 'capital' relate to the idea of 'habitus': the principles that generate particular practices, often in the form of preferences and skills, common to those who have certain forms and degrees of capital in a social 'field'.[68] Bourdieu encourages us to focus on the relations between people, the principles underlying their practices and their environments. In addition to these ideas, Nick Crossley suggests that Bourdieu recognises that, for a class to exist, people must 'form' it in reality by 'acting and identifying

[65] See, for a useful overview of the concept of capital in Bourdieu's work, R Moore, 'Capital' in Grenfell (n 9) 98.

[66] Crossley (n 9) 85.

[67] There also seems to be 'symbolic' capital, which refers broadly to the esteem in which people hold each other. See generally Crossley (n 9) 86. However, I do not consider that the idea of a further category of 'symbolic' capital adds much to the social and cultural, certainly bearing in mind the inspiration I seek to take from Bourdieu here. I, therefore, leave it aside.

[68] Crompton (n 7) 100. See especially on the danger of over-emphasis on 'habitus', C Burke, 'Bourdieu's Theory of Practice: Maintaining the Role of Capital' in J Thatcher and others (eds), *Bourdieu: The Next Generation* (Abingdon, Routledge, 2018) 8, 21.

collectively'.[69] There is, therefore, also a self-conscious, group-based quality to Bourdieu's work. Through this complex framework, Bourdieu illustrates how people accumulate capital, which interacts with their 'habitus' and brings them advantage in a particular 'field'.

Third, while the intricacies of Bourdieu's framework can pose difficult questions of theory and interpretation, his approach has proven to be immensely practical when applied. Mike Savage offers a compelling example of the application of Bourdieu's ideas to the issue of class in the twenty-first century.[70] Savage uses Bourdieu's idea of capital to move us away from an analysis of class that rests solely or mainly on occupation. Instead, he combines this with social connections and cultural knowledge. Savage notes how Bourdieu unlocks a convincing way to explain the depth of inherited advantages. It is not just 'the passing over of economic capital to one's kin: property, savings, tools, heirlooms'. It is also 'another kind of inheritance', which reflects educational qualifications, tastes and preferences.[71]

Fourth, Bourdieu does not necessarily require us to accept Marx's view that class is the *primary* form of division in societies. For instance, when discussing the relationship between class and the 'multiple oppressions' approach (eg class alongside race and gender), Wright summarises the Marxist view that class represents the 'pivotal lines of demarcation' in societies.[72] By contrast, Bourdieu's does not put class *above* race, gender or other categories. It allows the examination of interactions between class and race, for instance, without necessarily giving one analytical priority over the other.[73] Bourdieu's approach is, therefore, adept at answering scholars' criticisms of the biased norms of class analysis discussed in Chapter 1.

Overall, Bourdieu provides tools of analysis that reflect the various aspects of class through the accumulation and combination of forms of capital, which are malleable and can be assorted according to a person's setting. Savage shows this when he discusses Bourdieu and the ability of some classes to adapt themselves to use (traditional) 'highbrow' cultural capital, such as going to the opera, alongside (new) 'emerging' cultural capital, such as consuming popular television shows from a knowing distance as part of a 'plural and flexible' cultural palette.[74] By recognising the extent to which class concerns the principles that govern our preferences and practices (such as 'habitus'), Bourdieu's approach to class remains dynamic and allows class to evolve through the gathering of different forms and degrees of social, cultural and economic capital.

[69] Crossley (n 9) 90.
[70] Savage (n 62).
[71] Savage (n 62) 49.
[72] Wright (n 8) 32, 57.
[73] D Wallace, 'Reading "Race" in Bourdieu? Examining Black Cultural Capital among Black Caribbean Youth in South London' (2016) 51(5) *Sociology* 907.
[74] Savage (n 62) 121–25.

5.2. Legal Analysis

Bourdieu's approach can meet all three heuristics. First, the multi-dimensionality of Bourdieu's framework allows analysis to become very **precise**. If legal analysis should be able to articulate wrongdoing across a variety of contexts (such as employment, hostility-based crime, and governmental policy, as well as the role of class in the legal system more generally), there is much to draw from his idea of capital. Consider an example. One employee might be similar to a second employee in terms of their economic capital, such as (most obviously) their wages. But the ideas of social capital and cultural capital are key in emphasising why an employer still maltreats one employee because of *other* features that they have, which are associated with being lower-class. For instance, the first employee may have grown up in council housing and/or have a regional accent typically stigmatised as 'common' or 'rough'. That employee's social and cultural capital is likely to be perceived as lesser in quality than a colleague who was educated privately, grew up in an affluent area and who speaks with a socially and culturally prestigious accent. Bourdieu's approach allows us to be precise in identifying exactly how class-based divisions affect one person's treatment of another and how class may inform a specific person's identity. By comparison, Marx's emphasis on production and Weber's emphasis on the market do not offer that degree of texture.

Bourdieu's framework also allows us to be **accurate** when understanding class in legal analysis. Continuing with the example of two employees, missing (or, as Marx or Weber tend to do, de-emphasising) the social and cultural aspects of class prevents us from understanding why the treatment of that employee depends on associations with class. If we were to focus on 'production' as Marx might, or we were to give these aspects the separate label of 'status' as Weber might, we would likely misunderstand how class operates in this example. At its heart, Bourdieu's approach tells us about how people relate to each other. To borrow EP Thompson's words from his own discussion of class and interpretations of Marx, I suggest that Bourdieu's strength is that he understands class 'as something which in fact happens . . . in human relationships' rather than succumbing to 'an ever-present temptation to suppose that class is a thing'.[75] In this vein, Bourdieu's approach allows us to think of gradational norms of class – 'upper', 'middle' and 'lower' classes, for instance – in a relational way.

Remember that one of Wright's concerns (discussed above) is that gradational norms hinder our ability to identify the source of conflicts in societies, with 'upper' and 'lower' groups having no necessary connection with each other.[76] Using Bourdieu's approach, however, this is not so great a danger. A person who is highly advantaged by capital – an upper-class person – is constantly engaging with that capital to relate to others, including those who are much less advantaged. The link between grading and relating is firm.

[75] Thompson (n 11) 9–10.
[76] Wright (n 8) 35.

Against my arguments that Bourdieu offers the opportunity for precise and accurate analysis of class, you could say that the multi-dimensionality of Bourdieu actually *undermines* precision and accuracy. By pointing in various social and cultural directions, Bourdieu's approach loses the focus on the economic that anchors class in Marx and Weber. This is a forceful counter-argument. It may be difficult to imagine judges getting right the nuance of 'social' and 'cultural' aspects, and then integrating them coherently with the 'economic'. Would this just lead to confused analysis, with little guidance about which 'capital' is to be given priority, especially if they point in different directions? What about the Donald Trump-type situations in which a person has a lot of money but has other features associated with being lower-class (such as those that many call 'trashy' or 'tacky', like a lifestyle or way of talking)?

It is fair to wonder if judges could analyse these issues without misunderstanding them. However, this counter-argument needs to be treated with care. The answer is not to narrow class to relations of production. It is also not to constrict class to the 'market' and leave 'status' to describe other forms of ranking. Granted, when faced with more complex examples, those approaches may seem attractive. For instance, instead of grappling with ideas like social and cultural capital or internalised ways of classifying each other, we could characterise employees according to the nature of their occupation (borrowing from a scheme like Wright's) or their place in the market.[77] However, though simpler, these approaches are unlikely to be more precise or accurate than Bourdieu's approach. They do not offer the nuance to articulate why employees are mistreated because of the denigration of certain social and cultural features. Simplicity has a place, especially in the law, but only so far as it allows us to maintain precise and accurate analysis.

Last, there is the heuristic of striving for the **transformation of societies for the better**. Those who favour Marxist approaches might argue that they have more capacity to transform society for the better than Bourdieu's approach. If we are making law in a capitalist society, our approach to class should be tailored both to understanding how class operates in *that kind* of society and to redressing the wrongs peculiar to it. Marxist approaches could offer the law an opportunity to keep focus on the core of exploitation in relations of production, rather than drawing the law into a cosmetic exploration of the layers of class as if it were only a theoretical exercise or sociological study.

If the law were solely concerned with relations of production, I might agree with this argument. But this argument falls into the class trap, which I warned against earlier. The argument obscures the possibility that Marx's approach influences Bourdieu's own and can be used, to an extent, compatibly with it. Michael Grenfell, for example, notes that it is possible to see influences of Marx (and Weber) in Bourdieu's work, including in the origins of the idea of

[77] See also, on internalised systems of classification and the idea of 'doxa', Lane (n 9) 129.

'capital'.[78] Bourdieu's work also has radical possibilities, which are pertinent to the heuristic of transformation, so long as we take care with it. For example, some criticise Bourdieu's analysis of lower-class people in his book, *Distinction*. Bourdieu portrays lower-class people as having a set of needs-based, undeveloped cultural tastes.[79] It is right that Bourdieu sometimes mistakes informality for a lack of complexity. Jeremy Lane uses the example of Cockney rhyming slang: it is informal but hardly lacks linguistic complexity.[80] This mistake, however, can be corrected. Crossley illustrates the potential once it is corrected. Crossley argues that Bourdieu's use of capital emphasises that '[p]ower and dominance derive not only from possession of material resources but also from possession of cultural and social resources', with the idea of symbolic capital underscoring that 'the value of any form of capital depends, in part, upon social recognition'.[81] Money, for instance, gives us both spending power and a certain status. Crossley suggests that Marx, meanwhile, reduces capital to the economic.

I agree with Crossley that Bourdieu animates class in a way that Marx does not. Bourdieu's approach comfortably explains why class often forms part of personal and communal identity. His approach also captures aspects of the exploitation through relations of production (the wealthy boss, the poor worker) that Marx emphasises. Bourdieu's types of capital explain much about these relations and offer us a more developed toolkit for our analysis. However, Bourdieu's approach can still be read alongside some aspects of Marxist approaches. This reminds us of the class trap and the danger of assuming that we should pick one. It may be that, with the tools of Bourdieu's approach, legal analysis can still draw on some Marxist insights, such as exploitation in relations of production and correct the neutral (and, in respect of lower-class culture, apparently derogatory) approach that Bourdieu's work sometimes displays towards class-based differences. Altogether, then, Bourdieu's work satisfies the criteria of precision and accuracy and – perhaps with influence from other approaches – it can inspire reasoning that seeks to transform societies for the better.

6. 'STRATIFICATION' ANALYSES

6.1. Studies

This last sketch is not tied to a particular thinker. It moves away from specific theoretical traditions and, instead, considers a type of method. It concerns the

[78] M Grenfell, 'Biography' in Grenfell (n 9) 11, 20. It should be noted that Bourdieu would not necessarily have always accepted this: D Robbins, 'Theory of Practice' in Grenfell (n 9) 26, 38.

[79] See generally Lane (n 9) 161–65.

[80] Lane (n 9) 164.

[81] Crossley (n 9) 85–86.

more general category of 'stratification analyses'. Crompton identifies this category in her work. Having considered what she describes as the 'classic' influences of Marx, Weber, their modifiers and the 'cultural turn' in class, she describes the sociologists who measure forms of stratification understood as indicators of class divisions.[82] These approaches focus on giving empirical accounts of class structures, which Crompton understands as '[t]he division of the population into unequally rewarded categories' centring on types of work.[83]

Once more, note what these studies seek to do. Unlike the more theoretical frameworks that I have considered so far (and assessed, partly, in terms of how they can *explain* the reality of class), these approaches use work-based class schemes to describe 'the broad contours of occupational inequality'.[84] A good illustration of the more empiricist approach is the Office for National Statistics' Socio-Economic Classification (ONS-SEC, originally just NS-SEC). In a Weberian tradition, the approach offers a set of analytic classes and occupational categories – 'employers in large establishments', 'higher managerial and administrative occupations', 'higher professional occupations' – into which everyone might be sorted.

6.2. Legal Analysis

There is much to be said for such approaches, even if they seem mechanistic. Crompton correctly observes that the ONS-SEC is 'clearly constructed and operationalized, as well as being theoretically grounded'. It is **precise.** On the surface, it is attractive in a similar way to approaches inspired by Marx or Weber. We can take as a criterion a person's job, or the amount of property they control, and move from there. Again, for legal analysis, this has the appearance of ease. Presented with a dispute, a judge could apply these detailed schemes and determine how to classify each person involved. It is straightforward to imagine. Person A has a higher professional occupation, whereas person B has a lower technical occupation. In that scheme, person A occupies a more advantaged class position than person B. In addition to its precision, the ONS-SEC is well-established and has been applied in a range of studies, which suggests that it is measurable and can predict outcomes.[85] It might also be said that it is **accurate.**

Given these strengths, it may be tempting to swipe at the clouds of a theoretical approach like that of Bourdieu and go to ground. You could say that the

[82] Crompton (n 7) 42, 49–70.

[83] Crompton (n 7) 49.

[84] Crompton (n 7) 49; S Krutikova and others, *Intergenerational Mobility in the UK* (London, Institute for Financial Studies, 2023) 4–5: www.ifs.org.uk/publications/intergenerational-mobility-uk.

[85] See, eg, Social Mobility Commission, *Social Mobility Index* (London, Social Mobility Commission, 2024): www.gov.uk/government/publications/state-of-the-nation-2024-local-to-national-mapping-opportunities-for-all/chapter-1-introduction.

law should aspire to certainty and use a scheme like the ONS-SEC. Rather than relying on mazes created by Bourdieu and Marx, the law should avoid theoretical controversies and stick with a tabular system of categories, accepting that it may have to be less multi-dimensional in doing so. Yet we run into a similar problem faced by the Marxist schemes that Wright and others have developed. The appearance of both precision and accuracy is, in fact, limited by the focus on types of occupation. This cannot be – in all the contexts in which the law would consider class – a careful and complete approach to class. It would obscure, or at least sideline, the social and cultural aspects that Bourdieu correctly recognises as important.[86]

Perhaps there is a reply to my argument here. Why not use a stratification analysis of this kind in the context of employment law, for instance, and switch to Bourdieu's approach in other legal contexts better suited to it? What if legal analysis has different purposes in different areas, as do different approaches to class? For example, we might argue that the approach we take to introducing class as a 'protected characteristic' in the Equality Act 2010 should be different from the approach we take in other contexts, such as the criminal law or more general discussions of society and the law.[87]

My answer rests on more than a desire to have the neatness of a single approach for all legal analysis. The key is the ability of Bourdieu's approach to adapt. By using his idea of capital, the approach can unpick maltreatment in a specific employment context. It can *also* articulate why a person in the street might shout at another person in a way that displays hostility towards them based on their (actual or perceived) class. It has the granular quality needed to make sense of situations that occur between people. In addition to that, it has the overarching quality needed to identify what is wrong with structures and bigger decision-making, such as governmental policy that disadvantages those typically perceived as having low-quality social capital, or to dissect what part the law plays in maintaining and exacerbating classist inequality. This flexibility allows Bourdieu's approach to adapt across legal contexts while keeping a consistent overall framework.

7. TAKING INSPIRATION

Drawing these threads together, I suggest that Bourdieu's approach best meets the three heuristics of (i) precision, (ii) accuracy and (iii) transformation of

[86] Bourdieu's framework is also more consistent with an approach that does not presume that class is the most fundamental division or form of inequality, unlike Marxist approaches: see, on the 'pivotal lines of demarcation', Wright (n 8) 32.

[87] See, on the (misleading) association between lower-class people and criminality, Davis (n 16) 139.

societies for the better, so that it is most suitable to take forward to influence legal analysis. I should add to this conclusion in two ways.

There is, first, a point about *how* to use Bourdieu's approach in legal analysis. I have explored why this kind of approach should influence the law and legal scholarship in general. However, as I explained at the start of this chapter, the purpose of giving an overview of each approach to class was not so that we take one and transplant it wholesale into the law. Bourdieu's analysis was certainly never intended to be taken and dropped into legal doctrine. His framework is very complex, as I have emphasised. My preference for his approach is not, therefore, purist in some intellectual way. What I suggest is that legal analysis can take inspiration from the major aspects of his approach: class understood as a way we relate to each other in a distinctive system in societies, which has social, cultural and economic aspects that interact and overlap. To repeat the point: the place of Bourdieu's approach in legal analysis should be inspirational, not dogmatic. This is the part that Wolfenden, many years ago, got right: in legal analysis and law reform, we are not trying to produce 'a sociological treatise'.

There is a second point, which is about taking inspiration from approaches other than Bourdieu's. My arguments do not require us to ignore all other approaches to class, which may have used Marxist, Weberian or other schemes. We can still learn from them even as we draw mostly from Bourdieu's approach in the law. For example, when dealing with some contexts (such as wages and profit in labour), Marx may be able to give us some insights that are compatible with Bourdieu's general framework. Other approaches may still be relevant, especially when legal analysis must draw on studies which themselves use different approaches to explain why classist inequality can be so damaging and unjust. Indeed, you might not agree with my analysis of the approaches at all. You might prefer one to Bourdieu's or another that I have not even discussed. You could take inspiration from that approach for the purposes of legal analysis and have success. Different approaches will bring different insights. There may be instances in which Bourdieu's approach creates too much imprecision, leads to inaccuracy, or hampers legal reasoning's ability to transform societies for the better. However, I doubt that those issues would be significant enough to reject Bourdieu's approach entirely or to refute it as the leading approach in legal analysis. To that end, I have set out why I consider that Bourdieu's approach would, on the whole, work best in the law. My approach is not agnostic, but it is also not dogmatic.

8. IS CLASS WHATEVER YOU WANT IT TO BE, *REALLY*?

After touring the major approaches and settling on taking inspiration mainly from Bourdieu, it is worth revisiting this question. In a sense, class really might be what we want it to be. We have many approaches and taking 'inspiration' from them is hopelessly woolly. But, if that is true, it is similar to many ideas we already use in the law: 'race', 'sexuality', 'gender', 'disability' and other commonly prohibited grounds of discrimination. Ideas like this wield huge influence in the law and societies, even as they remain heavily contested. While these ideas are often influenced by what people who use them seek to achieve, they remain meaningful.

Accepting that there are diverging (and competing) approaches to an idea like class, I have argued that Bourdieu's approach is most suitable for legal analysis in the light of our three heuristics. Although some lawyers might think it necessary, I do not propose a 'definition' in the form of a context-free statement. Instead, I prefer an approach which takes class for the purposes of legal analysis **as a distinctive relationship between people in a society, best understood as involving unequal social, cultural and economic capital.**

So, taking inspiration from Bourdieu and Savage's development of his framework, class is relational and blends the social, cultural and economic. In the rest of this book, I take this as my working approach. Finding a way to approach class in legal analysis is only the first step in understanding it in the context of discrimination. From 'class', we still need to get to 'classism'.

3

Classism or Just Being Poor? Discrimination and Other Ideas

'But is it discrimination or is it just being poor?'

I HEARD THAT QUESTION when I was sitting in a seminar at university. I was studying discrimination law and had got into the habit of raising the topic of class almost every seminar. The habit was probably annoying to some of the other students and, maybe, my teachers. But it seemed that the law consistently missed the topic. In one seminar, I remember we were discussing a case (though – like any good lawyer – I forget which particular case). I suggested that the experience of the claimants in the case was an example of classism. Another student responded by asking that question.

Initially, the question struck me as dismissive. It seemed callous, as if we accept that being poor is inevitable or, worse, a morally acceptable part of life. I was tempted to ignore it, but it made me think. While the question may have come from a fellow student, it seemed to affect academics' work just as much. Thinking about it now, the instinct behind the question reflects a serious challenge when developing an idea of classism. There is a deep sense that class relates to problems *distinct* from discrimination. The theme is that class is better understood through ideas like 'maldistribution' and 'capitalism', not 'discrimination'. This chapter aims to answer the question – *discrimination or just being poor* – by looking at these ideas.

1. THEORISING DISCRIMINATION

Start with 'discrimination'. It is necessary to think about what it means. The law in the UK offers one approach. While the law's understanding of discrimination is often, at its core, individualistic, the law can make space for what are sometimes called the more structural aspects. For example, section 19 of the Equality Act 2010 prohibits indirect discrimination. This form of discrimination concerns policies, criteria and practices that put people with a certain protected characteristic at 'a particular disadvantage' when compared with those who do not share that characteristic (so long as the policy, criterion or practice in question is not 'a proportionate means of achieving a legitimate aim').[1] On one view, section 19 targets discrimination that is not confined to the way one person treats another. First, the framing is broad. Rather than taking as its starting point a single instance of treatment, section 19 concentrates on policies, criteria and practices. These encompass, by their nature, situations beyond a single instance of one person mistreating another. Second, section 19 does not require proof of intention or motive. A policy-maker does not need to intend disadvantage in relation to a protected characteristic, or be motivated by the protected characteristic, though evidence that a person intended to disadvantage a particular group may, of course, be highly relevant when assessing the facts of a case.[2] The lack of a requirement to prove intention or motive weakens the emphasis on a state of mind.[3] Instead, this part of the law shifts focus to the *effect* of the policy, criterion or practice.

On another view, however, even this framework remains individualistic. The Equality Act works in a particular kind of legal system. That system has broad regulatory and cultural influence, for instance in shaping how employers write their 'equality and diversity' policies. Nevertheless, the law's decisions and developments rely heavily on disputes between specific individuals and organisations. In the typical legal claim made against a public body's decision, for instance, the claimant needs standing to proceed: a 'sufficient interest', which usually requires someone to be directly affected by, or to have reasonable concern in, the decision in question.[4] Similarly, in a common type of dispute before an employment tribunal, it is the employee who sues the employer because of alleged wrongdoing, such as discrimination (alongside other claims, like those alleging unfair dismissal). Compared with the more theoretical literature on the meaning of discrimination, or other disciplines like political theory and sociology, the law tends to be less concerned with the *systems* in societies that create or embody discrimination. Rather, the law makes abstract an individual or a set of individuals. The language of section 19(1) of the Equality Act supports this interpretation: 'A person (A) discriminates against another (B) if A applies to B a provision, criterion or practice which is discriminatory in relation to a relevant protected characteristic of B's'. The statute's focus is still not on the broader ideas and systems that appear in theoretical literature. Those ideas and systems may lurk in the background of the legal framework (sometimes influencing

[1] Equality Act 2010, s 19(2)(b).

[2] *R (E) v Governing Body of JFS* [2009] UKSC 15, [195] (Hope L).

[3] See, for discussion of the blurring of the distinction in *James v Eastleigh Borough Council* [1990] 2 AC 75 and *JFS* between direct discrimination and indirect discrimination based on motive and reason, S Fredman, 'Direct and Indirect Discrimination: Is There Still a Divide?' in H Collins and T Khaitan (eds), *Foundations of Indirect Discrimination Law* (Oxford, Hart Publishing, 2018) 31, 39–40.

[4] Senior Courts Act 1981, s 31(3); *AXA General Insurance Ltd v Lord Advocate* [2011] UKSC 46 at [63]–[64] (Hope L).

certain doctrines, such as the 'meaning' of indirect discrimination), but they do not take centre stage.

Combined with the over-correction and the influence of party politics that I set out in Chapter 1, the law's individualistic focus might explain why many academics have ignored classism as a form of discrimination. Class-related issues tend to be understood as societal problems disconnected from the kinds of issues surrounding the protected characteristics in the Equality Act. If class is relevant, it is as a background to our legal analysis. Class is relegated to the maldistribution that provides the context for better known forms of discrimination, like racism. For example, when Bob Hepple, Mary Coussey and Tufyal Choudhury make one reference to 'social classes' in their review of anti-discrimination legislation, they do so only to discuss the higher '[u]nemployment rates for ethnic minorities' in comparison with white people in the same classes.[5] Too often, class is understood only through the lens of 'social mobility' or 'access to good-quality education and work opportunities'.[6]

The Social Mobility Commission's *State of the Nation*, published each year, has never referred to 'classism'. In its publication in 2024, the only references to discrimination are in footnotes, which take us to the list of protected characteristics (without class) in section 4 of the Equality Act.[7] The Commission regularly uses the idea of 'class' in its own writing, but it does so to make sense of the trajectory of 'social mobility' when children 'have different life outcomes from their parents'.[8] The report clumps together class, 'background, socio-economic status or any other personal characteristic'.[9] Perhaps, in all this, there is also the assumption that, unlike protected characteristics, class is so systemic that it cannot be reduced to individual instances or disputes. If class has a place anywhere, it is in 'the inequalities of outcome which result from socio-economic disadvantage' like the vague 'public sector duty regarding socio-economic inequalities' in section 1 of the Equality Act (yet to be brought into force in England).[10]

Beyond that specific statutory context, there are general patterns in the theory about the meaning of 'discrimination', both in legal academia and in other fields of study. Scholars disagree about what makes something discriminatory rather than more generally unfair, unjust or arbitrary. To illustrate the concern, take the classic example of a person with red hair. Prejudice against

[5] B Hepple, M Coussey and T Choudhury, 'Equality: A New Framework. Report of the Independent Review of the Enforcement of UK Anti-Discrimination Legislation' (Hart Publishing, 2000) 12.

[6] Social Mobility Commission, *State of the Nation 2024: Local to National, Mapping Opportunities for All* (2024) 43.

[7] Social Mobility Commission (n 6) 20.

[8] Social Mobility Commission (n 6) 20.

[9] Social Mobility Commission (n 6) 81.

[10] Although the Labour Party committed in its 2024 manifesto to bringing the section into force throughout the UK: *Change: Labour Party Manifesto 2024* (2024) 88: www.labour.org.uk/wp-content/uploads/2024/06/Labour-Party-manifesto-2024.pdf.

people with red hair has been around for many years. They may suffer bullying, particularly in childhood. They may feel less attractive or embarrassed because of the way that other people treat them. There are various insults for them. Properly understood, the disadvantage that red-haired people suffer is unfair, unjust and arbitrary. But it is not discriminatory.[11]

Why is that so? This question – about the distinction between discrimination and other kinds of wrongdoing – has kept many people occupied. By setting out an overview of different scholars' answers to the question, it may be easier to understand why classism has been ignored or misunderstood.

1.1. Individualistic Approaches

It is helpful to divide different academic approaches to the idea of discrimination into emphatic categories. By 'emphatic', I mean that the distinctions here are not rigid but rather capture the focus of particular approaches. The line between 'individualistic' and 'group' approaches is not rigidly drawn. Even within the loose category of individualistic approaches, there are many concepts at work: dignity, respect, autonomy, agency, identity.[12] Hanoch Sheinman summarises 'individualistic' approaches well. Such approaches accept that discrimination is often understood in a 'heavily comparative' way. However, they reject the argument that this comparative issue is what makes discrimination *wrong*. Rather, they emphasise an aspect of the treatment of a person, irrespective of the comparative treatment of other people. Sheinman, for example, refers to a range of approaches of this kind, including Sophia Moreau's idea of our interest in 'deliberative freedoms' about how we live our lives, an interest which does *not* depend on whether other people have been granted those freedoms.[13]

Although it is important to remember the nuances of each approach, there are some general points to make when thinking about classism. There is a point about **ignorance**. Scholars developing individualistic approaches rarely, if ever, consider class or refer to it in the examples they use to test their theory. By contrast, scholars consistently use categories like race, gender, sexuality and disability in their examples. For instance, while Deborah Hellman refers to homophobia, misogyny and racism in her theory of discrimination, she does

[11] See, eg (discussing the point about arbitrariness in a hypothetical society in which it is possible to separate eye-colour from race), T Khaitan, *A Theory of Discrimination Law* (Oxford, Oxford University Press, 2015) 31, 37–38.

[12] See, eg (discussing agency and autonomy), B Eidelson, *Discrimination and Disrespect* (Oxford, Oxford University Press, 2015) 144.

[13] H Sheinman, 'Two Faces of Discrimination' in D Hellman and S Moreau (eds), *Philosophical Foundations of Discrimination Law* (Oxford, Oxford University Press, 2013) 28, 29, citing S Moreau, 'What Is Discrimination?' (2010) 38 *Philosophy & Public Affairs* 143, 147, 174. See also S Moreau, *Faces of Inequality: A Theory of Wrongful Discrimination* (Oxford, Oxford University Press, 2020).

not use examples to do with class or classism.[14] Because scholars like Hellman prioritise the familiar ideas in anti-discrimination academia and activism (such as race and gender), they do not engage fully with the issue of class – let alone classism.

Then there is a point about **misunderstanding**. Individualistic theories hinder an accurate understanding of classism. They encourage us to locate the wrong of discrimination at the level of an individual: how it makes them feel, how it denigrates them, how it disrespects them, *irrespective* of the treatment of others. We could argue that these theories have got it right. They reflect what classism, in fact, entails. Consider Benjamin Eidelson's approach. It is one of the most classically individualistic: discrimination is, at its core, the failure to treat people 'as individuals'.[15] First, Eidelson puts forward the 'character condition': a person treats another person as an individual only if they give reasonable weight to the way in which that other person has exercised their autonomy in giving shape to their own life (where evidence is reasonably available and relevant to the determination).[16] Second, Eidelson offers the 'agency condition': if a person's judgements concern another's choices, these judgements should not be made in a way that disparages that other person's capacity to make those choices as an autonomous agent.[17] The violation of either of these conditions helps us to identify what discrimination is and what is wrong with it. Hellman's account, meanwhile, accepts that discrimination may highlight 'the relative treatment of groups', but the core of her approach is that discrimination violates 'an individual right' rooted in treatment 'with equal concern and respect'.[18] While there is some room for comparison with others in these approaches, discrimination is ultimately individualised.

It is certainly possible to sketch why classism counts as a form of discrimination under such approaches. Continue with Hellman's approach. Imagine that an incident occurs in London. One person mistreats a second person based on class-related attitudes, perhaps labelling them a 'chav'. In being dismissed as a 'chav', the second person is denied equal concern and respect based on traits associated with class. Eidelson's approach may also explain this, though it becomes a little strained. If a person displays traits associated with being a kind of lower-class person, such as their particular clothing and styling, dismissing them on that basis does not give 'reasonable weight' to the way in which they have chosen to live their life. If we understand these features as 'choices' in

[14] See, eg, examples relating to discrimination – understood as differentiation that 'demeans', ie 'denies [another] equal moral worth' – against those who contravene gendered expectations, transgender people and black people in D Hellman, *When Is Discrimination Wrong?* (Cambridge, Massachusetts, Harvard University Press, 2008) 29, 42–45, 59.

[15] B Eidelson, 'Treating People as Individuals' in Hellman and Moreau (n 13) 203; Eidelson (n 12) 144.

[16] Eidelson (n 12) 144, 155–58.

[17] Eidelson (n 12) 144, 158–59.

[18] D Hellman, 'Equality and Unconstitutional Discrimination' in Hellman and Moreau (n 13) 51, 55.

the way that Eidelson's agency condition does, the disparaging of those choices breaches his character condition.

However, the strain when applying Eidelson's approach indicates why individualistic approaches like his fail to understand the *character* of classism. Take my example of being called a 'chav' because of the way you present yourself. In a sense, these are 'choices', perhaps led by cultural examples or by a rejection of some traditional forms of etiquette and clothing. But they are often inseparable from wealth, exposure to stigma and different social rankings, alongside the influence of cultural figures and types of upbringing. Eidelson's approach encourages abstract ideas of 'autonomy' and 'choice'. As Bourdieu's approach to capital reminds us, our choices and autonomy are wrapped in the influences around us, the opportunities we have and the pressures on our decision-making. They may be reflexive or so much a part of our routine that we barely think about them.

These considerations should make us pause. They suggest why individualistic approaches pose the danger of making discrimination both too personal and (like with the focus on 'choice' in Eidelson's approach) too abstract. Such approaches tend to obscure the more structural aspects of discrimination. In addition to ignoring class in their examples, the most pressing problem with individualistic approaches is that they over-emphasise individual decisions to the point of minimising the layers of discrimination. Class is rarely about 'choice' in some personal or isolated sense; its core is unequal social, cultural and economic capital.

1.2. Structural or Group-Led Approaches

As with their individualistic counterparts, structural or group-led approaches vary significantly. Different ideas are, again, at the heart of each theory, but there remain features that put these approaches in a loose category. Most importantly, structural approaches refuse to reduce the wrong of discrimination to a question, at least primarily, of individual maltreatment. They prioritise concepts broader than the individual, such as the group or the system, and involve comparison.[19]

Tarunabh Khaitan's framework offers one example, which he uses to seek to understand and best conceive discrimination law. For Khaitan, the legal approach to discrimination should incorporate the 'Relative Disadvantage Condition': of those groups defined by a universal ground (such as 'race'), members of at least one group are 'significantly more likely to suffer abiding, pervasive and substantial disadvantage' than members of at least one other group.[20]

Structural approaches have an advantage when it comes to classism. They fit better with the understanding of class as systemic, not merely a collection of

[19] Sheinman refers to them as 'holistic' approaches: Sheinman (n 13).
[20] Khaitan (n 11) 31.

insults and stereotypes. In this way, they seem more consistent with Bourdieu's framework of our social field, internalised practices and forms of capital. Plus, such approaches do not ignore the individual. Instead, they see the comparison of individuals as important among the broader issues of groups, structures and disadvantages within society. They can explain why there is a distinctive quality to class-based maltreatment of individuals as opposed to other (non-discriminatory) forms of unfair or arbitrary treatment, but they do so by ensuring that these individualistic examples are kept in their group or structural context.

Nevertheless, even these approaches need care. They retain the potential to obscure classism as a form of discrimination. First, like the individualistic approaches, more structural or group-led approaches tend to **ignore** class in the examples that they give. Across the board, academics have rarely used class in their workings. Second, the notion of groups in some of these approaches (like Khaitan's) may encourage us to **misunderstand** what discrimination entails and, therefore, to exclude classism as a form of discrimination. Some might assume that groups are easy to define or that we must have a very precise notion of a 'group' in order to establish the existence of discrimination. This assumption returns us to the idea that, to achieve an accurate understanding of classism, we must be very precise. The reality is that class may often be imprecise and yet that imprecision is partly what makes up the very idea of class, as I set out in Chapter 2.

Khaitan's approach is useful here, but only if we are clear about the idea of 'disadvantage'.[21] His approach prioritises the connection between discrimination and disadvantage. For example, if I criticise capitalist society because of the big gaps between the rich and the poor, between those educated at huge private expense and those at low-performing state schools, some might say that I must be criticising 'disadvantage', which is different from – and much broader than – the idea of 'discrimination'. Yet this criticism seems not to accept that other forms of discrimination (like racism and misogyny) have structural aspects. Racism and misogyny are enmeshed in overlapping social, employment, educational, cultural and economic aspects of societies. While we may instinctively think of these forms of discrimination as slurs or stereotypes, they still have structural aspects, such as the gender pay gap and racial poverty.[22] Khaitan helps us to anchor discrimination in disadvantage. He uses 'disadvantage' to give a distinctive meaning to 'discrimination'. Adopting Khaitan's approach when we talk of disadvantage, we make sure that class disadvantage is kept firmly within the idea of discrimination. Disadvantage and discrimination are wrapped up together.

[21] It is also worth noting that Khaitan, among other aspects of his approach, attaches the proviso that the disadvantage must be unjustified, which is why groups who might otherwise meet his three criteria (eg people who are sexually violent to children) are excluded from protection under the law: eg Khaitan (n 11) 145, 180–92.

[22] See, discussing unemployed rates for racial groups in certain classes, Hepple, Coussey and Choudhury (n 5).

1.3. Mixed Approaches

As I have noted, categories like the 'individualistic' and the 'structural' may be reductive. Sheinman adopts an approach that rejects the wholeness of either an individualistic or comparative (between groups and so on) way of understanding the concept of discrimination. Instead, Sheinman suggests that each approach has 'some of the truth'. Sometimes, we may need to treat people well, no matter how we may treat others. Sometimes, the question is less absolute and more relative: the size of gaps in the treatment of different people may matter.[23] In a similar vein, Moreau notes that our concern in cases of wrongful discrimination is not with every act of treating people unequally, but only with some – those acts that disadvantage some people relative to others, those that treat them as the inferiors of others.[24] This is partly why Moreau calls her approach pluralist, as it accepts that discrimination may be related to inequality and yet wrong for different reasons. Moreau suggests that some older philosophical approaches to 'equality' tend not to capture the law's concern with giving people respect, rather than giving people *exactly the same*.[25] While I accept Moreau's analysis of pluralism and inequality here, I use the language of 'mixed approaches' to refer to the mixture of individual and structural concerns rather than the monism or pluralism of moral wrongs. 'Mixed' approaches can be monist or pluralist in Moreau's sense.

Tristin Green's work offers an example of a developed 'mixed' approach. Green rejects a strict line between individualistic and structural or group-led categories. While Green accepts that discrimination is a personal wrong that may occur in individual decision-making, she recognises the complexity of discrimination and the fact that individuals are guided and constrained by structures (such as those that organise the workplace).[26] Green stresses the enmeshing of individuals in these structural problems. In more recent work in the context of Title VII of the US Civil Rights Act 1964, Green argues that discrimination (at least at work) is best understood as organisational injustice through 'structures, systems, practices, and cultures' at work, rather than a set of moral failures between colleagues or abstract 'structures' operating alone.[27] Coming from a different context, Patrick Shin also identifies the problem of categories and offers a mixed approach. Rather than arguing for a single overarching idea with different parts (like Green's organisational injustice that blends individual and structural issues), Shin concludes that no one approach to the moral wrongness

[23] H Sheinman (n 13) 28, 36–37 and 50.

[24] Moreau, *Faces of Inequality* (n 13) 8. See, too, ch 3 (Moreau).

[25] Moreau, *Faces of Inequality* (n 13) 8, citing, eg, D Parfit, 'Equality and Priority' (1997) 10(3) *Ratio* 202.

[26] T Green, 'The Future of Systemic Disparate Treatment Law' (2011) 32(2) *Berkeley Journal of Employment & Labour Law* 395, 438–39.

[27] T Green, *Discrimination Laundering: The Rise of Organizational Innocence and the Crisis of Equal Opportunity Law* (Cambridge, Cambridge University Press, 2017) 65, 116.

of individual actions captures the 'legal' idea of discrimination. In fact, Shin suggests, it is 'probably futile' to reduce its dimensions to a formal set of moral principles.[28] This is likely because the law is not one philosopher's book. It is a blend, with many ideas floating around, not fully compatible with each other. Shin argues that the most we can suggest is that the law reflects a variety of attitudes about stopping behaviour that tends 'to reinforce or resonate with historic and persistent patterns of unjust inequalities'.[29] These observations suggest that law is more piecemeal or pragmatic than people often assume.

If this is true, it may explain why some scholars move to ideas that seem more positive or comprehensive than the idea of discrimination. One instance is a preference for 'equality law'. Editing a collection of essays on 'exponential inequalities' and the role of the law in addressing them, Shreya Atrey and Sandra Fredman use the language of 'equality law' rather than 'discrimination' or 'anti-discrimination law'.[30] Referring to Beth Gaze's contribution, they accept that 'it is disadvantage, not discrimination, then which seems to be the cause of exponential inequalities'.[31] Similarly, another contributor, Jessica Clarke, argues that the model of equality in the US has concentrated on a narrow, superficial idea of anti-discrimination, rather than pursuing more structural transformation.[32] Such an approach tends to view discrimination in a more individualistic or interpersonal form, rather than adopting a mixed approach.

Yet why have some scholars surrendered 'discrimination' to this narrow meaning? The capitulation supports Shin's reluctance to apply strict categories of individualistic and structural approaches. In truth, it is difficult, if not impossible, to understand either without using both. Bourdieu, for example, refuses to accept a strict division between the two. His approach accords with his broader rejection of common distinctions in political and sociological literature, including the sharp line drawn between the objective and the subjective as well as the individual and the structure.[33] Bourdieu's types of capital themselves are active as a person navigates their society, interacting with sources of power within that society, and drawing on them in their relationships with other people. The point here is that classism, as with other forms of discrimination, may operate at many levels and be wrong for many reasons.

Bearing in mind that discrimination may involve different wrongs across different contexts, and may involve beliefs and slurs among more 'structural' issues, Khaitan's approach comes closest to allowing for this possibility while

[28] P Shin, 'Is There a Unitary Concept of Discrimination?' in Hellman and Moreau (n 13) 164, 180.

[29] ibid, 181.

[30] S Atrey and S Fredman, 'Introduction' in S Atrey and S Fredman (eds), *Exponential Inequalities: Equality Law in Times of Crisis* (Oxford, Oxford University Press, 2023) 1.

[31] Atrey and Fredman (n 30) 5.

[32] J Clarke, 'A Public Policy Approach to Inequality' in Atrey and Fredman (n 30) 161, 169.

[33] See, eg, J Lane, *Pierre Bourdieu: A Critical Introduction* (London, Pluto Press, 2000) 100; M Grenfell, 'Introduction' in M Grenfell (ed), *Pierre Bourdieu: Key Concepts* (Abingdon, Routledge, 2012) 22 and 43.

still offering a useful framework that we can understand clearly. Granted, Khaitan's overall theory views the law in this area as having the general aim of protecting everyone's freedom 'to pursue a good life', which in part involves relatively equal access to the conditions needed for such freedom.[34] It is monist, in Moreau's sense, in that it appeals to a single value. However, I focus on Khaitan's use of disadvantage here, which I read as possible to separate from his reliance on an overall freedom to pursue a good life. I therefore do not take a view on Khaitan's monism; my main concern is with his idea of disadvantage helping us to understand discrimination as structural *and* individual.

First, Khaitan's idea of 'disadvantage' is **adaptable while remaining meaningful**. The specific type of disadvantage accounts for discrimination as a distinctively systemic phenomenon, rather than a set of unconnected harms that occur only on an individual-to-individual basis. In this way, his approach's flexibility is a considerable strength. It can squeeze into the confines of one person's interaction with another person, such as the disadvantage caused by the use of a slur or by the influence of a belief. It can also diffuse across wide-ranging issues, such as the disadvantage in inequalities in housing, for instance. While that flexibility might make 'disadvantage' appear empty, possibly applying to anything, Khaitan ensures that it remains meaningful by adding his three qualifiers: 'abiding', 'pervasive' and 'substantial'.[35] Disadvantage, then, does not capture anything and everything. It must be long-term, extensive and severe. This is not quite Sheinman's layered pluralism of different ideas, Shin's different wrongs mixing when the law addresses discrimination, or Moreau's approach to the different faces of inequality. Instead, Khaitan's approach provides a useful tool to pin down what we are trying to identify when we talk of discrimination as opposed to unfairness or arbitrariness in general. Khaitan's kind of 'disadvantage' encourages us to understand classism as necessarily including 'bigger' or 'tangible' issues (money, goods, physical property) which mingle with, cause, and are caused by, 'smaller' or 'intangible' issues (slurs, snobbery).

Second, Khaitan's approach is **compatible with various explanations of the cause or meaning of discrimination**. I read Khaitan's approach as compatible with, for instance, explanations that locate the wrong of discrimination in biased or otherwise wrongful attitudes, beliefs and ideologies. For example, the true cause of the layered disadvantage that Khaitan describes may be found, to borrow Jordan Scott's phrase, 'in the head'. Scott argues that, despite the trend in philosophy to move away from cognitive understandings of racism, racism is really about the biased attitudes that we hold and apply to others.[36] Scott is correct, clearly, that cognitive features are a part of discrimination, at least in ordinary language. We can be discriminatory in our thoughts as well as our behaviour. Yet – as a legal doctrine like indirect discrimination may reflect – we

[34] Khaitan (n 11) 5, esp 130–31.
[35] Khaitan (n 11) 31.
[36] J Scott, 'Putting Racism Back in the Head' (2025) 53(3) *Philosophy & Public Affairs* 218.

can be discriminatory without meaning to be or realising. A key advantage of Khaitan's reliance on 'disadvantage' is that it tells us why discrimination is distinctive while allowing for various explanations at the more theoretical level as to what causes or defines discrimination as a phenomenon (such as beliefs or ideologies). Discrimination may be in the head, but it is definitely in the disadvantage, too.

Third, given his focus on the law, Khaitan's approach has **significant explanatory value for legal analysis of discrimination in particular.** It makes sense of commonly protected grounds like race, disability and sexual orientation. It tells us why we tend to protect in law those groups rather than, for instance, people with red hair. Granted, this aspect of his approach is not as strong as the other benefits I have described: the law might be wrong to date in protecting many of the groups that it protects. However, when combined with other benefits, this adds a helpful explanatory layer to the theoretical aspects of Khaitan's approach. For these reasons, we should use his approach to develop an idea of classism as discrimination.

2. CLASSISM AS DISCRIMINATION

To do this, I take class and apply to it Khaitan's idea of disadvantage of a certain longevity, extent and severity, with the three criteria of 'abiding, pervasive and substantial'.[37]

2.1. 'Abiding'

Classism is 'abiding' because it has existed for a long time.[38] Even if class has changed over the centuries (including in the transformation into capitalist societies),[39] advantage and disadvantage relating to it go back centuries. Guy Shrubsole surveys aristocratic families who trace their influence and wealth to the Norman Conquest, including the Norfolks and the Percys, and to their role in colonial enslavement.[40] Other evidence supports this. Based on their research, Gregory Clark and Neil Cummins explain that families with surnames deriving from William the Conqueror's Norman French aristocracy are still found at

[37] I do not, however, adopt Khaitan's division between 'political', 'socio-cultural' and 'material' disadvantage: for that organisational approach, see Khaitan (n 11) 51–56. I prefer Bourdieu's framework here.

[38] Although Khaitan gives it simply the meaning of being 'likely to manifest itself over a certain length of time', I consider the better interpretation to require a long time: Khaitan (n 11) 35–36. This necessarily depends on the context. In other words, the disadvantage has neither materialised suddenly nor will it go away quickly.

[39] That shift being a significant one, rather than a quantitative one or a long, continuous process, as Ellen Meiksins Woods argues: *The Origin of Capitalism* (London, Verso, 2020) 13–17.

[40] G Shrubsole, *Who Owns England?* (Glasgow, William Collins, 2019) 76–78.

high rates in traditionally prestigious professions, indicating much lower levels of 'social mobility' than often estimated.[41]

In other contexts, divisions of advantage and disadvantage have long been drawn. The sumptuary laws of early modern England have broad equivalents in Scotland, under Louis XIII in France, Japan in the 1700s and the Tang dynasty of China from 618.[42] Across various groups, only the upper-class groups – whether royals, nobles, aristocratic samurai, depending on the time and the society – were allowed to wear certain fabrics or colours or, for example, to eat certain foods. Later, Victorian England remained 'a deeply classed society; everyone was aware of class, admitted that it was a meaningful social reality, and identified themselves as a member of a class'.[43] The ('new') Poor Laws and the workhouse took earlier themes of class division, of 'the rough-respectable divide' and 'the deserving-undeserving divide', and institutionalised them in ways that made them ever more important.[44] For centuries in some countries, the only form of representation in parliaments was restricted to upper-class men and, later, selected members of the upper part of the middle classes, such as prominent merchants (sometimes only through marriage to upper-class families), or extraneous property-owning groups.[45] In the UK, it was not until 1918 that all men – of *any* class – could, in principle, vote in parliamentary elections.[46] For much of the century following the Reform Act 1832, the right to vote had still rested on age, gender and property.

Today, the evidence generally supports the persistence of class advantage and disadvantage. Although class and classism have been largely ignored in discussions of the law and discrimination, it is nonetheless possible to find evidence of them. In Chapter 2, I referred to the arguments that class is still a meaningful category in people's lives, with significant consequences in societies. In recent times, there remain many examples of classism in popular media, from a former *The Apprentice* contestant 'sneering' on *This Morning* in 2013 about the class of families based on children's surnames to expressions of support for Scottish

[41] G Clark and N Cummins, *The Son Also Rises: Surnames and the History of Social Mobility* (Princeton, Princeton University Press, 2014), though see the criticisms of their methodology and the alternative proposed by F Torche and A Corvalan, 'Estimating Intergenerational Mobility with Grouped Data: A Critique of Clark's *The Son Also Rises*' (2018) 47(4) *Sociological Methods & Research* 787.

[42] See, eg, M Hayward, '"Outlandish Superfluities": Luxury and Clothing in Scottish and English Sumptuary Law from the Fourteenth to the Seventeenth Century' in G Riello and U Rublack (eds), *The Right to Dress* (Cambridge, Cambridge University Press, 2019) 96; and Rublack and Riello, 'Introduction' (in the same) 1, 8–10.

[43] S Steinbach, *Understanding the Victorians* (Abingdon, Routledge, 2012) 114.

[44] Steinbach (n 43) 120.

[45] See, discussing suffrage in France, the UK and Sweden, T Piketty, *A Brief History of Equality* (trans Steven Rendall, Cambridge, Massachusetts, Harvard University Press, 2021) 103–08. See also, on the composition of the House of Lords and the mingling of aristocratic and industrialist families, C Ballinger, *The House of Lords 1911-2011: A Century of Non-Reform* (London, Bloomsbury Publishing, 2014) 21–22.

[46] A Hobbs and FJ Ogden, *A Guide to the Representation of the People Act, 1918* (London, Butterworth & Co, 1918).

students in 2024, more likely to be lower-class, at Edinburgh University who suffer (English-centric) classism.[47] These examples reflect the academic research. The British Social Attitudes survey in 2023 found that people in the 2020s perceive barriers to moving between classes about as much as they did in the 1980s.[48] Lower-class people in traditionally prestigious professions – like law and medicine – remain likely to earn, on average, 17 per cent less than others.[49] Considering the persistence of classism alongside its long history, it is clearly 'abiding'.

2.2. 'Pervasive'

Classism is 'pervasive' because it affects many parts of people's lives. Khaitan frames this criterion in a similar way: '[t]he disadvantage must be pervasive in the sense that it should not normally be limited to a single, discrete sphere of human activity, but pervade several aspects of our lives'.[50] The disadvantage is likely across education, jobs *and* health, for instance, rather than limited to one aspect only.

Although the research does not often use the idea of 'classism', there is a great deal of evidence that disadvantage relating to class operates in a wide range of contexts. In the context of work, people experience it in terms of their expected income and their access to (and success within) traditionally prestigious professions. Research indicates that there is still prejudice against people with accents associated with being lower-class.[51] In formal education and healthcare, classism also operates in the barriers of access to them and experiences once inside. Valerie Walkerdine uses the idea of classism to describe how lower-class students at traditionally prestigious universities still suffer many aspects of classism, despite about 50 per cent of 18-year-olds now attending university compared with 13 per cent in 1965 and despite how well lower-class students can do in their studies once there.[52] Even in legal proceedings in the 2020s, Alice Paver and others found that stereotyping of participants based on accents and other class

[47] See, eg, the discussion of Hopkins's comments in M Savage, *Social Class in the 21st Century* (London, Pelican, 2015) 363–64, 387–88; R Keenan, 'Why Scottish Students at Edinburgh University Want More Support to Counter Classism', *Guardian* (2024): www.theguardian.com/uk-news/2024/dec/26/scottish-students-at-edinburgh-university-start-support-group-to-counter-alienation.

[48] J Curtice, *British Social Attitudes 40 – Overview: Secular or Cyclical?* (2023) National Centre for Research 15.

[49] D Laurison and S Friedman, 'The Class Pay Gap in Higher Professional and Managerial Occupations' (2016) 81(4) *American Sociological Review* 668.

[50] Khaitan (n 11) 36.

[51] See, discussing class barriers and bias against certain accents, Creative Access, *Class Barriers & Accent Bias Report* (2023): www.creativeaccess.org.uk/the-language-of-discrimination-how-you-can-work-to-remove-class-barriers-and-accent-bias-in-the-workplace.

[52] V Walkerdine, 'What's Class Got to Do with It?' (2020) 42(1) *Discourse: Studies in the Cultural Politics of Education* 60, 61–62.

markers still occurs.[53] Seventy-seven per cent of participants in Creative Access's research on class barriers and accent bias in the creative industries reported that they felt that they had to change their accents at work.[54]

Other studies tell us that lower-class people are more likely to suffer a range of harms. The Trades Union Congress's report in 2016 into housing and homelessness describes the vulnerability of lower-class queer people of all genders to poverty and homelessness, as a result of the mixing of homophobia, transphobia and classism (both in specific families and in more general forms, such as depriving certain communities of queer support networks and healthcare).[55] Alison Phipps examines the high rates of lower-class women's exposure to sexual violence and the particular forms of stigma attaching to it.[56] Savage, meanwhile, offers a detailed account of how Bourdieu's economic capital blends with the social and the cultural, so that the advantages and disadvantages reverberate across people's lives.[57] In the light of the research in a range of contexts, the correct view is that classism is 'pervasive'.

2.3. 'Substantial'

Classism is 'substantial' because it involves disadvantage that severely affects people's lives. I differ from Khaitan here, who suggests that 'substantial' means 'likely to be more than an inconvenience'.[58] Khaitan's interpretation accords with some legal contexts, such as the interpretation of 'substantial' in section 6 of the Equality Act 2010 as 'more than minor or trivial'.[59] However, it does not reflect other legal contexts, such as substantial being 'important or weighty' in the criminal law's partial defence of diminished responsibility.[60] Of the two, the more demanding interpretation better reflects the reality of classism. I have already set out much of the evidence in relation to what makes it 'abiding' and 'pervasive'. There are, clearly, severe impacts on people's likelihood of entry to and success in formal education and certain professions, wealth, health, and relationships with other people and with culture.[61] The more structural features mix, again, with the personal. There are also examples of severe impacts in

[53] A Paver and others, 'Stereotyped Accent Judgements in Forensic Contexts: Listener Perceptions of Social Traits and Types of Behaviour' (2025) 9 *Frontiers in Communication*.

[54] Creative Access (n 51).

[55] Trades Union Congress (TUC), *Housing, Homelessness and Young LGBT People* (TUC, 2016) 3: www.tuc.org.uk/sites/default/files/Housing%20policy_0.pdf (though again the report does not use the idea of 'class' in express terms).

[56] A Phipps, 'Rape and Respectability: Ideas about Sexual Violence and Social Class' (2009) 43(4) *Sociology* 667.

[57] Savage (n 47) 90–92.

[58] Khaitan (n 11) 36.

[59] Equality Act 2010, s 212.

[60] *Golds* [2016] UKSC 61, [27].

[61] See, eg, (on income) Laurison and Friedman (n 49), (on land and wealth) Shrubsole (n 40), (on cultural and social capital) Savage (n 47).

specific situations, such as the abuse based on class in the death of James Craig Anderson in Mississippi, as well as cases like *Stirling Council v Harris* (2009) in Scotland and *Keane* (2010) in England (which I discuss in more detail in Chapter 6).[62]

As well as existing for a long time and affecting many aspects of people's lives, classism is neither trivial nor easy to disregard. Rather, its impact is severe. Classism operates to preserve for some people the traditionally prestigious jobs, the formal educational achievements, certain social connections, cultural priority and other important aspects of life. It, therefore, meets the third and last criterion of 'substantial'. Classism accurately describes the state in which – for a variety of reasons – members of one class are significantly more likely to suffer abiding, pervasive and substantial disadvantage than members of another class.

3. DISCRIMINATION VERSUS OTHER PROBLEMS

3.1. Maldistribution, Inequality, Capitalism?

A. *Three Ideas*

Good intentions may be one explanation for the failure to develop an understanding of classism as a form of discrimination. Some academics talk of class regularly and strive to find solutions to the problems that overlap, in substance, with what I call classism. They may just be using different words in well-meaning ways.

A common one is 'inequality'. As I have noted, the contributors to Atrey and Fredman's collection of essays no longer ignore class in their examples, but they do not develop any understanding of 'classism' in addition to more general class 'inequalities'.[63] It seems that 'equality' is more desirable than 'anti-discrimination' because 'equality' is more positive. However, as Atrey and Fredman seem to accept elsewhere, the sources of these inequalities are not isolated to sudden problems arising in crisis.[64] Instead, they result from decisions made by successive policy-makers and governments to enlarge inequalities, whether through 'austerity' policies or by enhancing the private markets. It is also dubious to accept, even on its face, that there is a 'crisis', given that these inequalities have characterised societies for centuries.[65] Discrimination (understood using the idea of disadvantage) is wrapped up in these inequalities. It characterises them. The

[62] See, eg, T Dokoupil, 'The Devil Deryl Dedmon', *Irish Examiner* (2012): www.irishexaminer.com/lifestyle/arid-20192079.html; *Stirling Council v Harris* 2009 SLT (Sh Ct) 106; *Keane* [2010] EWCA Crim 2514.

[63] Atrey and Fredman (n 30).

[64] Atrey and Fredman (n 30) 3.

[65] See, eg, T Piketty, *A Brief History of Equality* (trans Steven Rendall, Cambridge, Massachusetts, Harvard University Press, 2021) 16–47.

approach that class is simply 'inequality' may tell us why it can be wrong and unfair, but it never recognises its discriminatory character: that it entails abiding, pervasive and substantial disadvantage in a way that, for instance, having red hair does not.

In these contexts, 'inequality' has a close relationship with 'maldistribution'. A common view understands class as societies' failure to apportion fairly the resources available in it. As a result, some people hoard resources (such as money and goods) at the expense of others, who have low-quality or very few resources. The main benefit of understanding class through the lens of maldistribution is that it offers a familiar vision. Class involves big problems of arrangements in societies. Class is about what people have, how societies organise their resources, and how we should rearrange societies in order to solve their problems. By contrast, classism could seem inadequate. In one sense, it might be too narrow, prioritising personal or only limited effects of bigger maldistributions and inequalities. In another sense, if applied to these broader features in societies, the idea of classism might become strained, stretched to the point of calling almost every arrangement classist, which in turn takes away its analytical usefulness.

It may also be that this is only a dispute about words. Perhaps it does not matter whether we use 'discrimination' or 'inequality' or 'maldistribution'. There is, after all, much common ground. One of Atrey and Fredman's contributing authors, Colm O'Cinneide, argues that the existing legal analysis (as well as being limited in scope and ambition) is rooted in an adversarial model rather than a more transformative and sweeping institutional model.[66] This is an observation that I accept, as I set out in more detail in Chapter 10. Fredman and Atrey add to this in their introduction: common 'indifference' to the use of the law is partly due to doctrinal issues, such as reliance on a restricted number of protected grounds required to make headway in court, as well as the practical difficulties of litigation. There is also the more fundamental 'architecture' of the law, which frames these ground- or group-based issues as 'individual rights or entitlements' within 'court-centred adjudication'.[67] Whichever words we use, we might conclude that the solution is not in the language but in the more practical question of how we deal with the various types of problems.

With debates like these looming large in the scholarship (both legal and otherwise), it becomes easier to understand why class has mostly appeared in discussions of maldistribution and inequality, rather than classism as a form of discrimination. This is especially strong if we introduce a third idea – capitalism – and its close links with class. In Chapter 2, I set out why class is specially associated with Marxism and capitalism. This association indicates why it is not surprising that class is often linked to questions of labour, property, resources,

[66] C O'Cinneide, 'New Directions Needed: Exponential Inequalities and the Limits of Equality Law' in Atrey and Fredman (n 30) 132–33.

[67] Atrey and Fredman (n 30) 8.

and certain economic systems. Attacking class is frequently understood as part and parcel of the attack on capitalism.

Indeed, Erik Olin Wright argues that a key feature of Marxist approaches is the view that class is *the* fundamental division in capitalist societies.[68] This feeds the sense that class is not something that we can, or should, reduce to legal rights and duties or resolve through the law. It is simply too systemic. We might even argue, as Fred Pincus and Natalie Sokoloff have done, that we should put energy into identifying the wrongs of capitalism and not be distracted by an idea like classism.[69] Pincus and Sokoloff contend that the meaning of classism is unclear and that the 'essence of class oppression is economic oppression where employers profit from the labor of employees', properly called 'capitalism'.[70] Using the idea of discrimination could draw focus to questions of interpersonal problems and away from the more fundamental exploitation in relations of production.

However, with the benefit of Khaitan's formulation, it becomes clear that we would be mistaken to use capitalism to brush aside classism or obscure the discriminatory character of class. Put class in the following terms: members of lower-class groups are significantly more likely to experience abiding, pervasive and substantial disadvantage because of their membership of those groups when compared with other class groups. This disadvantage helps to define discrimination. It is as evident in the differences in income between lower- and upper-class groups as it is in the stigma attaching to lower-class lifestyle and culture, such as in accents, residential areas and types of entertainment. Class inequality does not exist without classism: classism is a cause, an aspect of and a consequence of class inequality.

This is, clearly, a complex picture. It is true that class carries a strong connotation of broad inequalities, perhaps those inherent to the societies that exist across the world today. However, an accurate understanding of race, for example, would lead us to a similar conclusion. Although some might use an individualistic understanding of racism, such as an insult that one person uses against another, racism is properly understood as a complex phenomenon. Much of the force of it comes from systems of ideas and behaviours about certain 'races', which denigrate some races while elevating others. While the phenomenon may be identified in particular instances of conduct, such as the use of a slur, it remains an aspect of these systems. That is partly what distinguishes a racist insult from a more general insult about someone. Granted, all insults get some of their substance from the systems of meaning around us. If I call someone messy, it is because I am tapping into my understanding of their responsibility not to be messy, to clean up mess, to avoid mess, which relies on conventions of behaviour and expectations in society about tidiness and cleanliness. The nature of that substance, though, is

[68] EO Wright, *Classes* (London, Verso, 2023) 57.

[69] See, eg, F Pincus and N Sokoloff, 'Does "Classism" Help Us to Understand Class Oppression?' (2008) 15(1) *Race, Gender & Class* 9.

[70] Pincus and Sokoloff (n 69) 20.

not the same in kind as a racist insult, which relies on *particular sorts* of harmful practices, beliefs and systems. It is not convincing to suggest that racism – or classism – is confined to individual biases or stereotypes.

B. *Too Big?*

In this discussion, it may be that I am making the concept of classism too big. Older philosophical understandings of equality would likely suggest as much. In them, debates about equality tend to focus on having the same goods or resources rather the meaning of discrimination, so traditional egalitarianism tends to address arbitrary patterns of difference, like those linked with birth and talent.[71] Traditional egalitarianism might ask: if all inequalities relating to class are classist, what is discriminatory as opposed to simply unequal?

Clearly, this is another difficult question about the interaction between discrimination, equality, maldistribution and capitalism. A book could be written on it alone. It taps into the worry that expanding the idea of classism to cover such systemic problems over-extends the idea, meaning that it loses its explanatory and conceptual power. In response to it, I accept that we should be careful when using the idea of discrimination. However, the application of the idea in a broader way is theoretically coherent. It follows scholars like Green in resisting a dichotomy which disconnects instances of mistreatment of one person by another, or a policy that causes disadvantage to one group unjustifiably, from the bigger systems informing and constraining those behaviours and structures. Societies are made up of people, policies, practices, norms, institutions, structures, systems and so on, which incorporate ideas of class. While not every aspect is classist, many of them are. This complex picture helps to explain how a person comes to insult another with a class-based slur and what effect that may have on the other person. It helps to illustrate why a governmental agency implements a programme changing housing policies and practices without appreciating the disadvantage that the programme will cause lower-class people.[72] It recognises just how pervasive classism is in our inequalities, distributions and societies.

I accept that this complexity will not satisfy everyone reading this book, perhaps especially lawyers. Offering lists of tangled practices, systems and structures may be at home in sociological studies, but the intricate nature of this picture can seem difficult to pin down. However, I suspect that this is not something that we can reduce to neat lines of analysis or a set of terms orderly packaged. Even if hard to separate from ideas of (non-discriminatory) inequality, maldistribution and capitalism, classism captures the discriminatory character of class while those ideas do not.

[71] See, for reflections on these older approaches to equality, Moreau, *Faces of Inequality* (n 13) 2–11.

[72] See, for discussion of failure to treat people as equals in the form of indirect discrimination, Moreau, *Faces of Inequality* (n 13) 21.

3.2. Misrecognition

Related to the tendency to subsume classism in ideas such as inequality and maldistribution, there is also the tendency to reduce classism to a question of 'misrecognition'.

For example, if there is such a thing as class-based prejudice or stereotyping, it may be a form of petty snobbery or bigotry but not discrimination. Such an understanding of class goes as follows. People may have attitudes based on stereotypes and prejudice about class, which cause them to mistreat others. This kind of mistreatment disrespects others, it hurts their dignity, and it represents an unfair and unintelligent way to behave. However, it is no more than that: it does not meet Khaitan's criteria of abiding, pervasive and substantial disadvantage or a similarly demanding threshold. Instead, it falls within the dimension of misrecognition, rather than a more structural idea like maldistribution.

While the distinction between recognition and redistribution is not always a strict one, Fredman provides helpful guidance about the difference between the two. Fredman views misrecognition as that which mainly harms a person's identity (such as stereotyping and stigma), whereas maldistribution – discussed above – is more about a person's access to resources, such as money, education and jobs.[73] For example, Sarah Ganty elaborates on the 'issues of recognition' that the law might combat by introducing a protected ground of poverty, 'socioeconomic situation' or 'social condition'.[74] Ganty explains how stigma, prejudice and stereotype – typically associated with misrecognition – are both causes and consequences of discrimination against poor people.[75] Pincus and Sokoloff also seem to view classism as misrecognition: it is simply what some people call the 'prejudice and discrimination' that result from the more fundamental class 'oppression' of capitalism.[76]

Bearing this division in mind, I make two main criticisms of understanding classism as misrecognition. The first is **empirical**. Although there is often the risk that the failure to research classism has led to it being 'theoretically erased' (to borrow Kimberlé Crenshaw's phrase), the available research simply does not support the view that class is solely an issue of misrecognition.[77] As noted above, when lower-class people overcome the hurdles to access traditionally prestigious professions, such as law, medicine and finance, they are likely to earn, on average, 17 per cent less than others, even when the lower-class people in question

[73] S Fredman, 'Recognition and Redistribution: Reconciling Inequalities' (2007) 23 *South African Journal on Human Rights* 214, 221.

[74] S Ganty, 'Poverty as Misrecognition: What Role for Antidiscrimination Law in Europe'? (2021) 21 *Human Rights Law Review* 962, 964.

[75] Ganty (n 74) 964.

[76] Pincus and Sokoloff (n 69) 20.

[77] K Crenshaw, 'Demarginalizing the Intersection of Race and Sex' (1989) 1 *University of Chicago Legal Forum* 139.

did far better academically at university.[78] Lower-class women are more likely to suffer sexual and other physical abuse in their childhoods than other women.[79] Lower-class people, in general, especially those who are black and brown, are much more likely to experience police violence and to come into contact with the criminal justice system as suspects or defendants than other people.[80] Queer lower-class people, in general, are at particular risk of becoming homeless and experience violence.[81] Fredman's idea of misrecognition as a harm to identity hardly reflects the layered, pervasive harms that lower-class people suffer.

The second is more **conceptual**. Nancy Fraser argues that separating the harm of misrecognition from the harm of maldistribution creates 'false antitheses'.[82] This is a helpful criticism. Such a division suggests that we must choose between ideas when we do not, in fact, have to do so. For example, at one extreme end of the division, some Marxists locate the fundamental injustice of class in the 'economic structure'.[83] While they might accept some cultural and social injustices, redistribution (or transformation) and *not* recognition will end economic exploitation. By contrast, Fraser rejects this division and calls for 'a single, comprehensive framework' that integrates demands of both recognition and redistribution.[84] She argues that the same problem applies when we frame a choice between 'class politics' and 'identity politics'. While Fraser still locates the 'ultimate cause' of class injustice in 'the economic structure of capitalist society' (with the social and cultural aspects being 'subordinate'), she accepts that 'the resulting harms' include 'misrecognition' and 'cultural harms' with 'a life of their own'.[85] If we do not address 'class misrecognition', it 'may impede the capacity to mobilize against maldistribution'. To ensure 'economic transformation', we may need to attack 'cultural attitudes that demean poor and working people' and build 'a counter-"identity politics"' for 'class communities and cultures'.[86]

Building on Fraser's arguments here, it is right that class offers a sharp illustration of the dangers of these 'false antitheses'. Take the example of an admissions interview for a university place. An interviewer hears a candidate's Birmingham accent. The interviewer also knows, from the data gathered in the admissions process, that the candidate would be the first in their family to attend

[78] Laurison and Friedman (n 49) 668.

[79] A Phipps, 'Rape and Respectability: Ideas about Sexual Violence and Social Class' (2009) 43(4) *Sociology* 667.

[80] AY Davis, *Women, Race and Class* (London, Penguin, 2019) 179–80; L Gelsthorpe, 'Working with Women Offenders in the Community: A View from England and Wales' in R Sheehan, G McIvor and C Trotter (eds), *Working with Women in the Community* (Abingdon, Routledge, 2010) 127.

[81] Trades Union Congress (n 55).

[82] N Fraser, 'Social Justice in the Age of Identity Politics: Redistribution, Recognition, and Participation', *The Tanner Lectures on Human Values* (1996): www.tannerlectures.org/wp-content/uploads/sites/105/2024/06/Fraser98.pdf.

[83] Fraser (n 82) 12.

[84] Fraser (n 82) 12.

[85] Fraser (n 82) 19.

[86] Fraser (n 82) 20.

university. Because of these features, the interviewer perceives the candidate as less intelligent than other candidates and denies them a place at the university. In this example, there is clearly an aspect of misrecognition: a significant influence on the interviewer's decision is the stigma that the interviewer attaches to the accent and the family's educational history. Yet it is inaccurate to reduce the harm to misrecognition alone. Due to the negative, class-based ideas that the interviewer has, they associate the accent and the lack of a family history of formal higher education with low intelligence and unsuitability for the rigours of university. The source of the associations is, in part, the reality that lower-class people tend to have less money and less formal education than upper-class people, though the error comes when these features are mistaken for unsuitability and a lack of intelligence. It is the maldistribution that gives content to the prejudice and that gives the prejudice enough potency to influence the interviewer's decision. The maldistribution fuels the misrecognition. Notice, too, that this misrecognition then contributes to further maldistribution: the interviewer stops the candidate from attending the university, which is likely to have a negative impact – at least in the short term – on the candidate's prospects of formal education, future employment, income and social connections. Fraser is right to reject a strict division between misrecognition and maldistribution.

However, Fraser is less persuasive when she suggests that the cultural or social aspects of class are 'subordinate' and 'less weighty' than the economic.[87] She is not alone in this suggestion, with academics in other contexts arguing that we should understand class in 'specifically "economic" terms'.[88] I suggest three criticisms. First, Fraser assumes that class is tied to the economic more than the social or cultural. Although Fraser does not expressly define what she means by 'economic' here, her emphasis reflects a common assumption in political philosophy, which separates class (as economic) from race, gender and similar.[89] But Bourdieu's approach reminds us that, especially in modern times, the social and cultural aspects of class can be as influential on people's lives as the economic. Indeed, a person's economic capital can blur into their social and cultural capital.

Second, it is not clear if Fraser means 'subordinate' or 'less weighty' in the sense of how severely the 'economic' aspect harms people, or in the sense of what is the most important ingredient within the concept of class, or from the perspective of the people who suffer from class inequalities. For example, poverty is about 'much more than a lack of sufficient income', with it also involving the social degradation and cultural demeaning of those in poverty.[90] When we consider how poverty harms people's confidence, sense of self, health and their

[87] Fraser (n 82) 12.

[88] W Bottero, 'Class Identities and the Identity of Class' (2004) 38(5) *Sociology* 985.

[89] J Kaplan, 'Against Economy-Culture Dualism: An Argument from Raced Economies' (2021) 22(3) 381, 382–84.

[90] See, eg, S Atrey, 'The Intersectional Case of Poverty' (2018) 18(3) *Human Rights Law Review* 411, 416–17.

ability to find and use opportunities, it is not possible to say that the 'economic' does more damage than the social and cultural. They are inseparable here.

Third, when considering Fraser's remark in the light of Khaitan's idea of disadvantage, the disadvantage that we can identify in terms of stereotypes, biases and snobberies can be 'economic' in its content as well as in its effects. Stereotypes, biases and snobberies project on lower-class people ideas of inferiority; they help to create and sustain poverty and inequalities of wealth by hindering lower-class people's access to money, property, jobs and wellbeing. Yet they are often transmitted in social and cultural ways, such as through attitudes that people hold and representations that they consume in the media. Some of the most effective and lethal representations of lower-class people happen in our social activities and our media, for instance. How can we really say that this is 'less weighty' than the economic when it can be so pervasive and consequential?

For those three reasons, Fraser is mistaken to give primacy to the 'economic' aspect of class. That said, her overall arguments about the division between misrecognition and maldistribution remain compelling in the context of class. Abstracting, or isolating, misrecognition from maldistribution when considering class is a mistake. They are routinely aspects of, and explanations for, each other. By contrast, the idea of classism allows the mixing of misrecognition and maldistribution when understanding what makes up the abiding, pervasive and substantial disadvantage relating to class.

4. CLASSISM OR SOCIO-ECONOMIC STATUS, POVERTY, HOMELESSNESS

You might agree that classism is a form of discrimination (rather than some non-discriminatory problem). However, you might wonder if there is another idea that would be more suitable. Some scholars accept that discrimination is a relevant idea when discussing these issues, but they offer alternatives to class and classism. For example, what about 'socio-economic status', 'poverty' or 'homelessness'?

4.1. Socio-Economic Status or Disadvantage or Origin

In the place of class, we could use 'socio-economic status', 'socio-economic disadvantage' or 'social origin'. These concepts have appeared in academic proposals for new protected grounds in the law.[91] To explore this issue, take the example of the Trades Union Congress's report on classism in the workplace,

[91] See, eg, W Mackay and N Kim, 'Adding Social Condition to the Canadian Human Rights Act' (Final Report for the Canadian Human Rights Commission, 2009); Ganty (n 74); D Evans Peterman, 'Socioeconomic Status Discrimination' (2018) 104(7) *Virginia Law Review* 1283; JC Benito Sánchez,

published in 2019.[92] To date, it is probably the most high-profile proposal to introduce 'class' as a protected characteristic (or so it was reported).[93] It seems to have been one factor that influenced the Labour Party to include in its 2019 manifesto a commitment to 'create a new ground for discrimination on the basis of socio-economic disadvantage'.[94] The proposal is certainly insightful. It grasps useful examples of classism, such as mandating a candidate for a job to undertake an internship without pay or not shortlisting a candidate because their postcode is in a poorer area. Yet still the report uses the phrase 'socio-economic status' to refer to an idea that is, really, class.[95]

It may be that I am again tangling myself in semantics and connotations. There is certainly a more aseptic quality to phrases like 'socio-economic status' and 'socio-economic disadvantage'. They seem free of the difficult political and sociological history of class. They seem more scientific and measurable. They may be less controversial while still paying attention to issues of wealth, occupation and education.[96] They also seem more traditionally *legal*: more sterile, possibly more precise, and certainly easier to imagine being heard in courtroom argument than 'class'. However, the Trades Union Congress's report illustrates the problem with these ideas. When the proposal summarises the law under the Equality Act to mean that 'socio-economic status remains outside the groups that are explicitly covered by domestic equality legislation', it makes limited sense.[97] Is race, with its connections to stigma and poverty, not a 'socio-economic status'? Is gender, with its pay gaps and stereotypes, not one either?

They are forms of socio-economic status, too. The major problem with the language of socio-economic status is that it is broad enough to cover many things. It could cover race, gender, disability and sexuality. To solve this problem, we could adopt a technical interpretation of 'socio-economic status'. Accepting the criticism of breadth, we could argue that we mean 'socio-economic status' *to the extent* that it is not covered by the status of disability, sexuality and the other commonly recognised grounds. Unfortunately, this relegates class to residue. If we were to use such an interpretation of the phrase, class would become secondary, a category coming into play when the others have left. Such an interpretation also wrongly suggests that there is a conceptual barrier between the issues that make up this kind of 'status' and those that make up race and other familiar protected grounds.

'Towering Grenfell: Reflections around Socioeconomic Disadvantage in Antidiscrimination Law' (2019) 5 *Queen Mary Human Rights Review* 1.

[92] Trades Union Congress (TUC), *Building Working Class Power* (TUC, 2019): www.tuc.org.uk/research-analysis/reports/building-working-class-power.

[93] See, eg, CIPD HR-Inform, 'TUC: Make "Class" Discrimination Unlawful' (undated): www.hr-inform.co.uk/news-article/tuc-make-class-discrimination-unlawful.

[94] Labour Party, *It's Time for Real Change: the Labour Party Manifesto 2019* (2019) 66: www.ucrel.lancs.ac.uk/wmatrix/ukmanifestos2019/localpdf/Labour.pdf.

[95] TUC (n 92) 22.

[96] See, eg, Mackay and Kim (n 91) 21 and 37; Ganty (n 74) 5–6, 32.

[97] TUC (n 92) 22.

Consider another example: *da Silva Pimentel Teixeira v Brazil* (2011). Alyne da Silva Pimentel Teixeira was a poor, Afro-Brazilian woman who died during pregnancy because of a failure to provide proper, timely access to emergency obstetric care. Brazil had violated Article 12(2) of the Convention on the Elimination of All Forms of Discrimination Against Women by failing to ensure access to 'appropriate services in connection with her pregnancy'.[98] In its decision, the CEDAW Committee uses the language of 'socio-economic disadvantage' and 'background'.[99] But this is hardly precise or accurate. da Silva Pimentel Teixeira died because of the maltreatment generated by a misogynist, racist and classist system. Yet the Committee fails to refer to class, or indeed poverty, in its final recommendations. The language of 'socio-economic disadvantage' and 'background' is wide enough to cover all the ways in which the deceased suffered, while remaining shallow enough to gloss over them without articulating how each made her daily life and experience in healthcare worse.

More precise and accurate analysis would explain how she could not access safe healthcare because she did not have enough money. She did not have connections to those wealthy or formally educated enough to know doctors who would do them favours, or who would get her to a place with better facilities. Those charged with treating her disregarded her because of race, gender *and class*. She was not given access to an ambulance or hospital with enough space.[100] Medical staff left her in a corridor.[101] They transferred her without her medical records, which her mother had to retrieve herself from a health centre.[102] Without the language and concepts of class and classism, we would be unable to articulate how her treatment is distinctive from a woman of the same race, in the same health condition, but with much higher-quality social, cultural and economic capital: in other words, an Afro-Brazilian who was rich and well-connected. This argument is not just rhetorical. It is not merely a complication of semantics or connotations. Classism is an essential idea because it precisely and accurately explains her experience and the role of unequal systems in causing her death. 'Socio-economic status' (and its siblings) cannot do that without blurring all forms of discrimination under one unparticularised heading.

4.2. Homelessness

I make similar criticisms of proposals to introduce 'homelessness' as a protected ground in the law, such as in the criminal law.[103] The Law Commission has

[98] *Alyne da Silva Pimentel Teixeira v Brazil* (2011) CEDAW/C/49/D/17/2008.
[99] *Teixeira* [7.7], [8.2].
[100] *Teixeira* [7.4].
[101] *Teixeira* [2.8].
[102] *Teixeira* [2.9].
[103] M Al-Hakim, 'Making a Home for the Homeless in Hate Crime Legislation' (2015) 30(10) *Journal of Interpersonal Violence* 1755, 1770.

considered the possibility of homelessness in its work on reforming hate crime laws. The most insightful part of the Law Commission's work is found in its consultation paper from 2020. Applying the criteria, the Law Commission considers how protecting homelessness might work. In terms of the criterion of a 'demonstrable need', the paper refers to research showing long-standing levels of victimisation of homeless people in the UK.[104] In terms of 'additional harm', it relies on the work of the charity, Crisis, with its research into homeless people's experiences of both violence and other forms of harm. The evidence is clear that criminal behaviour against them causes significant damage to the health, safety and sense of self of homeless people.[105] Dealing last with the (vague) criterion of 'suitability', the paper notes a concern that legal protection might *reinforce* the reality of homelessness.

As with poverty (which I address next), some might think that protecting homeless people would be more persuasive than arguing for an understanding of classism in general. Both poverty and homelessness seem to offer more measurable standards by which to address discrimination. Rather than the complex meanderings of class, it would be much more precise to articulate who needs help and how we would analyse the effects of the discrimination against them. It is correct that homelessness is both an instrument and product of discrimination. However, homelessness is rooted in classism and other forms of discrimination. Although understanding homelessness as a form of discrimination (and making law on that basis) would be better than doing nothing, addressing it alone has limited justification in either theory or practice.

In theory, such an approach misunderstands the source of the maltreatment of homeless people – and, likely, the phenomenon of homelessness itself. The disadvantage experienced by homeless people, including prejudice towards them, traces to the relationship between homelessness and the class system. While homeless people often experience other forms of discrimination, such as ableism and racism, the core theme is classism. Stereotype and prejudice about homeless people have so much in common with those about lower-class people more generally: unclean, lazy, stupid, drunken, drugged, dangerous.[106] If we were to disconnect these ideas of homeless people from the same of lower-class people, we effectively cut a tree from its roots. Various forms of stereotype and prejudice affect homeless people in addition to the fact of being homeless, which operate both in becoming homeless and living homeless. Nonetheless, a necessary feature of both homelessness and the victimisation of homeless people is inequality because they are *very poor*. In other words, it is inequality

[104] Law Commission, *Hate Crime Laws*, Consultation Paper No 250 (London, TSO, 2020) 196–97.

[105] B Sanders and F Albanese, *It's No Life at all: Rough Sleepers' Experience of Violence and Abuse on the Streets of England and Wales* (Crisis, 2016) 17, cited in Law Commission (n 104) 332.

[106] A Whaley and B Link, 'Racial Categorization and Stereotype-Based Judgments about Homeless People' (1998) 28(3) *Journal of Applied Social Psychology* 189. See also, in the context of literary presentations, L Davis, *Poor Things* (Durham, North Carolina, Duke University Press, 2024) 105, 122.

because they have low-quality social, cultural and economic capital. Understood in this way, the type of disadvantage that homeless people experience is a severe and distinctive form of classism. It is part of a system that allows some to have so much and, necessarily, others to have so little. It is also part of a system that degrades those who are so poor. Without the idea of classism, legal analysis struggles to make sense of the reasons for homelessness and what sustains it, as well as the attitudes towards it.

In practice, consider the dislocation of homelessness from classism. If homeless people are not understood to suffer classism, they disappear as the most vulnerable group within the broader group of lower-class people. While they may need particular support, offering homeless people legal or other practical protection *to the exclusion of other lower-class people* means that we could only address a limited portion of classism. For example, it would not protect those who have a permanent address but still live in extreme poverty, as many do. It also encourages us to think about initiatives as if these categories do not relate to each other and as if the people within them do not change. A person in extreme poverty often lives in precarious accommodation, sometimes at the whim of friends or acquaintances and sometimes according to the limits of housing providers. They may have been homeless and they may become homeless again. Denying the connection between classism and homelessness makes it easier to end up at a cliff edge: if you are homeless, you receive protection, but if you are just beyond it, you do not. Even if the criterion of homelessness has a place for certain charitable organisations and initiatives, it cannot replace classism when considering what *form of discrimination* we are seeking to describe.

4.3. Poverty

Other scholars have considered the issue of poverty, both as a potential protected ground in the law and as a more general tool for legal analysis.[107] Shreya Atrey develops intersectional analysis in a way that is consistent with many of the arguments I make in this book about class, classism and the ways in which they mix with other forms of discrimination. Atrey identifies the 'dual intersectional character' of poverty, not necessarily suggesting that this prevents poverty from being a protected ground in law.[108] Rather, it is intersectional because it involves different dimensions of disadvantage. Poverty entails exclusion, lack of income and limited access to education. It is also intersectional in how it relates

[107] See, eg, M Jackman, 'Constitutional Contact with the Disparities in the World: Poverty as a Prohibited Ground of Discrimination under the Canadian Charter and Human Rights Law' (1994) 2(1) *Review of Constitutional Studies* 76; M Campbell, *Women, Poverty, Equality: the Role of CEDAW* (Oxford, Hart Publishing, 2018).

[108] Atrey (n 90) 417.

to what Atrey calls 'status groups'. As poverty affects the experiences of those who encounter forms of discrimination (such as racism and ableism), it ought to affect our understanding of the nature and extent of those forms of discrimination.[109] Atrey, therefore, analyses the ways in which poverty forms part of discrimination's context and a fuller concept of equality. She argues that courts can examine this, in part, through existing protected grounds.

I accept that poverty is essential to understanding discrimination of many forms, as well as for precise and accurate legal analysis of those forms. Without consideration of poverty, we lose our ability to articulate how discrimination works and what the most pressing, long-term solutions might be. In addition to that, unlike the Weberian conceptual shift, Atrey uses the language of status groups without separating them from the underlying economic disadvantage. The major problem, however, with an approach like that of Atrey is that it puts poverty too low in our conceptual framework. Atrey suggests that a full intersectional analysis is possible if it includes poverty, but not necessarily as a protected ground like race, sexuality or gender.

Most importantly, like homelessness, poverty does not come out of thin air. It has a number of sources. While Atrey does not over-simplify the causes of poverty, her approach cannot explain why some groups are significantly more likely to experience poverty than others. Although racism connects with poverty in Atrey's analysis, for instance, we struggle to explain where the poverty of the white, cisgender, straight and enabled man comes from. Is it simply a problem of society's maldistribution – an approach that I criticised earlier – or of that man's own laziness or ineptitude? Granted, it could be a wholly personal failing, depending on the specific facts. Yet this is rarely, if ever, the case. Properly understood, the source of that man's poverty is a *classist* system in which he is subject to abiding, pervasive and substantial disadvantage, one form of which is poverty. Putting poverty at the front or back of the analysis, as in Atrey's approach, is likely to obscure the causes of poverty, which are found in class.

5. NOT 'JUST' CLASS

In this chapter, I have aimed to show that academics have often understood issues of class as something other than discrimination. Some have focused on concepts like inequality, maldistribution and capitalism or used other ideas in place of class (like poverty). In doing so, they have missed the discriminatory quality of class. Others have assumed that mistreatment relating to class is really a form of misrecognition. However, the truth is that misrecognition mixes with maldistribution. Taking either alone obscures the real picture.

[109] Atrey (n 90) 421.

A more persuasive approach accepts that class has a discriminatory character, which entails disadvantage that is long-term, extensive and severe. While other ideas will always have a place (such as homelessness and poverty), they are no substitute for a form of discrimination relating to class.

Is it discrimination or just being poor? Although not particularly pithy, the answer to the question that opened this chapter is: it is a form of discrimination, which we should call classism.

4

Understanding Classism

So far, I have argued that we need the idea of classism, a form of discrimination. In short, members of one class are significantly more likely to suffer long-term, extensive and severe disadvantage when compared with members of another class. I set out both theoretical and empirical research to support the view that classism involves such disadvantage in Chapter 3.

However, I started this book with two lists of examples and I discouraged a search for abstract, context-free definitive statements. Building on that position, I aim to flesh out classism in this chapter. I argue that the best way to understand classism *as discrimination* is **by reference to examples**. I also argue that classism is distinctive as **a form of discrimination in itself** even if it blends or overlaps with more widely recognised forms of discrimination (such as racism). I then consider a trio of potential problems with my approach to classism: (a) people who 'change' class; (b) groups and their boundaries; and (c) a renewed argument that class is *really* an economic phenomenon, whereas classism is limited to the social and cultural aspects surrounding that phenomenon.

1. LED BY EXAMPLE

Like an attempt to define 'class', an attempt to define 'classism' may always end with dissatisfaction, especially for lawyers. As I argued in Chapter 2 in relation to class, classism is not something that we should treat as a rigid or formal rule. We can, of course, make headway by suggesting that classism is discrimination relating to class. Class involves a distinctive relationship between people involving unequal social, cultural and economic capital, which means that some groups of people are more likely to suffer disadvantage than others. But this remains somewhat abstract. You could query what it really adds. While this summary offers a high-level view, the idea of classism may remain unspecific and hard to apply.

However, it would be mistaken to view this as a weakness of the idea of classism. I used the analogy with defining a colour when discussing class. I suggest that the analogy also works for classism. Like a particular colour, if you see classism, you know it. But there is little point trying to create a definitive statement to summarise it, as we might for a concept in biological science. That perspective does not make the idea meaningless or less real; rather, it indicates that we need an approach tailored to what class is. In this way, though we can find a working approach inspired by Bourdieu, classism is best understood by reference to examples and by thinking about people's experiences and their lives.

In the Introduction, I gave two lists of examples of classism, with a focus on the UK. The first list offered specific examples of classism:

> *A person is refused a job, treated unfairly by the police or denied entry to a place because that person:*
>
> - *speaks with an accent or dialect considered to be 'common' or that does not make them sound 'polished';*
> - *lives or grew up in an area considered to be 'dodgy' or 'rough';*
> - *attended a state school, rather than a school that requires its students to pay fees (or obtain fees-based scholarships);*
> - *at one time received state benefit payments;*
> - *does not have an aristocratic family;*
> - *has a name considered to be 'chavvy' or 'trashy'.*

Each example refers to a feature associated with class. Of course, not everyone with a 'common' accent, or who grew up in a 'rough' area, is properly described as lower-class. But those features are still associated with being lower-class. The second list went on to give more general examples of classism across societies:

> *Some people:*
>
> - *enjoy huge wealth while some people have very little;*
> - *benefit from high-quality education while some people have little access to education or receive low-quality education;*
> - *expect much better health outcomes because of their region and wealth while some people have no such expectations;*
> - *benefit from connections with influential people in positions of power while some people have no such connections;*
> - *live in areas typically regarded as 'nice' and 'posh' while some people live in areas derided as 'rough' and 'dodgy';*
> - *enjoy culture and entertainment regarded by some as intellectual and valuable, while others enjoy culture and entertainment regarded by some as unworthwhile and 'tacky'.*

This list emphasises the more structural and systemic aspects of classism, which certain academics might call maldistribution or misrecognition (as discussed in Chapter 3).

What do these examples reveal about classism? Start with an example from the first list. A *person is . . . treated unfairly by the police because that person . . . lives in an area considered to be 'dodgy' or 'rough'*. This example tells us that classism operates in several senses. In a more general sense, it helps to explain why people are more likely to be poor and to experience other types of disadvantage, such as bad healthcare and lower life expectancy, if they live in certain areas.[1] If people in a society had equal social, cultural and economic capital, stark differences like those between 'rough' and 'posh' areas would not exist. In a more specific sense, people from lower-class areas are likely to suffer disadvantage in their daily lives. Sometimes, it will be more social and cultural: the stigma that those areas are not nice places to live and that the people who live in them must also be 'rough', unintelligent or objects of pity. It can also be more economic, shaping their opportunities for jobs and wealth. These aspects of classism mix and sustain each other: the 'rough' areas are partly a manifestation of the disadvantage that lower-class people suffer and a cause of further disadvantage to those people. Granted, there may be some people who leave; there may be 'gentrification' and 'regeneration'. Yet we can see the classism in the perceptions of those areas and the ways in which those perceptions harm the people associated with them.

Take another example from the first list. *A person is . . . denied entry to a place because that person . . . does not have an aristocratic family.* This example is easy to recognise as an example of classism. In a general sense, a system in which some families enjoy huge advantage because of their birth and inheritance is classist. Some families hoard social, cultural and economic capital to the exclusion of others. In many of their relationships, they hold positions of significant benefit because of the system. Once more, there will be nuances. Perhaps more than ever, aristocratic people consider it unfashionable or embarrassing to flaunt their family's credentials. Perhaps aristocrats' traditional sources of income (especially from land) do not bring in as much wealth as they once did, though there is much evidence to suggest that aristocratic families in the UK remain owners of large amounts of high-value property.[2] That is the product of the classist history: the amassing of land, the monopolising of certain industries, the influence of upper-class governance (including the history of hereditary peers and voting reserved to certain classes). Although it seems like a cartoonish anachronism, the endurance of aristocratic influence should not be under-estimated. As Guy Shrubsole argues in *Who Owns England?*:

> Once, when asked to give advice to young entrepreneurs on how they could succeed in modern Britain, the now-deceased 6th Duke of Westminster had some sage words. 'Make sure they have an ancestor who was a very close friend of William the Conqueror,' he said.

[1] Institute of Health Equity (IHE), 'England's Widening Health Gap: Local Places Falling Behind' (London, IHE, 2024) 3–5.

[2] See, eg, the Grosvenor family, commonly known as 'the Dukes of Westminster', have a fortune estimated to be worth around ten billion pounds in property, investments, hotels and other ventures: 'Gerald Cavendish Grosvenor & Family – Profile', *Forbes* (2016): www.forbes.com/profile/gerald-cavendish-grosvenor.

> Class runs deep in English society. Many of the aristocratic families who continue to thrive, prosper and own great swathes of the British Isles can date their bloodlines all the way back to the Norman Conquest . . . Today, the Duke of Westminster is consistently found towards the top of the annual *Sunday Times* Rich List, the inheritor of a £9 billion fortune made from owning a vast, 130,000-acre estate in land and property, built up over centuries.[3]

The example of denial of entry takes this bigger picture and makes it specific, offering a personalised instance of the general problem: aristocratic advantage may influence a specific decision to deny entry, for instance, to a lower-class person. It reminds us that classism operates in general and specific ways, in the arrangements of societies and in the decisions people make about each other. The mixing of the general with the specific, the 'maldistribution' with the 'misrecognition', is characteristic of it.[4]

The second list continues these themes, though its examples are more general in character. Some people enjoy culture and entertainment regarded by some as intellectual and valuable, while others enjoy culture and entertainment regarded by some as unworthwhile and 'tacky'. The tropes are familiar. Opera is good, valuable, educational; soap opera is bad, a waste of time, unintelligent. This reflects what Bourdieu and Savage call the demeaning of certain kinds of culture, though it has become more complex in recent years with the ability of class-advantaged people to flit between types of culture with ease and agility, 'a kind of ironic, reflexive and self-aware orientation towards knowledge and culture'.[5] But it can be straightforward to describe how this aspect of classism imbues these general issues of culture as well as specific interactions between people. It could feature in the first list, too. A person goes into an interview and, when asked, says that they enjoy watching reality TV shows in their spare time. The interviewing panel reacts to this badly, perhaps because there are other features about the candidate they perceive badly, such as their accent or details about their upbringing. Because of this, the panel decides to choose another candidate. The stigma attached to culture feeds into the denial of a job – a source of some economic advantage and possibly other forms. This is not woolly or abstract or empty. It is easily recognised as an example of classism, both in the general sense of demeaning lower-class culture and in the specific sense of mistreating the candidate because of their cultural habits.

The two lists could go on. For now, the point of them is to mix the specific and the general, building an approach to classism led by examples that are palpable and, to many people, easy to recognise. While more theoretical discussions of classism must have their place (especially in an academic book) and classism may be less clear-cut in some instances, neither should mask the many times when classism is blatant.

[3] G Shrubsole, *Who Owns England?* (Glasgow, William Collins, 2019) 76.
[4] For more detail, see the discussion of Nancy Fraser's arguments in Chapter 3 of this book.
[5] M Savage, *Social Class in the 21st Century* (London, Penguin, 2015) 90–92, 179–81.

2. THE CHARACTER OF CLASSISM

Taken together, as I set out in Chapter 3, the research (even while using different ideas of class) supports the argument that classism involves the type and extent of disadvantage that makes it a form of discrimination. Classism also has its own language, as I have noted, which helps it to convey distinctive ideas: 'posh', 'fancy', 'stuck up', 'common', 'rough', 'chav', 'scally'. But examples, analysis of disadvantage and even vocabulary only take us so far. You might accept that classism is, indeed, a form of discrimination. However, you might still ask what it is about the previous sections that makes classism *distinct* from better-recognised forms of discrimination. If any form of discrimination involves abiding, pervasive and substantial disadvantage, what separates classism from racism, misogyny and others? What is its vocabulary trying to convey?

Especially because classism mixes so closely with racism and misogyny, for instance, there might be an argument that it needs its own discernible features to exist as a form of discrimination *in itself*. Some qualities may be specific to certain manifestations of classism, such as the classism that has long existed in England, while other qualities may apply more generally. In addition to being led by examples, the challenge is to gain a more general sense of what those qualities may be. I suggest that it is possible to identify certain qualities that help to give this form of discrimination a distinctive character. I do not argue that other forms of discrimination have *none* of these qualities. Instead, I argue that they are particularly prominent in classism. Classism tends to be (1) regional and (2) inheritable while remaining (3) intersectional but not invisible.

2.1. Regional

Associations with particular regions, especially regions *within* nations, tend to be more marked in classism than in other forms of discrimination. In England, for instance, classism often connects with regional differences more prominently than other forms of discrimination do. Classist beliefs and structures have regional qualities. In England, for example, the best-known regional difference is the North–South divide. While criticised for being simplistic and geographically inaccurate, as Tom Hazeldine notes, it is difficult to deny the division's enduring role in people's perceptions of themselves and the country as a whole.[6] There is a primarily social and cultural aspect to the division: the idea that Northerners tend to behave in certain ways, perhaps seen as friendlier and more down-to-earth than Southerners, alongside stereotypes that Northerners are also less sophisticated and less intelligent. There is also the more economic aspect, which presents Northerners as poorer.

[6] T Hazeldine, *The Northern Question* (London, Verso, 2021) 17–18, 70.

Although the North–South divide is roughly drawn, the research bears out its contours. Northern towns and cities consistently appear on lists of the most deprived places in England. Paul Swinney and Andrew Carter identify figures as stark as a 45 per cent decline in jobs in Burnley, Lancashire, between 1911 and 2016 compared with a 307 per cent increase in Reading, Berkshire.[7] In other research, Swinney and Carter point to the fact that most of the towns and cities with the lowest average weekly wages are in Yorkshire and the North West.[8] England's A-level results in 2025 indicated that Northerners were still more likely to suffer worse educational outcomes, with those in the North East, Yorkshire and the Humber, and the Midlands less likely to achieve the highest grades than those in the South East and elsewhere.[9] Of course, these findings are not rigid rules. For instance, Carter and Swinney note the appearance of Southend-on-Sea in Essex on the list with the lowest average weekly wages.[10] However, the North–South divide retains deep social, cultural and economic features in the twenty-first century.

The regional aspect of classism also comes through in other ways. I discussed in Chapter 3 the extent to which people suffer discrimination relating to regional accents, reflecting the perceived 'class' of their family and 'social networks', which connects with classist stereotypes about intelligence, expertise and wealth.[11] It should be remembered that this is a question of the regional quality of classism being more prominent than in other forms of discrimination. Other forms may have regional qualities to them, too. Racism and homophobia, for instance, can be characterised by particular regions. Queer communities in Leeds, Bradford, Halifax, Hebden Bridge and nearby areas of West Yorkshire experienced police violence and press hostility, as their activities were expected in London but considered shocking for 'homely' Yorkshire.[12] Rather than suggesting that only classism is regional, the point here is that, if we aim to describe what *tends* to be prominent in classism but less so in other forms of discrimination, one feature is how regional it tends to be. There are close connections, between classist beliefs and regional differences, such as perceptions of wealth, intellect and cultural sophistication.

The prominence of the regional quality of classism does not mean that it applies across the board or without exception. For instance, the regional quality is consistent with the fact that some Northern people are rich and some Southern

[7] P Swinney and A Carter, 'The UK Towns and Cities Worse Off than 100 Years Ago', *BBC News* (2 November 2018): www.bbc.co.uk/news/uk-45952532.

[8] A Carter and P Swinney, 'The UK Towns and Cities with the Highest and Lowest Wages', *BBC News* (2 May 2018): www.bbc.co.uk/news/business-43729508.

[9] Ofqual, *Qualification Results in England: Summer 2025* (2025): www.gov.uk/government/publications/qualification-results-in-england-summer-2025/qualification-results-in-england-summer-2025-accessible.

[10] Carter and Swinney (n 8).

[11] See, eg, Accent Bias 'Britain, *Accent Bias in Britian* (2020) 5–6.

[12] M Cook, 'Split Scenes in Leeds' in M Cook and Al Oram, *Queer beyond London* (Manchester, Manchester University Press, 2022) 42, esp 47.

people are poor. It is also consistent with the fact that there are 'posh' areas in Yorkshire and Lancashire and 'rough' areas in Essex and Kent. Classism may deal in generalisations. The regional quality of it, though, means that people encounter it even when they move away from where they grew up. Even if people overcome barriers, they may still experience other barriers elsewhere, such as the bias of interviewers, who hold negative associations with the language and intellect of the North. It is a persistent regional quality like this that helps us differentiate classism, at least in England, from other forms of discrimination. They may also be regional, but they are not so linked with regional issues as classism tends to be.

2.2. Inheritable

Inheritance has long been associated with class. You are 'born' into your class; your birth indicates your class. Especially in societies with aristocratic systems, traditional understandings of class mean that certain ranks are reserved for those born into particular families. As we see with the British monarchy, part of the function of classism is to hoard advantage for some families to the necessary exclusion of others.[13] The idea of inheritance is broader, too. Although often overlooked, classism may involve falsehoods about genetics and bodies, though older stereotypes about inherited intellect and criminality seem to be weakening. For instance, Lennard Davis identifies numerous older literary portrayals of poor people as shorter, unhygienic, stunted and physically deficient.[14]

If the very idea of class goes back to features that we inherit, the strategic play here is self-serving: all aristocratic infants have to do is to be placed in their parents' arms and they may be assured a level of class advantage for a lifetime. Irrespective of their abilities, their intelligence, their hard work and their other qualities, they are advantaged by class. As societies change, it may be thought that the prominence of classism's focus on inheritability has begun to fade. Some might even argue that aristocratic birth, for example, now brings with it lower cultural and economic capital than simply being born into a wealthy but non-aristocratic family. The fading attractiveness of such birthright may mean that young aristocratic people seek to hide their heritage, perhaps to avoid the criticism that their success is only due to their family. Yet the research suggests that birth and family remain, in fact, prominent aspects of class advantage.[15] The phenomenon of 'nepo babies' reminds us of this.[16] The so-called next generation

[13] See, eg, A Benn, 'Besting Monarchy: The Anti-Classism Argument' (2023) 94(3) *The Political Quarterly* 393.

[14] L Davis, *Poor Things* (Durham, North Carolina, Duke University Press, 2024).

[15] S Krutikova and others, *Intergenerational Mobility in the UK* (London, Institute for Financial Studies, 2023): www.ifs.org.uk/publications/intergenerational-mobility-uk.

[16] See, eg, popular commentary on the topic: N Jones, 'How a Nepo Baby Is Born', *Vulture* (20 December 2022): www.vulture.com/article/what-is-a-nepotism-baby.html.

of judges, politicians, actors, musicians and directors already contains many examples of those who clearly grew up with the kind of social, cultural and economic capital that enabled them to amass wealth and prestige. The place of inheritance in classism remains strong.

Once more, this is a question of prominence rather than strict exclusivity. Racism, casteism and ableism also tend to involve the idea that there is an inheritable superiority and inferiority of different groups. Each form of discrimination has played a vicious role in eugenics.[17] The inheritable quality of homophobia and transphobia seems to be less prominent, but there are still examples of these forms of discrimination (sometimes internalised by queer people themselves) that rest on supposed genetic makeup, disease that may be passed on (such as HIV) and family history.[18] That said, if we seek to identify what is prominent in classism when compared with at least some other forms of discrimination, it is the marking of certain people as poorer, less intelligent and less culturally sophisticated, among other traits, due to their birth and family. Negative ideas of 'problem families' and attitudes to family names overwhelmingly attach to class (even as they may simultaneously attach to other forms of discrimination, like racism and the eternal question of where people are 'really from').[19] Classism often depends on the casting of certain families and upbringings as morally inadequate while others are presented as exemplary and successful by nature. Classism tends to frame everyone as if they are at a stage on a journey: it assesses – perhaps even obsesses over – their success compared with their family and their trajectory in relation to their 'background'.

2.3. Intersectional, Not Invisible

The risk of my emphasising even two qualities that make classism distinctive is that I start to dissociate classism from other forms of discrimination. That is partly inevitable. The nature of this exercise is to differentiate classism in order to understand it better. However, though it may be counter-intuitive in an analysis of what makes class distinctive, it is important to consider how classism is intersectional.

To explore this, note what happens when class is viewed too narrowly. Michael Lind's book, *The New Class War*, offers an example of what *not* to do. Granted, in some ways, Lind offers compelling commentary on the intergenerational nature of class, such as the lingering influence of certain aristocratic

[17] N Ordover, *American Eugenics* (Minneapolis, University of Minnesota Press, 2003); M Cortez, 'Compulsory Sterilisation and Reproductive Injustice in India: the Global Impact of the American Eugenics Movement' (2025 dissertation) 42–43.

[18] Ordover (n 17) 59–61.

[19] A Lapp and D Lapp, 'Stigmatizing the Working Class' (London, Institute for Family Studies, 5 October 2015): www.ifstudies.org/blog/stigmatizing-the-working-class/; A Nagesh, 'What Is It Like to Be Repeatedly Asked Where You Are From?', *BBC News* (1 December 2022): www.bbc.co.uk/news/uk-63822940.

families.[20] He accurately identifies that many political parties 'pretend that enduring, self-perpetuating social classes no longer exist'.[21] However, he labels efforts to combat racism, misogyny and transphobia as the trappings of the 'metropolitan elite' (even though he accepts that the lower class can be racially mixed and made up of migrants).[22] By setting class, race and gender in opposition, Lind uses the ideas of class and classism to undermine the seriousness of other forms of discrimination.

The image of the 'white, working-class man' – straight, cisgender, enabled – was a cause of the movement away from the idea of class in academic circles, as I set out in Chapter 1. It is especially important, then, not to make the same mistake when teasing out what it is that makes classism distinctive as a form of discrimination. It is wrong to think of classism as whatever is left over once other forms of discrimination have been considered. At the same time, it is essential to remember that class mixes closely with other ideas, such as race, gender and disability, so that it should not be treated in isolation from them.

This gives the impression of a tension. On the one hand, I suggest that classism is a form of discrimination *in itself*. A white lower-class person may suffer classism and no other form of discrimination – and still needs the language to say so. On the other hand, I accept that classism is closely related to, and even blends with, racism, misogyny and other forms of discrimination. The evidence tells us so. For example, class and race (and sometimes caste) heavily overlap, sometimes inseparably, in societies around the world. Research describes the concentration of black and brown people in the lower classes, including in poverty.[23] The distinctive and often severe effects of poverty on women of all races are also well-documented.[24] Classism and misogyny mingle to create gendered class prejudices, found in odd phrases like 'chav mum' and 'chavette' conjured in the early twenty-first century.[25] Sexuality and class, too, may pull in different directions and yet in doing so shape a person's experience. Didier Eribon reflects on this in the context of growing up gay and lower-class: 'in one case I needed to become what I was, but in the other I needed to reject what I was supposed to have been. Yet for me these two activities went hand in hand.'[26]

[20] M Lind, *The New Class War* (London, Penguin, 2020) 8.
[21] Lind (n 20) 1.
[22] Lind (n 20) 111.
[23] See, eg, Institute of Race Relations (IRR), 'BME Statistics on Poverty and Deprivation' (London, IRR, 2024): www.irr.org.uk/research/statistics/poverty.
[24] Women's Budget Group, *The Female Face of Poverty* (2018): www.wbg.org.uk/wp-content/uploads/2018/08/FINAL-Female-Face-of-Poverty.pdf; S Chant, 'The "Feminisation of Poverty" and the "Feminisation" of Anti-Poverty Programmes: Room for Revision' (2008) 44 *Journal of Development Studies* 165; J Kehler, 'Women and Poverty: the South African Experience' (2001) 3 *Journal of International Women's Studies* 41.
[25] I Tyler, '"Chav Mum Chav Scum": Class Disgust in Contemporary Britain' (2008) 8(1) *Feminist Media Studies* 17; A Nayak, '"Chavs, Chavettes and Pramface Girls": Teenage Mothers, Marginalised Young Men and the Management of Stigma' (2014) 17(10) *Journal of Youth Studies* 1330.
[26] D Eribon, *Returning to Reims* (M Lucey trans, London, Penguin, 2019) 219.

Intersectional analysis is a great help here. From the outset, though, it is crucial to understand intersectional analysis properly. It is worth going back to the basics. In relation to discrimination law, Kimberlé Crenshaw was the first to use the term 'intersectionality' in her 1989 article about the US legal system, though the idea has long existed in the substance of work by other authors.[27] In her article, Crenshaw criticises how discrimination law restricts analysis to a single protected ground. Black women must select either a claim based on misogyny (understood as the misogyny that white women experience) or a claim based on racism (understood as the racism that black men experience). As a result, the experiences of black women become 'theoretically erased'.[28]

Too often, academics and activists understand intersectionality in ways that mangle Crenshaw's concept. Two key features are worth bearing in mind. Intersectional analysis is **not mathematical.** It does not require us to add up forms of discrimination as if they were numbers. Instead, Crenshaw's focus is on recognising the distinctive experiences of people who suffer forms of discrimination not accurately understood as either 'racist' or 'misogynist' (or as some clunky compound of the two without nuance). Intersectional analysis has **a sense of priority.** Crenshaw encourages us to focus on the people most severely disadvantaged by discrimination. Those people are usually the ones who suffer distinctively intersectional discrimination, though in a given instance the facts may be otherwise. For example, a particular black man's experiences of racism may be more severe than a particular black woman's. The core of intersectional analysis is a different understanding of, and approach to, discrimination: it concentrates on identifying and dismantling power relations, including those within groups.[29]

Accepting that classism is a distinctive form of discrimination *is* consistent with intersectional analysis. The example of the Supreme Court of Canada's decision in *Gosselin v Québec* (2002) is worth discussing here.[30] The case concerned a social assistance scheme in Québec. The scheme paid recipients aged under 30 roughly one third of the amount paid to those aged 30 and over. Bringing a claim on behalf of many people against the Québec government, the claimant sought reimbursement of the difference, which would have been around $389 million (plus interest) for all those affected.[31] The Supreme Court's

[27] K Crenshaw, 'Demarginalising the Intersection of Race and Sex' (1989) *University of Chicago Legal Forum* 139; A Lorde, 'Scratching the Surface: Some Notes on Barriers to Women and Loving' in A Lorde, *Sister Outsider* (London, Penguin, 2007) 35, 42; AY Davis, *Women, Race and Class* (London, Penguin, 2019) 179–80. See generally A Hancock, *An Intellectual History of Intersectionality* (Oxford, Oxford University Press, 2016).

[28] K Crenshaw (n 27). See Chapters 5 and 6 of this book for discussion of this criticism in the context of the UK: eg the Equality Act 2010, s 4.

[29] S Cho, K Crenshaw and L McCall, 'Toward a Field of Intersectionality Studies; Theory, Applications, and Praxis' (2013) 38(4) *Signs* 765.

[30] *Gosselin v Québec* [2002] 4 SCR 429.

[31] *Gosselin* (n 30) [4].

majority held that the government's use of age as the relevant criterion aimed to help the young people in question to enter work-related training in order 'eventually to integrate into the workforce and become self-sufficient'.[32]

The case illustrates why the lack of a legal framework around classism and poverty impairs the quality of legal analysis. The Supreme Court evaluated the claim as a claim about ageism. In the judgment, McLachlin CJ struggles to articulate why the group was disadvantaged. For example, McLachlin CJ reasons that 'young adults as a class simply do not seem especially vulnerable or undervalued' or 'particularly susceptible to negative preconceptions'.[33] However, the 'class' in question was not merely based on age. It was not simply 'young adults'. The 'young adults' in question were not the ones from wealthy families, who had attended expensive private schools and started highly paid jobs. They were the recipients of a social assistance scheme.

By contrast, Bastarache J's dissenting judgment offers much more accurate reasoning: 'we are not dealing with a general age distinction but with one applicable within a particular social group, welfare recipients'.[34] Bastarache J highlights how the percentage of those under 30 had risen from 3 to 12 per cent in 1983, a reality that the government knew. The majority's singular focus on ageism obscured classism, failing to be precise and accurate in understanding the nature of the disadvantage that the recipients faced. The majority's reasoning could not transform the lives of the recipients for the better, as it misunderstood the problem and could not locate a solution. Rather, the mixture, the interweaving, of class and age identifies the problem and, in turn, the best ways for legal analysis to attempt to solve it. The case is a good example why classism – as with other forms of discrimination – needs to be understood *in itself* to do intersectional analysis.

Therefore, intersectional analysis does not require class to be invisible or to retreat into the background or anything of the kind. We can, and should, draw connections between classism and more commonly recognised forms of discrimination. We need the idea of classism to understand how discrimination towards a black family in Hartlepool, County Durham, with little money and little formal education, is in many ways different from discrimination towards a rich black family in Chelsea, London. Intersectional analysis shows us why we must be careful not to reduce forms of discrimination to their most advantaged versions. To do so would stop us from understanding all manifestations of discrimination. It would also prevent us from finding the solutions to help those who are most severely disadvantaged. These lessons are consistent with classism as a form of discrimination in itself. Classism can be distinctive, focused on the regional and the inheritable, *and* heavily intertwined with other forms of discrimination.

[32] *Gosselin* (n 30) [42].
[33] *Gosselin* (n 30) [33].
[34] *Gosselin* (n 30) [235].

3. POTENTIAL PROBLEMS

So, regional and inheritable qualities are prominent in classism, even as it blends with other forms of discrimination. Those qualities reflect the examples in the two lists I gave at the start of this chapter. Classism has its own vocabulary and entails long-term, extensive and severe disadvantage. However, some readers might point to outstanding issues, which cast doubt on my understanding of classism. To address some likely criticisms, I consider a trio of them: (a) people who 'change' classes; (b) the boundaries of groups; and (c) a renewed argument in favour of the economic core of class.

3.1. 'Changing' Class

In some cases and academic literature, there have been arguments that discrimination relates to 'immutable' traits.[35] These arguments reflect a common view that ideas such as race are immutable. The central point is that people are unable, or only able with difficulty and by drastic measures, to disguise or change their race.[36] Applied to class, the point would be as follows. By contrast with forms of discrimination we typically recognise, people can *change* class. They can develop social, cultural and economic capital and, in turn, shield themselves from classism. With a high-flying job, substantial property, new colleagues and friends as well as learnt cultural preferences, alongside changes of other class markers (such as dialect and accent), the lower-class person transforms into something else. How does this person fit within the idea of classism? If they have changed class, could they still be a victim of classism?

When considered in detail, this view does not pose a persuasive challenge to my understanding of classism. First, it is **flawed by relying on the concept of immutability.** It assumes that immutability – in the sense that something cannot change or be hidden – defines discrimination. It does not. This is primarily because the idea of immutability is inadequate.[37] It is inaccurate when identifying the trait in question. As Patrick Shin observes, '[i]t is not impossible to change . . . religion, sexual phenotype, or even skin colour'.[38] Yes, it may be

[35] See, eg, *Lyng* 477 US 635 (1971), 638. See also, for a now-historical discussion of the status of immutability in the context of discrimination against queer people and the US Constitution, and then the European Convention on Human Rights and Fundamental Freedoms, R Wintemute, *Sexual Orientation and Human Rights* (Oxford, Oxford University Press, 1993) 61–90, 119–49.

[36] See, eg, for discussion of racial, gender and sexual 'covering', K Yoshino, *Covering* (New York, Random House, 2006).

[37] See generally L Alexander, 'What Makes Wrongful Discrimination Wrong?' (1991) 141(1) *University of Pennsylvania Law Review* 149, 151.

[38] P Shin, 'Is There a Unitary Concept of Discrimination?' in D Hellman and S Moreau, *Philosophical Foundations of Discrimination Law* (Oxford, Oxford University Press, 2013) 163, 168–69.

difficult to change these features, but that fact does not make them immutable. Immutability is also inaccurate in the way that it conflates the trait with the protected ground, such as reducing 'race' to 'skin colour'. As I set out when citing Stuart Hall's work in Chapter 2, ideas like race are ideas made by people in societies.[39] The tendency to treat race as if it is 'as natural as complexion, or necessarily defined by pigmentation' is mistaken.[40] The 'social' approach to disability stresses a similar point. It emphasises that the primary *disabler* is an ableist society, not the traits of a person who is disabled. This is true even though some disabled people 'might still face particular struggles' if a society's ableist features were removed.[41] Class is similar. It is difficult, though not impossible, to change class. Even if people who grew up lower-class acquire considerable advantage, they will often retain associations with being lower-class. Manners, etiquette, accents, dialects, vocabulary, some cultural preferences, attitudes to spending and saving money, social norms – these are examples of practices that may persist, as they are habitual (even instinctive). This situation is partly due to classism's focus on the inheritable as well as the evidence that 'mobility' between classes is becoming less common.[42]

Second, even if it is in principle easier to change class than race, for instance, that is **not a reason to reject my approach to classism**. If there are examples of people changing class, my approach still makes sense of them. The idea of group-related disadvantage does not require all members of a group to be permanent or fixed at birth. The members of the group may change. In a specific instance, a person might no longer be properly described as 'lower-class' when we make an updated assessment of their capital. So long as we can still identify people who suffer abiding, pervasive and substantial disadvantage relating to their class, we can identify classism. This is true even if some members of a class may change over time. A person who changes class may still be mistreated in connection with features they retain that are still associated with being lower-class.

Once more, we can be led by an example. 'Changing' class is a complex process. People are often uncertain about their class at different stages of their life. A familiar example is my own. I grew up in a village near Bradford, West Yorkshire. My parents had left school to find jobs and joined the civil service as administrative assistants, later becoming officers. I went to a state primary school and then a state grammar school. I got into the University of Oxford and graduated top of my year. I am now a barrister and academic. I am writing

[39] See, eg, S Hall, 'New Ethnicities' in D Morley and K Chen (eds), *Stuart Hall: Critical Dialogues in Cultural Studies* (Abingdon, Routledge, 1996) 442, 444.

[40] A Shafi and I Nagdee, *Race to the Bottom* (London, Pluto Press, 2022) 9.

[41] P Dwyer, 'The Neurodiversity Approach(es): What Are They and What Do They Mean for Researchers?' (2022) 66(2) *Human Development* 73, 75, citing EP Ballou, 'What the Neurodiversity Movement Does – and Doesn't – Offer', *Thinking Person's Guide to Autism* (6 February 2018): www.thinkingautismguide.com/2018/02/what-neurodiversity-movement-doesand.html.

[42] See, eg, Krutikova (n 15).

this book, which is usually viewed as a socially and culturally prestigious activity, though one unlikely to bring me lots of money.[43] I spend most of my time in London and Oxford, sometimes back in Yorkshire. My accent is a blend of the Bradford and Halifax areas. I have friends with wealthy families and friends with poor families. I have friends who earn too much money and friends who earn too little. I do not describe myself as 'upper-class', though I know some people with influence and I have more money than I used to. Some of my features are still associated with being lower-class, not least my voice, but it is inaccurate to describe me as 'lower-class'. Yet I recognise little of myself in colleagues who grew up in million-pound houses, advantaged by substantial familial wealth.

Do people like me never experience classism? It depends on what traits we have. It also depends on the type of classism. If someone perceives me as less intelligent because of my accent or dialect, for instance, that is still classist. I do not need to put myself into the group of lower-class people to argue that. It is classist because, whether or not I am actually lower-class, the root of that perception is the abiding, pervasive and substantial disadvantage relating to class. The fact that people may change class does not mean that classism suddenly evaporates.

Here, it is necessary to distinguish between (i) the character of classism as a *systemic* phenomenon, entailing long-term, extensive and severe disadvantage, and (ii) particular manifestations of it. When a person who has become class-advantaged still has some features associated with being lower-class, for instance, they may suffer classism. Examples I have already used relate to stigmatised accents or to those who grew up in council housing. However, unlike lower-class people, people who change class to their benefit are usually able to isolate themselves from many manifestations of classism and much of its viciousness. A person who faces prejudice for their accent or upbringing in a workplace, but who has now acquired prestigious formal education, social connections, cultural knowledge and money, is likely to be confident and worldly enough to complain to the right people in the right ways. Do not confuse this with the absence or faltering of classism. Rather, it is an illustration that classism may work in different ways for different people. Its sting may be less keen, or its impact narrower, for those who gain huge class advantage. But it is not completely blunted. Association with being lower-class often lingers.

This is consistent with lower-class people being significantly more likely to suffer abiding, pervasive and substantial disadvantage relating to their class when compared with other people. The fact that even those who are not lower-class may still suffer some classism (in rarer and more limited ways) due to being perceived as or associated with lower-class people in general *supports* the existence of classism. A person 'succeeding' in the system means that the system is, nevertheless, intact.

[43] Understandably, my publisher might be more optimistic.

3.2. Groups and their Boundaries

Linked to the issue of changing class, another argument against my approach could point to my reliance on the idea of a group. This derives from Khaitan's 'relative group disadvantage', as it only makes sense if we can identify the groups in question.[44]

It is fair to note a tension here. On the one hand, I accept EP Thompson's view that class is not a 'thing' in the abstract but that class instead 'happens (and can be shown to have happened) in human relationships'.[45] Thompson reminds us that class is a dynamic in relationships in societies, not a stiff box or entity. In the context of Marxist analysis, Erik Olin Wright also identifies the challenge of categorising class groups for those in the 'middle', such as managers who occupy 'contradictory class locations' (advantaged by capitalist exploitation from one perspective, disadvantaged by it from another).[46] On the other hand, I follow Khaitan in understanding discrimination as relating to *groups*, not disparate individuals. At first glance, this seems to require us to abstract people into identifiable 'groups', which risks ignoring Thompson's warning that class is not a 'thing' or a 'category'.

This tension is not fatal. We can rely on groups to understand discrimination without making them into boxes or reifying them. This is a conceptual issue that Khaitan does not address, but it is consistent with his overall approach. The idea of disadvantage relating to groups allows the law to recognise and seek to address the correlation between disadvantage and certain people.[47] In this context, there is no neatly defined 'group' in a society. There are always complexities and exceptions. The challenge of exceptions for the boundaries of groups is already one that we are willing to address. Disability is one example. In academia and campaigning, there is much debate about how to understand the term 'disability'.[48] The law allows for flexibility too. Section 6(1) of the Equality Act 2010 treats disability as 'a physical or mental impairment' that 'has a substantial and long-term adverse effect on [a person's] ability to carry out normal day-to-day activities'.[49] To some people, the boundaries of the group are clear, such as the familiar image of a person who uses a wheelchair in daily life. To others, the boundaries are hazy: once we ask what are 'normal abilities', especially as societies change and technologies develop, we notice 'questionable, hidden assumptions'.[50]

[44] T Khaitan, *A Theory of Discrimination Law* (Oxford, Oxford University Press, 2015) 30–31.

[45] EP Thompson, *The Making of the English Working Class* (London, Penguin, 1968) 9–11.

[46] EO Wright, *Classes* (London, Verso, 2023) ch 2.

[47] See, eg, Khaitan (n 44) 28–29.

[48] See, for an example of 'disability' discussed in physical, intellectual and psychiatric contexts, J Hare, *Autism Is Not a Disease* (London, Verso, 2024) 14.

[49] See, discussing the law prohibiting discrimination relating to disability in the UK and the rest of Europe, S Fredman, *Discrimination Law* (Oxford, Oxford University Press, 2022) 156–57.

[50] J Beaudry, 'Theoretical Strategies to Define Disability' in A Cureton and D Wasserman (eds), *The Oxford Handbook of Philosophy and Disability* (Oxford, Oxford University Press, 2018) 3, 4.

When it comes to the challenge of group boundaries, my approach offers a reminder of this, not a revelation. There will always be hard cases. But my lists of examples tell us that many cases will also be clear-cut. Other cases might turn less on the boundaries of a class and more on the extent to which the person claiming discrimination has been associated with, or perceived as, lower-class. We might address these instances through an idea of classism in the form of association or perception, *even if* we are unsure about the class 'group' of a person. This is not, in truth, a new problem for analysis of discrimination or, indeed, the law.

3.3. But Economic?

A. *Class as Economic*

You might think: do we really have to return to class being, at its core, 'economic', whereas classism is limited to social and cultural prejudices about that economic phenomenon? After all, I addressed it in Chapter 3. I rejected Fred Pincus and Natalie Sokoloff's argument that the 'essence' of 'class oppression' is the economic exploitation that defines capitalism, not merely some understanding of 'prejudice' or 'discrimination' relating to class.[51] I also rejected Nancy Fraser's argument that the social and cultural aspects of class are 'subordinate' or 'less weighty' than the economic.[52]

The answer to this question is: yes, we do, but briefly. That is because my elaboration on the idea of classism in this chapter creates the opportunity for an adapted version of the argument that class is primarily economic. It stems from the issue of people changing class. When people change class to their benefit, I have explained that they may well gain advantage in social and cultural ways. But, as the revised argument might go, the key element is the economic advantage that they gain. The softer or narrower nature of classism for those people could be understood to support this view. If the wealthy owner of a company (who grew up lower-class) experiences classism, it will not be economic in its form. That aspect of disadvantage will have gone away with the owner's change of class. Instead, the classism could only now be social or cultural. It might relate to the owner's way of speaking or dressing, or her knowledge of culture or her tastes. That could tell us that class is primarily an economic phenomenon and that classism, at its core, relates to social and cultural aspects, biases or prejudices. In Pincus and Sokoloff's language, this argument might conclude that classism refers to the residual 'prejudice and discrimination' and not the central 'class oppression'. Borrowing Fraser and Sandra Fredman's language,

[51] F Pincus and N Sokoloff, 'Does "Classism" Help Us to Understand Class Oppression?' (2008) 15(1) *Race, Gender & Class* 20.

[52] N Fraser, 'Social Justice in the Age of Identity Politics: Redistribution, Recognition, and Participation' in *The Tanner Lectures on Human Values* (lecture, Stanford University, 30 April–30 May 1996) 12: www.tannerlectures.org/wp-content/uploads/sites/105/2024/06/Fraser98.pdf.

this argument might conclude that classism refers to 'misrecognition', not 'maldistribution'.

While this argument is attractive on the surface, it takes the exception and uses it to misunderstand the rule. The company owner who changed class has insulated herself from much of the economic disadvantage that classism entails. In fact, she may even contribute to the classism that some people suffer. Classism is likely able to hurt her only in social and cultural ways (though, should she ever lose her job and suffer financial hardship without family connections or savings to help her, the economic aspect would come to the forefront again). This is because of the *nature* of the limited classism that she may now experience. Once more, though, this exceptional case does not make classism, in general, 'more' social and cultural and 'less' economic.

Consider a connection with racism. Oprah Winfrey, the billionaire, once described an experience she had in a shop. She had grown up lower-class in the US, mostly in poverty. Starting in the 1980s, she gathered huge fame and wealth. Later, in 2013, she went to a shop in Switzerland to buy a handbag then worth about £25,000.[53] In spite of Winfrey's fame in many countries, the shopworker appeared not to recognise her. Assuming a black woman could not afford an item for sale, the shopworker refused to show her the item she wanted to look at, Winfrey said.

Analysing what happened in this situation, it seems that the shopworker reduced Winfrey – despite her vast estates and money, her social and cultural prestige, the classist and racist economic barriers that she had overcome, the huge advantage that she had gained – to a black woman who could not possibly afford the item in question. By 2013, Winfrey had been able to isolate herself from many forms of racism and classism, given her wealth and fame. She could hire security guards, gain access to exclusive spaces, and develop powerful links with the rich and famous. By 2013, Winfrey was suffering little economic disadvantage. After all, she was shopping for an absurdly expensive handbag. She was able to spend money elsewhere that day. The incident did not affect her broader power in the media and corporate worlds. Nevertheless, in that shop, she suffered classism and racism. Of course, it was not of the most severe kind. The aim of eradicating classism or racism is not so that billionaires like Winfrey can buy £25,000 bags in peace. Even so, the treatment of her was discriminatory. Notably, it hardly makes sense to call the incident in the shop 'less' economic and more 'social' or 'cultural'. It was about perceived wealth, expensive goods and retail shopping. An exceptional case like this, involving a person who has changed class drastically, does not support the view that class is primarily economic or that classism is only social and cultural. The lesson we should draw from these exceptional cases is different, if a little watery: certain aspects of classism are more salient in some contexts than others. In some, the economic comes to the fore, but not to displace or cast aside the social and cultural.

[53] 'Oprah Winfrey "Racism Row" a "Misunderstanding"', *BBC News* (9 August 2013): www.bbc.co.uk/news/entertainment-arts-23633768.

B. *Classism as **Unusually** Economic: Paradox of the Rich Lower-Class Person*

On the role of the economic, there is a further argument that I should address. Rather than suggest that class is solely or primarily economic in nature and that classism is limited to social or cultural prejudices, this version suggests that the economic has a place in the idea of classism that differs from its place in other forms of discrimination. It does not ask us to determine that classism is *more* or *less* economic in its character than other forms of discrimination. Instead, it wonders if economic disadvantage has an *unusual* role in classism when compared with other forms of discrimination.

Consider the following summary. *You can't have a rich lower-class person. If a person is rich, they are not lower-class. Even though a rich person may still experience some limited forms of classism (such as by association), they are not on the whole a victim of classism. Therefore, the economic aspect of classism is really what defines who is advantaged and disadvantaged by it in a way that, for example, homophobia does not.*

This is complex and worth unpicking, especially because it may reveal something about the meaning of class. In Chapter 2, I discussed different approaches to class. Some of the most famous, such as those of Marx and Weber, centre on class as a relationship within production or the markets. By primarily locating class there, rather than in the home or in education or in traditional social settings, those approaches prioritise issues of income, wealth and property in the idea of class. As Weber suggests, though class may come with social and cultural markings, it is at its core an economic concept, rooted in relations within markets. Similarly, the idea of class associated with Marxism is found in the exploitation of production relations (though he preserves the more general meaning of class as hierarchical ranking). Even a multi-dimensional approach like that of Bourdieu includes economic capital as a discrete category, though interacting and blending with other forms of capital. With all that material in mind, the focus seems squarely on the economic. It is therefore unsurprising that people baulk at the prospect that a lower-class person could be 'rich'.

In principle, I agree. I do not need to adopt a Marxist or Weberian approach to do so. If a person acquires such a high degree of economic capital, they will be able to use it to isolate themselves from much of the disadvantage that classism comprises. They would be likely to afford a significant amount of property, goods and services, the lack of which is closely connected with the worst instances of classism. Once more, this point illustrates what is helpful about Bourdieu's multi-capital framework: the accumulation of one form of capital is likely to compensate for the absence of others, and, as Savage makes clear in his interpretation of Bourdieu, the accumulation of one form will often mean that a person acquires the others, too.[54]

[54] Savage (n 5).

That said, it is possible to imagine a rare situation in which a lower-class person suddenly becomes rich. The example that comes to mind is winning the lottery. Imagine that a person with little money, perhaps who lives in crowded council housing in Hartlepool, wins millions of pounds in the lottery. Would they suddenly become middle- or upper-class? This is a scenario for which usual class analysis is ill-suited. It is extremely rare and counters the broader patterns of class disadvantage, which provide fairly accurate predictions of people's wealth, employment, education and health over the course of their lives. Considering such a scenario, the person does not occupy a different class overnight. However, it is likely that what they do with that money will change their class status. Their interests may change, unless they donate significant portions of that money to charity shortly after receiving it. They may spend it to acquire property, with social connections and access to culture accompanying their new wealth. In time, then, their class is likely to change. As I have argued, the features that associate them with lower-class people may not disappear; they may retain a stigmatised accent, for instance, and they still have their family and heritage, which more traditional class hierarchies would use to exclude them from true class prestige.

Evaluating this kind of scenario does reveal the distinctive role of wealth in classism when compared with other forms of discrimination. The issue of wealth occupies an unusual place in class and classism. Even if racism is in part economic, people of all racial groups can, in theory, be rich; members of some groups are rich for their entire lives. The same observation applies to people of all sexualities and genders, for example, as well as disabled people. Although the forms of discrimination relevant to those groups have economic aspects, there is no seeming contradiction in the idea of a rich straight woman or a rich gay man. Yet the position does seem different when it comes to the idea of a rich lower-class person. While all forms of discrimination share economic aspects, that aspect helps to define class *and* classism in a way that it does not for other forms of discrimination.

This suggests why it is not possible to speak of a rich lower-class person, except in some very rare scenarios (such as winning the lottery). It may also indicate why there are special terms to describe those who acquire wealth in a way that is unusual in a long-standing class system, such as 'nouveau riche'. In this sense only, the economic does play a distinctive role in classism. It does not make class primarily economic or classism *more* economic than other forms of discrimination, but wealth does occupy an *unusual* place in the meaning of both class and classism.

4. GROUNDWORK

Classism remains best understood by reference to examples. It is also possible to provide some more abstract guidance, as I have done in this chapter. Even engaging with some challenging issues (like the place of the economic), it is correct that classism is a form of discrimination. It should be acknowledged as one.

With the groundwork done, Part I draws to a close. In Part II, my aim is to build on the analysis of class and classism in specific legal contexts. If you read ahead expecting that class and classism will always be easy to apply in the law, you should be given credit for your optimism – but you may be disappointed. That warning aside, there are also several opportunities to use the law in ways that will contribute to the end of classism.

Part II

5

Classism and the Equality Act 2010

In Part II, I consider how prohibiting classism might work in the law of England and Wales (or, where appropriate, the UK as a whole):

- This chapter addresses class as a protected ground in the UK Equality Act 2010 (concentrating on employment, education and public bodies' decision-making).
- Chapter 6 addresses class as a protected ground in the criminal law, commonly known as hate crime.
- Chapter 7 addresses classism as the basis of a ground for review in constitutional and administrative contexts.
- Chapter 8 moves away from a specific area and considers the law in more general terms, exploring some features that might be used (or removed) to address classism.

With its peculiar legal contexts and features, this mixture of subjects showcases the different challenges that arise when trying to use the law to protect people from classism. Although my analysis of classism is flexible enough to apply to different jurisdictions, and I will draw on the law of other countries at points in my analysis, I concentrate on the law of England and Wales for two main reasons. First, it is the jurisdiction I know best. Second, focusing on a particular legal system brings the opportunity to take the more abstract issues of Part I and test them in a specific, doctrinal setting. The aim, overall, is to think about *how* we might use the legal framework we have in order to combat classism.

—

1. EQUALITY ACT 2010

In the UK, the best-known piece of legislation concerning equality and discrimination is the Equality Act 2010. It came into force on 1 October 2010. In its current form, it has more than 200 sections and 20 Schedules. While it addresses a range of topics, the most relevant for my analysis are those of employment (or situations akin to employment), education, and public bodies' decision-making.

There may be other aspects of the Equality Act that are important for analysis of discrimination. For example, section 175(1) takes the unusual step of introducing a criminal offence to address discrimination, namely the contravention of regulations which seek to ensure that public service vehicles are accessible.[1] However, this chapter prioritises the aspects of the Act that deal with the question of which protected 'characteristics' can be used to claim discrimination.

When considering class and classism, the Equality Act cannot be overlooked.[2] Not only is it a central feature of the law, but it also has a significant impact on many aspects of the UK. It does not sit in dust on a shelf in Parliament. It has become a (if not *the*) point of reference for countless initiatives and policies.[3] Many reflect the list of nine protected characteristics in the Equality Act – but no more. Although some go further and include reference to class, this is rare.[4] Such a situation may be predictable: if legislation requires a closed list of characteristics, many organisations will follow it without question. A policy that goes beyond such a list would be ambitious. Worse, a policy going beyond the list might be regarded as excessive or laden with risk. It is not difficult to imagine legal executives and compliance officers worrying about the potential liability of including a protected characteristic within a policy that does not, by the letter of the law, need to be there.

This chapter's key question is *whether or not to amend the Equality Act to introduce class as a protected ground* (or, as the Act calls it, a 'protected characteristic').[5] The list in section 4 of the Equality Act contains nine protected characteristics: age; disability; gender reassignment; marriage and civil partnership; pregnancy and maternity; race; religion or belief; sex; and sexual orientation. Class is absent. Under the main piece of legislation on equality and discrimination, people cannot claim that they have suffered classism. To attempt to redress this kind of discrimination, a person would have to try other legal tools, such as the existing protected grounds, unfair dismissal in the context

[1] See generally (on the rarity of criminal sanctions in this area) S Fredman, *Discrimination Law* (Oxford, Oxford University Press, 2022) 434–92.

[2] Earlier versions of the arguments in this chapter appeared in A Benn, 'The Big Gap in Discrimination Law: Class and the Equality Act 2010' (2020) 3(1) *Oxford Human Rights Hub Journal* 30.

[3] See, eg, Advisory, Conciliation and Arbitration Service (Acas), 'Equality, Diversity and Inclusion Policy Template' (7 January 2022) [2]: www.acas.org.uk/equality-policy-template; UK Home Office, 'Equality and Diversity' (undated): www.gov.uk/government/organisations/home-office/about/equality-and-diversity; University of Oxford, 'Equality Policy' (19 June 2025) [4]: www.edu.admin.ox.ac.uk/equality-policy; University of Manchester, 'Equality, Diversity and Inclusion Policy' (July 2022) [1.3]: www.manchester.ac.uk/connect/jobs/equality-diversity-inclusion.

[4] See, eg, Compass Group UK, 'Diversity, Equity & Inclusion Policy' (21 November 2024): www.compass-group.com/content/dam/compass-group/corporate/Who-we-are/Policies/diversity-equity-inclusion.pdf; Red Lion Chambers, 'Equality & Diversity' (undated): www.redlionchambers.co.uk/about/equality-diversity.

[5] The term 'characteristic' can misdirect us: it is not necessarily true that all the protected grounds relate to a 'characteristic' (eg disability) and, even if they do, the emphasis should be on the way in which decision-makers and societies *approach* them, rather than on a 'characteristic'-based classification: Fredman (n 1) 29.

of employment, or claims against public bodies (such as judicial review for irrationality). The Equality Act does not recognise a form of discrimination relating to class.

There are, however, some aspects of the Act that touch on issues *to do* with class. Section 149, for instance, provides for a 'public sector equality duty'. However, it rests on the same list of nine protected characteristics. Section 1 seems more promising. It requires public authorities to have 'due regard' to reducing 'the inequalities of opportunity which result from socio-economic disadvantage'. That said, section 1 has at least three problems. First, and most important, it is not in force in England (though it is, in certain contexts, in Scotland and Wales).[6] Second, its language is woolly. Section 1(1) only requires 'due regard' to be given to 'the desirability' of 'making decisions of a strategic nature' in a way that is 'designed to reduce the inequalities of outcome which result from socio-economic disadvantage'. This is hardly a clear or firm commitment. Third, section 1 rests on the idea of 'socio-economic disadvantage' which remains vague and, it seems, separate from discrimination. Section 1 does not refer to the nine protected characteristics in section 4. This suggests that 'socio-economic disadvantage' is understood as something different from them, as if 'race' and 'sex' do not also entail that kind of disadvantage. Section 1 therefore suffers from the problems with ideas of the 'socio-economic' that I set out in Chapter 3. The Equality Act offers no real substitute for class and, importantly, no clear and direct protection against classism.

2. 'WHAT' AGAIN?

Earlier in this book, I considered the 'what' objection in a more theoretical way: *what* is class? Can we ever come to a sensible understanding of it? One that is comprehensible, usable, workable? I set out how and why we could. The Equality Act brings us back to the objection, though. You may agree that my rebuttal of the objection works in a theoretical sense, but you may think that it comes into difficulty in practice. The task is harder, you might say, when we are confronted with the prospect of drafting a new statutory provision to define class.

However, the 'what' objection is no stronger in practice than it is in theory. The objection shows little knowledge of the Equality Act and the case law concerning it. Consider the protected characteristic of religion or belief. Section 10(1) provides that '[r]eligion means any religion and a reference to religion includes a reference to a lack of religion'. Yes, religion includes no religion at all. Section 10(2) adds to the expanse when providing for the category of 'belief', which includes 'any religious or philosophical belief and a reference to belief includes a reference to a lack of belief'. So, believing includes not believing.

[6] Equality Act 2010 (Commencement Order No 13) (Scotland) Order 2017, art 2; Equality Act 2010 (Commencement Order No 15) (Wales) Order 2021, art 2.

These quips are, perhaps, unfair. The point of including the 'lack' of religion or belief is, of course, to protect those who are agnostic or atheist or who refuse to adhere to orthodoxy. Nevertheless, the room for debate under section 10 is substantial. In the subsequent case law, courts and tribunals have had the task of deciding if beliefs about ethical veganism,[7] democratic socialism[8] and environmentalism,[9] as well as wearing poppies in November, fall within section 10.[10] The Equality Act already deals with complex notions, such as 'religion' and 'philosophical beliefs', and uses definitions of those notions that include their non-existence. It seems odd, then, that *class* supposedly poses a level of definitional difficulty that the law cannot overcome.

It may be that I have selected the easiest example. 'Religion or belief' seems abstract, after all. Yet the difficulties of definitions apply to other protected grounds, such as 'race' and 'sex'. Section 9(1) defines race as including 'colour', 'nationality', and 'ethnic or national origin'. Section 9(3) goes on to define a racial group as 'a group of persons defined by reference to race'. While these concepts clearly relate to race, they do not offer the kind of granular, definitive statement that lawyers might expect to find in the law. Instead, courts and other decision-makers must decide what 'race' is by applying the statutory words to specific facts. For instance, in *Chandhok v Tirkey* (2014), the Employment Appeal Tribunal had to decide if 'caste' fell within 'race'. The tribunal held that it did.[11]

Despite the apparent vapidity of some of the drafting, there has been little suggestion that race is either too vague or too difficult an idea to include in the Equality Act. This may be because of a prevailing reduction of race to skin colour or nationality. However, as I have argued, it is widely accepted that race remains 'a politically and culturally constructed category'.[12] The inclusion of race also reflects its place in older legislation and the prominence of anti-racism campaigns in the evolution of the law relating to discrimination, both in the UK and in other countries (such as the US civil rights movement).[13] Plus, even with definitional questions, many examples of racism will be blatant. They will be straightforward for the law to analyse. Where the cases are more complicated, courts have been expected to cope (such as in *Chandhok v Tirkey*). While these concepts may be challenging at their most abstract, they nonetheless exist in our world and we identify them every day without significant problems. The commitment to address racism has prevailed over challenges about definition.

[7] *Casamitjana Costa v The League Against Cruel Sports* (2020) ET/3331129/18, [33]–[39] (Postle J).

[8] *The General Municipal and Boilermakers Union v Henderson* (2015) UKEAT/0073/14/DM (though the Employment Tribunal's conclusion on this issue was not challenged on appeal: [62]).

[9] *Grainger plc and ors v Nicholson* [2010] IRLR 4.

[10] *Lisk v Shield Guardian Co Ltd* (2011) ET/3300873/11.

[11] *Chandhok v Tirkey* (2014) UKEAT/0190/14/KN, [2015] IRLR 195.

[12] S Hall, 'New Ethnicities' in D Morley and K Chen (eds), *Stuart Hall: Critical Dialogues in Cultural Studies* (Abingdon, Routledge, 1996) 442, 444.

[13] See, eg, Race Relations Act 1965, s 1 (repealed); Race Relations Act 1968, s 1 (repealed); Race Relations Act 1976, s 1 (repealed); Race Relations (Amendment) Act 2000 (repealed); US Civil Rights Act 1964, Title VII.

3. HOW THE EQUALITY ACT GOT HERE

Even though the 'what' objection is false (both in theory and in the specific context of the Equality Act), it seems to have influenced lawmakers. To explore this, it is necessary to consider the legislative process that led to the Equality Act as we know it today.

3.1. Causes

A. *Assuming Class Is Something Else*

When it comes to class, difficulties with definition seem to be implicit or assumed in much of the material that records the legislative process. It does not appear that any politician ever expressly rejected a 'protected characteristic' of 'class' because it was hard to define. Rather, during debates of a public bill committee about the socio-economic duty in what became section 1 of the Equality Act, politicians across the major political parties tended to understand discrimination as 'all about perpetrators and victims'.[14] By comparison, 'socio-economic disadvantage' required 'quite different' solutions.[15] This may have been a consequence of the Equality Act being, in part, a consolidation and modernisation of existing statutes, meaning that politicians were following what was already protected.[16] But it seems also to reflect the frequent dissociation of class from discrimination considered in Part I. The injustice of class seems to have been understood as a problem of maldistribution or general inequality, rather than of discriminatory beliefs, systems and practices. One response during a committee debate in June 2009 encapsulated this view: 'lack of social mobility and people trapped in disadvantage' had to do with 'the reasons for disadvantage', which related to 'an equal opportunity to succeed' and not proposals in discrimination law.[17] Earlier in the debates, a committee witness and a director at the Equality and Human Rights Commission, John Wadham, adopted a slightly different position, though still distinguishing discrimination from 'disadvantage'. He argued that the 'core mandates' ('race, women and gender, disability, sexual orientation, religion, belief and age') involve 'poverty' and 'discriminatory treatment [that] has significant socio-economic consequences'.[18] Rather than considering this to be *part* of discrimination or of the 'core' protected characteristics, Wadham supported a 'socio-economic duty' to address these 'consequences' so that groups could 'compete on equal terms'.[19] Influenced by

[14] PBC Deb (Equality Bill), 5th sitting, cols 128–29 (John Penrose).
[15] PBC Deb (Equality Bill), 5th sitting, cols 129–30 (Mark Harper).
[16] B Hepple, 'The New Single Equality Act in Britain' (2010) 5 *The Equal Rights Review* 11, 21.
[17] PBC Deb (Equality Bill), 5th sitting, cols 129–30 (Mark Harper).
[18] PBC Deb (Equality Bill), 1st sitting, cols 4–5 (John Wadham).
[19] PBC Deb (Equality Bill), 1st sitting, cols 4–5 (John Wadham).

witnesses like Wadham, politicians appear to have narrowed the idea of discrimination to one of individuals harming each other, rather than something more systemic (despite the indirect discrimination, concerned with policies, criteria and practices, already present in the Bill as introduced in April 2009).[20]

The theme continues in the material that informed the parliamentary process. There is a moment of hope in the report of the Equalities Review in 2007. The report makes a rare reference to class by name: inequality is considered in relation to 'socio-economic status and social class' as well as gender, disability and race.[21] That hope quickly fades. The report uses the idea of discrimination to describe the last three, whereas 'socio-economic status and social class' are left to float into some other conceptual space.[22] When the Department for Communities and Local Government's Discrimination Law Review outlined its proposals later that same year, it omitted class.[23] Its report refers to 'class barriers hav[ing] shifted' but does little to develop the point.[24] The trend carried on. The government's response to the consultation about the Equality Bill also omitted class.[25] The government's policy paper in 2009 mentions it only in the context of a duty placed on public authorities, arguing that 'persistent inequality of social class' is interwoven with 'specific inequalities' relating to gender, race, sexuality and disability.[26] It makes the unwarranted assumption that inequality relating to the latter categories is more 'specific' than that relating to class. From these references, it is possible to conclude that politicians and others misunderstood class in the lead up to the Equality Act. To them, apparently, class was not a matter of discrimination.

B. *Political Interests*

The less forgiving interpretation is that this was insidious rather than a genuine misunderstanding. It may be that there was a deliberate effort to exclude issues of class from the scope of the Equality Act. If, for instance, class were to have been proposed as a protected characteristic, politicians may have seriously worried about the implications for employers and public bodies who wished to use policies, practices and criteria that would put lower-class people at a disadvantage, which could then amount to indirect discrimination under section 19. With the

[20] Equality Bill, clause 18 (24 April 2009).

[21] The Equalities Review, *Fairness and Freedom: The Final Report of the Equalities Review* (2007) 1, 26.

[22] See, eg, as 'beneficiaries of equality policies' and a relevant addition to 'membership of [disadvantaged] groups', The Equalities Review, *Fairness and Freedom* (n 21) 26, 28.

[23] Department for Communities and Local Government, *Discrimination Law Review: A Framework for Fairness: Proposals for A Single Equality Bill for Great Britain* (2007).

[24] Department for Communities and Local Government, *Discrimination Law Review* (n 23) 15.

[25] UK Government, *The Equality Bill: Government Response to the Consultation* (Cm 7454, 2008).

[26] UK Government, *New Opportunities: Fair Chances for the Future* (Cm 7533, 2009), 10.

vast inequalities in the UK, linked closely with regional differences, it is not beyond imagination to suspect that there was concern about this in some quarters.

An example is a set of policies commonly known by the term 'austerity', such as cuts to funding and public services, though representing deeper ideological changes.[27] Austerity's public message is that, in order to save the government money (and to stop the people in a country suffering in the long term), the funding for public services must be cut. Lower-class people tend to rely more on those services than upper-class people, who can pay for alternatives, such as education and different types of care. In preparing the Equality Act, perhaps the worry was that giving class a legal footing would endanger commonplace techniques in politics and government policies. If a prohibition of classism were to have been seriously contemplated in the Equality Act, the implications of it could have been far-reaching. If, for example, public bodies' decisions could be challenged as unlawful when they rationalised an increase in poverty as a necessary sacrifice to ensure a better standard of living for all in the long term, some politicians would have viewed that as an intolerable prospect.[28] There may also have been interests closer to home: prohibitions of classism could jeopardise the personal wealth and opportunities of politicians. For some, there may have been a simpler, self-serving goal: the less class came up in debate and 'fix[ed] . . . in people's minds', the better.[29]

C. *Academics*

As I set out in Chapter 1, those in legal scholarship must also accept their share of the responsibility for the absence of class in the Equality Act. For reasons both personal and institutional, class has not had the attention that the existing protected characteristics have had (perhaps especially sex, race and sexual orientation).

First, there is the issue of *who*. Who is writing legal scholarship? As with many areas of academia, legal scholars tend to have grown up with significant class advantage. Many major legal scholarships are not means-tested, and various academic positions, especially at traditionally prestigious institutions like Oxford and Cambridge, have little regard for the class of their applicants. In addition to that, even if academics grew up lower-class, for example, they inevitably acquire a degree of social and cultural capital by the time they write scholarship and teach. With professional membership of higher educational institutions comes a level of social and cultural influence. As Angela Harris observes in her work on feminist legal theory, the fact that many academics have long been advantaged by both classism and racism means that they tend to overlook the role of classism and racism in misogyny.[30]

[27] See, eg, B De Oliveira, *Austerity* (Abingdon, Routledge, 2025) esp 48–74.
[28] See generally De Oliveira (n 27) 46–47, 102–03.
[29] M Thatcher, 'Don't Undo My Work', *Newsweek* (27 April 1992). See too Chapter 1.
[30] A Harris, 'Race and Essentialism in Feminist Legal Theory' (1990) 42(3) *Stanford Law Review* 581, 588–91.

Second, there is the issue of *where*. I do not mean geographically (though, clearly, scholarship suffers from distortions in favour of Oxford, Cambridge, London and the South East of England).[31] Instead, I mean *from where* much of legal scholarship has drawn its inspiration. As I argued in Chapter 1, especially in the literature about discrimination in the legal context, the most influential sources have come from movements like feminist and anti-racist work. In brief, with class perceived (often accurately) to presume a white, straight and masculine norm, scholars and activists developed new modes of analysis and new emphases, such as gender, queerness and race.

This may be unfair to those involved in legal scholarship, especially in the years just before the Equality Act came into force. For instance, class makes an appearance in the output of the Equality and Human Rights Commission around that time.[32] In a review of statistics relating to equality in 2008, Sylvia Walby, Jo Armstrong and Les Humphreys discuss 'socio-economic status (social class)', noting that it is important but 'not one of the equality strands'.[33] However, class then seems to disappear from the material. Examples like that of Walby, Armstrong and Humphreys remained the exception in the legal scholarship surrounding the Equality Act.

The theme continued in the academic literature written after the Equality Act came into force. Bob Hepple, one of the authors of the influential Cambridge Review in 2000, followed the theme in 2010. While he accepted that discrimination in part caused 'social disadvantage', he made no attempt to consider what this 'social disadvantage' was, as distinct from the disadvantage that racism, homophobia and other forms of discrimination involve.[34] In the years since, the theme has not gone away. Sandra Fredman's work in 2016 offers a useful illustration. Fredman develops a concept of 'substantive equality' with four dimensions but without mention of class or classism.[35] To be fair to her, Fredman's work often refers to the substance of class, such as by considering how to approach poverty in the law.[36] Nevertheless, Fredman's article draws a distinction between 'socio-economic' disparity and the disparity involved in racism, misogyny and other forms of discrimination.[37] Responding to Fredman's article, Catherine MacKinnon criticises its 'bafflingly narrow concept of disadvantage'.[38] This is

[31] M Donnelly and S Gamsu, *Home and Away* (The Sutton Trust, 2018) 19–20, 23–24.

[32] A Donald, P Leach and A Puddephatt, *Developing a Bill of Rights in the UK* (Equality and Human Rights Commission, 2010) 70.

[33] S Walby, J Armstrong and L Humphreys, *Review of Equality Statistics* (Equality and Human Rights Commission, 2008) vi.

[34] Hepple (n 16) 21.

[35] S Fredman, 'Substantive Equality Revisited' (2016) 14(3) *International Journal of Constitutional Law* 712.

[36] See, eg, S Fredman, 'The Potential and Limits of an Equal Rights Paradigm in Addressing Poverty' (2011) 22 *Stellenbosch Law Review* 566.

[37] Fredman (n 35) 734–35.

[38] C MacKinnon, 'Substantive Equality Revisited: A Reply to Sandra Fredman' (2016) 14(3) *International Journal of Constitutional Law* 739, 743.

a justifiable criticism: I have already argued against the dissociation of 'socio-economic disadvantage' from the disadvantage involved in racism, misogyny and widely recognised forms of discrimination. Although some of Fredman's more recent work has begun to recognise more expressly the concept of class itself, her approach reflects a wider failure to acknowledge classism as discrimination in legal theory and in practice.[39] Elongating this theme in 2021, the fourth edition of *Blackstone's Guide to the Equality Act 2010* makes no attempt to engage with class or classism, perhaps because they are still assumed to be outside the scope of the Act.[40] Drawing these threads together, it seems that academics not only contributed to the sidelining of class and classism in the lead up to the Equality Act, but they have also continued to do so in the years since it came into force.

D. *Courts*

Alongside the factors I have discussed, the courts have a share of responsibility. There has been a failure to develop jurisprudence to address class or classism. Having regard to the law before the Equality Act, there was no common law protection in the UK against classism (though there has been some speculative consideration of it in the context of administrative law, which I will discuss in Chapter 7). The Equality Act should itself be understood against the background of earlier statutes and legislation, which in part reflects human rights developments. The Human Rights Act 1998 incorporates Article 14 of the European Convention on Human Rights (ECHR), which includes the (unfocused) reference to 'social origin'. However, this article requires another right under the ECHR to be engaged (though not necessarily breached) before it comes into play and applies to public authorities.[41] In addition to that, the jurisprudence surrounding the ECHR has not developed an understanding of class or classism, meaning that it has not used the opportunity to influence the drafting or subsequent interpretation of the Equality Act.[42]

Moving to the decisions of judges themselves rather than broader legislative issues, it is unsurprising to see a similar lack of consideration of class. Due to the constraints on those bringing claims, the courts tend to consider class-based issues through the existing protected characteristics in section 4. Two cases before the UK Supreme Court show one problem within typical judicial analysis. In *R (SG) v Secretary of State for Work and Pensions* (2015) and *R (DA) v Secretary of State for Work and Pensions* (2019), the UK Supreme Court had to consider whether or not caps on state benefit payments indirectly discriminated against

[39] See, eg, S Atrey and S Fredman, 'Introduction' in S Atrey and S Fredman (eds), *Exponential Equalities* (Oxford, Oxford University Press, 2023) 1.

[40] A Robinson, D Ruebain and S Uppal (eds), *Blackstone's Guide to the Equality Act 2010* (Oxford, Oxford University Press, 2021).

[41] ECHR, Art 14; *Carson and Ors v UK* [2010] ECHR 338, [63].

[42] See, eg, addressing disparities in pension age and financial inequality relating to gender without addressing class or classism, *Stec v UK*, App no 65731/01, [62]–[66].

women and against single parents with young children. In *SG*, the majority held that the cap was not discriminatory against women, despite women representing the majority of single parents. The majority of the court went to considerable lengths to frame the issue as 'political' rather than 'legal'.[43] In *DA*, the majority held that reducing benefit payments below the threshold of poverty was not a policy manifestly without reasonable foundation. Again, the court reasoned that, given the nature of the issues and the role of the political branches of government, it was necessary to give them 'appropriately generous ... leeway'.[44]

In this pair of decisions, we see the courts keen to characterise these questions as 'political' (and, therefore, not for courts readily to interfere with). This is, in part, because of the absence of a characteristic expressly about money in section 4 of the Equality Act. It also indicates the judicial tendency to understand these issues as matters of economic policy, which fall squarely within the legitimate remit of political decision-makers and not courts.

It is possible to put forward many criticisms of the artificial distinction between the 'political' and the 'legal'.[45] For now, my point is narrower: the absence of class has exacerbated the courts' reluctance to tread on areas that they consider the legitimate territory of politicians. This may be another cause of the absence of a concept like class in the Equality Act. If class is purely a question of broad 'socio-economic disadvantage' or 'inequality', surely it would be for politicians and not judges to answer that question? Yet we see judges engage with difficult questions of money and economic decision-making on a daily basis, whether they are hearing litigation worth billions of pounds or awarding compensation to large numbers of people in group actions.

The perception that class-based issues are solely questions of economic policy (and are therefore conceptually ill-suited to judicial analysis or more appropriately left to other institutions) is not limited to courts in England and Wales. Here, it is useful to draw connections with other jurisdictions, being careful to note the different legal contexts. An instructive example comes from the US Supreme Court's decision in *San Antonio Independent School District v Rodriguez* (1973).[46] The Supreme Court decided that the school district's funding system, which used local property taxes in addition to a minimum level of state funding, was compatible with the Fourteenth Amendment.[47] It reached this conclusion despite clear disparities in educational standards due to such a system. Indeed, the majority held that the US Constitution did not protect a

[43] *R (SG) v Secretary of State for Work and Pensions* [2015] UKSC 16, [69].

[44] *R (DA) v Secretary of State for Work and Pensions* [2019] UKSC 21, [118].

[45] See, eg, V Fikfak, 'Protecting Human Rights in Austerity Claims in the UK' (2016) 8(2) *Hague Journal on the Rule of Law* 205, 219.

[46] *San Antonio Independent School District v Rodriguez* 411 US 1 (1973).

[47] *Rodriguez* (n 46) 8–9, 62.

fundamental right to education.[48] The funding system, therefore, did not require a higher standard of scrutiny.

In part, *Rodriguez* rests on a peculiarity of legal heritage. This is the US law's formulation of a protected group as 'a discrete and insular minority' in *US v Carolene Products* (1938).[49] With this formulation looming large, the majority held that people of lower wealth could not be such a group, as they were neither discrete nor insular.[50] However, it would be wrong to reduce *Rodriguez* to this detail of precedent. The case offers a more general lesson for legal analysis of class and classism. It reflects the worry – also seen in *SG* and *DA* – that questions of class would require courts to intensify their constitutional role, encroaching without good reason on the territory of executive or legislative decision-making. Justice Powell's reasoning is littered with these suggestions: it frames the Supreme Court as an institution lacking the justification (and possibly the capability) to scrutinise the 'infinite variables' within education, especially as the Texan legislature had granted partial funding for the system in question.[51]

Although this pattern gives one insight into the absence of class in a statute like the Equality Act, it is not as if courts are inherently unable to undertake reasoning about issues like class and the distributive aspects of discrimination, which often involve money and property.[52] The Indian Supreme Court offers an example for comparison. In *Indra Sawhney v India* (1993), for instance, the court held that a 27 per cent reservation of governmental jobs for members of designated 'backward classes' was lawful.[53] There, the judges were able to rely on an article of the Indian Constitution, namely Article 16(4), on the basis that it enabled the identification of backward classes in terms of both economic status *and* caste. Labelling caste 'nothing but a social class', the court recognised that 'caste, occupation, poverty and social backwardness are closely inter-twined'.[54] However, this is where attention to the legal context explains the difference from the patterns we see in the UK and US cases. With India's relatively strong constitutional recognition of casteism and its commitment to the tool of reservations, the Indian Supreme Court was willing to view itself as institutionally appropriate and capable of justified, protective decision-making. The Indian Supreme Court also remains one of the few worldwide to recognise that there *can* be discrimination relating to class.[55]

[48] *Rodriguez* (n 46) 37.

[49] *United States v Carolene Products Co* 304 US 144 (1938) (US Supreme Court).

[50] *Rodriguez* (n 46) 60.

[51] *Rodriguez* (n 46) 9, 24, 40–41.

[52] See, eg, the 'fair distribution' of physical resources in a fuller concept of equality in S Moyn, *Not Enough* (Cambridge, Massachusetts, Harvard University Press, 2018) 204.

[53] *Indra Sawhney v Union of India* AIR 1993 SC 477.

[54] *Indra Sawhney* (n 53) [83].

[55] *State of Maharashtra v India Hotel and Restaurants Association* (2013) 8 SCC 519.

Although the courts have approached their role in these contexts in a narrow way, there is another option available to them. Concerns about courts overreaching their role have appeared in many areas of the law, including in relation to longstanding protected grounds. They have, for example, arisen in the context of caps on welfare payments and the impact on women.[56] Yet these concerns seem to be sharpest when it comes to issues that are to do with class – especially money. On the one hand, some courts understand misogyny, ableism, transphobia, homophobia, racism and ageism by elevating the 'socio-' part of the disadvantage and diminishing the '-economic' part. Some courts consider the discrimination on such grounds through a primary lens of misrecognition, such as stigma and prejudice.[57] On the other hand, when some courts address the loosely conceived category of 'socio-economic disadvantage', it is the '-economic' part that obscures the other.

Yet, with accurate analysis, so-called 'socio-' disadvantage is not isolated from the economic. I have already noted a range of available research, some of which indicates the higher rates of black and brown lower-class people than white lower-class people, as well as the severe and distinctive reality of poverty for women of all races.[58] Granted, judges may have well-founded concerns about the legitimacy and effectiveness of the courts when answering these questions, as I explore in Chapters 9 and 10. However, the failure to engage with the economic has led to a misshapen understanding of discrimination and an oddity when considered against a statute that already prohibits forms of discrimination – such as racism, misogyny and ableism – with substantial economic aspects. It may be, rather, that courts are willing to understand forms of discrimination so far as they are about what some may call 'misrecognition' but no further. This is not, though, a problem unique to class and classism. Rather than realising these connections between misrecognition and maldistribution (analysed in Chapter 3), courts have compounded the sidelining of class by politicians and scholars.

4. HOW TO INCLUDE CLASS

These factors explain why class and classism have been ignored in the Equality Act. They do not, however, justify that omission. Having developed an understanding of classism as a form of discrimination in Part I, it is now possible to imagine what a provision about class in the Equality Act would look like. This is

[56] See, eg, M Campbell, 'Capping Motherhood: Equality-Based Analysis of UK Benefit Cap Cases' in M Davis, M Kjaerum and A Lyons (eds), *Research Handbook on Human Rights and Poverty* (Cheltenham, Edward Eldgar, 2021) 156, 169–70.

[57] See, eg, *SG* (n 43) and *DA* (n 44).

[58] See Chapters 3 and 4 of this book.

a more technical question. One approach would be to follow the drafting of the provisions on 'age' and 'sex'.

5 Age

(1) In relation to the protected characteristic of age—

(a) a reference to a person who has a particular protected characteristic is a reference to a person of a particular age group;

(b) a reference to persons who share a protected characteristic is a reference to persons of the same age group.

(2) A reference to an age group is a reference to a group of persons defined by reference to age, whether by reference to a particular age or to a range of ages.[59]

11 Sex

In relation to the protected characteristic of sex—

(a) a reference to a person who has a particular protected characteristic is a reference to a man or to a woman;

(b) a reference to persons who share a protected characteristic is a reference to persons of the same sex.[60]

In this vein, the equivalent provision for class would be simple, inserting a new section 12A after the provisions listing the existing protected characteristics, which currently end with section 12.

12A Class

In relation to the protected characteristic of class—

(a) a reference to a person who has a particular protected characteristic is a reference to a person of a particular class;

(b) a reference to persons who share a protected characteristic is a reference to persons of the same class.

This draft has some benefits. It is flexible. It does not specify in statute my particular approach to class. If lawmakers were not persuaded to take inspiration from Bourdieu, for example, a provision of this kind might be least controversial. It would allow courts to develop their own understanding of class, perhaps guided by parliamentary debate. It is also wide enough to accommodate different interpretations, like the existing provisions concerning 'age' and 'sex'.

However, the lack of detail in this draft creates some drawbacks. It does not offer much guidance. Like 'sex', it gives us only circular guidance that, simply put, a 'reference' to class is a reference to 'a particular class'. Granted, the Equality Act has many provisions like this. But we may criticise those provisions

[59] Equality Act 2010, s 5.
[60] Equality Act 2010, s 12.

as well and call for a more detailed approach across the board, even if it risks controversy. The alternative approach would answer this call by adding a subsection about the meaning of class. This would resemble other provisions in the Equality Act, such as that concerning religion or belief.

10 Religion or belief

(1) Religion means any religion and a reference to religion includes a reference to a lack of religion.

(2) Belief means any religious or philosophical belief and a reference to belief includes a reference to a lack of belief.

(3) In relation to the protected characteristic of religion or belief—

(a) a reference to a person who has a particular protected characteristic is a reference to a person of a particular religion or belief;

(b) a reference to persons who share a protected characteristic is a reference to persons who are of the same religion or belief.'[61]

Taking inspiration from this, we could add a subsection to tell us what class means. Predictably, my suggestion reflects my preference to take inspiration from Bourdieu and Savage, who understand class via social, cultural and economic capital. The new provision, then, would incorporate this approach.

12A Class

(1) Class means social, cultural and economic capital.

(2) In relation to the protected characteristic of class—

(a) a reference to a person who has a particular protected characteristic is a reference to a person of a particular class;

(b) a reference to persons who share a protected characteristic is a reference to persons of the same class.'

Instead of avoiding any attempt to give meaning to class, this version of the provision has the benefit of offering greater guidance. It commits to the understanding of class as social, cultural *and* economic (and, therefore, rejects understandings that reduce class to a person's occupation).

However, this version could run into a number of problems. First, it may need clarification that 'capital' is not, as in other legal contexts, entirely about money, wealth or equity. A sensible reading of the new subsection may tell us this already: 'social' and 'cultural' qualify 'capital' to ensure that it is not reduced to the 'economic'. Nevertheless, putting complex sociological concepts into statute may be considered confusing and risk inviting difficult interpretive disputes.

Second, with the emphasis on 'capital', this version of section 12A also risks over-simplifying the complex issues surrounding approaches to class discussed in Chapter 2. Bourdieu would not, for instance, agree that it is right to summarise

[61] Equality Act 2010, s 10.

class as 'social, cultural and economic capital'. Those concepts depend on other ideas in his work, such as practices, habitus and the places of people within a given social field. In a similar way, EP Thompson would criticise the impression of class as 'capital', ie a 'thing' that exists rather than a distinctive relationship *between* people.

Third, this version is wide enough to be symmetrical, as the meaning of class here could include upper-class people as well as lower-class people. This issue taps into the broader debate about protection of the advantaged groups as well as the disadvantaged groups in the law, which I will address in Chapter 9. At this stage, the point can be put in summary: the worry is that this provision would protect those who enjoy significant class advantage, which would entrench classism rather than reduce it.

Do these criticisms mean that we should revert to the first version of section 12A, which offers less detail? That is not necessarily correct. First, dealing with clarification and the question of drawing inspiration from complex academic contexts, **the Equality Act *already* does this.** Its approach to disability, for example, takes a particular position in the layered and evolving debate about the meaning of 'disability' and diverging medical, social and diversity models.[62] Once more, we risk forgetting the thorny background of the existing provisions by assuming that class alone would not be possible to put in a statutory 'definition'.

Second, there is definitely a risk of over-simplification, but it is **a risk worth taking.** Putting in statute reference to the social, cultural and economic would ensure that all the aspects of class are included while deterring approaches that simplify class to money or income. The possibility of competing interpretations based on technical detail from academic debates certainly exists, yes, but this possibility should not bar the offer of some further detail in a statutory provision. The benefit of framing class in this way may invite theoretical argument and yet so do race, philosophical belief and sex.[63] Again, it is the nature of such ideas. They exist in society and, if litigants and others wish to draw on the wealth of sociological, political and philosophical literature available to support competing interpretations, the nature of these ideas permits that. It would have to be for judges and other decision-makers to evaluate the merit of technical interpretations in applying the terms of the statute. But this challenge is not substantial enough to omit the proposed subsection.

Third, **symmetry in this context is easily resolved.** In the place of 'social, cultural and economic capital', an asymmetrical approach – one protecting only disadvantaged groups – would propose a draft such as 'disadvantage relating to social, cultural and economic capital'. Such an approach would restrict the meaning of class (and the statutory protection of class) to disadvantaged people,

[62] See, eg, Fredman (n 1) 150–52.

[63] See, eg, the discussion of the meaning of 'philosophical' in *Grainger* (n 9) [10]–[11], [20], [25]–[31].

which would exclude those who are advantaged. Properly understood, this is not an argument against further detail in the provision but an argument about how we word that detail. I return to this argument in Chapter 9.

For now, the second version of section 12A offers the better illustration of how we might formulate a provision for class as a protected characteristic. In many ways, even accepting the risks, it would not be that different from provisions currently in force.

5. IS INTERSECTIONALITY STILL NOT THE ANSWER?

In Part I, I considered why relying on intersectionality as a substitute for the idea of class is inadequate. That was mainly in the context of more theoretical issues about classism as a form of discrimination. The main theme of this chapter is plainly more doctrinal: class as a protected characteristic in the Equality Act. Even accepting that the use of intersectionality at a more theoretical level is inadequate, you might argue that the position changes when we are considering the specific question of class as a protected characteristic. Given how class may blend with other protected characteristics (such as race), there may be good reasons to argue for an intersectional approach to the existing protected characteristic rather than the introduction of a new, separate ground of class.

To explore this argument, it is necessary to consider the drafting of the Equality Act alongside the role of protected characteristics within its scheme. We should also bear in mind the issue of how to achieve the most effective protection for lower-class people.

5.1. Drafting and the Role of Protected Grounds

If the Equality Act were to recognise class only when an idea of 'intersectionality' called for it, it would become internally inconsistent. The starting point for this argument is the Act's current scheme. The Act proceeds on the basis that a protected characteristic (such as 'race' and 'sex') requires its own provision and is not properly addressed by some general reference to intersectional discrimination. This does not necessarily preclude intersectional analysis. For instance, going back to Kimberlé Crenshaw's framework of 'race' and 'sex', she accepts that each has a distinctive meaning, albeit a meaning that includes the most disadvantaged members of a group as well as the most advantaged members.[64] Understanding race and sex in an intersectional manner, according to her argument, does not mean that we do away with race and sex as independent ideas.

[64] K Crenshaw, 'Demarginalizing the Intersection of Race and Sex' (1989) 1 *University of Chicago Legal Forum* 139, 145, 151–52; K Crenshaw, 'Mapping the Margins: (1993) 43 *Stanford Law Review* 1242, 1243.

Crenshaw also suggests that, in some contexts, the only precise (and accurate) form of analysis is to accept that racism and misogyny can be 'crosscurrents', thus not being ideas isolated from one another.[65]

However, in the context of protected characteristics, you may wonder if there is an inherent tension with intersectionality. At least in the Equality Act, a protected 'characteristic' is singular, not intersectional. Section 14 – yet to be enacted – concerns 'combined discrimination: dual characteristics'. It is restricted to 'a combination of two relevant protected characteristics', thus not extending to situations involving, for example, disability, race *and* age.[66] While the provision makes clear that a person does not need to establish direct discrimination on the basis of each characteristic ('taken separately'), it falls short of a proper intersectional analysis. It simply offers the opportunity to put together two 'characteristics' and make a claim on that joint basis. It contemplates little about the priority, if any, to be given to the most disadvantaged members of a group. Section 14 is also supposed to function as an addition to the list of protected characteristics in section 4, rather than as an alternative approach or a challenge to the paradigm of a 'characteristic'. Section 14 seems to be a provision designed to deal with the exceptional case, rather than the usual one.[67] This reflects much of the debate during the legislative process, such as Stephen Whittle's argument before the public bill committee that, if someone has experienced 'multiple discrimination', their 'award is multiplied as well'.[68] Theo Gavrielides called this 'impractical'. John Penrose MP remarked that it would be 'hideously complicated'. Ben Summerskill thought that lawyers would consider it 'Christmas . . . come early'.[69] These views encourage a false logic of multiplication, merely 'adding' together characteristics as if they were numbers. They mangle the true nature of intersectional analysis.

To see why this is a problem, consider the issue of class as a new protected characteristic. If we were to introduce such a characteristic, would we not just contribute to existing problems within the law? Adding class would extend the theme of a list of characteristics, each representing a narrow understanding of the discrimination that members of a group face. For example, litigants would select one or more 'characteristics' and advance them, perhaps in addition to each other or in the alternative to each other, without being able to articulate their experiences in a truly intersectional way. This would be neither precise nor accurate. On this approach, introducing a characteristic of 'class' would not offer the law a *more* intersectional analysis. Rather, it would add a sectional understanding of class to a statute that is already sectional. With section 14

[65] See, eg, Crenshaw, 'Demarginalizing the Intersection of Race and Sex' (n 64) 155.

[66] Equality Act 2010, s 14(1).

[67] A point reinforced by the fact that the provision has remained prospective since the rest of the Act came into force more than 15 years ago.

[68] PBC Deb (Equality Bill), 3rd sitting, cols 49–50 (Stephen Whittle).

[69] PBC Deb (Equality Bill), 3rd sitting, cols 49–50 (Theo Gavrielides, John Penrose and Ben Summerskill).

representing no more than a gesture towards intersectional analysis, you might conclude that introducing class as a protected characteristic would further take attention away from this problem within the Equality Act. Instead, if we wish to address classism and other forms of discrimination in an intersectional way, a bigger doctrinal transformation is needed. This would move the law away from fixed lists of characteristics entirely.

Addressing these concerns, there are two rebuttals. One is based on the drafting of the Equality Act. The other rests on the role of a protected characteristic in intersectional legal analysis in general. Dealing with **the drafting of the statute**, it is important to identify the cause of the existing problems. It is not the *nature* of the characteristics, as such, that causes these analytical and procedural problems. As I have noted, intersectional analysis like Crenshaw's uses 'class', 'race' and related ideas, rather than rejecting them in favour of some unparticularised 'discrimination'. Instead, the cause of the current problems lies in how the law understands the protected characteristics and enshrines them in its doctrine. Each characteristic is understood in isolation from the others (as section 14, while not being in force, confirms). The law's default model, in effect, is to use them separately and not in an intersectional way. However, even if this is correct, introducing class would not make these problems worse. The solution to them has little to do with the continued exclusion of class or the restriction of it to a background or additional factor in the analysis of the existing protected characteristics. The solution would be to re-draft the statute in an intersectional way, not least by amending section 14 to make possible claims beyond a model of 'dual characteristic' claims and then bringing into force the amended version. This would make clear, at least, that a person can claim discrimination based on the interaction of several protected characteristics. This argument favours amending the whole Equality Act to offer a more intersectional understanding of discrimination (including, not excluding, classism). Viewed in this way, intersectionality is still not an argument against class as a protected characteristic in particular.

In terms of **the role of protected characteristics in intersectional analysis**, they can be consistent with such analysis – so long as they are not interpreted as alternatives or provisions tightly sealed from each other. Such an understanding offers another answer to those who criticise some scholarship about discrimination for its tendency to reify and over-simplify groups of people.[70] Critics suggest that some scholars and activists rely on essentialised portrayals of groups, such as all black people being stereotyped as subjected to police violence or women of Pakistani heritage being presumed to be subservient to their husbands, or whatever stereotype is prevalent at a given time. Protected characteristics always pose this risk, but it is nonetheless possible to have statutes that both depend on protected characteristics *and* avoid reifying groups. Class as a protected characteristic, in fact, offers much nuance to intersectional analysis. When approached

[70] See, eg, C Phillips, 'Negotiating Identities: Ethnicity and Social Relations in a Young Offenders' Institution' (2008) 12 *Theoretical Criminology* 313.

alongside other characteristics, we can use the idea of class to develop the law's understanding of how discrimination manifests and to introduce nuances to legal arguments about discrimination. By contrast, if class remains an accessory or part of the background, certain ideas – like race and gender – are always put *above* class in legal analysis. In cases where class, race and gender mix with each other, without one being more prominent than the other, treating class as equal in the order of priority allows legal analysis to be more accurate. It helps legal analysis to be intersectional by ensuring that it has the tools to explain, as Crenshaw and others do, the experiences of the most disadvantaged people *within* disadvantaged groups. Lower-class women, for instance, may be more in need of protective measures than upper-class women. Class must be on an equal footing for legal analysis to maintain nuance and identify those most in need.

5.2. Effective Protection

Even if you accept my arguments so far, you might still say that in common usage class continues to raise questions. You might also point to the possibility that some judges could be reluctant to apply the idea of class, which could lead to the watering down of class as a protected characteristic. By contrast, if class remains a flexible consideration but not a formal characteristic in the law, judges and others may be less reluctant to consider it, which might actually allow the law to combat classism more effectively.

Discussed in Chapter 3, Atrey's approach to poverty offers an example of this kind of approach.[71] Instead of committing to poverty as a protected characteristic, independently understood, Atrey offers a sophisticated analysis of the 'intersectional character' of poverty, which complements and improves our understanding of existing protected characteristics like race, gender and disability. If we bear in mind the examples of misunderstanding that I have already considered (such as that of the Supreme Court of Canada in *Gosselin v Québec* in Chapter 4), such an approach would offer courts analytical nuance without the more pointed difficulties of addressing class outright as a protected characteristic.

There is some force to this argument. While it would still deny class the status of a protected characteristic (and such a denial may have the unfortunate result of downgrading class when compared with the recognised characteristics), it is justifiable to make such a sacrifice in favour of the overall progress that the law could make. The style of analysis that Atrey, for instance, adopts could still allow courts to distinguish between upper-class and lower-class people when assessing claims based on discrimination. On this view, then, the introduction of

[71] S Atrey, 'The Intersectional Case of Poverty' (2018) 18(3) *Human Rights Law Review* 411.

class as a protected characteristic might not be necessary – strictly speaking – for the law to offer protection against classism.

While attractive, the reality of such an argument would be unlikely to be as effective as introducing class as a protected characteristic. To locate class in the background of analysis is not merely a problem for theory or connotation. The practical effect of such a position would be to make class an additional, even *desirable* feature of analysis, but one that ultimately relies on whoever is doing the legal analysis to remember to consider it. One judge may do a good job of incorporating consideration of issues of class when deciding a claim based on the protected characteristic of race. Another judge may not. By contrast, a claim based on class as a protected characteristic would require a judge to confront class in its own terms. It would not be open to a judge to sidestep class entirely or omit it because of more pressing factors in the scheme of analysis. If class were only an analytical consideration, in the vein of Atrey's approach, it would be optional for judges to consider class. Not only is there this strength in class as a protected characteristic requiring consideration in legal analysis, but there is also the question of the quality of the protection that results from it. If class sits in the background or features only to supplement a protected characteristic, the quality of the protection against classism is likely to be lower.

Consider the point in the specific context of the Equality Act. Direct discrimination occurs 'because of a protected characteristic'.[72] Indirect discrimination is 'discriminatory in relation to a relevant protected characteristic'.[73] If class were not such a 'characteristic', it could only be an accessory or ornament of legal analysis, however well-intentioned or well-integrated. The 'protected characteristic' takes primacy, and, if class did appear, it would feature only to the extent helpful to advance arguments for or against the engagement of the 'characteristic' in question. Evidence relating to class in such a case would be very unlikely to establish direct discrimination, as courts would need evidence concerning the characteristic in question. Indirect discrimination would also require proof of 'a particular disadvantage' in respect of those who share a protected 'characteristic' when compared with those who do not.[74] Class might assist as part of the evidence explaining why there is broader disadvantage for a certain group, but the court would not be assigning class any particular doctrinal role.

Here, the doctrinal problem goes back to the theoretical. In a characteristics-based scheme like the Equality Act, class as a consideration achieves, at best, a skeletal version of intersectional analysis. In the Act, the relationship between a protected characteristic and an unspecified analytical consideration must be hierarchical. A protected characteristic rests on the express words of a statutory section. An analytical consideration does not. A protected characteristic offers the foundation for a claim or a policy, being

[72] Equality Act 2010, s 13(1).
[73] Equality Act 2010, s 19(1).
[74] Equality Act 2010, s 19(2)(b).

a gateway for claims and providing the main heading under which claimants narrate their experiences. An analytical consideration is merely an elaboration. It remains parasitic on the (distinct) protected characteristic. Such a doctrinal structure continues to contradict intersectionality's internal logic. Class, like intersectionality, should be more than a 'buzzword'.[75] If the law is to strive for true intersectional analysis while retaining protected characteristics, it cannot achieve that goal without a protected characteristic of class.

6. FILLING THE GAP

If the Equality Act is going to be internally coherent, the gap of class needs to be filled. This would entail amending the Act by inserting a new section, which would introduce class as a protected characteristic. Yes, there would still be other questions, including whether class should be protected in an asymmetrical way (as is, for example, disability). I aim to answer some of these questions, complex as they are, in Chapter 9.

This chapter's purpose has been narrower. Although there are hurdles to overcome, there are compelling arguments in favour of inserting the proposed section 12A in the Equality Act. So long as a legal framework about discrimination rests on protected characteristics, class needs to be recognised as one, even if this represents only the first step of many.

That is the case for introducing class (and classism) to the Equality Act, with its specific scheme and emphasis on areas like employment and public bodies' decision-making. But what about a starkly different context, such as the law concerning hate crime?

[75] H Potter, *Intersectionality and Criminology* (Abingdon, Routledge, 2015) 41.

6

Classism and Hate Crime

THERE ARE SOME obvious connections between (civil) discrimination law and certain topics in the criminal law, especially the idea of a 'hate crime'. However, because of the criminal law's distinctive features, arguments about including class in the criminal law may be quite different from those about including it in employment and administrative law, for instance. The criminal law brings with it the most severe stigma and punishment of any area of the law. The state often occupies a distinctive role in the criminal law, acting as a party to the proceedings or a 'punisher' rather than merely as a 'facilitator' of disputes.[1] Given these differences, some of the arguments in Chapter 5 might not be convincing when it comes to the criminal law. It is this chapter's aim to consider the question of protecting class afresh in this context.

1. 'HATE CRIME' IN ENGLAND AND WALES

To explore classism in the criminal law, I again take as my focus the law of England and Wales, though my arguments may apply across jurisdictions.[2] When writing about so-called 'hate crime' in this jurisdiction, some basic observations help to avoid confusion. Discussing the law of 'hate crime' implies a coherent set of doctrinal elements in the law, perhaps neatly defined. It might suggest that there is a discrete area of the law, with a uniform list of protected grounds or one clear, overarching purpose. That impression is misleading.

Strictly understood, there is no law of 'hate crime' in England and Wales. No statute refers to a 'hate crime'. While the Racial and Religious Hatred Act 2006 makes reference to hatred in its title, 'hate' itself does not appear as an element of an offence. The closest a statutory provision comes to using hatred as an element of an offence is in the meaning of 'racial hatred' in sections 17 and 29A of the Public Order Act 1986, the latter having been inserted by the 2006 Act.[3]

[1] B Zipursky, 'Philosophy of Private Law' in J Coleman and S Shapiro (eds), *The Oxford Handbook of Jurisprudence and Philosophy of Law* (Oxford, Oxford University Press, 2004) 623, 651.

[2] Earlier versions of the arguments in this chapter appeared in A Benn, 'Classism as Hate Crime: Proposing Class as a Protected Ground in Criminal Law' (2021) 10 *Criminal Law Review* 809.

[3] Public Order Act 1986 (POA 1986), ss 17 and 29A.

But all section 17 offers us is that racial hatred means 'hatred against a group of persons ... defined by reference to colour, race, nationality (including citizenship) or ethnic or national origins'.[4] Similarly, section 29A provides that religious hatred means 'hatred against a group of persons defined by reference to religious belief or lack of religious belief'.[5] There is no attempt to define hatred or 'hate' itself. Instead, the law relies on the idea of 'hostility'. It does so in a variety of ways.

First, there are aggravated offences. Such prohibitions take a 'base' offence that already exists in the criminal law. For example, the offence of assault is contrary to section 39 of the Criminal Justice Act 1988. It becomes racially or religiously aggravated assault by virtue of section 29 of the Crime and Disorder Act 1998. Section 29(1) of the 1998 Act tells us what the additional element means. It must be proved that either: the offender, at the time of committing the offence, or immediately before or after doing so, demonstrated towards the victim hostility based on the victim's membership (actual or as presumed by the offender) of a racial or religious group; or the offence was motivated in whole or in part by hostility towards members of a racial or religious group based on their membership of that group.[6] Section 29(2) makes clear that the membership in question may include association with members of that group.[7]

Second, there is the aggravation of sentences. Section 66(1) of the Sentencing Act 2020 applies when a court is considering the seriousness of an offence aggravated by hostility relating to race, religion, disability, sexual orientation or transgender identity.[8] Section 66(2) requires the court to treat such hostility as an aggravating factor and state so in open court.[9]

Third, there is an assortment of offences addressing hostile or hateful behaviour in specific contexts, which include what many people might describe as discriminatory behaviour. Parts III and 3A of the Public Order Act 1986 provide for a variety of offences concerning oral and written expressions of racial hatred, religious hatred and hatred on the ground of sexual orientation. Again, though the term 'hatred' appears, the statutory provisions focus on the definitions of 'racial', 'religious' and 'sexual orientation' rather than the definition of 'hatred' itself. Elsewhere, section 3 of the Football Offences Act 1991 prohibits 'indecent or racialist chanting' at designated football matches. Subsection 2(b) defines 'of a racialist nature' as 'threatening, abusive or insulting to a person by reason of [their] colour, race, nationality (including citizenship) or ethnic or national origins'.[10]

[4] POA 1986, s 17.

[5] POA 1986, s 29A.

[6] Crime and Disorder Act 1998 (CDA 1998), s 29(1).

[7] CDA 1998, s 29(2).

[8] Note that, by virtue of s 66(3) of the Sentencing Act 2020 (SA 2020), the section does not apply to an offence under ss 29–32 of the CDA 1998, as that would be to double-count the form of aggravation.

[9] SA 2020, s 66(2).

[10] Football Offences Act 1991 (FOA 1991), s 3. I have grouped the law into three categories, though others view the FOA 1991 and similar statutes as an additional miscellaneous category: Law Commission, *Hate Crime Laws: Final Report* (2021) 13.

Given this overview, the idea of 'hate crime' should be approached with caution. It has evolved in a piecemeal way and, despite proposals by academics and the Law Commission, there has been no statute collecting the law's fragments and drawing them together with a sense of the overall purposes of these offences.[11] Rather, successive governments have enacted new statutes, or amended existing ones, in order to respond to concerns emerging at particular times. Indeed, in the changes over the years, the law seems to have been gesturing to a number of purposes. One persuasive purpose has been the use of the criminal law to stop discrimination. There is certainly support for this on the law's surface. The protected grounds reflect categories linked with discrimination: race, religion, disability, sexual orientation and transgender identity.[12] They also feature in the Equality Act 2010 (though the Act itself uses 'gender reassignment' rather than 'transgender identity', which has since been interpreted in a broader way in the case law).[13] Anti-discrimination is an obvious candidate for one of the purposes of this area of the law, though some scholars advocate for an approach based on vulnerability or difference.[14]

However, the current law does not fulfil an overall aim of reducing discrimination – interpreted at its widest – for at least two main reasons. First, the law is **under-inclusive in terms of the grounds protected.** Compared with the Equality Act's protected characteristics, the list in the criminal law is much shorter. In the place of nine protected characteristics, there are five. That is the case in section 66 of the Sentencing Act. It is even more limited in other statutes, with only three specified in the Crime and Disorder Act.[15] Second, it is **under-inclusive in terms of the aspects of discrimination that it addresses.** The criminal law in this area does not seek to address, at least directly, discrimination in terms of the broader structures within society, such as inequalities of pay, living conditions, or educational biases. There is no attempt to formulate a duty like the public sector equality duty in section 149 of the Equality Act, for example.[16] Instead, if the criminal law does address discrimination, it only addresses certain manifestations of discriminatory behaviour. It primarily targets manifestations that cause a specific person physical or psychological harm. It also targets manifestations that threaten public safety or morality in designated contexts, such as the offences concerning football matches.[17] While the law here does have some connection with discrimination, this connection is highly circumscribed in terms of both *who* is protected and *what* conduct is prohibited.

[11] See, eg, Law Commission (n 10).
[12] See, eg, CDA 1998, Pt III; SA 2020, s 66.
[13] *Taylor v Jaguar Land Rover Ltd* (2020) ET 1304471/2018.
[14] N Chakraborti and J Garland, 'Reconceptualizing Hate Crime Victimization through the Lens of Vulnerability and "Difference"' (2012) 16(4) *Theoretical Criminology* 499.
[15] CDA 1998, Pt III; SA 2020, s 66.
[16] Equality Act 2010, s 149.
[17] FOA 1991.

Another purpose of this area may be the countering of violence and threats based on a more general kind of vulnerability or difference. Unlike an understanding centred on discrimination, Neil Chakraborti and Jon Garland advance the idea of vulnerability or difference as the core of hate crime laws.[18] Other purposes include tackling prejudice while building community cohesion,[19] protecting minority groups from 'intimidation',[20] and punishing certain forms of public disorder.[21] There are also more prosaic understandings of the law's purposes. A series of governments has attempted to signal concern for groups who suffer discrimination by enacting statutes, often in response to high-profile incidents. In England, the murder of Stephen Lawrence is a widely discussed example of murder based on racism.[22] Yet, despite section 66 of the Sentencing Act, there has not been a move to designate murder of this kind as a separate offence of 'racially aggravated murder', for instance. This seems inconsistent with the introduction of aggravated offences for less serious offences, such as those in the Crime and Disorder Act. It may be that governments have had reservations about the introduction of aggravated offences at the more serious levels. It may also be, in simpler terms, that governments have not thoroughly considered such reform. As the Law Commission has observed, some provisions 'replace previous legislation' and others 'expand . . . protection to further groups'. The Crown Prosecution Service itself has suggested that prosecutors find the legal framework 'fragmented and potentially confusing'.[23]

This is the context in which we approach class and classism as topics of 'hate crime' in England and Wales. When compared with the Equality Act and the civil law relating to discrimination, hate crime laws show even less of a sense of their overall purposes. Helpfully, the Law Commission's work on this topic has attempted to establish more rigorous criteria. In its consultation on hate crime laws in 2020, the Law Commission proposed three criteria: demonstrable need to protect the group in question; additional harm to the group; and the suitability of including it in the law in this area.[24] By applying these criteria, which bear some resemblance to Khaitan's concept of relative group disadvantage, it is possible to develop a more coherent and consistent framework for hate crime laws rather than the collection of divergent purposes that I have set out so far. I shall now apply the three criteria to the issue of class.

[18] Chakraborti and Garland (n 14) 500.

[19] Independent Advisory Group on Hate Crime, Prejudice and Community Cohesion, *Report of the Independent Advisory Group on Hate Crime, Prejudice and Community Cohesion* (2016) 5, 18.

[20] Labour Party, 'New Labour because Britain Deserves Better' (1997).

[21] UK Government, *Review of Public Order Law* (Cmnd 9510, 1985) [6.5].

[22] H Petersen, 'The Ambivalence of the "Macpherson Moment": Re-examining the Political Struggles Following the Racist Murder of Stephen Lawrence' (2025) 6 *Ethnic and Racial Studies* 1, 5–13.

[23] Law Commission (n 10) 532.

[24] Law Commission (n 10) 14.

2. CLASS IN SCHOLARSHIP AND IN PRACTICE

2.1. The Analytical Place of Class

Apart from an article that I wrote for the *Criminal Law Review* in 2021, there has been very little – if any – analysis of class and classism within hate crime. As with scholarship concerning the civil law, those researching the criminal law have only referred to class in a limited way. For instance, published before its final report in 2021, the Law Commission's 2020 consultation paper only touches on class. It refers to Chakraborti and Garland's work, which suggests that those who commit 'hate crime' tend to come from families with little formal education, often with material deprivation, and with health- and drug-related issues.[25] However, these observations are common when analysing criminality. They often appear in the broader criminological and sociological literature concerning the criminal law. The Law Commission's paper also refers to class in the context of misogyny, commenting that experiences are 'not homogenous' and vary according to 'race, gender identity, sexual orientation, disability status and class'.[26] The Law Commission's final report cites my article to note that class 'has also been proposed', but it declines to consider class because there is 'very limited precedent' for recognising such a ground.[27] In these assertions, the Law Commission makes no mention, for instance, of jurisdictions that already criminalise the incitement of hostility 'between social classes', such as Türkiye.[28]

On this topic, there are obvious similarities between the criminal and civil contexts. First, in the criminal law, class is also treated as a matter of background. While class appears more frequently than in civil law contexts (possibly due to the influence of sociology and criminology in the literature concerning hate crime laws), class is not treated as a possible ground on which people are hostile to others.[29]

Second, class tends to appear only as an ingredient of intersectional analysis. The Law Commission's consultation paper, for instance, cites work by Kimberlé Crenshaw and Angela Davis.[30] In doing so, the paper includes a relatively superficial understanding of intersectionality, namely that experiences of hate crime depend on a number of factors, rather than one alone. As I set out in Chapters 4 and 5, such an approach is better than nothing, but it remains no substitute

[25] Law Commission, *Hate Crime Laws* (2020) Consultation Paper No 250, 117.
[26] Law Commission (n 25) 253.
[27] Law Commission (n 10) 245.
[28] Turkish Penal Code 2004, Art 216(1). See, eg, *Ceylan v Turkey* [1999] ECHR 161, [15], [28].
[29] See, eg, N Lacey and L Zedner, 'Criminalization: Historical, Legal and Criminological Perspectives' in A Liebling, S Maruna and L McAra (eds), *The Oxford Handbook of Criminology* (Oxford, Oxford University Press, 2023) 53; T Jones, T Newburn and R Reiner, 'Policing and the Police' in A Liebling, S Maruna and L McAra (eds), *The Oxford Handbook of Criminology* (Oxford, Oxford University Press, 2023) 806.
[30] Law Commission (n 25) 253.

for class as its own concept. While recognising that experiences of class may affect people's experiences of misogyny, the Law Commission still erases class by failing to see the complement: that gender may affect people's experiences of *classism*. By declining to consider class because of 'very limited precedent' for it, the Law Commission reflects the failure in the academic literature to evaluate class as a protected ground.[31] Despite the Law Commission's claims, there has been no truly intersectional analysis of class in the criminal law, either.

2.2. The Doctrinal Place of Class

A. *Absent*

In the current criminal law, 'class' has no formal place. There is no element of an offence or principle of sentencing anywhere in the criminal law that expressly uses the idea of class. The same observation applies to the more particular context of hate crime. However, as with the process that led to the Equality Act 2010, there has been some consideration of ideas similar to class in the criminal law. The most notable has been that of 'socioeconomic status'. In the final report of the Independent Review of Hate Crime Legislation in Scotland, Alastair Campbell concludes that 'socioeconomic status' is 'a very difficult concept to define and not an inherent personal characteristic', one 'likely to change over time'.[32] Campbell shows little engagement with opposing arguments, such as those that suggest that it may be 'inherent' or that it is in fact no more difficult to define than another 'characteristic' like disability. For example, Campbell does not address the common view among scholars (which I have discussed) that race and gender are politically and culturally constructed categories, which evolve over time. Instead, he quickly dismisses 'socioeconomic status' as vague and changeable.

As in the civil law, it seems that those working in the criminal law have assumed that class is just too difficult to define. Even in this context, this is an odd position to adopt. Consider the criminal law's approach to the meaning of a 'racial group'. The courts have interpreted it as wide enough to include Spanish people, 'African' people, 'foreigners' and 'immigrants'.[33] Similarly, the Law Commission and some scholars have been comfortable with the prospect of a category of 'alternative subcultures' in the light of the high-profile death of Sophie Lancaster.[34] Such a category is littered with definitional challenges. Yet the Law Commission and scholars have given it significant consideration.

[31] Law Commission (n 10) 245.

[32] A Campbell, *Independent Review of Hate Crime Legislation in Scotland: Final Report* (2018) 52.

[33] *Rogers* [2007] UKHL 8, [18]; *White* [2001] EWCA Crim 216, [17]–[18]; *DPP v M* [2004] EWHC 1453 (Admin), [30]; *Attorney General's Reference (No 4 of 2004)* [2005] EWCA Crim 889, [24].

[34] Law Commission (n 10) 260–73.

By contrast, perhaps because of the absence of a similarly high-profile case combined with lingering assumptions about definition, class and classism have been ignored.

That said, it is not the case that classism has been absent outside the law. In 2020, reports surfaced of a group of young men, who were incoming students at Durham University.[35] Messaging each other by WhatsApp, they discussed sexual assault being part of 'lads' culture. It seems that the 'posh lads' were competing to have sex with the 'poorest girl' that they could find. In this example, classism and misogyny blend, with neither dissolving into the background or sitting in the shadow of the other. Class and gender were the qualifications that the men chose in their category of the 'poorest girl'. You might suggest that this example reveals some hazier kind of snobbery or masculine stupidity. Whatever their character, the classist aspects of such behaviour are plain and yet they have often been ignored. Even though examples like this exist, class and classism have been left out of the criminal law.

B. *Misdiagnosed*

The criminal law also tends to misdiagnose examples of classism. In a sense, this tendency contributes to the general absence of class: by diagnosing classism as other forms of discrimination, the criminal law erases it. Although the examples from the case law are relatively limited, there are indications that class is a ground on which people commit hate crime. One example appears in *AA* (2018).[36] Shortly before the appellant raped the victim, he called her 'white trash'.[37] Then, as he raped her, he told her that someone else must have penetrated her before him because she was 'white'.[38] The prosecution put its case on the basis that the offence was 'racially aggravated', an analysis that the Court of Appeal later accepted.[39]

However, such analysis represents, in part, a misdiagnosis. The appellant's conduct certainly raises issues of both race and misogyny. But, properly understood, 'white trash' is often a classist slur that originated in the US. It refers to white people, yes, but specifically those who are lower-class.[40] It has notable

[35] E Menendez, 'Freshers Planned Competition to Have Sex with the Poorest Female They Could Find', *Metro* (9 September 2020): www.metro.co.uk/2020/09/09/freshers-planned-competition-to-have-sex-with-the-poorest-female-they-could-find-13243854; J Halliday, 'Durham University Withdraws Fresher's Place over "Abhorrent" Online Posts', *Guardian* (23 September 2020): www.theguardian.com/education/2020/sep/23/durham-university-withdraws-freshers-place-over-abhorrent-online-posts.

[36] *AA* [2018] EWCA Crim 1758.

[37] *AA* (n 36) [9].

[38] *AA* (n 36) [11].

[39] *AA* (n 36) [24].

[40] M Wray and A Newitz, 'Introduction' in M Wray and A Newitz (eds), *White Trash: Race and Class in America* (Abingdon, Routledge, 1997) 4. It may, of course, be used in a way that is not necessarily *intended* to be classist, eg it is difficult to understand if it is intended to be classist in the summary of the facts in the judgment in *Babbs* [2007] EWCA Crim 2737, [3].

connotations of poverty and a lack of formal education.[41] While 'white trash' is not always a gendered phrase, it is frequently used against women. It has appeared, for instance, in other cases that concern violence against women. In *Singh* (2005), the appellant had called the victim 'white trash' and hit her in the face with a saucepan. He was later convicted of assault occasioning actual bodily harm, contrary to section 47 of the Offences Against the Person Act 1861.[42] Applying the approach in *AA*, the conduct in *Singh* would be understood as racially aggravated, ie a *racist* hate crime. The issue of gender (or class) would not feature anywhere in the analysis.

Perhaps the answer to this criticism would be to introduce a protected ground of gender, given the misogyny often present in these cases.[43] However, the inclusion of gender would fail to convey accurately the meaning of 'white trash'. The power of that phrase lies in its classism. While there is a racist implication that 'white' people ought to be ashamed for occupying such a low rank in society, marking them as a kind of failure by racist standards, the principal objects of insult are supposed poverty and lack of cultural sophistication, intelligence and education – not whiteness.[44]

The misdiagnosis of classism as racism appears not to be limited to England and Wales. *Stirling Council v Harris* (2009) offers a stark example in a decision by a court in Scotland.[45] Stirling Council sought an anti-social behaviour order (ASBO) under the Antisocial Behaviour etc (Scotland) Act 2004. The defender knew one of his neighbours from her time housekeeping and cleaning the premises before she had moved in with her family. Against a background of tensions, the defender labelled his neighbours 'chavs'.[46] The council officers described this comment as 'racist'. In its judgment, the Sheriff Court refers cryptically to a 'culture clash'.[47] Yet 'chav' is one of the most obvious classist slurs. It has been a feature of popular culture and language in the UK for decades.[48] The stigma attaching to a culture of 'chavs' was part of the context that led to the repackaging of the ASBO as the criminal behaviour order.[49] Given that 'chav' is a familiar classist slur, analysing it as racist is likely to misunderstand it. Meanwhile, characterising it as a 'culture clash' is not so much a

[41] Cambridge English Dictionary, 'White Trash': www.dictionary.cambridge.org/dictionary/english/white-trash. See generally N Isenberg, *White Trash: the 400-Year Untold History of Class in America* (London, Atlantic Books, 2017).

[42] *Singh* [2005] EWCA Crim 96, [10].

[43] There have been calls for the addition of 'gender' to hate crime laws: see, eg, J Schweppe and A Haynes, 'You Can't Have One without the Other: "Gender" in Hate Crime Legislation' (2020) 2 *Criminal Law Review* 148.

[44] Wray and Newitz (n 40) 4.

[45] *Stirling Council v Harris* 2009 SLT (Sh Ct) 106.

[46] *Stirling Council* (n 45) [14].

[47] *Stirling Council* (n 45) [44].

[48] I Tyler, '"Chav Mum Chav Scum": Class Disgust in Contemporary Britain' (2008) 8(1) *Feminist Media Studies* 17.

[49] J Kelly, 'Asbo: The End of an Era', *BBC News* (23 May 2012): www.bbc.co.uk/news/magazine-18164426.

misunderstanding but an indication of the courts' tendency to euphemise, or otherwise obscure, the nature of the conduct.

It may be that the Sheriff Court in *Harris* considered it improper to tangle itself in what exactly the tensions were between the people involved and why they had arisen. Perhaps, too, there were themes of both race and class involved, with 'chav' being an insult that the defender had used to express – in truth – racist sentiment. Whichever the explanation, the Sheriff Court took the most famous classist slur in the UK and turned it into some other idea.

3. PROTECTING CLASS

3.1. Criteria for Inclusion: The Law Commission's Approach

Building on the proposal in its consultation paper, the Law Commission's first recommendation in its final report on hate crime laws identifies the three criteria by which lawmakers should choose groups to protect:

> We recommend that decisions to include, or not to include further groups in hate crime laws should be based on the following criteria:
>
> 1. **Demonstrable need:** evidence of the prevalence of the criminal targeting of the characteristic group based on prejudice or hostility. A balance of the following considerations should inform this determination of need:
>   a. Absolute prevalence: the total amount of criminal behaviour that is targeted based on hostility or prejudice towards the characteristic.
>   b. Relative prevalence: the amount of criminal behaviour that is targeted based on hostility or prejudice towards the characteristic, as compared with the size of the group who share the characteristic.
>   c. Severity: the nature and degree of the criminal behaviour that is targeted towards the characteristic based on hostility or prejudice.
> 2. **Additional harm:** there is evidence that criminal targeting based on hostility or prejudice towards the characteristic causes additional harm to the victim, members of the targeted group, and society more widely.
> 3. **Suitability:** protection of the characteristic would fit logically within the broader offences and sentencing framework, prove workable in practice, represent an efficient use of criminal justice resources, and is consistent with the rights of others.'[50]

It is not clear what exactly the Law Commission means by the notion of a 'balance' between the ideas of 'absolute prevalence', 'relative prevalence' and 'severity'.

[50] Law Commission (n 10) 77 (emphasis in original).

If the severity of such behaviour is significant, but the absolute prevalence low, how should we 'balance' the considerations? For instance, the Law Commission recognises concerns by Stonewall and the Magistrates' Association about 'the risk of a disproportionate emphasis' on absolute prevalence, as it 'might exclude smaller minority groups'.[51] While this lack of clarity should be resolved, for now it does not stop me from using the three criteria to evaluate class.

A. *Demonstrable Need*

The first criterion poses a problem for class. That is not because it gives a reason, in principle, to reject class as a protected ground. Rather, it is because of the word 'demonstrable'. One of the main arguments in this book is that there has been too little research into class in legal scholarship (and even less into classism). The requirement of a demonstrable need means that we have to overcome the hurdle of evidence. As the research into hate crime laws has paid limited attention to class, it is more difficult to find evidence from academic studies in this area to support a form of criminal targeting and hostility relating to class when compared to, for instance, race and sexuality. By contrast, take an example from the context of gender. Jennifer Schweppe and Amanda Haynes rely on a series of studies about gender-based hostility in criminal behaviour in order to make arguments about the demonstrable need to include gender as a protected ground in hate crime laws.[52] Class, meanwhile, is more similar to homelessness in this respect. As Mohamad Al-Hakim emphasised when arguing for the inclusion of homelessness in the law in 2015, the lack of empirical studies significantly impairs those who try to draw attention to issues that have passed under many people's radar.[53] However, unlike class, research into hostility towards homeless people has vastly increased since Al-Hakim's article.[54] Not only has classism been 'theoretically erased', but it has also been obscured by the lack of empirical work specifically addressing class-based hate crime.[55]

Despite this difficulty, I will try to identify empirical research that suggests, even provisionally, that class satisfies this criterion. As I have set out, criminological research tends to understand class as a feature of the background, which may increase a person's likelihood to suffer or commit certain kinds of crime (though it is questionable if there is any link between increased criminality *in general* and class).[56] There is evidence that some groups are targeted, or made more

[51] Law Commission (n 10) 74.

[52] Schweppe and Haynes (n 43) 153.

[53] M Al-Hakim, 'Making a Home for the Homeless in Hate Crime Legislation' (2015) 30(10) *Journal of Interpersonal Violence* 1755, 1759.

[54] Law Commission (n 25) 328–37.

[55] K Crenshaw, 'Demarginalizing the Intersection of Race and Sex' (1989) *University of Chicago Legal Forum* 139, 140.

[56] See also, for discussion of statistics of the class background of those tried at the Old Bailey in London, L Davis, *Poor Things* (Durham, North Carolina, Duke University Press, 2024) 139.

vulnerable, partly due to their class. For example, as I discussed in Chapter 3, Alison Phipps argues that lower-class women are more likely to suffer sexual and other forms of abuse in their childhoods than others.[57] This is because of their increased vulnerability, not least because figures who are supposed to protect them fail to do so.

The case law gives other indications that, if further research were done, there is a high prospect that we would identify a clear empirical basis for the 'demonstrable need' to protect class. Alongside *AA* and *Stirling Council v Harris* (above), there are examples of criminal behaviour based on classist hostility. One example is the case of *Keane* (2010).[58] The decision is typically cited as authority for the elements of self-defence.[59] But an aspect of the facts of the case tends to go unnoticed. Before punching the eventual victim, the defendant called another person a 'stupid bitch' and a 'chav'.[60] Those slurs helped to start the physical fight, which involved shoving and knocking that other person to the ground.[61]

The case law also supports the argument that classism and misogyny often blend. Alongside *AA*, the case of *Willoughby* (2014) saw the defendant break into his former partner's home in Doncaster.[62] As he dragged her by her hair from her bed, he called her both a 'slag' and a 'skank'.[63] Properly understood, 'skank' expresses hostility towards *a particular kind of woman*. 'Skank' typically refers to women perceived to behave in lower-class ways, with the stigma of bad hygiene and sexual activity considered shameful by traditional standards of femininity.[64] Similarly, 'slapper' is a term for a 'vulgar or coarse woman' said to have sex in ways that violate certain moral conventions.[65] It is a word that appears throughout the case law on violence against women.[66]

Examples exist outside the UK, too. One case reported in the press comes from the US. In Jackson, Mississippi in June 2011, Deryl Dedmon beat James Craig Anderson and crushed him to death under a pick-up truck.[67] Dedmon was white and Anderson was black. An investigator's discussions with schoolfriends of Dedmon emphasised that the murder had occurred because of hierarchies of 'social status' seemingly distinct from racism.[68] The schoolfriends' attempt to

[57] A Phipps, 'Rape and Respectability: Ideas about Sexual Violence and Social Class' (2009) 43(4) *Sociology* 667.

[58] *Keane* [2010] EWCA Crim 2514.

[59] See, eg, J Herring, *Criminal Law: Text, Cases, and Materials* (Oxford, Oxford University Press, 2020) 658.

[60] *Keane* (n 58) [9].

[61] See also, for a bystander's use of the word 'chavs', *Appleby* [2010] EWCA Crim 926, [7].

[62] *Willoughby* [2014] EWCA Crim 1902.

[63] *Willoughby* (n 62) [2].

[64] Merriam-Webster Dictionary, 'Skank': www.merriam-webster.com/dictionary/skank.

[65] Oxford Languages Dictionary, 'Slapper': www.lexico.com/definition/slapper.

[66] See, eg, *D* [2002] EWCA Crim 2784, [18]; *CB* [2018] EWCA Crim 2146, [7].

[67] 'Ten Sentenced in Hate Crime Case', *FBI News* (16 June 2015): www.fbi.gov/news/stories/ten-sentenced-in-hate-crime-case.

[68] T Dokoupil, 'The Devil Deryl Dedmon', *Irish Examiner* (28 April 2012): www.irishexaminer.com/lifestyle/arid-20192079.html.

downplay racism may indicate their willingness to dismiss the topic in general. However, it may also be an attempt to describe a quality of Dedmon's attitude towards Anderson that differed from the way in which Dedmon had treated his black schoolfriends. In contrast from his black schoolfriends, Dedmon's hostility towards Anderson appears to have blended classism and racism. He had sought out a poor area of Jackson in which most residents were black. He then used his racist language towards Anderson as someone targeted because he was a black person in a poor area. It seems that Dedmon reserved his racist hostility for *poor* black people.

Drawing these examples together, they suggest that there is evidence to demonstrate the need to prohibit classist hate crime. It seems that harmful behaviour arising from class-based hostility exists. The lack of empirical research into the issue stops me from concluding, in firm terms, that there is a clearly documented 'need' to include class as a protected ground in the sense that the Law Commission intends. The Law Commission's references to prevalence and severity suggest more is required than the collection of examples I put forward. That said, the Law Commission has been content to accept the limits of the available research in other contexts (in relation to 'alternative subcultures', for instance) and to recognise the importance of a contextual interpretation of 'relative prevalence'.[69] Bearing that approach in mind, the examples above should be enough to demonstrate the need that the first criterion has in mind.

B. Additional Harm

Referring to its earlier proposals, the Law Commission gives the rationale for this criterion as 'the additional harm that hate crimes cause: to individual victims, other members of the victimised group, and to the community more widely'.[70] This reflects the observations in its consultation paper that there is increased harm to the primary victim, secondary harm to other members of the same group, and a wider form of harm to society in terms of impairing social cohesion and equality.[71]

Classist hostility, particularly in forms of violence, involves these harms. The hostility invokes hierarchies in which some people are deemed desirable, intelligent and successful through their social, cultural and economic capital, whereas others are deemed distasteful, stupid and unfortunate. The example from Durham University given earlier illustrates how these harms manifest. If the behaviour that the students discussed had in fact occurred, there would have been humiliation and degradation of those women based on gender and class, with the 'posh lads' targeting them. This perspective reflects Kellina Craig-Henderson and L Ren Sloan's arguments, linking hate to the greater harm

[69] Law Commission (n 10) 262–63.
[70] Law Commission (n 10) 67.
[71] Law Commission (n 25) 323–24.

because the hostility taps into entrenched and ongoing discrimination (rather than expressing merely personal dislike, for example).[72]

When it comes to the second and third aspects of the 'additional harm', the example from Durham University also illustrates how they may operate. In terms of the harm to the group, other lower-class students (perhaps particularly women) would likely have thought in terms of 'people like me'. This is similar to the way a black Muslim woman described her view of hate crime when giving an answer to the Law Commission. She detailed the emotional response to hate crime in the sense of hostility towards anyone who falls into a given category.[73] It does not stretch the imagination that, in the example from Durham University, there would have been an increased sense among some lower-class students that they were less safe at university alongside a feeling of reluctance to be associated with lower-class features (such as speaking in particular dialects or discussing their family circumstances). Of course, some might have persevered and responded to such an incident bravely, such as by being even more open about their class and refusing to diminish themselves. But that is bravery because it is *in spite of* potential harm.

This connects with the third aspect of harm, namely wider harm to society. The Law Commission outlines ways in which criminal behaviour of this kind hinders a group's participation in economic and social life, politics and culture.[74] The Durham University example illustrates the type of behaviour that could reinforce the sentiment of class-based divisions and entrench lower-class students' sense of their 'outsider status' in university and beyond.

Overall, then, classist hostility involves the different aspects of harm that the Law Commission identifies in its second criterion. Although this conclusion should again be tentative given the limited empirical research, it seems highly likely that further empirical research would show the 'additional harm' that the criterion requires.

C. *Suitability*

The Law Commission describes this as 'designed principally as a common-sense check', meant 'to avoid unintended and negative consequences', and 'necessarily broad'.[75] While references to 'common sense' rarely bode well in legal analysis, the Law Commission really seems to mean a more holistic consideration of different issues. For example, while there might be strong arguments in favour of protecting class based on stopping harm to lower-class people, there may be

[72] K Craig-Henderson and L Ren Sloan, 'After the Hate: Helping Psychologists Help Victims of Racist Hate Crime' (2003) 10(4) *Clinical Psychology: Science and Practice* 481.

[73] Law Commission (n 25) 201.

[74] Law Commission (n 25) 203.

[75] Law Commission (n 10) 74.

arguments based on other factors (perhaps to do with the role of the criminal law) which are more persuasive.

As with the Equality Act 2010, there may be arguments that class is vaguer than the existing protected grounds. This is consistent with the concern in the Independent Review of Hate Crime Legislation in Scotland that class is 'a very difficult concept to define'.[76] That vagueness could make class unsuitable to include in the law, falling foul of the Law Commission's third criterion. However, there is some irony to an argument based on vagueness. The 'common-sense check' of 'suitability' could, really, mean many things. The Law Commission also gives consideration to a ground based on 'alternative subcultures', though ultimately rejecting it due to a combination of the lack of 'available evidence … establish[ing] a strong demonstrable need to extend protection to this group', concerns about the breadth of such a ground from the perspective of 'suitability', and a lack of 'clear community support' for the inclusion of such a group.[77] Notably, it was not the vagueness of the category alone that proved fatal.

When considering the criterion of suitability, it is difficult to foresee what unique problems a protected ground of class would pose for the criminal law. As with the Equality Act, it is once more necessary to separate problems specific to class from those shared by all protected grounds. Due to the importance of showing hostility (whether by demonstration or motivation) in relation to a protected ground, it can already be a struggle to prove an aggravated offence, for instance. In part, this may be because the criminal standard of proof is high when considering an element like hostility. For this reason, among others, the Law Commission considered expanding the law's approach to aggravation in this area so that it includes 'prejudice' as well as 'hostility'.[78] Yet this challenge applies to the existing protected grounds. Here, class rises and falls with the others. For example, when seeking to prove hostility (or, hypothetically, prejudice), the prosecution often relies on evidence about the defendant's language or behaviour towards another. The most familiar examples are discriminatory slurs and threatening actions towards others. In this context, evidence of terms like 'chav' and 'white trash' would perform the same function as evidence of other types of slurs: it is evidence from which the fact-finder infers the demonstration or motivation. Depending on the context, they fall to be interpreted as evidence consistent with hostility in the same way as, for instance, racist or homophobic slurs.

I accept that prosecutors may also refer to the alleged victim's identity alongside such aspects of evidence. A case may not be so much about what is said or done by the defendant. Instead, evidence that it was said or done *against a particular person in a particular context* allows a court to be sure that there was hostility based on a protected ground. In this sense, it might be true that

[76] Campbell (n 32) 52.
[77] Law Commission (n 10) 273.
[78] Law Commission (n 25) 10–11.

a court would find it more difficult to conclude that this was because someone was lower-class rather than, for instance, because of a person's race. However, this is not a compelling objection. First, even if there are some cases in which it is difficult to categorise the alleged victim into a specific class, many will be straightforward. Second and more importantly, it is not necessary to put everyone into boxes of 'class' for the purposes of the law concerning hate crime. If there is evidence of language which is hostile based on class (such as 'chav' and 'benefit scrounger'), that will show classist hostility even if the alleged victim is not *in fact* lower-class. The current law makes this point clear in its references to actual or perceived membership of a group.[79] Therefore, class would be unlikely to pose more difficult evidential problems than the existing grounds.

4. CAUTION: CRIMINAL LAW'S CHARACTER

It is worth taking stock of where this analysis has taken us. So far as criminal and civil contexts go, some of the same arguments are forceful. Class is not too difficult to define. Class could be introduced as a protected ground in a sensible way in both areas, with enough precision and with fulfilment of criteria specific to each legal context.

That being said, it remains crucial to recognise the distinctive character of the criminal law. It is uniquely stigmatic, coercive and punitive. Because of its nature, there are concerns I must address when considering the use of class in the criminal law, which may not exist in the context of the civil law.[80] Chara Bakalis identifies one such issue: the principle of 'minimum criminalisation'.[81] Minimum criminalisation means that crimes are only to be created, or aggravated, if necessary *and* if other (non-criminal) methods cannot combat the harms in question.[82] There is no principle directly equivalent in the civil law. This concern links to one that Crisis, the homelessness charity, has raised in relation to protecting homelessness as a ground in the criminal law. Although recognising the severity of the victimisation of homeless people, Crisis expressed concern to the Law Commission that using the law in this way would actually reinforce homelessness in society.[83] One point here is that there may be solutions to such victimisation without resorting to the heavy mechanisms of the criminal law. Rather than erecting a protected ground of homelessness or class, we should focus on other tools, perhaps beyond the law.

It is not clear, though, that acknowledging the existence of criminal behaviour based on classist hostility would entrench that behaviour. Discrimination

[79] See, eg, SA 2020, s 66(4) and (6).
[80] Zipursky (n 1) 623, 651.
[81] C Bakalis, 'The Victims of Hate Crime and the Principles of the Criminal Law' (2017) 37(4) *Legal Studies* 718, 722.
[82] Bakalis (n 81) 724.
[83] Law Commission (n 25) 163; Law Commission (n 10) 276.

law has seen similar arguments over the years, with some scholars and judges suggesting that the use of the law to address racism would actually entrench racial categories and lead to more division.[84] I do not disregard concerns like those raised by Crisis, which may have special weight in the context of the criminal law. I discuss them in more detail in Chapter 9. For now, I simply make the point that these are concerns about the law entrenching problems in societies by recognising them or by making legal rules about them. The law has a legitimate role in 'symbolic denunciation': to express that such criminal behaviour not only exists, but also has long been a harmful part of society.[85] To put class on a lower rung, without legal recognition of this kind, would ultimately send an unjustifiable message that class is less important than the existing protected grounds. Questions about the criminal law's character apply across the protected grounds and, in themselves, do not justify the exclusion of class.

5. CLASSIST HATE CRIME

Drawing this chapter to a close, there are clearly bigger themes here. Some of those themes concern the symmetry or asymmetry in how the law protects certain categories, the role of the police, and limits of the law in general. I will come to them in more detail in Chapters 9 and 10. In this chapter, I have instead concentrated on outlining – in what are, I hope, forceful and persuasive terms – the need for, and the suitability of, class as a protected ground in hate crime laws.

The arguments on this issue weigh in favour of including class. They reveal that there has been no good reason for excluding it. The sparseness of the theoretical or empirical research that understands 'hate crime' in terms of class and classism hinders us, but it is not conclusive. This chapter offers a framework to start to bring class and classism into hate crime laws.

[84] See, eg, R Siegel, 'From Colorblindness to Antibalkanization: An Emerging Ground of Decision in Race Equality Cases' (2011) 120(6) *Yale Law Journal* 1278, 1281, 1300.

[85] M Walters, A Owusu-Bempah and S Wietlizka, 'Hate Crime and the "Justice Gap": The Case for Law Reform' (2018) *Criminal Law Review* 961, 963.

7

Classism and Administrative Law

THE ADMINISTRATIVE LAW of England and Wales offers a third doctrinal setting in which to assess the law's potential. In this chapter, I begin by considering if administrative law, as it stands, *does* protect class in the context of discrimination. I then explore if this area of the law *could* protect class in that context. Here, the debate surrounding a so-called principle of consistency or equal treatment in administrative law may help. As the principles of administrative law tend to be framed in wider ways than doctrines like direct discrimination or aggravated criminal offences, there may be scope for a general principle against classism in public bodies' decision-making – but only after much ambition and effort.

Before diving in, I should make clear that I use 'administrative law' to mean the set of legal rules and principles concerning the mechanisms of governance and the institutions typically considered to be part of the running of the state.[1] This meaning overlaps with the Equality Act 2010. Indeed, administrative law can be difficult to pin down, given that it takes in legal topics as wide-ranging as constitutional, tort, criminal, labour, employment and housing matters. The focus of this chapter is on the principles that guide and monitor public bodies' decision-making, often via the 'central control mechanism' of judicial review.[2]

1. DOES ADMINISTRATIVE LAW PROTECT CLASS?

In a word, the answer to the question is 'no'. To explain that answer, with all its nuances, it is helpful to set out the place of class and classism in the administrative law of today. To many working in this area of the law, the issues of class and classism may prompt one of two reactions. Some may find it odd to encounter the issues in this area. What has administrative law got to do with discrimination against lower-class people? Others may find the issues more familiar but only in the sense that they may be relevant to certain types of administrative law claims (such as local authority housing or provision of education). However, on a closer look at the law, there may be more room for arguing about classism than expected.

[1] See generally P Craig, *Administrative Law* (London, Sweet & Maxwell, 2021) 1-001.
[2] M Fordham, *Judicial Review Handbook* (London, Hart Publishing, 2012) 5.

1.1. Common Law Recognition of Class and Classism

A passage in *Kruse v Johnson* (1898) raises questions.[3] The appellant was convicted of singing hymns near to a house. A by-law made by the county council in Kent prohibited singing within 50 yards of a dwelling if a constable asked the person in question to stop. According to the law report, the appellant submitted that the by-law was bad because it was unreasonable, which also meant that the conviction needed to be quashed: the power given by it could easily be abused.[4] The respondent submitted that the county council had properly passed the by-law under the relevant legislation. A court could not simply decide that a by-law was unreasonable because it did not approve of it, the respondent argued, rather than finding it to be 'manifestly unjust, capricious, inequitable, or partial in its operation'.[5]

The Divisional Court held that the by-law was valid. The by-law was reasonable. Checks and safeguards accompanied the imposition of it. Although the presence of those safeguards did not remove the court's responsibility to assess the by-law's validity, by-laws of this 'class' ought to be supported if possible, interpreted 'benevolently' and with credit to those administering them that they be reasonably administered.[6] Although this particular by-law was reasonable and valid, Russell LCJ observed that by-laws 'partial or unequal in their operation as between different classes' were likely to be unlawful.[7]

In the passage, Russell LCJ first uses the word 'class' in a sense distinct from the one I have focused on in this book. The judge means 'class' in the sense of a category, here the category of by-laws made by public representative bodies ('of the class we are here considering').[8] In the case, by-laws of the 'class' in question were those of 'a public representative character entrusted by Parliament with delegated authority' rather than those of railway and dock companies.[9] Indeed, the judge uses 'class' twice before the passage I quoted at the beginning in the sense of 'class' as a category, set or group – not necessarily a social, cultural and economic relationship between people. Because of that, we might argue that Russell LCJ must be using the word 'class' as a synonym for category. Yet 'class' seems to have been in regular use in the sense of a ranking in a society long before the judgment in *Kruse v Johnson*. James Lawrence's *On the Nobility of the British Gentry* (1840) discusses 'the nobility of a class in society' in the context of the establishment of the Heralds' Office to record

[3] *Kruse v Johnson* [1898] 2 QB 91 (Russell LCJ).
[4] *Kruse* (n 3) 93.
[5] *Kruse* (n 3) 94–95.
[6] *Kruse* (n 3) 99.
[7] *Kruse* (n 3) 99.
[8] *Kruse* (n 3) 96.
[9] *Kruse* (n 3) 99.

the gentry's births, alliances and deaths.[10] This may well have been a sense in which Russell LCJ was familiar with the term when he was giving judgment in *Kruse v Johnson*.

There is another interpretation of the passage, though. This interpretation takes a more generic notion of 'class' when considering the phrase 'partial and unequal in their operation as between different classes'. The phrase would not make sense if it were interpreted as referring to by-laws operating in a partial and unequal way between categories (classes) of *by-laws*. The judgment must mean another sense of 'class' here. More likely, class in this sense refers to groups of people. The question, then, is whether the judge is referring, first, to 'classes' of people in my sense of class relationships or, second, to a wider idea of categories, sets or groups of people. Ewan McGaughey supports the first interpretation. In his discussion of the case, McGaughey describes *Kruse v Johnson* as 'a remarkable endorsement of a prohibition of discrimination "between different classes"'.[11] He asserts that 'there is not yet a clear codified provision against "class discrimination" in the UK', but that 'it is recognised at common law, and probably in EU and ECHR norms'.[12]

It is possible to find further support for McGaughey's interpretation in both historical and modern literature. In the historical literature, there is a great deal of evidence of the sense of class as a ranking in societies by 1898. For instance, a 'rank or order of persons' was included as the first definition of class in Samuel Johnson's *A Dictionary of the English Language* in both 1755 and 1773.[13] It was also included as an element of other words associated with the more specific sense of 'class': 'gentility' as 'the class of persons well born'; 'gentry' as 'class of people above the vulgar; those between the vulgar and the nobility'; and 'underservant' as 'a servant of the lower class'.[14] Both in the UK and elsewhere, by 1898 there were many instances of 'class' being used in the sense of division between groups in society according to social, cultural and economic features (being more specific than merely a synonym of 'category' or 'kind').[15] In more recent legal scholarship, some authors have suggested that *Kruse v Johnson* gestured towards, or even established, a principle of equality or non-discrimination as

[10] J Lawrence, *On the Nobility of the British Gentry* (London, James Fraser, 1840) 5.

[11] E McGaughey, *A Casebook on Labour Law* (Oxford, Hart Publishing, 2018) 536.

[12] McGaughey (n 11) 536.

[13] 'Class' in S Johnson, *Johnson's Dictionary Online* (undated): www.johnsonsdictionaryonline.com.

[14] 'Gentility' in Johnson (n 13); 'Gentry' in Johnson (n 13); 'Underservant' in Johnson (n 13).

[15] See, eg, J Bowen, *The Russell Predictions on the Working Class, the National Debt, and the New Poor Law, Dissected* (London, Hatchard & Son, 1850) 1–2; S Earnshaw, *The Attitudes of the Working Class Towards Religion* (Sheffield, Leader & Sons, 1870) 5–6; JL Diman, *The Alienation of the Educated Class from Politics* (Cambridge, Massachusetts, Riverside Press ,1876) 29; F Engels, *The Condition of the Working-Class in England in 1844* (F Kelley Wischnewetzky trans, Penguin, 2009).

part of rationality review.[16] Colm O'Cinneide, for instance, cites *Kruse v Johnson* first in a list of authorities in support of the argument that 'the courts have been prepared to treat the equality principle as informing the application of irrationality review' and 'differential treatment of similarly situated persons that lacks objective justification may be struck down on the basis that it is *Wednesbury* unreasonable'.[17]

However, it seems unlikely that Russell LCJ had in mind an idea associated with the radical politics of the time. Class has many meanings, including hierarchical, scientific, educational and generally categorical.[18] Marx's works, for example, only gained prominence outside limited political circles after his death in 1883.[19] Even if Russell LCJ had in mind relationships or hierarchies along lines I associate with class, it is unlikely that he had an idea more sophisticated than that (let alone an approach like Bourdieu's framework of social, cultural and economic capital). The more plausible intention behind the judge's use of 'classes' is simply to mean sections or groups of the population, the boundaries of which would depend on the case. For example, if a by-law were to apply both to owners and tenants, those two groups would be the kind of 'classes' that Russell LCJ's reasoning envisages. Most difficult for an interpretation like McGaughey's is the fact that, in more than a century since *Kruse v Johnson*, there has been no authority expressly supporting the view that the decision refers to class in my sense or, more radically, a form of discrimination relating to class. This is perhaps unsurprising. Before statutory protections against racism came into force, for instance, the common law did not recognise any principle of equal treatment in access to services or equal access to accommodation.[20]

While *Kruse v Johnson* is more likely authority for protection against arbitrary distinctions between 'classes' in the more general sense of groups and categories, we should not entirely dismiss McGaughey's observations. The historical literature and more recent scholarship remind us that the general sense of class as a group in societies may still incorporate the more specific sense of class that I use in this book. McGaughey's commentary reminds us of the multiple senses that Russell LCJ's passage can accommodate. Even if the judge did not mean class in the sense that this book has set out, his use of 'classes' may still be broad enough to include it. This offers at least a foundation that lawyers might build on. I return to that foundation later in this chapter.

[16] See, eg, McGaughey (n 11) 534; A Pillay, 'Reinventing Reasonableness: The Adjudication of Social and Economic Rights in South Africa, India and the United Kingdom' (doctoral thesis, University College London, 2011) 100.

[17] C O'Cinneide, 'Equality: A Core Common Law Principle, or "Mere" Rationality' in M Elliott and K Hughes (eds), *Common Law Constitutional Rights* (Oxford, Hart Publishing, 2020) 167, 181.

[18] See, eg, the entries for 'Order', 'Genus', 'Fellow-Student' and 'Kind' in Johnson (n 13).

[19] G Steenson, *After Marx, Before Lenin* (London, University of Pittsburgh Press, 1991) 11, 24, 47–48.

[20] *Scala Ballroom (Wolverhampton) Ltd v Ratcliffe* [1958] 3 All ER 220; *Constantine v Imperial Hotels Ltd* [1944] KB 693. See generally A McColgan, *Discrimination, Equality and the Law* (Oxford, Hart Publishing, 2014) 10–12.

1.2. The Convention and the Human Rights Act 1998

Although sometimes (unhelpfully) labelled 'human rights law' as if it were parcelled off from domestic administrative law, my analysis would be incomplete if it were to ignore the role of the European Convention on Human Rights and Fundamental Freedoms in the United Kingdom. The Convention – a 'living instrument' – has been pivotal in the development of the nation's administrative law in recent decades.[21] Section 1(2) of the Human Rights Act 1998 (HRA 1998) gave effect in the UK to the Articles of the Convention.[22] Section 2 of the HRA 1998 requires a court or tribunal deciding a question in connection with a Convention right to 'take into account' a number of sources, including any judgment of the European Court of Human Rights (ECtHR).[23] The case law on this issue has been considerable, with the UK Supreme Court repeatedly stressing the continued role of the common law.[24]

Within the scope of enjoyment of the Convention's rights and freedoms, Article 14 prohibits discrimination:

> The enjoyment of the rights and freedoms set forth in this Convention shall be secured without discrimination on any ground such as sex, race, colour, language, religion, political or other opinion, national or **social origin**, association with a national minority, **property**, **birth or other status**. (emphasis added).[25]

This prohibition does not exist in a standalone sense. *Carson and Others v UK* (2010) saw the ECtHR emphasise this point.[26] The ECtHR considers Article 14 *alongside* the rights and freedoms of the Convention, though non-discrimination is integral to each of them. Non-discrimination is not necessarily limited to the right or freedom in question.[27] It may also impose on states obligations to act in a manner that ensures the protection of a Convention right, possibly by what might be known as positive action in the UK's Equality Act 2010.[28] In this context, the main concept of discrimination is differential treatment if it lacks 'an objective and reasonable justification'.[29] Such a concept requires consideration of the pursuit of a legitimate aim by proportionate means.[30] The case law

[21] See, eg, E Bjorge, *Domestic Application of the ECHR: Courts as Faithful Trustees* (Oxford, Oxford University Press, 2015) 101–04

[22] HRA 1998, s 1(2).

[23] HRA 1998, s 2.

[24] See, eg, *Horncastle* [2009] UKSC 4; *R (Osborn) v Parole Board* [2013] UKSC 61; *Kennedy v Charity Commission* [2014] UKSC 20; *R (UNISON) v Lord Chancellor* [2017] UKSC 51.

[25] In the French version, 'such as' is '*notamment*' and 'any other status' is '*toute autre situation*'.

[26] *Carson and Others v UK* (2010) 51 EHRR 13, [63].

[27] *Marckx v Belgium* (1979) 2 EHRR 30 [32]; *Carson* (n 26) [63].

[28] See, eg, in the context of the interpretation of a deceased person's will, *Pla and Puncernau v Andorra*, App no 69498/01 (ECtHR, 13 July 2004), [59]–[63]. See also, in the context of a failure to protect people from homophobic violence, *Members of the Gldani Congregation of Jehovah's Witnesses v Georgia*, App no 71156/01 (ECtHR, 3 May 2007). See also, on positive action, *DH and Others v Czech Republic* App no 57325/00 (ECtHR, 13 November 2007), [175].

[29] *DH* (n 28) [175]; *Molla Sali v Greece*, App no 20452/14 (ECtHR, 19 December 2018), [135].

[30] *The Belgian Linguistic Case* (1968) 1 EHRR 252, [42]; see, more recently, *Molla Sali* (n 29) [135].

of the ECtHR has developed notions of 'direct' and 'indirect' discrimination, an influence seen in the related concepts in the Equality Act 2010.[31] It has also prohibited discrimination by association.[32] Article 1 of Protocol 12 prohibits discrimination in a more general way, not being limited to enjoyment of the rights and freedoms of the Convention.[33] However, the UK has not signed or ratified this Protocol.[34]

The language of Article 14 is broad. Discrimination must not occur on any ground, including 'social origin', 'property', 'birth' or 'other status'. I highlight those phrases, in particular, because they have the most obvious connection with the ideas of class and classism developed in this book. 'Social origin' and 'birth' are wrapped up with class. Especially in a country like England, with its long heritage of class according to birthright, the potential breadth of such a prohibition seems radical. 'Property' appears to go even further, capturing the aspects of class beyond where a person comes from. Property, after all, is one of the key differentiating tools in society and a concept that many theorists of class, like Marx, make central to their writing. To round off, 'other status' emphasises the open-endedness of Article 14. If class is understood as a type of (social, cultural, economic) 'status', it seems to be included here, too.

Reading that paragraph alone, it is tempting to expect a firm conclusion: Article 14 prohibits classism so long as it occurs within the scope of the Convention's rights and freedoms. The language seems broad enough. McGaughey, for instance, suggests that classism is 'probably' recognised 'in EU and ECHR norms'.[35] Yet the case law of the ECtHR, at least, does not live up to that expectation.

A. *Birth*

'Birth' has primarily been interpreted in terms of a child born in or out of marriage, with the main authorities addressing differences in the context of inheritance.[36] It has not been interpreted in the sense of birthright, aristocratic status, or birth as part of class systems.[37]

[31] See, eg, *Carson* (n 26) [61]; *DH* (n 28) [184]; Equality Act 2010, ss 13 and 19.

[32] *Molla Sali* (n 29) [134]. See also, in the domestic context, *EBR Attridge Law LLP v Coleman* [2009] UKEAT 0071/09/3010.

[33] Protocol No 12 to the Convention for the Protection of Human Rights and Fundamental Freedoms, Art 1.

[34] See, eg, Joint Committee on Human Rights, *Review of International Human Rights Instruments* (17th Report of Session 2004–2005, HL 99/HC 264), [29]–[34].

[35] McGaughey (n 11) 536.

[36] *Marckx* (n 27) [59].

[37] See also, as to the related issue of birth registration and Art 8 of the Convention, *GTP v Spain*, App no 3041/19 (ECtHR, 16 November 2023).

B. *Social Origin*

'Social origin' has been swept up with questions of national origin, rather than origin *within* a society, a social hierarchy or system. The major cases have considered status in the context of national distinctions, such as differences between residents and non-residents in relation to particular entitlements.[38] The ECtHR has not developed jurisprudence to the extent that 'social origin' has a broader meaning than that identified in this specific context.

C. *Other Status*

In relation to 'other status', the ECtHR claims to give the words a broad meaning.[39] However, though the ECtHR has interpreted 'other status' to include ideas such as age and disability, it has not done so for class or a similar idea.[40] A useful illustration is *PC v Ireland* (2022).[41] The ECtHR had to decide whether or not remand prisoners were in a position comparable to serving prisoners in relation to social security pension payments. The parties' submissions appear to have made no mention of class (perhaps because there is not always a clear link between imprisonment and class). The clear vulnerability in the case was that remand prisoners had not been convicted but were still deprived of their freedom on other grounds (such as concerns about the commission of further offences if granted bail). More generally, both remand and convicted prisoners would often, on release, have lost employment and financial support, making social security payments particularly important to them. The applicant argued that he had suffered discrimination based on age, based on being a prisoner whose only income came from the payments, and based on being a convicted prisoner. In respect of age (caught by 'other status' in Article 14), the ECtHR held that there was no evidence of a disproportionate impact on the group of older people.[42] In respect of the 'source or level of income', the ECtHR followed its reasoning in an earlier case that 'the fact of having, or not having, acquired a right to a welfare benefit' was not 'an aspect of personal status' within Article 14.[43] It was neither 'an innate characteristic which applies from birth' (like 'race') nor relevant to 'a core or personal belief or choice' (like 'religion' or 'political or other opinion').[44] This last point is the most important for my concern with class. A common indication of class (being in receipt of social security payments) is disregarded

[38] *Savickis and Others v Latvia*, App no 49270/11 (ECtHR, 9 June 2022).
[39] *Carson* (n 26) [70]; *Clift v UK*, App no 7205/07 (ECtHR, 13 July 2010), [56].
[40] *Schwizgebel v Switzerland*, App no 25762/07 (ECtHR, 10 June 2010); *Glor v Switzerland*, App no 13444/04 (ECtHR, 30 April 2009).
[41] *PC v Ireland*, App no 26922/19 (ECtHR, 1 September 2022).
[42] *PC* (n 41) [74].
[43] *PC* (n 41) [78]–[79].
[44] *PC* (n 41) [78]–[79].

under Article 14 because it is neither 'innate' nor relevant to 'core or personal belief or choice'. Such an approach suggests why the ECtHR's jurisprudence on Article 14 has consistently missed class.

D. *Property*

The only glimmer of real possibility is found in the jurisprudence concerning 'property', even if this line of cases has not articulated more than an indirect, skeletal idea of class. In *Chassagnou and Others v France* (1999), the ECtHR addressed landholders' mandatory inclusion within the hunting grounds of the local hunters' group.[45] There was a long history wrapped up in class. According to the ECtHR's summary, before the French Revolution of 1789, 'the right to hunt was a privilege of the nobility'.[46] For a long time afterward, it was a matter for any landholder to decide on their own land. In 1964, a piece of legislation was enacted. It required the owners of land smaller than a given measure to be a member of the local hunters' association. Those smaller landowners were required to transfer to that association the hunting rights over their land.[47] Reading Article 14 alongside Article 11 of the Convention and Article 1 of Protocol 1 (on the right of every natural or legal person to peaceful enjoyment of their possessions), the ECtHR held that the distinction between small and large landholders was unjustified.[48] Requiring smaller landholders to act incompatibly with their own beliefs represented 'a disproportionate burden', which was not justified.[49]

Later, in *Chabauty v France* (2012), smaller landholders brought a case before the ECtHR. They could not stop their land being used by approved hunting associations, unless they did so as a result of 'being opposed to hunting as a matter of personal conviction'.[50] The ECtHR interpreted *Chassagnou* as resting 'to a decisive degree' on the applicants' opposition to hunting 'on ethical grounds'.[51] The ECtHR framed the earlier decision as one, at its heart, about 'issues of conscience'.[52] By contrast, the ECtHR reasoned that the present case concerned understandable reasons for pooling the smallest hunting areas to create hunting grounds governed by shared rules of stock management, which enabled 'sustainable' hunting. In those circumstances, the state had adopted a proportionate means in pursuit of a legitimate aim.[53] The effect of *Chabauty* was to narrow the scope of *Chassagnou* to matters of conscience.

[45] *Chassagnou and Others v France*, App nos 25088/94, 28331/95 and 28443/95 (ECtHR, 29 April 1999).

[46] *Chassagnou* (n 45) [11].

[47] *Chassagnou* (n 45) [13].

[48] Protocol No 1 to the Convention for the Protection of Human Rights and Fundamental Freedoms, Art 1.

[49] *Chassagnou* (n 45) [85].

[50] *Chabauty v France*, App no 57412/08 (ECtHR, 4 October 2012), [45].

[51] *Chabauty* (n 50) [41].

[52] *Chabauty* (n 50) [41].

[53] *Chabauty* (n 50) [54]–[56].

Despite the potential of recognising the role of property in discrimination, the case law has not realised it. The ECtHR has not interpreted the Convention to redress more general inequality between bigger and smaller landholders, for instance, or protected smaller landholders from disparate burdens of the state based on the size of the land alone. The focus on the size of land in *Chassagnou* and *Chabauty* is a product of the details of French history that led to the disputes. Wrapped up in that history, it is difficult to argue that either case offers a plausible argument that 'property' includes class here. Without further information, for example, it is difficult to understand what relevance the size of land has to class. Those owning huge swathes of land may well be upper-class people. It is also possible to imagine a farmer who owns a relatively large patch of land, but whose income is relatively low, whose formal education is little and who has few social contacts. Absent further detail, combined with the existing case law, the ground of 'property' does not – at present – address classism.

E. *Class in the Background*

Article 14 of the Convention is not alone in failing to protect people against classism. The case law of the ECtHR more generally echoes the domestic picture by ignoring or misunderstanding classism.[54] Take two cases as instances of the pattern.

In *DH and Others v Czech Republic* (2007), the main issue was whether the application of legislation meant that, in practice, Roma children were placed in separate schools disproportionately and, in being there, put at significant disadvantage compared with other children. As a result of the design of the educational tests used to select schools and the tests' failure to take account of Roma children's traits, the ECtHR found that there was indirect discrimination against those children.[55] Given the significant connection between the Roma population, education, social contacts, money and property, there is a reasonable argument that this judgment – in effect – protects a part of the lower classes in the Czech Republic. However, the ECtHR did not do so expressly or, it seems, consciously. Indeed, even if its judgment has that effect, the ECtHR's reasoning was tied to Roma children rather than the broader category of lower-class children. It is, therefore, an elaboration to suggest that *DH and Others* is an example of the ECtHR prohibiting classism, even if the treatment of Roma children was in fact racist and classist.

Another example comes from *BS v Spain* (2012).[56] Police officers abused a black woman who was a sex worker. The officers' language and behaviour

[54] The same could be said for class itself. Although some cases have raised the topic of class (eg *Ceylan v Turkey*, App no 23556/94 (ECtHR, 8 July 1999), [28] and *Ayoub and Others v France*, App nos 77400/14, 34532/15 and 34550/15 (ECtHR, 8 October 2020), [17], the court has never attempted to analyse the idea itself.

[55] *DH* (n 28) [200]–[201].

[56] *BS v Spain*, App no 47159/08 (ECtHR, 24 July 2012).

indicated their contempt for her and their sense that they could act without repudiation because she was a black woman in public who did sex work. The ECtHR held that the investigations carried out were insufficient and violated Article 3 of the Convention under its procedural limb. In the light of the state's failure to examine the connection between racist behaviour, the 'vulnerability in her position' and the abuse, the ECtHR also found a violation of Article 14.[57] Its reasoning here is accurate and persuasive. However, it reveals no consideration – certainly not in express terms – of the classism that a black woman in sex work might face, together with racism and misogyny. Classism may be covered by the ECtHR's references to her 'vulnerability', granted, but that is by implication only.

Taking stock of a bleak picture, a final observation can be made. There has been no challenge before the courts of England and Wales in which litigants have used 'social origin' or the other terms to argue that the Convention, by virtue of the HRA 1998, prohibits forms of classism. Perhaps this is because of a lack of imagination by lawyers and litigants. Perhaps it has been contemplated but put aside because it would be too risky or unrealistic. More generally, it may be a direct product of the ECtHR jurisprudence to date: it is difficult to make an argument for an idea that the case law has yet to acknowledge.

2. COULD ADMINISTRATIVE LAW PROTECT CLASS?

Aside from the passage in *Kruse v Johnson*, there is little basis to suggest that administrative law (even under the ECtHR's influence) protects class or prohibits classism. This leads to a different question. Could administrative law protect class? There is a need to be realistic. A system of administrative law fully committed to the eradication of classism would look very different from the one in the UK today. In all likelihood, it would take considerable shifts – transformations, really – across politics, the economy and the law more generally. In the UK, there has never been a government committed to ending classism in all its forms. The highest courts tend to understand their role as one of interpreting Parliament's intention and (more occasionally) protecting the common law tradition rather than leading societal change. Even accepting that need for realism, it remains possible that we have tools in administrative law (particularly in the context of judicial review) that could address classism. Alongside the kinds of societal changes I have mentioned, we would still need protections against classism in the law, a theme to which I will return in Chapter 10.[58] To that end, I focus now on the possibility of a principle against classism in administrative law.

[57] *BS* (n 56) [47], [62].

[58] As I will develop in Chapter 10, I accept the suggestion that many current legal principles rest on a particular political perspective. Nevertheless, with broader societal changes accompanying it, the law can be reshaped in a way that realises its emancipatory potential: see, eg, A Piekarska,

2.1. What Administrative Law Offers

Unlike some areas of the law (such as the principles governing a person's culpability in criminal law), administrative law tends to address topics, institutions and entitlements as they relate to governance of societies. This gives me the sense that administrative law may provide fertile ground for a protection of classism in wider senses, such as in general class inequality in societies. The criminal law is consistently retrospective and punitive, with individualistic norms unlikely to provide well-considered, systemic transformation of the kind that would eliminate classism. Meanwhile, under the Equality Act, the law tends to be less directly punitive and more concerned with a system of entitlements harnessed in litigation. Both areas, especially when realised in litigation, tend not to address directly societal structures and the distribution of resources. By contrast, administrative law is often concerned with themes of governance and constitutional importance, politics and the functioning of prominent institutions in society. Well-known cases in administrative law have concerned issues of the reasonableness of decisions by public bodies, exercise of a minister's discretion, parliamentary sovereignty, access to justice, and the UK's exit from the European Union.[59] The familiarity of administrative law with these bigger questions might, in turn, mean that it is better at addressing the full extent of classism when it comes to more general rights and entitlements (especially social security payments), resources, property, education, and poverty.

These observations reflect the focus of Shreya Atrey and Sandra Fredman's collection – discussed earlier – about equality law in different jurisdictions. In the introduction to their collection, Atrey and Fredman give an overview of the contributors' various criticisms of the law's limited, adversarial nature and prioritising of formal equality. They highlight equality law's reliance on the concepts of direct and indirect discrimination (as opposed to wider-ranging ideas), the legal remedies (often prospective, monetary and individualistic), and the law's emphasis on individual rights and duties as opposed to, for instance, communal or societal entitlements.[60] In one chapter, for example, Diane Elson and Marion Sharples look beyond the law and outline approaches to address inequalities connected with class, gender and race, such as the establishment of a 'caring economy'.[61] When it comes to constitutional and administrative law in particular, Aleta Sprague, Amy Raub and Jody Heymann argue that '[c]onstitutional

---

'Challenging the Rule of Law Universalism: Why Marxist Legal Thought Still Matters' (2023) 34 *Law and Critique* 269.

[59] *Associated Provincial Picture Houses Ltd v Wednesbury Corporation* [1948] 1 KB 223; *Padfield v Minister of Agriculture* [1968] AC 997; *R (Jackson) v Attorney General* [2006] 1 AC 262, [2005] UKHL 56; *R (Miller) v Secretary of State for Exiting the European Union* [2017] UKSC 5; *UNISON* (n 24).

[60] S Atrey and S Fredman, 'Introduction' in S Atrey and S Fredman (eds), *Exponential Inequalities* (Oxford, Oxford University Press, 2023) 1.

[61] D Elson and M Sharples, 'Addressing Intersecting Inequalities through Alternative Economic Strategies' in Atrey and Fredman (n 60) 43–60.

guarantees of equality and fundamental social and economic protections can provide an important practical and normative foundation for protecting the equal rights of marginalized workers amidst and in the wake of crises'.[62] Such guarantees combine prohibitions on discrimination with minimum standards of social protection and labour, for example.

Sprague, Raub and Heymann cite the South African Constitutional Court's decision in *Mahlangu v Minister of Labour* (2020). Domestic workers had been excluded from the definition of 'employees' under South Africa's legislation on workers' compensation. The Constitutional Court held that the exclusion violated constitutional guarantees of equality and social security. Noting the 'gendered and racialised system of poverty', the Constitutional Court stressed the role of social security in ensuring 'basic necessities' and 'dignity'.[63] In doing so, the judges connected the values of equality and minimum standards with the historical context of poverty (though they did not refer expressly to class). While Sprague, Raub and Heymann note the 'substantial variation' across countries in constitutional protections of equality and non-discrimination, they argue that constitutional enshrinements have benefits including by providing the basis for limits on cuts to benefits and services. Such enshrinements also offer a foundation for more detailed protections of social and economic rights in addition to more specific legislative provisions, such as introducing class as a protected characteristic in the Equality Act.[64]

2.2. What Administrative Law Lacks

Administrative law does not exist in isolation from the wider legal system. Certainly in England and Wales, without a singular constitutional document, it is still marked by: (i) the adversarial nature of administrative law disputes; (ii) the limited role of evidence in appellate and review proceedings; and (iii) the role of appellate and reviewing courts.

First, it is not as if issues of administrative law occupy an entirely distinct place in our legal system or in our courts. The proceedings are still, for the most part, adversarial, as were all the cases I listed above as examples of the bigger themes that administrative law raises.

Second, appellate and reviewing courts tend to have more stringent rules as to when they will hear evidence in comparison with courts of first instance.[65] A high-profile example is *For Women Scotland v The Scottish Ministers* (2025).[66]

[62] A Sprague, A Raub and J Heymann, 'Protecting Workers' Equal Rights during Crisis and Recovery' in Atrey and Fredman (n 60) 19.

[63] *Mahlangu v Minister of Labour* [2020] ZACC 24, [63].

[64] Sprague, Raub and Heymann (n 62).

[65] See, eg, CPR, Pt 54, rr 54.16–54.17 (concerning judicial review proceedings).

[66] *For Women Scotland Ltd v The Scottish Ministers* [2025] UKSC 16.

The Supreme Court had to consider the meaning of 'sex' and related terms in the Equality Act. In the usual way, the judges did not adopt an inquisitorial approach. They did not hear evidence of the supposedly 'unworkable' aspects of the Equality Act, such as 'single-sex spaces' and sports. Instead, the judges heard submissions from counsel on behalf of For Women Scotland and then the Scottish Ministers. The judges also allowed submissions from four interveners: the Equality and Human Rights Commission; a group called 'Sex Matters'; a number of groups claiming to represent lesbian interests; and Amnesty International.[67] Of those four, the judges only heard oral submissions from the first two.[68] The reasons for the selection are unclear. The parts of the judgment dealing with them do not set out the rationale. It may be that groups closely connected with transgender people did not wish to make submissions or that the judges considered that Amnesty International could give them the necessary assistance.

Significant portions of the judgment concern questions of the effectiveness and clarity in practice of certain provisions of the Equality Act.[69] The EHRC made a significant point of the problems with the functioning of those provisions without a clear resolution, but the judges did not hear any evidence from people actually organising 'single-sex' spaces and similar.[70] Although counsel for 'Sex Matters' made a positive impression on the judges by offering a route through statutory provisions, there was no evidence admitted to show the effect in practice, though some census data was quoted in a written submission.[71] By a combination of submissions and a selection of interveners, the Supreme Court assumed facts that informed its conclusions about what would be 'unworkable' interpretations of the Equality Act.[72] This is an example of appellate and reviewing courts' tendency to determine issues – even those that turn on highly contested facts – without hearing evidence. For questions about classism and discrimination, the rarity of the admission of evidence could contribute to context-free reasoning, providing little information about what class actually means to real people.

Third, linked to this concern, there is the distinctive role of appellate and reviewing courts in administrative law. In part, this is clearest in assessments of proportionality in the highest courts, which I will consider later. More generally, for now, the tendency of appellate and reviewing courts in England and Wales is to emphasise their institutional function in order to restrict their intervention. This can take the form of adopting a less intense form of review depending on the issues under consideration (such as 'controversial' matters of 'social' and

[67] *For Women Scotland* (n 66) [31]–[35].
[68] *For Women Scotland* (n 66) [33] and [35].
[69] See, eg, *For Women Scotland* (n 66) [152], [156], [160], [182], [188], [210], [234].
[70] *For Women Scotland* (n 66) [33], [247].
[71] *For Women Scotland* (n 66) [26], [35], [101].
[72] *For Women Scotland* (n 66) [264].

'economic' decision-making) or determining that the issues are not for a court to decide (due to the respect given to democratic bodies, for instance), or different techniques sometimes labelled 'deference'.[73] In addition to those features, apart from one division of the High Court, there is no set of courts or judges in England and Wales that is specifically 'constitutional' or 'administrative'. The judges who make administrative law are often the judges who make other kinds of law or who, in practice, dealt exclusively in other areas.[74]

These three features tell us that there are big questions about whether or not the UK's legal system, and the kinds of senior judges that it tends to reproduce, is an effective system in which to develop the administrative law to combat classism. These features are not conclusive, however. While administrative law in the current legal system has features that make it difficult to address classism, these have to be set against the positive features that this area of the law does have. It could be used to combat classism, even if it has features that might make that task a challenging or sometimes ineffective one.

To consider how we might build a principle against classism from the doctrinal framework, the ideas of consistency and equal treatment may provide an opening.

3. CLASS AND ONGOING DEBATES: CONSISTENCY AND EQUAL TREATMENT

3.1. The Current Position

In England and Wales, the current position is that there is no general administrative 'right' or 'entitlement' to equal treatment under the law and in relation to the government's use of its powers.[75] Despite the influence of cases like *Kruse v Johnson* on challenges to the reasonableness of legislation and public bodies' decision-making, the law has never enshrined a standalone right or entitlement to equal treatment. In *Matadeen v Pointu* (1999), Hoffmann L reasoned that, though equal treatment was a fundamental feature of a democratic society and 'a general

[73] See, eg, P Daly, *A Theory of Deference in Administrative Law* (Cambridge, Cambridge University Press, 2012) 7–10 (giving weight as 'epistemic deference', allocating authority as 'doctrinal deference', both grouped under 'curial deference').

[74] At the time of writing this book, the UK Supreme Court comprises Robert Reed JSC (civil and criminal law), Patrick Hodge (commercial and property law and assorted judicial review claims), David Lloyd-Jones (international, EU and assorted public law), Michael Briggs (commercial and chancery law), Nicholas Hamblen (commercial law, shipping and insurance law), Philip Sales (commercial, chancery and assorted public law), George Leggatt (commercial law), Andrew Burrows (academic specialising in civil law), Ben Stephens (insurance and other civil law), Vivien Rose (commercial law), David Richards (company and insolvency law) and Ingrid Simler (tax, employment/discrimination and other civil law): www.supremecourt.uk.

[75] *Webster v Attorney General of Trinidad and Tobago* [2015] UKPC 10 (Hale JSC), relying on, in turn, *Matadeen v Pointu* [1999] 1 AC 98 (cited in *Gallaher* at [25]).

axiom' of rational behaviour, it was not necessarily 'a justiciable principle'.[76] In sum: equal treatment is of course important, and likely essential, for a truly democratic society, but it is not necessarily suitable for, or open to, the courts to determine. There is some haziness here, since Hoffmann L may intend 'justiciable' to be (i) a question of a phenomenon's suitability to adjudication by courts, (ii) a question of courts having permission – whether institutional, constitutional, legal, conceptual – to adjudicate on it, or (iii) both. Without addressing this haziness, Carnwath JSC relied on the same passage in *R (Gallaher Group Ltd) v Competition and Markets Authority* (2018).[77] With the majority, Carnwath JSC concluded that issues of consistency could arise in administrative law but 'generally as aspects of rationality'.[78] Giving his separate judgment, Sumption JSC reasoned that '[t]he common law principle of equality is usually no more than a particular application of the ordinary requirement of rationality imposed on public authorities'.[79]

Gallaher is a key case when it comes to the possibility of a common law principle of equality or 'equal treatment', especially when looking for a way to develop existing constitutional law doctrine to address classism. It concerned a judicial review claim arising from 'early resolution agreements' after an investigation by the Office of Fair Trading (OFT) into alleged arrangements to fix prices in the tobacco market.[80] The Supreme Court overturned the Court of Appeal's finding that the OFT's decision had to comply with 'the principle of equal treatment in all steps leading up to the imposition of a penalty'.[81] The Court of Appeal had reasoned that the OFT had failed to offer a similar assurance to the claimants and others in the same position as it had to another party, such that there was 'stark and manifest' unequal treatment.[82] The Court of Appeal had also relied on the ideas of resiling from a legitimate expectation, abuse of power and unfair (alongside unequal) treatment.[83] In the Supreme Court, the parties again adopted the language and ideas of equal treatment and kinds of fairness.[84] Despite the parties' common ground, Carnwath JSC reasoned that it was important 'to be clear as to the precise content and attributes of the relevant legal principles'.[85] Similarly, Sumption JSC observed that it was 'important not unnecessarily to multiply categories'.[86] Addressing a principle of equal treatment in

[76] *Matadeen* (n 75) [9].

[77] *R (Gallaher Group Ltd and Others) v Competition and Markets Authority* [2018] UKSC 25.

[78] *Gallaher* (n 77) [26] (Carnwath JSC). On the facts of *Gallaher*, in any event, there was a commitment to equal treatment expressed in terms to certain parties: [29] (Carnwath JSC).

[79] *Gallaher* (n 77) [50] (Sumption JSC).

[80] See also M Elliott, 'A "Principle" of Consistency? The Doctrinal Configuration of the Law of Judicial Review' (2018) 77 *Cambridge Law Journal* 444. The OFT later became the Competition and Markets Authority.

[81] *Gallaher* (n 77) [15] (Carnwath JSC), quoting *R (Gallaher Group Ltd and Others) v Competition and Markets Authority* [2016] EWCA Civ 719, [34] (Dyson MR).

[82] *Gallaher* (n 77) [15] (Carnwath JSC), *Gallaher*, CA (n 81) [59] (Dyson MR).

[83] See, eg, *Gallaher*, CA (n 81) [60] (Dyson MR).

[84] *Gallaher* (n 77) [19]–[20].

[85] *Gallaher* (n 77) [23].

[86] *Gallaher* (n 77) [50] (Sumption JSC).

particular, Carnwath JSC considered that, whatever the position in other jurisdictions, 'the domestic law of this country does not recognise equal treatment as a distinct principle of administrative law'. While 'consistency' was 'generally desirable', it was 'not an absolute rule'.[87]

When deciding if there is scope for a distinct principle of equality (or, at least, equal treatment) at common law, the observations in *Gallaher* deserve careful attention. The Supreme Court's reasoning does not sit easily with earlier decisions by other courts that appear to give equality a status independent from rationality.[88] In his commentary on *Gallaher*, Mark Elliott identifies the disagreement between Carnwath and Sumption JJSC about the existence of such a principle but suggests that they agree as to its relevance to questions of rationality. While Elliott is correct here, it is worth looking a little closer at the language that Sumption JSC used. Although the judge referred to '[t]he common law principle of equality', he conceived it as 'usually no more than a particular application of the ordinary requirement of rationality'.[89] This aspect of Sumption JSC's observations is telling in two ways. First, as Elliott notes, Sumption JSC seems to preserve a distinct common law principle concerned with 'equality', though one found under the heading of 'rationality'. But the second and more pertinent point is that Sumption JSC's use of the adverb 'usually' suggests that he accepted that there may be some situations in which the principle exists *beyond* the requirement of rationality. This differs slightly from Carnwath JSC's analysis.

Why does this abstract, taxonomical debate matter for classism? It matters when we consider where a protection against classism might come into administrative law. If a fundamental feature of classism is unequal capital as I have suggested, an administrative law principle committed to equal treatment might offer the root from which anti-classism arguments could grow.

The case of *Carmichael and Rourke v Secretary of State for Work and Pensions* (2016) offers an example of this possibility.[90] The appellants argued that the restrictions on housing benefits violated Article 14 of the Convention, alongside Article 8, and Article 1 of Protocol 1. Criticising the Supreme Court's approach to the issue of justifying such a policy, Meghan Campbell asks the question: 'Should disabled people bear the burdens of mistakes made in the financial sector?'[91]

Rather than ask such a question, the Supreme Court held by majority that there was a justification for the policy on the basis that, given that there was no 'objective' need for a higher number of bedrooms, the government's approach

[87] *Gallaher* (n 77) [24]. Similarly, the majority of the Supreme Court cautioned against acontextual notions of 'unfairness' or the prospect of 'substantive fairness' (in contrast to the settled idea of 'procedural unfairness') as a freestanding administrative principle: see [40] and [41].

[88] See, eg, *Gurung v Ministry of Defence* [2002] EWHC 2463 (Admin), [55].

[89] *Gallaher* (n 77) [50] (Sumption JSC).

[90] *Carmichael and Rourke v Secretary of State for Work and Pensions* [2016] UKSC 58.

[91] M Campbell, 'The Proportionality of Economic Crisis' in Atrey and Fredman (n 60) 79, 85.

was not manifestly without reasonable foundation – a low standard of scrutiny to apply.[92] However, the Supreme Court's reasoning lacked a logical connection. The judges, and it seems the government, failed to question with rigour why such a policy would assist in resolving a situation created by the financial industries (especially the banks).[93]

The advantage of a separate principle of equal treatment would be twofold here. First, there is its distinctness in analysis. It would require the court to address directly the issue of the inequality *independent of* the question of justification under the assessment of proportionality, which pulls in various factors. Of course, it may be that courts would approach this by making some vague references to 'striking a balance' of different principles. But, if a principle of equal treatment is elevated to an important administrative principle in its own right, it would certainly be harder to ignore. Second, it would lend force to the considerations about non-discrimination that Article 14 of the Convention captures, which could have changed the court's assessment of proportionality. If we were then to combine this understanding with a prohibition against classism (including, as I have argued, inequality between classes), the Supreme Court's decision in *Carmichael and Rourke* would be much harder to sustain.

A. *Precision and Accuracy*

To develop this argument, I return to the three heuristics of legal reasoning that I set out in Chapter 2. I start with precision and accuracy. On the one hand, you might argue that treating equality simply as a factor within more general rationality review achieves both precise and accurate reasoning. So long as the reasoning makes clear when it refers specifically to equality and is transparent about what importance it gives equality among other considerations in rational decision-making, equality can happily be part of general rationality review.

On the other hand, distinguishing equality from more general rationality would save courts from analytical muddles. As Elliott suggests, there are benefits for both doctrinal coherence and the transparency of reasoning by recognising a distinct principle.[94] As a matter of doctrinal coherence, distinction would enable courts to undertake a focused and clearer development of the idea and how it should be understood. As a matter of the transparency of reasoning, the courts would avoid jumbling together different concepts, particularly when that jumbling prevents a precise explanation of which one is most instructive in a given case. For example, when Dyson MR brought together the ideas of unfair treatment, unequal treatment, objective justification and resiling from assurances in the Court of Appeal in *Gallaher*, it was not obvious how those

[92] *Carmichael* (n 90) [53]–[56]. See also *AIB Group (UK) Plc v Mark Redler & Co Solicitors* [2014] UKSC 58, [53], [56].
[93] Campbell (n 91) 85.
[94] Elliott (n 80) 447–48.

considerations related to each other.[95] Put another way: if one factor disappeared from Dyson MR's reasoning, would his conclusion be the same? It is not possible to find the answer when reading the judgment of the Court of Appeal in *Gallaher*, as the Supreme Court correctly observed.[96] A distinct principle of equality in administrative law would be more likely to ensure such clarity and precision in judicial analysis, rather than the filing of equality under a wide and often unwieldy category of rationality.

This last point suggests how such a principle might be fashioned to address classism. If the reference in *Kruse v Johnson* to 'classes' is broad enough to include class in my sense, a standalone idea of equality has more potential than merely equality as one consideration among others in rationality review. With that standalone idea, many of the appellate decisions about the distribution of resources, especially welfare payments, would have had to name and consider the issue of inequality between classes in a way that they simply have not done to date.[97] Granted, this is an argument about doctrinal clarity. It does not address the questions about the role of the law in driving radical changes within societies, or the relationship between the courts and governments, or the composition of the judiciary (discussed in Chapters 9 and 10). For now, the benefit I envisage is more limited. By recognising a standalone principle of class equality, the courts would have to reason about classism in its own terms.

B. *Capacity for Transforming Society*

Considering the third and last heuristic of the capacity for transforming society by eliminating classism, the existence of a distinct principle of equality – not subsumed within general ideas of reasonableness or rationality – would tell us that it is a value that the law itself prizes. Recognising it independently would, therefore, have a symbolic advantage. Elliott makes the argument that recognising 'consistent/equal treatment as a free-standing principle would be fitting recognition of its normative importance'.[98] If administrative law places value in equality itself, it tells us that, even if the decision-making is otherwise rational and justifiable, the law may still regard that decision-making as deficient. Placing separate emphasis on the value of equality indicates that it may have to be protected even above other considerations.

In addition to the symbolic significance of the law adopting that position, a distinct principle of equality would likely be more effective in its protection. This would work in a similar way to the existence of class as a protected characteristic in the Equality Act, for example, and not merely one consideration in an overall analysis. I have already set out that Elliott argues that 'carving out a

[95] *Gallaher*, CA (n 81) [60] (Dyson MR).
[96] *Gallaher* (n 77) [44] (Carnwath JSC).
[97] See later in this chapter for further discussion in the context of proportionality.
[98] Elliott (n 80) 447.

principle of consistent/equal treatment from the generality of the rationality review would place less weight on the latter and, as a result, would aid legal transparency'.[99] Rather than making another argument based on transparency, it is better to pause at Elliott's suggestion that the separation would 'place less weight' on the idea of rationality. This can be understood as an argument about the effectiveness of this ground of review, especially if we were to use it to seek to address classism. If we extract equality from broader considerations of rationality, it takes on the status of a distinct principle and not just a factor we visit on the way to determine something else. To that end, it would likely be much more effective if parties could argue that, even if a public body's decision-making were rational, it still violates the principle of equality. Courts would then have to reconcile the reasons for concluding that decision-making is rational with the importance attached to equality. This is not, then, a question of the transparency of legal reasoning alone; it is also a question of increasing the analytical place of equality in order to encourage more rigorous review.

To make this more concrete, take an example from the case law. There has been some debate about a right to access to justice. The courts have recognised the importance of access to justice and have quashed regulations on the basis that they violate it. In *R (UNISON) v Lord Chancellor* (2017), the Supreme Court quashed the Employment Tribunals and the Employment Appeal Tribunal Fees Order 2013, a statutory instrument that imposed certain fees on claimants in proceedings before those tribunals.[100] The instrument came from section 42(1) of the Tribunals, Courts and Enforcement Act 2007. That provision gave the Lord Chancellor the power to prescribe fees by order.[101] Emphasising the importance that the common law has long attached to 'the right of access to the courts', the Supreme Court held that the order was unlawful because the fees effectively prevented access to justice without proper justification.[102]

Discussing *UNISON*, some suggest that the existence of a 'free-standing' legal principle of access to justice in the common law is unlikely to make 'a practical difference' in many cases. For example, measures made pursuant to statute will be unlawful by either route, whether by interpreting the statute not to intend disproportionate hindrance of access to justice or by violating the common law principle. However, in some cases, they consider that 'the difference of view may matter when the hindrance to access comes from a source other than a statute'.[103] Connecting this with the discussion about a 'free-standing' principle of equal or consistent treatment, it indicates an advantage beyond both the symbolic and effective dimensions I have identified. Recognition of a distinct principle may

[99] Elliott (n 80) 448, citing concern about the obscurity allowed by the *Wednesbury* doctrine's 'ample cloak': J Jowell and A Lester, 'Beyond *Wednesbury*: Substantive Principles of Administrative Law' (1987) *Public Law* 368.

[100] *UNISON* (n 24) [2] (Reed JSC).

[101] *UNISON* (n 24) [5].

[102] *UNISON* (n 24) [68]–[71], [98], [100]–[101].

[103] H Woolf and others (eds), *De Smith's Judicial Review* (London, Sweet & Maxwell, 2024) 6-082.

enlarge the scope of protection under it. Such a principle would allow litigants to bring challenges against unequal treatment from sources other than statutes.[104]

There are, then, at least three advantages to a principle of equal treatment, rather than merely approaching such treatment as one factor of several in other grounds of review. It would be beneficial in terms of (i) symbolism, as well as (ii) effectiveness, and (iii) the scope of protection under it.

3.2. Consistency, Equal Treatment, Equality

A. *Consistency versus Equal Treatment*

You may note the references to both equal treatment and consistency in my discussion so far. My arguments in this book, however, depend on an idea of classism that is not solely about different or inconsistent treatment. It is about long-term, extensive and severe disadvantage. To explore how these pieces fit together, it is necessary to consider how inequality between classes relates to both consistency and equal treatment.

The courts have tended to conflate the ideas of consistency and equal treatment. Responding to Sumption JSC's remark that we should not 'unnecessarily' multiply categories of principles in the law, Elliott observes that difficult situations always raise complex questions, such as when the 'creation or acknowledgement of a new category' may aid 'legal transparency or predictability'.[105] Elliott argues that the reasoning in *Gallaher* is surprising, given the reference to a 'free-standing' principle of public bodies dealing 'straightforwardly and consistently' with the public in *R (Nadarajah) v Secretary of State for the Home Department* (2005), related to the law of legitimate expectations.[106] Complexity of a new category is not, and has not been, a good reason to reject outright a standalone principle.

While Elliott is right about this, his argument reflects the law's conflation of consistency and equal treatment. Consider the language in Elliott's analysis of *Gallaher*: 'recognising consistent/equal treatment as a free-standing principle would be fitting recognition of its normative importance'.[107] In the scholarship on equality and discrimination, it is widely accepted that consistency of treatment is an inadequate approach to equality of treatment.[108] Sameness in approach can be unequal, as in the well-known example of requiring everyone to use the stairs including people who are physically disabled. More sophisticated readings

[104] See, eg, the Divisional Court's quashing of a regulation prohibiting the bringing of certain legal proceedings without the consent of a minister in *Chester v Bateson* [1920] 1 KB 829, 836, cited in *UNISON* (n 24) [76].

[105] Elliott (n 80) 445.

[106] *R (Nadarajah) v Secretary of State for the Home Department* [2005] EWCA Civ 1363, [68] (Wilson L); Elliott (n 80) 445.

[107] 447.

[108] See, eg, S Fredman, *Discrimination Law* (Oxford, Oxford University Press, 2022) 9–15.

of both equality and consistency might understand them not as instances of exact sameness but perhaps of a more abstract sameness of quality. Different approaches and outcomes when making decisions can, for example, still reflect equality and consistency, as those values require attention to individual circumstances and adjustment of general policies to reflect those circumstances. This should be intuitive. Person A may need more help than person B because of their circumstances, but this does not make the treatment of A unequal or inconsistent when compared with B.

That being said, even if they are understood as involving more nuance than merely a mechanical commitment to 'sameness', conflating consistency with equal treatment is dangerous. While both are features of good, logical decision-making, we could have a government that was consistent *and* terrible. Across the board, it could make decisions that violate people's dignity, undermine their quality of life and erode the good values in a society. Such a government would be consistent in its evil. By contrast, at least when understanding equal treatment in its common senses of equal respect, equal dignity or similar (rather than, for instance, equal awfulness), we can understand why equal treatment is likely to capture features about the treatment that consistency does not. Therefore, while consistency and equal treatment are related, they should not be used interchangeably. There is a benefit to be found in treating people equally that is not necessarily present when treating them consistently.

B. *Equal Treatment versus Equality*

It is also important to distinguish the 'generic term' of 'equal treatment' (which appears in some of the case law) from 'equality'.[109] As Sandra Fredman argues, equal treatment often refers to the idea of the sameness or comparability of the process, rather than the sense of equal outcomes or a more sophisticated understanding of equality.[110] The problem with the sketching of a principle of equal treatment in the law to date is that it really is concerned with the *manner* in which decisions are made, rather than the *content* of the decisions themselves. This is familiar territory for theorists of discrimination and the law: administrative law has contemplated a principle of equal treatment, certainly, but it has not developed any sense of equality in outcome, in results or in distribution.

In order to address classism in its more structural and systemic aspects (as opposed merely to instances of disagreement or maltreatment between individuals), we would need to establish a standalone principle of equality between classes of this kind. At present, as I have accepted, the basis in precedent for this principle is thin. As Colm O'Cinneide puts it, 'the courts have not recognised

[109] O'Cinneide (n 17) 168.

[110] S Fredman, 'Substantive Equality Revisited' (2016) 14(3) *International Journal of Administrative Law* 712.

the existence of a common law right to non-discrimination'.[111] The courts have not substantially elaborated on a standalone principle of consistent or equal treatment, let alone a more transformative (or, to use Fredman's language, 'substantive') idea of equality between classes.[112] With only a skeletal framework found in the case law, a principle of equality between classes needs significant imagining.

3.3. A Principle of Equality between Classes

There are also much bigger questions about the role of the courts here, especially in legal systems and societies as they are at present. I consider these issues in Chapters 9 and 10. Although a comprehensive analysis would be a considerable task, it is possible to provide the contours of a principle of equality between classes. For now, read alongside my arguments about understanding class and classism so far, I suggest the following steps in making the argument for such a principle.

First, the passage in *Kruse v Johnson* is a tool open to scholars and practitioners. In the passage, Russell LCJ did not have classism specifically in mind in his reference to 'classes', but his sense of the word remains general enough to include class groups. Such divisions – social, cultural, economic – fall within the prohibition of 'partial' or 'unequal' distinctions between 'classes'. As a matter of precedent, *Kruse* offers the root of the argument that administrative law is legitimately concerned with equality between classes, including classes in my sense. It is open to lawyers to re-animate – or re-imagine – Russell LCJ's 'classes'.

Second, lawyers should push for the recognition of a standalone principle of equality within the administrative law. As I have argued, this is a doctrinal step that goes beyond mere tidiness or transparency. A distinct principle would bring a symbolic benefit as well as greater effectiveness and scope of protection when compared with situating questions of equality in general rationality.

Third, lawyers should prefer an idea of equality more sophisticated than the current focus on consistent or equal treatment. The latter ideas are more formal, concerned with the nature of the treatment rather than the quality of that treatment and the outcomes that it generates. In particular, if equality becomes in itself a principle in administrative law, it will need its own jurisprudence. As O'Cinneide argues, even though the idea of equality has several meanings 'clustered around' a general idea of people being equal in 'status' or 'worth', *Gallaher* was 'a wasted opportunity' for the Supreme Court to recognise such a principle and 'delineate its substantive and formal dimensions' (and how those dimensions relate to each other).[113] The various meanings might give

[111] O'Cinneide (n 17) 168.
[112] Fredman (n 110).
[113] O'Cinneide (n 17) 170, 191.

a basis to the objection that a distinct principle of equality – let alone equality between classes – would be too vague. But this objection is not persuasive. An approach such as Fredman's four-dimensional 'substantive equality' is one of many models now well-established in the academic literature and apt for use by the courts.[114]

Fourth and most vital to my arguments in this book, equality *between classes* should be emphasised as a necessary aspect of the common law's guarding of equality. This could either be done by the establishment of a further distinct principle of equality between classes or by incorporating it as part of a newly distinct principle of equality. The benefit of a distinct principle about classes, in particular, would be to put class and classism on its own terms and require courts to engage with questions on those specific issues. For this, lawyers can rely on an approach to class inspired by Bourdieu and an approach to classism using Khaitan's three criteria for disadvantage. The principle would recognise class in accordance with unequal social, economic and cultural capital. It would recognise classism in accordance with the abiding, pervasive and substantial disadvantage that lower-class people suffer relating to class.

It is also possible to sketch its dimensions by taking Fredman's framework of substantive equality.[115] Such a principle would require public bodies not to make decisions that sustain, or worsen, inequality between classes. It must be assessed by four interactive dimensions:

(1) It would require public bodies to redress disadvantage by ensuring their decisions reduce 'the cycle of disadvantage' that lower-class people experience across contexts, including in housing, work and education.[116]
(2) It would require public bodies to address stigma, stereotyping, prejudice and violence by considering these issues in the making of decisions and policies and avoiding reliance on them in doing so.
(3) It would require public bodies to enhance participation and the voice of lower-class people in the procedures by which public bodies make decisions and take actions that affect lower-class people.
(4) It would require public bodies to accommodate difference by accurately understanding the needs of lower-class people, including by recognising differences within that category, and by tailoring decisions and policies to those needs, even if that tailoring results in lower-class people being treated differently and even if that includes transforming the structures that exist.

Plainly, this is only a sketch. Further work needs to be done to consider how such a principle might apply to the various contexts that administrative law touches. More modestly, my purpose here has been to offer the contours of a workable and compelling principle of equality between classes. Many questions

[114] Fredman (n 110).
[115] Fredman (n 108) 29–30.
[116] Fredman (n 108) 29.

remain, including important issues of the realism of the prospect of such a principle developing in the law, the potential burden on public bodies of these considerations, and the appropriateness of courts attempting to resolve these issues. However, as important as they may be, those questions do not mask the ability to state such a principle, using the ideas of class and classism within a well-established approach to equality. Drawing on Fredman's work shows one cogent and exciting way to do so.

4. EVEN SO: PROPORTIONALITY'S SHADOW

Imagine that we can enshrine a principle of equality between classes, then, perhaps by choosing Fredman's four-dimensional substantive equality. This would not only make a distinct principle relating to equality, but it would also enhance that principle (or even create a further principle) with equality between classes in mind. This would be an impressive development. However, it would not be the end of the matter. The question of what is 'justifiable' would likely become the next hurdle. Even when equality has been considered as a distinct issue in the existing case law, it has certainly not been clear to date what is the correct standard of review to apply.[117] To consider the prospect, the culture of administrative law needs some further attention.

By contrast from jurisdictions that have a constitution in a single formal document (or set of formal documents), with a supreme status among legal sources, the UK's constitution is a mixture of written and unwritten sources, conventions and complex relationships between powerful institutions.[118] Instead, there is the Supreme Court, which has limited power when compared with some equivalent courts in other countries (such as the US Supreme Court or South African Constitutional Court). In addition to that, there is a good argument to suggest that the analytical culture of the UK Supreme Court's judges is conservative. There are various explanations for this, including the cultivation of apparent political neutrality among the UK's most senior judges in a way that is not maintained in the US, for instance.[119] Whatever the precise causes, the tendency of the UK Supreme Court is to claim a role as a 'policy'-free interpreter of statutes according to Parliament's intent.[120]

The issues of proportionality and review of public bodies' actions closely link with the role of judges. With this in mind, Meghan Campbell considers

[117] O'Cinneide (n 17) 183–84.

[118] See, eg, The Constitution Society, 'The UK Constitution' (undated): www.consoc.org.uk/the-constitution-explained/the-uk-constitution.

[119] E Delaney, 'Searching for Constitutional Meaning in Institutional Design: the Debate over Judicial Appointments in the United Kingdom' (2016) 14(3) *International Journal of Constitutional Design* 752, 753, 757.

[120] Delaney (n 119) 758. See also, for a recent example, *For Women Scotland* (n 66) [2], [8]–[14].

four major decisions of the Supreme Court in the context of austerity.[121] Most notably, in *SG and Others v Secretary of State for Work and Pensions* (2015), the appellants argued that the Benefit Cap (Housing Benefit) Regulations 2012 were unlawful under the HRA 1998 because they discriminated against women in exercising their right to peaceful enjoyment of their possessions (contrary to Article 1 of Protocol 1 alongside Article 14 of the Convention itself). By a majority of three judges to two, the Supreme Court held that it was correct to subject the benefit cap on lone mothers to limited scrutiny. The reasoning of Reed JSC, in particular, rested on the argument that the cap raised 'controversial issues of social and economic policy', which were more appropriately left to Parliament and institutions with democratic credentials.[122] Assessing whether or not the cap was manifestly without reasonable foundation, Reed JSC reasoned that there was a rational basis for the cap (to encourage people to obtain work and not continue to rely on such payments) and it was a legitimate method to reduce public spending when necessary to do so for economic reasons.[123]

It is straightforward to imagine what robust administrative protections of equality (and prohibitions of inequality between classes, in particular) would do in a case of this kind, whether statutory or common law in nature. Such a change would be, in effect, a culture shock, starkly different from the type of reasoning that presents itself as politically neutral but contains strong indications of the images within the judges' minds. Campbell points out that, underlying the sheen of so-called political neutrality, the Supreme Court's majority viewed 'the large fiscal debt [as] a function of welfare dependency and the work-shy behaviour of individuals'.[124] In addition to Campbell's argument about the stereotyping influencing the judgment, alongside the inaccurate suggestion that such a cap will actually work in this way, there are the dissenting judgments of Hale and Kerr JJSC. Reasoning that the cap needed to be considered with the interests of the children affected in mind, both judges stressed the extent of the impact on those children to find that it was neither necessary nor proportionate.[125] Here, we see the absence of the analytical lens of class, since it was *lower-class* women who were disproportionately disadvantaged by the cap in question. Because of the absence of class as a protected ground under the HRA 1998 and the Convention, though, the arguments had to rest on the simplistic ground of 'sex'.

The detail of *SG and Others* aside, Campbell's review of the four decisions illustrates the role of proportionality even in the context of these broader 'administrative' or 'human rights'-based challenges. It is evident that, even with the benefits of administrative law's broader framing of issues, much would depend on how courts scrutinise issues through the tool of proportionality. For example,

[121] M Campbell (n 91). See also M Campbell, *Hanging in the Balance* (Oxford, Hart Publishing, 2025) esp ch 6.
[122] *SG and Others v Secretary of State for Work and Pensions* [2015] UKSC 16, [93] (per Reed JSC).
[123] *SG* (n 122) [93], [96] (Reed JSC).
[124] Campbell (n 91) 84.
[125] *SG* (n 122) [229] (Hale JSC), [268]–[269] (Kerr JSC).

even when moving from the lower standard of scrutiny in *SG and Others* to a higher standard when considering the two-child limit for child tax credit in *SC and CB v Secretary of State for Work and Pensions* (2021), the Supreme Court still treated the aim of curing the country's economic ill-health as sufficiently important to find the measure proportionate.[126]

This is the essential challenge for a principle of equality between classes. Unless there are significant changes in administrative law's culture in this sense, whether by outright statutory reform or a transformation in senior judges' habits, the courts may take any principle of equality (even a class-based one) and let it disappear into proportionality's shadow. Rhetoric of the 'balance' of rights, of 'democratic' functions of the legislature and the executive, of 'controversial' issues of social and economic policy – these would gather together to identify many reasons why, even with a new and important principle in administrative law, courts should not intervene. In this respect, administrative law could fall victim to a similar problem faced by class as a protected characteristic under the Equality Act, which I will discuss in Chapter 9: the diluting role of 'justification'.

That brings me to the end of considering three areas of the law: the Equality Act, the law relating to hate crime, and administrative law. Before moving ahead to the thorny issues like those of justification and the role of judges in Chapter 9, Chapter 8 takes a different approach. Rather than being limited to the introduction of a protected characteristic or a principle, as Chapters 5, 6 and 7 have been, the last chapter in Part II considers other ways we could use the current law, or remove parts from it, to address classism.

[126] *SC and CB v Secretary of State for Work and Pensions* [2021] UKSC 26, [199].

8

Using and Removing Classism in the Current Law

IN THIS CHAPTER, I seek to do something different from the previous three. I look at a pair of issues: (i) what we might *use* in the law, as it is, to address classism; and (ii) what we might *remove* from the law to further our aims to eradicate classism. My discussion will not be exhaustive; it may even be disparate. The issues scatter across the Equality Act 2010, the criminal law relating to employment, certain crimes and policing, and more entrenched legal rights – *class rights* – that benefit upper-class people at the expense of others. They all offer illustrations of how we might take the law that we have and make it more protective against classism. What features of the law, as it is, might we use to address classism? What features might we remove or restrict?

1. USING WHAT WE HAVE

1.1. The Public Sector Duty Regarding Socio-Economic Inequalities

Section 1 of the Equality Act is a good place to start. Section 1(1) provides for a public sector duty 'regarding socio-economic inequalities' (not to be confused with section 149's public sector equality duty, the PSED):

> An authority to which this section applies must, when making decisions of a strategic nature about how to exercise its functions, have **due regard** to the desirability of exercising them in a way that is designed to reduce the inequalities of outcome which result from socio-economic disadvantage.[1]

By virtue of section 1(3), the duty applies to authorities including Crown ministers, government departments (apart from the Security Service, the Secret Intelligence Service or the Government Communications Headquarters), and county and district councils.[2] However, the provision is not in force in England,

[1] Emphasis added. See also the further provision made about relevant guidance: Equality Act 2010, s 1(2) and (2A). A Crown minister may also issue regulations to amend s 1 in certain respects: Equality Act 2010, s 2.

[2] It excludes from its definition, however, inequalities experienced by a person as a result of immigration control within the Immigration and Asylum Act 1999, s 115(9).

though some local authorities have adopted it voluntarily.[3] It is only in force in certain contexts by virtue of a statutory instrument in Scotland from 1 April 2018 (as the 'Fairer Scotland Duty') and in Wales from 31 March 2021.[4] This is in spite of the Labour Party's manifesto commitment in 2024 to enact the provision in England.[5]

Section 1's language is wide:

(1) Having 'due regard' to something is a duty of observation, not necessarily of action.
(2) 'Due regard' is not directed to the eradication or reduction of inequality but rather to the issue of 'desirability'. It is at some distance from the inequality in question.
(3) 'Desirability' is broad enough to allow decision-makers to pull in many issues, such as the importance of 'social cohesion' and any need to avoid entrenching divisions.[6]
(4) Even if there has been due regard to desirability and the approach is deemed to be desirable, the idea of equality here is a *procedural* one: what is 'designed' matters, not the outcomes that result.
(5) Even when 'outcomes' are mentioned, the cause of them is not framed as arising from forms of discrimination as they permeate society. Instead, the cause of them is generic 'socio-economic disadvantage'.

Despite these issues, section 1 retains potential. If it is read properly, it may target the issue of classism. 'Socio-economic disadvantage' (though broad enough to cover most of the protected 'characteristics' in section 4 of the Equality Act) boils down to class.[7] Some texts support this interpretation, describing the provision as the Labour government's 'attempt to address the inequality that arises from a person's social class or family background'.[8] In the Equality Act's Explanatory Notes, it is suggested that such authorities will be required to consider how to reduce inequalities 'associated with socio-economic disadvantage' through decisions about priorities and objectives.[9] Those Explanatory Notes tellingly refer to inequalities in 'education, health, housing, crime rates, or other matters associated with socio-economic disadvantage'.[10] In January 2010, the Government Equalities Office published guidance about how the duty

[3] S Bailey (ed), *Cross on Local Government Law* (London, Sweet & Maxwell, 2025) 1-79F.

[4] Scottish Government, 'Fairer Scotland Duty: Guidance for Public Bodies' (19 August 2022): www.gov.scot/publications/fairer-scotland-duty-guidance-public-bodies; Equality Act 2010 (Commencement No 13) (Scotland) Order 2017; Equality Act 2010 (Commencement No 15) (Wales) Order 2021.

[5] Labour Party, *Change: Labour Party Manifesto 2024* (2024) 88.

[6] See, eg, the US Supreme Court drawing such considerations into the law in that jurisdiction, *Grutter v Bollinger* 539 US 306 (2003) 332.

[7] See my arguments in Chapters 3 and 4 of this book.

[8] IDS Employment Law Handbooks, vol 5, ch 41, 41.1.

[9] Explanatory Notes to the Equality Act 2010, para 23.

[10] Explanatory Notes (n 9), para 23.

was drafted and how it could function in relation to different types of public bodies, but the guidance has since been withdrawn.[11] It seems to have suggested that such disadvantage related to, for example, 'getting on, getting education, getting a job' as a result of 'one or more of a range of external factors'. Those factors included poverty as the most prominent among a combination of others, including health, housing, education and familial background.[12] There seems to have been an effort to collect indicators of class and use legislation to address them when public authorities make certain decisions.

Even with its boundaries, section 1 offers one tool to combat classism in its more structural senses. Properly understood, section 1 focuses on what public authorities can do to reduce the disadvantage that lower-class people suffer. The Equality and Human Rights Commission's evaluation of the duty in Scotland and Wales found that (with clear criteria) the duty helped public bodies to set 'priority areas'.[13] Those areas included lowering poverty (such as low pay), area- and community-based disadvantage, gaps between rich and poor people, boosting educational attainment, and improving health. Although not themselves authoritative, the Explanatory Notes bolster this interpretation of section 1. They give examples of providing primary care services to ensure 'people suffering socio-economic disadvantage' can access them outside typical working hours, encouraging business development and jobs in 'deprived areas', and additional work in 'more deprived . . . neighbourhoods' to improve children's chances of securing a place at a school of their choice.[14] This is consistent with studies of public bodies that have voluntarily adopted the duty. Megan Isaac and Anna Lopez describe, for instance, how Hackney Council recognised the impact of the Covid-19 pandemic on the most disadvantaged people, directly referring around 500 households to its Community Partnerships Network for funding for food and other essentials.[15] At least for local authorities like these, the watery language of section 1 has not prevented them from making practical changes. Its strength is not found in the vapours of its words. Instead, the section's importance is that it emphasises considerations of class and poverty: it indicates to public authorities that these considerations must not be ignored and that they should foster an approach that puts class disadvantage and poverty at the centre.

There is also a compelling argument that, once brought into force, the duty could then be expanded. For example, the Equality Trust has called for a number of increases in the scope and rigour of the duty. The increases would include widening the public bodies subject to the duty, moving the focus to delivering outcomes (rather than merely opportunities in the abstract), effective enforcement

[11] IDS Employment Law Handbooks (n 8) 41.3.

[12] IDS Employment Law Handbooks (n 8) 41.3.

[13] E Wilson Smith, D Garcia Rodriguez and J Brawner, *Evaluating the Socio-Economic Duty in Scotland and Wales* (EHRC, March 2021) 27, 43, 53.

[14] Explanatory Notes (n 9), para 27.

[15] M Isaac and A Lopez, 'The Socio-Economic Duty in Action: Case Studies from England and Wales' (Just Fair, 2023).

and broader investment to ensure that the duty makes a difference.[16] However, as attractive as the proposals for expansion may be, first we need to have a statutory provision in effect. Bringing into force section 1 in England remains the obvious first step to begin to combat classism, especially in its more structural senses.

1.2. Protection via Existing Protected Grounds

Another way to use the current law lies in the list of protected characteristics in section 4 of the Equality Act. While I have rejected the argument that we can *adequately* protect class through the existing characteristics alone, we should not wholly dismiss their potential.

Courts could guard vigorously the existing characteristics, so that the lives of lower-class people who have protected characteristics are considered and given priority in legal decisions. Some of the decisions of the UK Supreme Court that I considered in Chapter 7 touch on this potential. In *SG and Others v Secretary of State for Work and Pensions* (2015), for example, the Supreme Court relied on the characteristic of 'sex' to address discrimination against women.[17] The Supreme Court was content to give 'due weight' to Parliament due to the contentious issues of social and economic policy involved.[18] Yet, if the Supreme Court were to realise more rigorously the legal mandate of the Equality Act (alongside, for instance, my suggested administrative law principle of equality between classes), it could ensure that policies like this fall foul of the legislation. Rather than cast these issues as 'economic and social policy' beyond the parameters of the statute, the courts should be more protective of the characteristics that already exist. For instance, in a case like *SG*, the poorest women should be given priority in the analysis because this is partly why they suffer the worst kinds of misogyny. While such an approach would be imperfect in prohibiting classism for the reasons I have already explained, it would offer at least some protection for certain lower-class people. The point takes us back to *Alyne da Silva Pimentel Teixeira v Brazil* (2011).[19] Although the CEDAW Committee did not expressly conceive her treatment in terms of classism, it nonetheless arrived at the right outcome by stressing the vulnerability of women of 'lower socio-economic backgrounds'.[20]

It will not always be the case that the existing protected characteristics align with the interests of lower-class people. There may sometimes be tension, as

[16] Equality Trust, 'Socio-Economic Duty Briefing' (26 June 2025): www.equalitytrust.org.uk/socio-economic-duty-briefing.

[17] *SG and Others v Secretary of State for Work and Pensions* [2015] UKSC 16. See also, for a more recent example of the same deference to 'the social and economic sphere' and 'policy choices', *R (Jwanczuk) v Secretary of State for Work and Pensions* [2025] UKSC 42, [138].

[18] *SG* (n 17) [93].

[19] *Alyne da Silva Pimentel Teixeira v Brazil* (2011) CEDAW/C/49/D/17/2008.

[20] *Teixeira* (n 19) [5.5].

we find between queer people and those expressing certain religious beliefs, for example.[21] However, on the whole, recognising how much poverty connects with gender, race and disability (for instance) will show why classist treatment and decision-making are also likely to be discriminatory in relation to existing characteristics. Recognition of this within a more intensive protection of the existing protected characteristics should be, therefore, a priority in the current law.

1.3. Prosecuting Wage Fraud by Employers

A. *Theft or Fraud?*

The existing criminal law also offers some tools to address classism. In *Criminality at Work* by Alan Bogg and others, Sarah Green analyses the idea of wage theft in the context of the current criminal law.[22] Noting that the phrase 'wage theft' has been applied to various 'unscrupulous' employer practices, Green identifies its core meaning as the deprivation of 'what is lawfully due . . . as remuneration for [workers'] labour'.[23] However, Green suggests that the current law of theft poses problems for prosecuting such a crime.[24] There are, for instance, complications surrounding ownership and possession when it comes to wages, given that the employer usually holds the funds and they have not yet been released to the employee. Although the employee may have an interest in them (under a contract of employment, for example, or via a claim for damages), there are challenges when arguing that the wages *belong* to the employee.[25] Related to this problem, while the employee may be entitled to the funds in a sense, there has been no valid transfer in the sense of the civil law. As a result, it is difficult to conclude that the situation involves an employee's loss of their own property.[26]

Green's points are persuasive here. The structure of property-related duties in law and the legal concept of ownership are rooted in a narrow understanding money and objects. Without a wholesale restructuring of the legal framework (and, likely, the ideas behind it), it is hard to argue that theft occurs in these contexts. To do so would require a significant movement towards Marxist understandings of property and theft, for example, which criticise the law's tendency to defend only 'private property rights' limited to 'power distribution among people in power'.[27]

[21] See, eg, *Lee v Ashers Baking Co Ltd* [2018] UKSC 49.

[22] S Green, 'Wage Theft as a Legal Concept' in A Bogg and others (eds), *Criminality at Work* (Oxford, Oxford University Press, 2020) 134–50.

[23] Green (n 22) 134.

[24] Green (n 22) 134.

[25] Green (n 22) 136, 138.

[26] Green (n 22) 136–137.

[27] See, eg, Z Wenxi, *Property and Justice: A Trend Towards Marxist Political Philosophy* (Abingdon, Routledge, 2023) 203–04.

Instead, Green finds more hope in the offence of fraud, contrary to section 1 of the Fraud Act 2006. The principal benefit of such an offence is that it does not entangle the prosecution in complex questions about ownership, property and transfer. Green focuses on the version found in section 4 of the Fraud Act: fraud by abuse of position, noting the Law Commission's reference in its report to 'employee and employer' as an illustration of the kind of relational position in section 4. Green suggests that the advantages of the concept of 'wage fraud' (via the Fraud Act) include its 'inchoate nature' (as no loss actually needs to be proven), the broad meaning of 'gain and loss' in section 5, and the express inclusion of omissions as well as acts in section 4(2).[28] For these reasons, the existing criminal law offers a tool by which to target employers who withhold wages or underpay their employees.

B. *In Practice*

To put Green's argument into practice, consider how we might prosecute such crimes. It seems unlikely that the Crown Prosecution Service (CPS) would start prosecuting such cases, given that it would represent a novel reading of the law and one likely to be controversial. However, there is another avenue that exists in the law to prohibit wage fraud: private prosecutions.

In simple terms, a private prosecutor (ie not an agent or body of the state) acts for itself or another. The phrase excludes the police and other prosecuting authorities. Section 6(1) of the Prosecution of Offences Act 1985 provides that nothing in the Act 'shall preclude any person from instituting any criminal proceedings or conducting any criminal proceedings to which the Director's duty to take over the conduct of proceedings does not apply'. The reference here is to the Director of Public Prosecutions (DPP), the head of the CPS.

While the CPS comes first to mind when discussing prosecutions, private prosecutions have a long history in England and Wales. Contrary to many people's perceptions, research suggests that most prosecutions brought in the last eight hundred years have been private.[29] This has of course changed in recent decades, given the increased prominence of the CPS as the main prosecuting authority. There is no requirement that private prosecutors be members of a particular professional association, for example, or regulator. This has been one of the sources of significant concern in the ongoing Post Office scandal in relation to the use of the Horizon system in the prosecutions of sub-postmasters. There is, however, the Private Prosecutors' Association (PPA), which attempts to provide guidance in its Code for Private Prosecutors.[30] The PPA defines a 'private prosecution' as 'prosecutions instituted and conducted other than by the state'.[31]

[28] Green (n 22) 147.
[29] *Glanville Williams and Dennis Baker Treatise of Criminal Law* (2021) 2.61.
[30] At the time of writing this chapter, the extant version dates from 2019.
[31] *PPA Code for Private Prosecutors* (2021) 1.1.5.

Of note here is the PPA's suggestion that 'the criminal justice system must not be used solely or primarily to achieve a purpose for which it is not designed'.[32]

On one view, this last suggestion would include actions that deploy the criminal law to make 'purely political' statements about classism. On another view, given the language of the Fraud Act, Parliament clearly intended to use the criminal law to punish fraudulent conduct in a very wide sense. Dishonestly depriving workers of pay for their labour falls within this sense. Although there may be some practical risk of the CPS taking over such a prosecution and discontinuing it, there are strong arguments in favour of the public interest.[33] The CPS, exercising the DPP's powers, may continue or discontinue (or otherwise stop) the prosecution. The CPS's 'Full Code' test is applied: (a) whether or not there is a realistic prospect of conviction; and (b) whether or not it is in the public interest to pursue proceedings. There is a further step: that there is 'a particular need for the CPS to take over the prosecution'.[34] The CPS's policy is that, unless there is a request specifically to take over conduct, it will usually intervene only if there are exceptional circumstances justifying such a course of action. While orchestrating refusals to pay workers or arrangements to underpay workers for their labour is plainly exploitative conduct, such circumstances are unlikely to meet the criterion of 'exceptional' to justify the CPS's intervention. Therefore, private prosecution poses the most realistic option for putting prosecutions of wage fraud into practice.

1.4. Prosecuting Employers Who Frustrate Industrial Action

Not only could the mechanism of private prosecution address wage theft and fraud, it could also extend to other violations of workers' rights by employers. As this would likely occur in cases involving low-paid workers, often in the context of trade union disputes, it closely connects with the issue of classism and the structural aspects of lower-class people in work.

In general, the criminal law has a limited role when it comes to industrial action.[35] A notable exception is the Conduct of Employment Agencies and Employment Businesses Regulations 2003, which were made pursuant to sections 5(1), 6(1) and 12(3) of the Employment Agencies Act 1973 (EAA 1973). Regulation 7 prohibits employment businesses from introducing or supplying a work-seeker to a hirer to perform (a) 'the duties normally performed by a worker who is taking part in a strike or other industrial action'; or (b) 'the duties normally performed by any other worker employed by the hirer and who

[32] *PPA Code* (n 31) 2.2.2.

[33] Prosecution of Offences Act 1985, s 6(2).

[34] Crown Prosecution Service, 'Private Prosecutions' (1 November 2025): www.cps.gov.uk/prosecution-guidance/private-prosecutions. The CPS may also take over conduct of a prosecution to stop it if it is considered vexatious: Senior Courts Act 1981, s 42.

[35] But see, eg, Trade Union and Labour Relations (Consolidation) Act 1992, ss 240–241.

is assigned by the hirer to perform the duties normally performed by the first worker'.[36] This prohibition applies unless, in either situation, 'the employment business does not know, and has no reasonable grounds for knowing, that the first worker is taking part in a strike or other industrial action'. Section 5(2) of the EAA 1973 provides that any person who contravenes or fails to comply with any of the regulations shall be guilty of an offence (the maximum penalty being a fine).

However, note that it would be the *agency* who is the principal offender here: the agency's breach of the regulation attracts criminal liability. That said, a further avenue exists in the criminal law already, which would be open to trade unions here: accessory liability, which has two stages. First, a person or (where appropriate) body must do an act that encourages or assists the principal in the commission of the offence.[37] Second, the person or body must do the act intentionally, with the intent to encourage or assist the principal to act with whatever mental element is required by the offence (eg, in the context of murder, this is the intention to kill or cause really serious harm), knowing the facts necessary to make the conduct criminal.[38] Accessory liability applies to all criminal offences, unless the statute expressly (or by necessary implication) excludes it.[39]

In a simple example to which regulation 7 would apply, accessory liability would work as follows:

(1) The act of encouragement or assistance: the employer asks the agency to provide workers to replace workers on strike.
(2) Intentional act: as is obvious, the employer's act is intentional.
(3) Intention that the principal has the relevant mental element: the employer has informed the agency of the strike and, therefore, intends the agency to act in the knowledge that the agency workers would be provided to replace the striking employees.

The elements of accessory liability are, therefore, met and the employer is liable for the breach, rather than solely the principal. Granted, there would be complexity in proving corporate liability in cases where only a manager or lower-level official had direct knowledge. However, accessory liability offers the potential to turn the criminal law on employers who undermine workers' industrial action.

As I have discussed in relation to wage fraud, the CPS could be more rigorous in prosecuting employment businesses for breach of the regulation concerning interference with industrial action. The route of accessory liability could allow for the prosecution of the employer working with the agency in order to undercut its employees' industrial action and, accordingly, their negotiating power.

[36] Conduct of Employment Agencies and Employment Businesses Regulations 2003, reg 7.
[37] *Jogee* [2016] UKSC 8, [9].
[38] *Jogee* (n 37) [9] and [16]; *Pop* [2026] EWCA Crim 774, [36].
[39] Accessories and Abettors Act 1861, s 8.

But such efforts could still encounter institutional problems within the CPS and its unwillingness to prosecute such breaches, especially when governments are hostile to trade unions. In those circumstances, it would be open to trade unions to use the current law to address this problem. The avenue of private prosecution persists. This could be done by an 'in house' set of investigators or lawyers, though it would need careful adherence to the requirements of independence, lawful disclosure and fair investigation. It could also be done by working with an investigative organisation or solicitors' firm. Such organisations or firms may be more likely to have the resources and expertise in the law of disclosure to ensure that such investigations are conducted thoroughly and fairly.

Clearly, prosecuting employers who frustrate industrial action is a niche area of the current law. My analysis so far has addressed other issues about the existing criminal law and justice system and what negative effects further prosecutorial initiatives could have. That said, when exploring areas of potential change, steps like this which seem small could still have a big practical impact. By taking this approach, the trade union movement could take up a tool in the law that has never been used in this way. Innovations and symbolic steps of this kind, in turn, would help to press class issues of fair wages and robust industrial protections into legal frameworks in which they have not been recognised to date.

1.5. Changing Prosecutions of Lower-Class People in Certain Contexts

Before turning to what might be removed from the current law to address classism, I consider a third aspect of the criminal law that we might use. I have explored a handful of ways to prosecute more classist wrongdoing. When it comes to using the current law's existing framework to target classism, however, the inverse may also help. We may need to prosecute less.

To expand on this statement, take the example of shoplifting. In my discussion of hate crime laws in Chapter 6, I noted the strong association between the criminal law and the policing of lower-class people, both now and in the past. However, we should not restrict our analysis to the abolition of certain crimes. We should also consider *how* we decide to prosecute those crimes that justifiably exist in the law.

It is common to see magistrates' courts filled with prosecutions for shoplifting. By its nature, shoplifting tends to be low-level. It is usually treated as an offence to be tried summarily, meaning that it may only be tried in a magistrates' court.[40] If the property allegedly stolen is high in value (or if the defendant elects), it may be tried by judge and jury in the Crown Court. Alongside the broader arguments made by Marxists and others about the unjust system of private property that the law protects (including

[40] Magistrates' Courts Act 1980, s 22A.

by criminalising shoplifting), there are also more instinctive or moral reactions. You could suggest, for example, that the prohibition on theft reflects the importance of property as a condition of our autonomy, at least while we have societies that use ideas of private property. Yet you could also say that a system of private property is merely a political choice and one that is unjust.[41] You might not want to delve into these more philosophical issues but accept that there is a moral difference between a poor person who takes a loaf of bread from a large supermarket and a rich person who does so. You could also distinguish between stealing from a large supermarket and stealing from a small, family-run shop.

At present, the law does not tend to recognise moral differences like these.[42] It has the tools to do so, however. One challenging option would be to create defences of hunger, duress by poverty and economic compulsion. A more straightforward option is prosecutorial guidance.[43] Such guidance is a useful mechanism because it does not have to be written at the same universal level as a statute or concerned with fact-specific anomalies like the common law. It can be fact-sensitive while being general in pointing prosecutors in the right directions.

Prosecutions for theft and fraud, and similar property-related offences, should be addressed with greater humanity – and, in this context, that means not using prosecution as a tool to make classism worse by punishing lower-class people for these kinds of wrongs. The guidance should instruct prosecutors to consider, so far as they can gather relevant information: (i) the relative means of the people, businesses or organisations involved; (ii) the extent of the goods taken; and (iii) the circumstances of the person who is suspected to have taken the goods.

Addressing (i), this criterion would differentiate the nature of the effect of loss of goods on someone who owns a small, family-run shop from the chief executive of a large chain of supermarkets. Prosecutors might argue that these considerations would be unnecessary. There is already the 'public interest' stage of the test that prosecutors in the CPS must apply. While that is correct in principle, the CPS concedes the usefulness and importance of topic-specific guidance by issuing it in other areas of the law.[44] One advantage of topic-specific guidance is that it focuses the mind of prosecutors. Rather than applying generic notions of 'public interest', it requires prosecutors to apply special criteria tailored to the topic, which would in this instance be the issue of property-related allegations. In turn, it would be more difficult to justify the continuation of a prosecution

[41] As Marx does: Wenxi (n 27).

[42] See generally N Lacey, 'Responsibility and Modernity in Criminal Law' (2001) 9 *Journal of Political Philosophy* 249.

[43] Another option, which is not about using what we have in the law's doctrine at present nor about abolishing parts of that doctrine, might be to develop the existing, but very limited, defence of necessity (or, as it is sometimes known, duress of circumstance) to such conduct.

[44] See, eg, Crown Prosecution Service, 'Disclosure Manual' (14 July 2022): www.cps.gov.uk/prosecution-guidance/disclosure-manual.

against a very poor person who has stolen low-value goods, as it would likely be apparent to the court and the defence that the criteria have not been properly applied in such a case.

To this proposal, one objection would likely rest on deterrence. If the guidance were developed and applied as I suggest, wouldn't it encourage shoplifting sprees? If those who often shoplift knew that their means and the low value of goods were relevant considerations, for example, they might proceed on the basis that they would not be prosecuted. This would then be very difficult in practice for shopworkers and, eventually, for the overall profits of the organisations themselves. In response to this objection, it is worth making two points. First, theories of punishment based on deterrence (whether general or individual) remain widely criticised, especially by scholars who study the effect of punishment on reoffending.[45] The application of those criticisms to some examples of shoplifting is straightforward: people desperate enough to take bread from a shop may be less likely to be concerned about a conviction on a record or a short term of imprisonment than someone who may have stable housing and ample money. Second, even if deterrence is effective, it is unpersuasive when considering what crime and punishment should reflect about society.[46] Assuming deterrence actually works, why do we want to subject a poor person who takes bread from a shelf to a criminal conviction and the subsequent fine, community penalty or time in prison? Is that further exclusion and destabilisation a justifiable way to treat someone who has taken the bread, even putting aside the exclusion and further destabilisation the system has on their lives once the punishment is over?

I suggest that the answer to the first question is that it is more convenient for people in power to deploy the usual model of criminality rather than to address the underlying causes. I suggest that the answer to the second question is negative. Using a harsh prosecutorial model in this area, as opposed to specifically written guidance, has been a serious error. Using the criminal law to address classism should involve asking questions like this. The answers must pay attention to what would actually better the position of lower-class people and not contribute to a cycle of policing, charge, punishment and instability.

2. ASPECTS TO REMOVE

Those are some illustrations – in the context of the Equality Act and the criminal law – of how we might use existing aspects of the law to address issues for

[45] See, eg, the criticism of a range of general and specific deterrence theories (though resolving the issues in favour of a rights-protection theory that results in effective deterrence) in H Lee, 'Consequentialist Theories of Punishment' in MC Altman (ed), *The Palgrave Handbook on the Philosophy of Punishment* (Basingstoke, Palgrave Macmillan, 2023) 149.

[46] See, eg, H Carvalho and A Chamberlen, 'Why Punishment Pleases: Punitive Feelings in a World of Hostile Solidarity' (2017) 20(2) *Punishment & Society* 217.

lower-class people and, in turn, attack classism. I now turn to explore some features that we might remove from the current law.

2.1. Class Rights: Aristocratic Peerages and Honours

I have addressed the potential for the abolition of certain crimes. There is a corresponding, and potentially more radical, argument that concerns the abolition of certain rights.

Abolishing rights? A sentence of that kind might sound alarming. But it depends which rights we mean. The selection of rights is a process that reflects much about a society. For example, in the Charter of Fundamental Rights of the European Union, Article 16 protects the 'freedom to conduct a business'.[47] Some might consider the freedom to do business a good or interesting aspect of life; some might accept that, yes, it can be important, but it is hardly something that we should include in a definitive legal document containing 'fundamental' rights and freedoms. The inclusion of that right in such a document reflects the social, cultural, economic and political aims and functions of the EU. It reveals a lot about the EU as an institution and an international framework.[48]

When it comes to the UK, there is an unusually entrenched system of class rights. I use this phrase to refer to the set of legal entitlements that favour upper-class people in England and Wales. In particular, peerages, aristocratic honours, monarchical prerogative, hierarchies of landowning and fierce protection of wealth have long been features distinctive to the national legal system.[49] These rights cross many of the doctrinal boundaries of the legal system, affecting ownership and inheritance of property, political status and judicial ranks (both in their customs and their composition). Given the continued pervasiveness of this system, it could easily overwhelm this chapter. Others have dealt comprehensively with the history of changes to the feudal law of real property in the medieval and early modern period and the supremacy given to a so-called 'right to property', for instance.[50] To illustrate the general theme, I limit my discussion to a small but well-known aspect of class rights: aristocratic peerages and associated honours.

To get a sense of how the UK ended up with a maze of peerages and associated honours, it is necessary to sketch the history. Based on the archaeological

[47] CFREU, Art 16.

[48] See generally, for broader criticism of the neo-liberalism apparent in EU funding of civil society, H Muehlenhoff, *EU Democracy Promotion and Governmentality* (Abingdon, Routledge, 2019).

[49] To avoid overloading this chapter and to keep clarity of focus, I leave aside other class issues, like the English system of 'public schools', though they are also an illustration of such entrenched classism. On the classist nature of monarchy in general, see A Benn, 'Besting Monarchy: The Anti-Classism Argument' (2023) 94(3) *Political Quarterly* 393.

[50] See, eg, ME Tigar and MR Levy, *Law and the Rise of Capitalism* (New York, Monthly Review Press, 2000) 174–75.

evidence, it appears that a hierarchy with an advantaged class ('*thegns*') existed in Anglo-Saxon society.[51] After centuries of development, a significant change came after the Norman Conquest of 1066. Having succeeded in his invasion, William the Conqueror ensured his power by transferring property (and, with it, greater power) to those loyal to him.[52] The main distinction became that between (i) barons (some also being known as earls) and (ii) knights. Barons held their property 'per baronium', one aspect of which seems to have been the duty to provide military support to the monarch when required. They had other rights and duties distinguishing them from those lower in the hierarchy, including a place at the king's council and an ability to hold their own courts. They also appear to have had some exemptions, including restrictions on who could decide what financial penalties might be imposed on them. Knights held their property by virtue of their corresponding duty of military service. Later, duchies were created, the first being the Duchy of Cornwall in 1337.[53] Nearly seven hundred years later, the Duchy of Cornwall still covers more than 128,000 acres across 20 counties in England and Wales.[54]

In fourteenth-century England, it seems that a key privilege was a hereditary entitlement to a writ of summons to Parliament by the monarch.[55] Along with it, status at birth, inherited land and rank, and military place were 'probably the most important determinants of status'.[56] Chris Given-Wilson offers the further observation that the most advantaged group's 'bundle of rights and . . . series of connections' were not 'immutable' but rather changed hands with frequency.[57] Together with the elaboration of the feudal system, privileges attached to land (and, in turn, concentrated power in the monarch who was able to grant 'fiefs') or, where land was not available, they attached to services.[58]

By various developments, peers – as they became known – formed an upper house, distinguished from the lower house by the principle of primogeniture.[59] The requirement of the consent of both Houses of Parliament for a bill to become law was recognised in the time of Henry VII; the notion of the 'House of Lords' came into use in the time of his son, Henry VIII.[60] With many others, a significant change came during the English Revolution. In 1648, under

[51] See, eg, R Rodrigues da Silva, *The Anglo-Saxon Elite: Northumbrian Society in the Long Eighth Century* (Amsterdam, Amsterdam University Press, 2021) 24–50; K Ulmschneider, 'Settlement Hierarchy' in D Hinton (ed), *The Oxford Handbook of Anglo-Saxon Archaeology* (Oxford, Oxford University Press, 2011) 156.

[52] C Given-Wilson, *The English Nobility in the Late Middle Ages* (Abingdon, Routledge, 1996) 20–22.

[53] *Black's Guide to Duchy of Cornwall* (Edinburgh, Adam and Charles Black, 1889) xi.

[54] See generally Duchy of Cornwall, 'About the Duchy': www.duchyofcornwall.org/page/about-us.

[55] C Ballinger, *The House of Lords 1911-2011: A Century of Non-Reform* (London, Bloomsbury, 2014) 19–21.

[56] Given-Wilson (n 52) 8–9.

[57] Given-Wilson (n 52) 1.

[58] J Lawrence, *On the Nobility of the British Gentry* (London, James Fraser, 1840) 7.

[59] Ballinger (n 55) 15–18; Given-Wilson (n 52) 15–16.

[60] Ballinger (n 55) 18–19.

the influence of Oliver Cromwell, the House of Commons passed an Act of Parliament abolishing the House of Lords. Yet the House of Lords was shortly re-established, only then to be dissolved alongside the Commons by Cromwell. The number of peers expanded hugely in the years of the Stuart and early Hanover monarchs. It became a source of tension whenever the issue entered the centre of political debate, though legislation was never passed to limit the creation of peerages.[61] Of special importance to the topic of class rights, even the membership of the House of Commons was significantly influenced by those in the House of Lords (despite the passing of the Reform Act 1832).

The relationship between classism and the law should not omit the place of senior lawyers in the development of what became the House of Lords. It appears that senior legal officials were summoned by writ by the monarch alongside the lay and spiritual peers. While lawyers then appear to have faded away, Chris Ballinger suggests that the House of Lords required such expertise in its judicial capacity by the middle of the eighteenth century.[62] Later, the Parliament Act 1911 abolished the veto of the House of Lords over Acts of Parliament in most contexts. Much later, in the 1990s, the New Labour government began some notable reforms to the House of Lords. The House of Lords Act 1999, for example, had the effect of stopping hereditary peers sitting automatically in the House of Lords. However, it still permitted a considerable number of hereditary peers. This continued until the abolition of the remainder in 2026.[63]

It is not only the composition of the Houses of Parliament that this broader system of class rights characterises. There is also the particular case of the judiciary of England and Wales. I deal with the issue of *who* makes up the judiciary in Chapter 10. Here, I focus on the customs of the judiciary. Following the Wensleydale case in the 1850s about the ability of the Crown to create judges effectively as life peers, there was some delay until the Appellate Jurisdiction Acts of 1876 and 1887. As a result of those pieces of legislation, the 'Law Lords' came into being. They obtained the rank of baron and could sit and vote in the House of Lords for life. The Constitutional Reform Act 2005 created the Supreme Court, moving the 'Law Lords' from the House of Lords. However, though there were various amendments made to substitute 'Justice of the Supreme Court' for 'Lord of Appeal in Ordinary', nothing today prevents the ongoing custom of aristocratic honours to be given to the senior judges. The smooth transition for those judges sitting in the House of Lords was ensured by a variety of provisions in the Constitutional Reform Act, including section 60(2)'s definition of 'high judicial office', which includes 'a Lord of Appeal in Ordinary'. Judges of the High Court and above (and some other judges, such as resident judges at some Crown Court centres) are still addressed as 'my Lady' or 'my Lord'.[64] The symbolic and

[61] Ballinger (n 55) 19–20.

[62] Ballinger (n 55) 21–23.

[63] House of Lords (Hereditary Peers) Act 2026.

[64] There is, at the time of writing this book, no example beyond this binary. Hopefully, that will change.

historical connection between the aristocracy and the law imbues the customs and the language of courtrooms today. The oath of allegiance to the monarch is yet another mark of a historically classist system.

From this sketch, it is easy to gain a sense of the strength of the law's connection with peerages and associated honours, both in governance and the judiciary. Plainly, there are many other instances of class rights, including property directly attributed to a monarch's gift or hereditary title. There is much to consider. But, at the least, the abolition of these class rights would require the enactment of statute to remove:

(a) all forms of peerage, including hereditary peerages; and
(b) all titles or honorifics relating to an aristocratic system across all contexts, including in courtrooms and in the legal system.

2.2. Class Crimes: Repeal of the Vagrancy Act 1824

In addition to firmly settled class rights, the law of England and Wales furthers classism through 'class crimes'. This is related to the issue of prosecutorial guidance that I have considered, but it focuses on the content of the crimes we have. To accept this, we should first take a step back and think about the process of criminalisation. It rests on the idea of criminality. People give meaning to this idea rather than it being the product of some self-evident, universally accepted and naturally occurring truths.[65]

With classism in mind, there are many crimes that exemplify the disadvantage that lower-class people experience. The criminalisation of certain drugs and of activities connected with sex work and homelessness are just some examples of this problem.[66] A marked instance of this problem is the Vagrancy Act 1824 (repealed in the later stages of the writing of this book). Section 3 provides for the punishment of 'every petty chapman or pedlar wandering abroad, and trading without being duly licensed, or otherwise authori[s]ed by law', 'every common prostitute wandering' in public and behaving 'in a riotous or indecent manner' and 'every person wandering abroad, or placing himself or herself in any public place, street, highway, court, or passage, to beg or gather alms, or causing or procuring or encouraging any child or children so to do so'. Section 4 adds that such people are 'convicted as an idle and disorderly person' and continues a succession of winding clauses about various categories of 'rogue and vagabond'.

These words, of course, leap from centuries past. Indeed, in 2022, the UK Parliament passed the Police, Crime, Sentencing and Courts Act. Section 81(1)

[65] A Sanders, R Young and M Burton, *Criminal Justice* (Oxford, Oxford University Press, 2010) 1–13.

[66] See, for an example of recommendations on decriminalisation in the US context, C Cunneen, *Defund the Police* (Bristol, Policy Press, 2023) 173.

makes provision to repeal the Vagrancy Act. For years, that section remained prospective. It was at last implemented in 2026. It was not the case that we saw prosecutions under the sections every day in England and Wales. But the risk was not solely theoretical, even in recent years. According to figures that the Metropolitan Police disclosed in 2023, there were nearly 480 charges under sections 3 and 4 of the Vagrancy Act in 2014, reducing to 11 in 2023. However, the figures did not include those who may have been arrested and then de-arrested.[67] There was an ongoing practical effect. In 2014, section 4 was used to prosecute a number of people who took food that had been put in skips and bins outside a supermarket in Kentish Town in London, though the CPS – after public pressure, including from the supermarket itself – decided to discontinue the case.

As I have argued in relation to class and the Equality Act, there is more to the law than the practice. The fact that the Vagrancy Act remained in force for so long meant that it was not just a historical object of wonder. The lingering of the Act meant that, for nearly two centuries, it was a crime to beg for money in public. The Act's legacy of formal and symbolic degradation will take years to subside. Although commendable, the removal of this piece of the law in 2026 took far too long. While the removal at least shows that Parliament can take decisive action in the form of repealing statutes that criminalise lower-class people, such action must be quicker next time.

2.3. Policing

Last, I turn to the broader issue of enforcement, with a special focus on the criminal law and policing. Much has been written about the injustices of the law's mechanisms of enforcement, especially the current systems of policing and imprisonment that exist in countries across the world.[68] When focusing on policing, London's Metropolitan Police have become a notorious centre of the problems. In spite of many years of supposed reforms and improvements, the Casey Review in 2023 found that widespread discrimination continued alongside serious dysfunction.[69] It is perhaps no surprise that calls to the effect that policing does not work have grown louder in recent years. Although there are aspects of the Metropolitan Police that other police forces in the UK (and indeed those in other countries) do not necessarily share, it is difficult to deny that policing continues to have fundamental cultural problems.

[67] Metropolitan Police, 'Arrests, Prosecutions and Convictions under the Vagrancy Act 1824 from 2014 to 2023': www.met.police.uk/foi-ai/metropolitan-police/disclosure-2024/april-2024/arrests-prosecutions-convictions-vagrancy-act1824-2014-2023.

[68] See, eg, AS Vitale, *The End of Policing* (London, Verso, 2018).

[69] L Casey, *An Independent Review into the Standards of Behaviour and Internal Culture of the Metropolitan Police Service: Final Report* (March 2023) 9.2.

Thinking about classism, the issue of the culture of policing connects with the questions of what policing is *designed* to achieve and what it *does* achieve. With the origins of policing in Britain found in a disparate collection of 'constables' claiming expenses and fees, it became an institutionalised and waged workforce in the nineteenth century.[70] As Trevor Jones, Tim Newburn and Robert Reiner argue, especially in the transformation from communal monitoring to state-centred mechanisms, policing is often an exercise in 'class control'.[71] Upper-class people – with prestigious formal education, high incomes and private property in affluent areas – can remain distant from the police in ways many lower-class people cannot. The result is that lower-class people are 'over-policed and under-protected', especially those who are black and brown.[72] So long as there is policing in this way, the enforcement of the criminal law in particular – whatever its content – is likely to cause its own harms to lower-class people.

Similar debates surround imprisonment.[73] If you accept these arguments, you are probably now asking what the solutions are. On the topic of policing, critics approach this question as if removing the police requires 'violent anarchy', with no highly trained professionals offering protection from harm.[74] Responding to such critics, proponents of the abolition movement like Ruth Wilson Gilmore emphasise that the focus of the movement is on what we can *add* to society instead of policing.[75] For example, community-led approaches might better ensure treatment of those accused of crimes and other misconduct in a way that maintains dignity and fairness. In addition to that, abolitionists stress the divestment of resources, moving away from funding policing, imprisonment and related systems and going towards funding care, education and work in disadvantaged communities. Chris Cunneen sets out a number of practical recommendations. They range from education about the harms of policing to the replacement of police officers in contexts like public transport and schools, as well as targeted decriminalisation and other strategies to address gendered violence.[76] To this end, Cunneen identifies several propositions, two of which lawyers would do especially well to keep in mind when thinking about what to remove to address the role of policing in the furthering of classism. First, the key point is 'presence, not absence': defunding is not about the stripping away of society but the enriching and bettering of it. Second, there is a need 'to find ways of doing things that do not involve the police' and these are found in areas like community-based organisations, social welfare, education

[70] C Williams, *Police Control Systems in Britain, 1775–1975* (Manchester, Manchester University Press, 2014) 24–25.

[71] T Jones, T Newburn and R Reiner, 'Policing and the Police' in A Liebling, S Maruna and L McAra (eds), *The Oxford Handbook of Criminology* (Oxford, Oxford University Press, 2017) 769–70.

[72] Jones, Newburn and Reiner (n 71) 769–772.

[73] See, eg, AY Davis, *Are Prisons Obsolete?* (New York, Seven Stories Press, 2003).

[74] Cunneen (n 66) 43–45.

[75] Cunneen (n 66) 168.

[76] Cunneen (n 66) 171–74, 178–80.

and health.[77] Removing features of the law to address classism will include not only technicalities of doctrinal reform (such as repeal of legislation) but also these more systemic questions of how we police people, if we even should, and how to enforce the law in a way that does not in itself harm lower-class people.

3. FURTHER CHANGES

At its heart, this chapter has set out a list of issues of classism within the current law. The discussion so far indicates that it will not be enough to introduce new grounds and principles and leave the topic there.

My emphasis has been on areas I know best, such as the Equality Act and the criminal justice system. My purpose in switching between examples has been to push beyond my earlier focus on issues like introducing a single 'protected characteristic' or principle of review in a recognised 'area' of the law. A more holistic approach encourages us to think about how much of the law – *as it is* – fosters classism. I have given some examples of actions we might take:

(a) prosecuting employers who commit wage fraud;
(b) prosecuting employers and employment businesses who frustrate industrial action;
(c) changing prosecutions of lower-class people in some areas, such as shoplifting;
(d) removing 'class rights', such as peerages and other aristocratic honours;
(e) repealing 'class crimes', as with the Vagrancy Act 1824; and
(f) de-emphasising the police in favour of other ways to address problems in societies.

Many other issues deserve consideration, such as the system of private property, imprisonment and contract law.[78] Whatever those other issues may be, one message is clear. Lawyers should adapt what the law already has and, more significantly, remove features of it that hinder us.

—

Bringing Part II to an end, I have now analysed the law's doctrine in some detail. At points, my discussion has been technical. At others, it has gestured towards deeper issues without delving into all the detail, partly in the hope that illustrating these points might prompt further study in the area.

In Part III, my goal will be to take a step back and look across the law. I will consider the law as an instrument of change and, sometimes, of great harm. Even with all these doctrinal additions, developments and removals, what if the law will *never* be the right way to tackle classism?

[77] Cunneen (n 66) 168–69.
[78] See, eg, concerning contract law, Tigar and Levy (n 50) 186.

Part III

9

More Harm than Good?

WHETHER IT IS done by statute or judicial decision, legal reform often has consequences that campaigners for it cannot predict. Some consequences are welcome. Others are counter-productive and harmful, undermining the goals of the reform. This reality means I should consider carefully the possible negative results of reforms surrounding classism. In a phrase, the law must not end up doing more harm than good. The task of this chapter is to assess if the law would do more harm than good in the struggle against classism, even with all the reforms suggested in Part II.

There are some provisional points to remember when considering the issue of doing more harm than good. First, harms and goods are multiple and overlapping. Reform to the law may create many goods, but the danger of a single harm might mean that reform should not, on reflection, be pursued. There may also be situations in which many harms, taken in isolation or together, are not enough to overcome a single good that reform would achieve. Second, we may also ask about doing harm or good *to what*. The subject could include people, organisations, cultural norms and abstract issues like harm to the law's legitimacy and authority. Taking these points into account, the ultimate question is whether the law would help or hinder progress towards the end of classism.

—

This chapter will consider the question through a series of topics: (1) symmetrical or asymmetrical protection; (2) affirmative or 'positive' action and the law's double-edge; (3) justification in law and watering down protections; and (4) harm by distraction or complacency. Learning lessons from each topic, I argue that legal protections against classism will *not* do more harm than good – but only if those protections are asymmetrical, not diluted by low standards of justification, and accompanied by robust affirmative action and broader changes in societies.

1. SYMMETRICAL OR ASYMMETRICAL PROTECTION

1.1. The Current Position

One debate in the law concerns how we frame the grounds or 'characteristics' we protect. A central choice is between symmetry and asymmetry. Symmetrical protection includes anyone who falls in a given category, even if they are on the whole advantaged compared with others in that category. Take a simple example. A protected ground of 'race' is a type of symmetrical protection: people of any 'race' are included, even if they are on the whole advantaged by racism. By contrast, a protected group of 'black people' is a type of asymmetrical protection. Black people are protected because racism on the whole disadvantages them. White people are not protected because racism on the whole advantages them.

The Equality Act 2010 adopts a mostly symmetrical approach. Some of the best-known grounds are framed so that anyone in a given category is included: race, sexual orientation, sex, religion or belief (or none), and age.[1] The Sentencing Act 2020 also uses mostly symmetrical protection in the context of hostility and criminal law sentencing: race, sexual orientation and religion.[2] Even though symmetrical protection seems to ignore how some groups benefit while others suffer, there is a range of common justifications for it:

1. It avoids the practical problem of drawing fine distinctions between different groups.[3]
2. It avoids, or at least reduces the risk of, essentialising or stereotyping groups of people.
3. It gives the law symbolic strength in treating people the same, even if the reality of disadvantage is different, because the law signals that this is *how* we should treat people.
4. It maintains the law's legitimacy and authority (partly because of what the law symbolises) by refusing to draw controversial distinctions between groups which might fuel resentment and encourage claims that the law is itself discriminatory.

The last two points are especially thorny. Reva Siegel's work is insightful here. Siegel identifies a theme in decisions of the US Supreme Court concerning claims about equal protection over the decades. Moving from a rationale of colour-blindness, the court (particularly its right-wing constituents) adopted a justification based on the potential entrenchment and worsening of divisions in society. If the law were to recognise such divisions and favour one group over the other in its reasoning, it would add to those divisions. Siegel describes this argument as one of 'antibalkanization'.[4] Drawing on concerns about the law's giving of priority to some groups over others, anti-balkanisation justifies a lack of intervention by judges on the basis that it avoids making existing divisions worse.

I take a different view. The disadvantage that some groups experience means that the law is justified in protecting certain groups and not others. Sandra Fredman discusses this issue in her work on 'formal' and 'substantive' ideas of equality. While

[1] Equality Act 2010, s 4.

[2] Sentencing Act 2020, s 66.

[3] See, for concern about the precision of categories in the context in the US law on affirmative action, *Students for Fair Admissions v Harvard* 600 US 181 (2023), 25.

[4] R Siegel, 'From Colorblindness to Antibalkanization: An Emerging Ground of Decision in Race Equality Cases' (2011) 120(6) *Yale Law Journal* 1278, 1281, 1300.

formal equality confuses equality with sameness, substantive equality may require us to treat different people differently.[5] The current law in the UK reflects this to a degree. The Equality Act operates in some asymmetrical ways. There are settled examples of an asymmetrical approach: disability, gender reassignment, pregnancy and maternity, and marriage and civil partnership.[6] The Sentencing Act is also asymmetrical in part: it protects disability and transgender identity.[7] Disability, for instance, is a widely used ground in the law of work disputes and claims against public bodies. The law does not use the idea of 'ability or disability', which would be the symmetrical equivalent. It is not clear from the legislative material why this approach was considered justifiable for disability but not for grounds such as race and sexual orientation. It may be the result of lawmakers following earlier statutes. The Disability Discrimination Act 1995 (DDA 1995) used the term in both its title and provisions.[8] The definition in section 6(1) of the Equality Act mirrors that found in section 1(1) of the DDA 1995. Asymmetrical protection may also be the result of one influential model of disability. In this book, I have used the language of 'enabled' and 'disabled' because I accept the arguments that disability is largely a product of society's structures *disabling* certain people (though the 'social' model of disability does not capture all the experiences of disabled people, particularly those with chronic pain).[9] By contrast, the idea of 'physical or mental impairment' in the Equality Act indicates a biological or medical model of disability.[10]

This model frames disability as something intrinsic, or stemming from, disabled people's bodies, rather than something to do with society's structures. As a result, it may be that the willingness to protect disability asymmetrically stems from the medical model, which has been accepted by politicians who would otherwise oppose the use of the law to 'balkanise' us (using Siegel's word) and entrench divisions. The medical model allows disability to look deceptively simple and unthreatening. Although the reasons for the protection of disability may, then, be specific to this intellectual history, it nevertheless shows that the current law in the UK already permits some asymmetrical protection.

1.2. How to Frame Class

A. *Equality Act 2010 and Upper-Class Misuse*

If class were to be protected under the Equality Act, lawmakers might take one of two approaches. First, if they were to put a purely economic idea of class at

[5] S Fredman, 'Substantive Equality Revisited' (2016) 14(3) *International Journal of Constitutional Law* 712, 716–19.

[6] Equality Act 2010, ss 6–8, 17–18.

[7] Sentencing Act 2020, s 66.

[8] DDA 1995, s 1.

[9] See, for a critical analysis of the social model, S Symeonidou, 'Researching Disability Politics: Beyond the Social Model and Back Again' in S Symeonidou and K Beauchamp-Pryor (eds), *Purpose, Process and Future Direction of Disability Research* (Rotterdam, SensePublishers, 2013) 45.

[10] S Fredman, *Discrimination Law* (Oxford, Oxford University Press, 2022) 156.

the centre, lawmakers could easily choose an asymmetrical model. If lawmakers were to treat class as entirely about income thresholds, the line would be straightforward to draw. People earning below a specified amount of money would be the ones protected. Second, if lawmakers were to take inspiration from Bourdieu and recognise the social, cultural and economic aspects of class, they could accept that various classes should be protected, since upper-class people can also encounter prejudice and negative attitudes towards them. The question of symmetry or asymmetry is very much left open.

To work through the issue, consider an example from UK government policy. A bastion of the traditional upper class in the UK is expensive private schooling (especially famous 'public' schools like Eton and Harrow). When the Finance Act 1972 introduced value added tax (VAT), private schools were exempt from charging it.[11] The Value Added Tax Act 1994 (VATA 1994) preserved that exemption. However, the VATA 1994 was amended with effect from 1 January 2025. Private school fees were no longer exempt. The new Part 3 of Schedule 9 removed private school fees from the exemption. Those fees included those for education, vocational training and services of board and lodging.[12] This was later accompanied by further changes, including the loss of private schools' eligibility for charitable business rate relief.[13] In response, many private schools increased their fees (though some actually lowered their basic rates and then increased other payments).[14]

The changes to the VATA 1994 were the subject of various claims for judicial review in *R (ALR and Others) v Chancellor of the Exchequer* (2025).[15] Without class as a protected characteristic, the claimants advanced arguments relating to religion, disability, sex and nationality. The claimants included children adhering to certain religions, some who had special educational needs, some who said they required 'a single-sex environment' and some who said they needed access to a foreign curriculum.[16] The Administrative Court dismissed the claims and refused to declare the national law incompatible with the European Convention on Human Rights under section 4 of the Human Rights Act 1998. The changes did not contravene Article 1 or 2 of the First Protocol to the ECHR (which provide for peaceful enjoyment of a person's possessions and the right to education) or Article 14 of the ECHR read alongside them.[17] Although Article 2 of the First Protocol was engaged as well as Article 14, the government's reform did not impair a right under Article 2 and it fell within the margin of appreciation. That margin was broad because the issues fell 'squarely into the fields of economic or social strategy', the measure's aim was 'redistributive', the measure was a

[11] Finance Act 1972, Sch 5, item 1 (repealed).
[12] VATA 1994, Pt 3, Sch 9, group 6.
[13] Non-Domestic Rating (Multipliers and Private Schools) Act 2025, s 5.
[14] Independent Schools Council, *ISC Census and Annual Report 2025* (2025) 4–5, 21–22.
[15] *R (ALR and Others) v Chancellor of the Exchequer* [2025] EWHC 1467 (Admin).
[16] *ALR* (n 15) [3].
[17] *ALR* (n 15) [3], [5].

'manifesto commitment' and the key issues had been debated in Parliament.[18] To the extent that the reform engaged Article 14 and discrimination based on religion, sex, nationality and disability, it was within the government's margin of appreciation (and, seemingly, justified in law).[19] When two of the claimant groups appealed to the Court of Appeal in 2026, they were again unsuccessful, with the judges emphasising in part the 'objective justification' for the VAT measure.[20]

Now imagine that a claim of this kind takes place after the development of an administrative law principle in favour of equality between classes or after the introduction of a protected characteristic of class in the Equality Act. Imagine, too, that the protection of class is symmetrical. It therefore includes children from very wealthy and aristocratic families who send their children to expensive private schools. Imagine that the claimants use class to argue that there is inequality between classes here and indirect discrimination against upper-class children. Despite the Administrative Court's emphasis on the government's 'policy' and 'redistributive' aim, as well as the margin of appreciation, a new administrative law principle about class may change the outcome in a case like *ALR* for the reasons I set out in Chapter 7.

On the particular facts of *ALR*, a possible claim alleging direct or indirect discrimination under an amended Equality Act raises other questions. Such a claim would not strictly engage the margin of appreciation. It would also not apply directly to a statute. So, tweak the facts slightly. Imagine that the change to VAT had been brought about by a government department's new policy rather than Parliament amending a statute. If the claimants were to allege indirect discrimination against upper-class children, arguments of a similar kind could arise. The claimants could emphasise the effect on upper-class children and the proportionality of the means adopted. Faced with such arguments, a court's conclusion might be similar to the one it reached in *ALR*. Much would turn on the aims and means of the change and the judges' deference to government 'policy'. However, if the claimants were to argue that the policy *directly* discriminated against upper-class children, this could be more dangerous. If a court were to accept this argument, the policy would contravene section 13 of the Equality Act. As direct discrimination cannot be justified in law, the policy would be unlawful. Such reform to the financing of private education would be found to be discriminatory. Symmetrical protection of class in this way would cause damage. Upper-class people could use it to *entrench* classism, primarily in the form of broad educational inequality relating to class.

On the one hand, an anti-balkanisation argument might accept this danger, but it could claim that avoiding the entrenching of divisions and worsening of resentments in societies are more important objectives. On the other hand, the damage here is easy to foresee. If courts were to consider a decision to be within

[18] *ALR* (n 15) [85]–[88].

[19] *ALR* (n 15) [160], [168], [176], [185].

[20] *R (BYL and Another) v Chancellor of the Exchequer* [2026] EWCA Civ 170, [85] and [97].

a margin of appreciation or an area of (non-legal) 'policy' (whether under the Human Rights Act or the Equality Act), a decision to reduce upper-class people's enjoyment of certain advantages could be less favourable treatment because of their class. Class would become an effective way in which upper-class people could challenge measures designed to eradicate classism. Those people would certainly have the money to do so. This would significantly undermine the good the law could do to end classism, as opposed to entrenching a robotic requirement to treat each class the same. Being open to misuse in this way, the law could do more harm than good.

To avoid such misuse, we should build asymmetrical protection of class. The answer is to define class in terms of *disadvantage relating to* social, cultural and economic capital. Revisit Chapter 5 and my suggested draft of a new section 12A of the Equality Act. We can insert the idea of disadvantage into subsection 1.

12A Class

1. Class means **abiding, pervasive and substantial disadvantage relating to** social, cultural and economic capital.
2. In relation to the protected characteristic of class—
   (a) a reference to a person who has a particular protected characteristic is a reference to a person of a particular class;
   (b) a reference to persons who share a protected characteristic is a reference to persons of the same class. (emphasis added)

Such an approach would be **conceptually coherent** within the overall framework I have been developing. It would further reflect Khaitan's formulation of 'abiding, pervasive and substantial disadvantage'.[21] Although it might cause some confusion with other uses of 'disadvantage' elsewhere in the Equality Act (such as in relation to indirect discrimination), Khaitan's criteria keep its meaning here demanding. Under such a formulation, people who *benefit* from a form of discrimination connected with a protected characteristic would not be able to claim discrimination using that characteristic.

The approach would also have a subtler advantage in its **drafting**. The name of the characteristic is still not an express declaration of its asymmetry. The 'characteristic' is 'class', not 'being lower-class'. Rather, the asymmetry comes in the detail of the provision, as it is in the detail that the characteristic is defined in asymmetrical terms. The difference between the name of a characteristic and the detail of a statutory subsection may seem small – perhaps even trivial. For instance, those seeking to vilify the law could quickly see past this and still criticise the law for instituting an 'unequal' approach that favours lower-class people over upper-class people. However, if we consider the symbolic importance of the law, using the label of 'class' but then defining it asymmetrically

[21] T Khaitan, *A Theory of Discrimination Law* (Oxford, Oxford University Press, 2015) 155.

would avoid giving the characteristic a simple, easily distorted label such as 'lower-class people'. At the same time, it would ensure that the law's protection is limited to those who are, in fact, disadvantaged. Although it may be naïve to hope that this would reduce objections by those who would seek to stir up widespread resentment to such reform, it offers a more nuanced approach that anchors the law to the idea of 'disadvantage' rather than an express label of 'lower-class people' only. The subtler detail of the statutory provision would be doing the work.

B. Relevance of Potential Criticisms and Distortions

These worries tap into a broader issue with symmetrical protection of grounds, which is not limited to class. Politicians and interest groups caricature asymmetrical protection of class and other protected grounds as social warfare and a kind of discrimination in itself. While a practical consideration, this is not a good argument in favour of protecting class symmetrically. Unless we change the Equality Act's wider approach to protection (which is internally divergent, given the presence of asymmetrical grounds like disability), we risk distorting the understanding of discrimination as a whole. Class simply reinforces the point that asymmetrical protection is a more accurate approach, even though there are genuine concerns about entrenching divisions and creating trouble.

When considering doing more harm than good in the mission to end classism, these concerns nevertheless deserve attention. Since some people conflate equality with sameness before the law, it would be easy for politicians and campaigners to promote the view that the law is 'unequal' if it is asymmetrical and only protects lower-class people. They could say that we should all be 'equal' (understood here to mean 'the same') before the law. In the words of one politician speaking about legal protections against racism and homophobia, 'I want to live . . . in a country that is literally colour-blind. I couldn't care less what colour you are. I'm not interested in what sexuality you have. Let's treat everybody equally. That is my agenda.'[22]

Notice, though, that these kinds of criticisms are not always specific to the issue of symmetry. They are attacks on the general premise of discrimination law: that legal protections are necessary to combat discrimination. These criticisms rail against the notion that the law should protect some groups more than, or to the exclusion of, others. It is fair to anticipate that introducing new and broader asymmetrical protection would add fuel to this fire. Critics could rely on asymmetrical protection of class as another clear example of the law treating a group of people in one way (ie protecting them from discrimination)

[22] F Brown, 'Reform Candidate Quits and Backs Tories – as Nigel Farage Says Some BNP Supporters "Gravitate" to His Party' (30 June 2024): www.news.sky.com/story/reform-candidate-quits-and-back-tories-as-nigel-farage-says-some-bnp-supporters-gravitate-to-his-party-13161281.

and another group in another way (ie not protecting them from discrimination). This would be characterised as inequality – difference – before the law.

While it is essential to stop tactics like this from becoming distractions, they should not be ignored. In the theoretical sense of doing more harm than good, asymmetrical protection best reflects one of the purposes of discrimination law, specifically to reduce and even eliminate the fact that members of some groups are significantly more likely to experience abiding, pervasive and substantial disadvantage than members of other groups.[23] This argument can be put even higher: asymmetrical protection is the *only* **theoretically coherent** way forward in this area of the law. Otherwise, the law would give protection to the very groups who are advantaged by discrimination. However, in the practical sense of doing more harm than good, we should recognise the **potential political consequences** of asymmetrical protection. Even if asymmetrical protection would be theoretically coherent, would it be weaponised by those who want to abolish discrimination law and, in doing so, ensure their own advantage?

This is what Donald Trump, Nigel Farage and those deploying similar techniques have been trying to do. Khaitan discusses a similar theme when he develops the idea of 'expressive salience'. It exists when membership of a group is 'a source of important (and usually valued) personal identity to a critical mass of its members, and when this importance is recognized by a critical mass of the rest of the population of that society'.[24] Expressive salience is 'symbiotic' with relative group disadvantage.[25] When both the advantaged and disadvantaged groups have expressive salience – that important and usually valued sense of identity – symmetrical protection may be desirable.[26] These ideas are concerned with whether or not asymmetrical protection 'can result in damaging societal consequences (for the protected group itself, as well as for the society at large)'.[27] Sometimes, asymmetrical protection may add 'fuel to … politics of competitive debasement between rival groups' and 'catalyse retaliation'.[28] For example, the law tends to use 'race' to protect white people as well as black people because the absence of protection for white people 'may exacerbate the relative group disadvantage suffered by black people' (alongside collateral harms to several groups and a failure to encourage 'social solidarity and cohesion' across groups).[29]

In one sense, if asymmetrical protection of class were adopted, such a reform would need robust defence by politicians, lawmakers and campaigners. There would be little use in introducing such an asymmetrical protection without a persuasive defence by those implementing it. Much has been written in recent years about the failure of political parties 'across the ideological spectrum' to

[23] Or, at least, as I suggest by adopting Khaitan's criteria.
[24] Khaitan (n 21) 172.
[25] Khaitan (n 21) 175.
[26] Khaitan (n 21) 179.
[27] Khaitan (n 21) 172.
[28] Khaitan (n 21) 177–78.
[29] Khaitan (n 21) 178–79.

articulate policies in order to overcome 'populist' criticisms.[30] In the context of classism, the worry is that, without such a defence, critics would have an easy task extracting asymmetrical protection of class from its context and demonising it. Although this danger is not in itself fatal, it could become so if it were to lead to a political shift undermining discrimination law more generally or fuelling harms suffered by certain groups, as Khaitan explains.

Reflecting on these concerns, I accept that upper-class people may have expressive salience in Khaitan's sense (though, again, some may reject the label of 'upper-class' or feel ashamed by it). However, this is not a good reason to prefer symmetrical protection. Such an approach would remain incoherent. A white woman is not on the whole disadvantaged by racism but is so disadvantaged by misogyny. The better response for her is to distinguish between worries about potential distortions of the law and the principled, justifiable reform of that law. Even accepting those worries to be genuine, I am reluctant to allow them to defeat otherwise much needed and theoretically coherent reforms. A lot of these concerns could apply to a variety of features of discrimination law that already exist, such as positive (affirmative) action – discussed below – and the selection of protected grounds in the first place. Critics attack these features as much as they attack asymmetry or 'two-tier' justice. Some people will always want to demonise such aspects of the law. Lawmakers should not allow fears of potential political or social reactions to pre-determine our legal analysis or, indeed, our reforms. If they did so, lawmakers would struggle to use the law for anything transformative or controversial.

The blunt truth is that asymmetrical protection is the only position that makes theoretical sense when considering discrimination as closely connected with *dis*advantage. With a robust defence, like other issues in discrimination law, it will withstand the criticisms that may come.

C. *What about Line-Drawing?*

There is a further discrete point to consider in the light of doing more harm than good. It is more about the law's doctrine than its place in broader political movements. If lawmakers were to choose asymmetrical protection of class, how well would they actually define who to protect?

I covered some of this ground in Chapters 2 and 3, arguing why class is *not* more difficult to define than existing ideas like race. In the context of asymmetrical protection, the law would have to draw a distinction based on advantage and disadvantage. In simple terms, lower-class people would receive protection whereas upper-class people would not. As I have argued, this would not necessarily require a hard and fast categorisation of each person's class status: if

[30] See, eg, A Grzymala-Busse, 'Failure of Europe's Mainstream Parties' (2019) 30(4) *Journal of Democracy* 35, 39–42; M Ivanovic, D Byrd and J Morelock (eds), *The Many Faces of Populism: Perspectives from Critical Theory and Beyond* (Boston, Brill, 2024).

a person is *perceived as* or *associated with* lower-class features, and badly treated as a result, the law is likely still to protect them by some means. In hate crime, perception is undoubtedly enough, even if a person is not *in fact* a member of the perceived group or if a person is merely associated with the group.[31] In civil contexts, there is less clarity on the issue of associative discrimination, but I accept the interpretation of section 13 of the Equality Act which holds that direct discrimination can occur by association, as section 13 does not expressly require claimants to possess a characteristic themselves.[32] Nonetheless, the issue of line-drawing puts the question of what being disadvantaged by classism means into a stark light. I have – in a way that, I hope, has been persuasive – dealt with that more general issue of definition. It is not necessary to put us all in 'class' boxes in order to protect class in the law and to do so effectively. Yet the reason asymmetrical protection revives this difficulty is because it requires the drawing of some kind of line in statute between those protected and those who are not.

There will forever be difficult cases in the law. Accepting that, the best answer is as follows. Those who are significantly more likely to experience abiding, pervasive and substantial disadvantage relating to lower-quality social, cultural and economic capital should be protected. Those who are not so likely should not be protected. This general position would be subject to the exceptions of perception and association. For instance, if a person were perceived as having such lower-quality capital and mistreated on that basis, but who in fact did not, they could still seek legal recourse.

A reader might consider those sentences and think that they are too vague, too weak, too open to different interpretations. Once more, though, the law *already* does this kind of difficult line-drawing. Disability is an example. Although some may have an archaic idea of disability as permanent use of a wheelchair, for example, the more compelling idea of it is fluid and social. Therefore, the line-drawing can, in some circumstances, require careful consideration, including by drafters and judges. Once again, this challenge should not cause you to reject the ground of disability entirely or asymmetrical protection. You can accept that there are difficult questions of line-drawing in some cases and – nevertheless – argue that these potential harms do not detract from the overall goods to be gained by the law concentrating on *dis*advantage and protecting class accordingly.

D. *What about 'Poverty'?*

In response to asymmetrical protection, you might also say that this only gives another example of why class is not the right idea. Even if we would otherwise prefer class to be a protected characteristic, the problems of implementing asymmetrical protection reinforce why a concept other than class would be better.

[31] See, eg, Sentencing Act 2020, s 66(4), (6)(c) and (6)(f).
[32] *IDS Employment Law Handbooks* (London, Sweet & Maxwell, 2025) 15.114.

Perhaps a more suitable idea would be inherently asymmetrical. For example, the law could revisit 'poverty' or 'socio-economic disadvantage' as possibilities, which I discussed in Chapters 3 and 4. They are both asymmetrical: they protect the *dis*advantaged. Consider poverty in particular. Poverty is inherently asymmetrical. Across definitions, poverty refers to the lack, denial and degradation of certain goods. A committee of the United Nations in 1998 defined the core of poverty to be 'a denial of choices and opportunities, a violation of human dignity'.[33] An asymmetrical idea like this could ensure that (i) the law's focus is confined to those most in need, here those in poverty, and (ii) those who are out of poverty cannot misuse the legal protection, which would bolster the law in contributing to the end of poverty.

Despite these arguments, I suggest two main reasons to keep class over an asymmetrical idea like poverty. The most important reason concerns the **scope of protection**. While poverty is always an example of classism, poverty does not capture the full range of classism. Discrimination law should still protect a person from classism, even if they are out of poverty. If an employee is paid below the average salary in this country, but above the poverty threshold, that employee can still suffer classism. Even in high-status professions, such as banking and law, classism is rife, though few bankers and barristers are in poverty. Those kinds of cases may not be our main priority, but they remain examples of classism. As a matter of law, we should protect anyone who suffers classism, including people who live in poverty or who have lived but no longer live in poverty. Research also shows how cyclical poverty can be. A person who acquires a level of money above a given 'poverty' threshold may still suffer precarity and lingering harms of poverty (such as the more psychological and social harms) and may easily return to poverty.[34] The 'poverty line' is a misleading metaphor: there is no line neatly drawn and fixed in place. Asymmetrical ideas like poverty would not protect some people who suffer classism. By contrast, class could protect all people in poverty *and more*.

A supporting reason relates to **connotations**. While there is overlap between the language and themes surrounding class and an asymmetrical notion like poverty, the connotations differ. Poverty (in common with some models of class) can be over-simplified to a question of an income threshold or amount of money. Although both are rightly connected with income and money, they are both more complex. Yet, even in everyday language, class bears a closer connection with social and cultural issues than poverty does, at least in the UK. Class and

[33] UN Administrative Committee on Coordination, *Statement of Commitment for Action to Eradicate Poverty (Press Release ECOSOC/5729)* (20 May 1998): www.press.un.org/en/1998/19980520.eco5759.html.

[34] SP Jenkins, *Changing Fortunes: Income Mobility and Poverty Dynamics in Britain* (Oxford, Oxford University Press, 2011) ch 8. See also, for discussion of the relative nature of poverty and income when compared with the general level of prosperity in a community, A Sen, 'Conceptualizing and Measuring Poverty' in DB Grusky and R Kanbur (eds), *Poverty and Inequality* (Stanford, California, Stanford University Press, 2006) 30, esp 35–36.

classism, particularly in the UK, are strongly associated with snobbery, prejudice and disadvantage concerning certain regions and accent bias as well as attitudes in education and employment. These aspects remain part of everyday language, which class is quicker to accommodate than an asymmetrical idea like poverty. I accept that these arguments about connotations are fragile and are not in themselves decisive. However, when combined with the greater scope of protection that class offers, they reinforce the point that the law should prefer class over a concept like poverty.

E. *What about the Criminal Law?*

Before I leave the issue of symmetry, there is the further question of the criminal law. The arguments for symmetry might differ in the context of the criminal law. In its work on hate crime in 2020 and 2021, the Law Commission paid little attention to the issue of symmetry, though its consultation paper made a brief reference to it in the context of 'suppressed minorities'. The Scottish review also considered it in passing when discussing gender.[35] In the criminal law, it may be appropriate to be particularly cautious, more so than when approaching the Equality Act, for example. Coercion, policing, imprisonment and stigma are prominent in the criminal law. There are distinctive considerations to take into account. Concerns about 'fair labelling' play a particularly important role, such as the question of whether the language and stigma attached to a crime reflect fairly the nature and extent of the wrongdoing.[36] Unlike in the law concerning contracts and trusts, for instance, the criminal law is thought to be unusually concerned with its own capacity to limit freedom and cause its own harms. Discussing hate crime, Chara Bakalis points out the peculiar principles of the criminal law, specifically 'minimum criminalisation' and the law's adoption of John Stuart Mill's 'harm principle'.[37] Elsewhere, analysing the law of theft and the criminal law's interest in protecting vulnerable people from exploitation, Alan Bogg and John Stanton-Ife emphasise that we may need differences in approach between criminal and civil law. They suggest that we may conclude that the two areas of law should use concepts and approaches that diverge from each other.[38] While authorising differences between areas of law, such a view does not endorse inconsistency. It may simply reflect the goals and features of the area of law in question.

[35] Law Commission, *Hate Crime Laws* (2020), Consultation Paper No 250, 184; A Campbell, *Independent Review of Hate Crime Legislation in Scotland: Final Report* (2018) 41.

[36] A Ashworth, 'The Elasticity of *Mens Rea*' in C Tapper (ed), *Crime, Proof and Punishment: Essays in Memory of Sir Rupert Cross* (London, Butterworths, 1981) 45, 53; J Chalmers and F Leverick, 'Fair Labelling in Criminal Law' (2008) 71(2) *Modern Law Review* 217.

[37] C Bakalis, 'The Victims of Hate Crime and the Principles of the Criminal Law' (2017) 37(4) *Legal Studies* 718, 723–24.

[38] A Bogg and J Stanton-Ife, 'Protecting the Vulnerable: Legality, Harm and Theft' (2003) 23(3) *Legal Studies* 402, 418–21.

Thinking about its particular features, the criminal law can be a blunt tool, dividing people into the good and the bad. In its crudeness, the criminal law may be especially susceptible to distorted claims about a 'two-tier' justice system. Criticism of this kind emerged in 2025 when the Sentencing Council tried to encourage the use of pre-sentence reports for 'ethnic, cultural and faith minority groups'.[39] Because of this, some might argue that we should be more cautious in using asymmetrical protection in the criminal law than in other areas. If there were any area that might provoke the strongest public reaction, which could in turn jeopardise the safety of the most vulnerable people, it could be the criminal law. It might be better to allow a simplistic view of 'equality before the law' (as sameness) in the criminal law than to risk negative reactions.

While these concerns should not be underestimated, an asymmetrical approach remains the most compelling, even in the criminal law. Remember that symmetrical protection is not a neutral alternative. It is itself a stance about the role of the law and the way in which people should be treated. To illustrate the point, take an example of a person who is homeless and very hungry. Desperate for money to buy food, the person enters a wealthy neighbourhood in Chelsea, London. It is owned by a straightforwardly upper-class family. Spotting an open window in a large townhouse, the person climbs in, takes some jewellery from a nearby chest of drawers and runs away with it. A passer-by overhears the person mutter, 'Serves the rich right.'

It is possible to understand this example as involving a crime (domestic burglary), motivated by hostility towards the owners of the townhouse. Under the reform suggested in Chapter 6, this would be motivation by hostility related to class. The burglar's conviction and sentence could be aggravated on that basis. But are we really content with using the criminal law's stigma and coercion in this way, especially given that the burglar is the one overall who suffers the greater harms of a classist society? The owners may be the victim of this crime and yet they are, on the whole, the ones advantaged by classism. If we go back to the idea of abiding, pervasive and substantial disadvantage, the owners would not satisfy the criteria here.[40] Understood in an asymmetrical way, while the burglar may have thought about the owners' class and even made negative decisions based on their class, the burglar was not classist.[41] They should not be labelled as classist. They should not be punished more severely on such a basis.

[39] See W Davis, 'Letter to Shabana Mahmood MP' (27 March 2025): www.sentencingcouncil.org.uk/media/yktcmblz/2025-03-26-letter-to-the-lord-chancellor-from-william-davis-lj-1.pdf; Sentencing Council, *Imposition of Community and Custodial Sentences Guideline* (not brought into force); H Zeffman and J Nevett, 'Sentencing Guidelines Ditched after "Two-Tier" Row', *BBC News* (31 March 2025): www.bbc.co.uk/news/articles/c5yg887m6qdo.

[40] Khaitan (n 21) 155.

[41] See also, on the point of the likelihood of the law eliding 'class-related' and 'classist', Kay Goodall's analysis of the relationship between 'racial' and 'racist' hate crime, alongside the 'woolliness in the criminal law's conception of ... protected minorit[ies]': K Goodall, 'Conceptualising "Racism" in Criminal Law' (2013) 33(2) *Legal Studies* 215, 218–22.

Symmetrical protection conflates behaviour relating to class with *classist* behaviour. This is an error that the criminal law already makes. When the criminal law allows a black person to be prosecuted partly based on racial hostility for calling a police officer 'stupid' and 'white', the law appears to endorse the view that this is as much a question of racial hostility as a white person calling a police officer 'stupid' and 'black'.[42] Yes, that approach is the more 'inclusive' approach in the literal sense of the word, but it pays no attention to the asymmetrical nature of racism. Once more, the law must not be timid because of the risk of criticism by those who want to do away with anti-discrimination protections entirely. Even in the criminal law, asymmetrical protection is the theoretically coherent and defensible approach.

2. AFFIRMATIVE OR 'POSITIVE' ACTION AND THE LAW'S DOUBLE-EDGE

2.1. The Current Picture

The debate surrounding asymmetry connects closely with the topic of affirmative action or (to use the language of the Equality Act) positive action.[43] The typical meaning of such action concerns initiatives and programmes aimed at reducing the effects of discriminatory systems in certain settings, most often admissions, recruitment and promotions.[44] Most initiatives and programmes of this kind focus on improving the likelihood of success of certain groups in these settings.

In some ways, the presence of a strong and effective system of affirmative action can mitigate the concerns about symmetry and misuse. While, for example, symmetrical protection might allow some straight people to assert discrimination based on sexual orientation, the law would have affirmative action programmes for queer people aimed at changing workplaces, universities and other organisations. Of course, some jurisdictions do affirmative or positive action better – more transformatively – than others. South Africa is a good example. The trend in South African decisions reveals the courts' understanding of the law's role in redressing 'past exclusion, dispossession, and indignity'.[45] The Constitutional Court's reasoning has not always been convincing, but it has shown an impressive ability to grapple with potential conflicting interests between protected groups, such as the complexities around promoting white women and promoting black men in *South African Police Service v Solidarity obo Barnard*.[46] In that case, the National Commissioner refused to promote a white woman to the rank

[42] See, eg, 'Striker Called PC "Stupid and White", Court Hears', *BBC News* (3 February 2025): www.bbc.co.uk/news/articles/c8xqyrlpnl4o.

[43] Equality Act 2010, ss 158–159.

[44] S Fredman (n 10) 367–68. See also, discussing the meaning of affirmative action in the US, S Meyer, *Affirmative Action* (New York, Rosen, 2018) 4.

[45] *Minister of Finance and Other v Van Heerden* [2004] ZACC 3, [25] (Moseneke J).

[46] *South African Police Service v Solidarity obo Barnard* [2014] ZACC 23.

of superintendent. The refusal was on the basis that the promotion would not improve racial representation at that level (and it was not a post that needed to be occupied immediately due to demand for service delivery). The decision in the end turned on whether or not the claim for review of the Commissioner's decision was properly before the court.[47] More relevant to this chapter, the majority of the Constitutional Court held that the police service's Employment Equity Plan (EEP) was the kind of measure permitted by section 9 of the South African Constitution and section 6 of the Employment Equity Act 1998.[48] The separate judgment of Van der Westhuizen J offers careful treatment of the various issues, recognising the effect on the police officer's dignity and the reality of her experience of misogyny, but ultimately deciding that the EEP was justified in pursuit of the broader aim to end discrimination in all forms in society.[49]

By comparison, the UK approach is limited. 'Positive action' is less developed than the equity plans of South Africa or even the older ideas of affirmative action in the US. In the UK, it amounts to a kind of 'tie-break' between applicants which has led some to argue that it is not really positive action at all.[50] It is optional, not required. Section 158(1) of the Equality Act applies if a person (P) reasonably thinks that:

(a) persons who share a protected characteristic suffer a disadvantage connected to the characteristic,

(b) persons who share a protected characteristic have needs that are different from the needs of persons who do not share it, or

(c) participation in an activity by persons who share a protected characteristic is disproportionately low.

The three focal points are disadvantage, difference and participation. So far, it is promising. Section 158(2) sets out further detail:

> This Act does not prohibit P from taking any action which is a proportionate means of achieving the aim of—
>
> (a) enabling or encouraging persons who share the protected characteristic to overcome or minimise that disadvantage,
>
> (b) meeting those needs, or
>
> (c) enabling or encouraging persons who share the protected characteristic to participate in that activity.

This framework offers the foundation for responding to worries about upper-class people, in particular those wealthy people who are privately educated,

[47] *Barnard* (n 46) [59]–[60].
[48] *Barnard* (n 46) [62]–[70].
[49] *Barnard* (n 46) [130]–[132], [148], [155]–[156], [170]–[176] (Van der Westhuizen J).
[50] See, eg, N Johns and others, 'When Is Positive Action Not Positive Action? Exploring the Conceptual Meaning and Implications of the Tie-Break Criterion in the UK Equality Act 2010' (2013) 33(1) *Equality, Diversity and Inclusion: An International Journal* 97, 104–09.

misusing class in order to undercut positive action. It would also interlock with the asymmetrical approach to class I have proposed. Section 158(2) would still enable educational decision-makers to prioritise class-disadvantaged people in their access initiatives.[51] In the context of recruitment and promotion, though, section 159(4) of the Equality Act limits positive action situations to those in which 'A is as qualified as B to be recruited or promoted' at the time of the action.

With the introduction of protections against classism, there would be new risks for positive action. As a matter of strategy, those decision-makers who currently use class as a measure to prioritise more disadvantaged applicants might find their efforts undermined by bad judicial interpretation of terms such as 'proportionate'.[52] More pressing still is the potential impact on 'recruitment and promotion'. These provisions have received relatively little consideration by the higher courts.[53] The Equality and Human Rights Commission has issued codes of practice, which courts are required to take into account.[54] Even reading those codes, though, it does seem that there is limited room for a contextual interpretation of the idea of qualification (such as recognising that a person may have achieved more relative to their context than someone else relative to their context).[55]

With section 159 and the language of 'as qualified as', the Equality Act hinders the transformative potential of positive action in the important setting of recruitment and promotion. This is especially so when the idea of what makes up a qualification or merit can itself be discriminatory. This is another problem that is not specific to class, though. It is, instead, a problem for protected characteristics across the board. The same logic applies to those decision-makers who might otherwise seek to address, for instance, homophobia, racism and/or misogyny in their recruitment processes. When considering the issue of causing more harm than good, the answer does not turn on protections against classism but rather on how we interpret affirmative or positive action. Instead of concluding that such protections would do more harm than good, we should again be more precise. If we maintain a contextual interpretation of qualification and merit, taking into account how they themselves may be defined in discriminatory ways, we can apply positive action in a way that allows the law to be effective in contributing to the end of classism.

The focus must be on moving towards an understanding of affirmative action that is truly transformative. Here, the law must be **neither too narrow nor too**

[51] See, on the restriction of a benefit to people with a particular protected characteristic in the context of charities, Equality Act 2010, s 193.

[52] See, eg, *SG and Others v Secretary of State for Work and Pensions* [2015] UKSC 16, [67]–[77] (Reed L).

[53] See, eg, *R (Z) v Hackney LBC* [2020] UKSC 40, [17]–[23], [80]–[81].

[54] Equality Act 2006, s 15(4)(b).

[55] Equality and Human Rights Commission, *Equality Act 2010 Code of Practice: Employment Statutory Code of Practice* (2019) 175–82.

modest. To explore these two features within a specific example, take student admissions to higher education. Universities in the UK may use positive action in their admissions processes, though they are not required to do so.[56] Many higher education institutions use what is known as 'contextualised admissions' for their candidates.[57] The information is often imprecise. It is certainly imperfect. It gives assessors and interviewers a sense of the candidate's geographical area, the rates of poverty there and the rates of progression to higher education (though it is not always clear as to what *form* or *status* of that higher education).[58] It also gives some information about the kind of schools attended.[59] The broad aim is to have regard to the candidates' achievements in their context and to 'widen participation'.[60]

Imagine a candidate who has achieved top grades in a poor area, with parents who have not gone to university and who are not rich, and in a low-achieving school; they have done a lot more than a candidate who has achieved similar grades in a rich area, with wealthy parents who have had prestigious education, while attending an expensive private school. The question of causing more harm than good puts focus on what anti-classist affirmative action could do. If we were to incorporate class as a protected ground, the use of 'contextual information' could trigger greater legal scrutiny. This is where affirmative action meets the question of symmetrical protection. Educational organisations would have to comply with the legal requirements in a way they have not had to do to date. If class were protected symmetrically, it may be that this kind of reliance on contextual information would become unlawful as it would be counter to upper-class candidates' interests. If class were protected asymmetrically, though, taking into account contextual information would likely become a legal requirement. More emphasis would, then, fall on the specific construction of the protection of class and its relationship with affirmative action.

With this in mind, we can understand why the regime of positive action under the Equality Act is both too narrow and too modest. On narrowness, it only applies in a very limited set of circumstances. It also concentrates entirely on who is where in the existing structures, whether in employment or education. It rests on the premise of sameness or similarity between people and, only then, it allows the preference for one person over another in order to advance equality. Yet, in the context of class, we are often dealing with quite different grades or pieces of information. We are justified in preferring lower-class candidates because they have done better than their upper-class comparators. On modesty,

[56] See, eg, Equality and Human Rights Commission, *Guidance: What Equality Law Means for You as an Education Provider–Further and Higher Education* (2014) 9.

[57] See, eg, Universities and Colleges Admissions Service, 'Contextualised Admissions – How It Works in Practice' (undated): www.ucas.com/advisers/help-and-training/guides-resources-and-training/tools-and-resources-to-help-you/contextualised-admissions-how-it-works-in-practice.

[58] V Boliver and others, *Admissions in Context* (Sutton Trust, 2017) 10–11.

[59] Boliver (n 58) 11.

[60] Boliver (n 58) 6.

the existing provisions do not necessarily require structures to change, as a duty to make reasonable adjustments might do to a greater extent. The law would not require the admissions process to change. It would only offer a greater opportunity for more lower-class people to be successful in that process.

2.2. A Way Forward?

These problems suggest a way forward in at least three steps. First, there should be a contextual approach to questions of similarity *by reference to class*. It is important to consider class because, without it, we would have a distorted image. A lower-class student has achieved the same – or, indeed, more – than an upper-class student when interpreted in their context. Understood in this way, they will have the same qualifications and, often, better qualifications than their comparators.

Second and more ambitiously, it may be that we need to do away entirely with a standard based on sameness or similarity. The analytical exercise of determining whether a lower-class student is in the 'same' context as an upper-class student, for instance, becomes artificial. It may be a necessary feature of a comparative or competitive process to consider candidates' profiles in the light of each other. But, as a matter of analysis, it becomes strained when we conduct that assessment via an idea of sameness. It may be that the problem here, then, is best solved not by the argument based on sameness. The more persuasive way forward may be to revise the standard of positive action, certainly in the form it exists in the UK. As I have noted, attempts to be more transformative may bring bad consequences, as evident in the US when the Supreme Court effectively demolished affirmative action in *Students for Fair Admissions v Harvard* (2023).[61] However, in order to ensure the effectiveness of an anti-discriminatory system, it must be as well-considered in the context of what it *permits* as what it *prohibits*.

Third, lawmakers should consider a different approach to positive action, perhaps by resort to a different legal mechanism, such as other proactive measures and positive duties.[62] The law's approach should be both structural and outward-looking. To borrow an argument from a more philosophical context, it is mistaken simply to focus on increasing the diversity of those who sit around a table in a room and then defer to their accounts. Rather, we should transform the architecture of the room: open it up, take apart its bad hierarchies, diffuse and restructure its resources.[63] At present, the Equality Act's idea of positive action does nothing to achieve this. It merely tries to improve the likelihood

[61] *Students for Fair Admissions v Harvard* 600 US 181 (2023).
[62] See, eg, Fredman, *Discrimination Law* (n 10) 465–72.
[63] OO Táíwò, *Elite Capture* (London, Pluto Press, 2022) 81.

of entry for certain people. This is not as intensive, for example, as a duty to make reasonable adjustments, which concerns disabled people. It is in this vein that lawmakers should consider how, as part of protections against classism, we should replace the current idea of positive action with a more contextual approach, one not dependent on ideas of sameness or similarity, and perhaps by resorting to a stronger legal mechanism that scrutinises the structures themselves.

3. JUSTIFICATION: HARMS OF WATERING DOWN

Symmetry affects any protection of a characteristic or ground of class. Affirmative or positive action affects such protections in areas of the law apart from the criminal law. In addition to them, there is the role of justification, which has special importance when considering changes to the Equality Act and administrative law. The effectiveness of the law in combatting classism depends, both in practice and more symbolically, on the issue of justification. At least under the current scheme of indirect discrimination, there would then be instances where people seek to justify what would otherwise be classism.[64] The key would be how rigorously the law would assess justifications. If the law were too lenient in permitting behaviour to be justified, for example, then the protection of class would become weaker. This could impact on how effective the law would be in practice and in its symbolism.

Indirect discrimination is the main venue for this debate. Section 19(1) of the Equality Act gives the idea meaning:

1. A person (A) discriminates against another (B) if A applies to B a provision, criterion or practice which is discriminatory in relation to a relevant protected characteristic of B's.

Section 19(2) adds further detail:

2. For the purposes of subsection (1), a provision, criterion or practice is discriminatory in relation to a relevant protected characteristic of B's if—
   (a) A applies, or would apply, it to persons with whom B does not share the characteristic,
   (b) it puts, or would put, persons with whom B shares the characteristic at a particular disadvantage when compared with persons with whom B does not share it,
   (c) it puts, or would put, B at that disadvantage, and
   (d) A cannot show it to be a proportionate means of achieving a legitimate aim.

[64] I assume that class would be subject to justification in cases of alleged indirect discrimination: Equality Act 2010, s 19. I leave open the question of whether class, like age, should be a characteristic susceptible to justification even in cases of direct discrimination, though that option seems undesirable: Equality Act 2010, s 13(2).

How would these provisions apply to class? The Trades Union Congress has done some work on the unfairness of unpaid internships.[65] Imagine that an employer in central London requires all applicants for a job to complete an unpaid internship for two weeks. The employer applies the criterion, in principle, to applicants of all classes. The applicants include 'B' from a poor area in Essex. B works part-time in a supermarket and cannot do the internship as they cannot afford travel fares or accommodation. B does not have connections in London to stay with. The criterion puts B and other lower-class applicants at a particular disadvantage when compared with other applicants, which makes them much less likely to be able to complete such an internship.[66] The legitimate aim is, for the sake of argument, to ensure the employer has a thorough opportunity to evaluate applicants' performance in a place of work. The key issue would then be: can the employer show that it is a proportionate means of achieving that aim?

On the one hand, a court could consider all the options available to the employer. There might be evidence, for instance, that the employer could provide online resources about its work and require applicants to complete an online course instead. There might be evidence that the employer could afford to pay applicants to do the internship if it were to last for one week rather than two weeks. There might be other evidence that the employer could pay applicants to do a two-week internship if it reduced the overall number per year. Therefore, a court could conclude that the criterion – at least without changes made to it – is not 'a proportionate means' of achieving that aim.

On the other hand, it is not difficult to imagine a court watering down the standard of justification required. The employer might adduce evidence of its financial constraints. The employer might argue that niceties of monetary arrangements and recruitment processes are fundamentally questions of organisational and financial policy for employers. There will often be no stark right or wrong. Courts might place a lot of weight on this aspect. Courts might be reluctant to subject employers' finances to rigorous scrutiny (though they plainly do this in many contexts of litigation at present). While courts would recognise the disadvantage for the lower-class applicants, they would nonetheless find the criterion to be justified. The reasoning may sound familiar. It goes back to the entrenched perception that courts are not the appropriate scrutineers and decision-makers, especially for questions of financial policy and organisation. It is not a world apart from the reasoning of the UK Supreme Court in *SG* and *SC* discussed in Chapter 7.[67] The protection against classism in the form of indirect discrimination would be a kind of lip service.

[65] Trades Union Congress (TUC), *Making Work Pay: Call for Evidence on Unpaid Internships (TUC Submission)* (TUC, 13 October 2025): www.tuc.org.uk/research-analysis/reports/making-work-pay-call-evidence-unpaid-internships.

[66] TUC (n 65).

[67] *SG* (n 52); *SC and CB v Secretary of State for Work and Pensions* [2021] UKSC 26.

To avoid the harms of watering down, the courts should establish and develop jurisprudence which centres on two principles. First, at least in the context of the Equality Act, judges should make clear that **the economic aspects of discrimination fall within a credible interpretation of the courts' statutory mandate.** Taking the first point, for all the statute's emphasis on formal equality, the language of the Equality Act nevertheless refers to 'disadvantage', 'needs', 'adjustment' and 'participation'.[68] It is legislation full of concepts closely connected with economic issues. Disadvantage often means money and income. Participation depends, in part, on money and income. These are not difficult ideas, especially for courts that regularly calculate compensation, hear submissions about salaries, and some of which deal with allegations of complex fraud. Courts should stress the economic aspects of discrimination firmly caught by the provisions of the Equality Act as well as their co-dependent relationship with the social and cultural aspects. Courts should no longer treat the category of 'money' or 'economic' as inherently a place in which they cannot tread or can only go exceptionally.

Second, especially under a protection against classism in the Equality Act, courts are not being asked to write the government's budget from scratch. The Equality Act focuses more on the relationships between an individual and an organisation, though sometimes that organisation is the state. The easier example is the typical litigation that arises from employment disputes. If a court or tribunal finds discrimination, it should not doubt its institutional legitimacy simply because there will be economic consequences. Parliament has assigned courts and tribunals the role of the key decision-makers under the Equality Act for a reason. Properly understood, their task is **to develop an intellectually rigorous and effective regime of discrimination law in line with the statute.** Their task is not to shy away from discrimination when situations get complicated or raise issues about money. (The context of administrative law may be more complex and involve a tailored approach to proportionality, as I considered in Chapter 7.)

These arguments clearly pose controversial questions about the role of the courts. They also feed into the bigger debate about the source of the judiciary's legitimacy and raise the issue of who makes up the judiciary. As I discussed in Chapters 1 and 5, as with certain positions in academia, once people enter the judiciary, they can often insulate themselves from suffering classism. While there may still be features that cause them to experience some persisting examples of classism (such as bias against them based on their presentation or their accent), they are likely to have been exposed to upper-class environments and etiquettes. The bigger problem is that some judges will never have suffered classism. Instead, they will have spent their lives advantaged by it. The response to this, of course, comes from legal practice. Available tools include the use of expert evidence and properly informed legal argument. There are many topics

[68] Equality Act 2010, ss 19A, 20, 149(3)(b), 158(1)(c).

that judges have neither considered academically nor suffered in their personal lives. They may have limited knowledge of many issues. Yet we are still right to accept their legitimacy because we expect the process of adjudication to have brought them sufficient information by way of parties' submissions and, if appropriate, evidence from both lay and expert witnesses.

Whichever the precise source of judges' legitimacy (whether intellectual expertise, depth of experience, or another), the point is that courts should not shy away from recognising the extent of discrimination because it will disrupt governmental policy or arrangements by employers. Courts in the UK often pride themselves, correctly or otherwise, on their intellectual rigour. However, allowing justification to water down protections against classism would be intellectually timid and leave reform nugatory.

4. BEING DISTRACTED AND COMPLACENT

4.1. Harm by Distraction?

I have spent most of this chapter considering potential symbolic and practical effects of protections against classism. However, the question of doing more harm than good also raises a further issue about legal protections against classism. The issue is more of a conceptual one, with some consequences for our strategy. It suggests that, if we focus on building a legal understanding of classism, we will become distracted from the more urgent challenges of socio-economic inequality and poverty.

Andrew Fagan makes an argument of this kind in his article, 'Taking Class Seriously'.[69] As I have argued in this book, Fagan agrees that the law has failed to recognise, or engage with, class. While Fagan does not delve into the various analyses of class in 'academic and political domains', he accepts that there are 'discriminatory and stigmatizing attitudes and beliefs' amid the 'overtly material, socioeconomic effects of poverty and inequality', which in turn affect access to healthcare, spaces and amenities, housing, exposure to the criminal justice system and care of children.[70] Fagan grounds his analysis in 'the lack of social mobility' of 'the poor as a distinct class'.[71] Repackaged in terms of the question of doing more harm than good, Fagan suggests that using the law to protect against classism would do little to better the situation of lower-class people. What we truly need, Fagan argues, is not a legal understanding of classism that distracts us from the 'underlying causes' of 'the injustices the poor suffer'.[72] We need the de-gentrification of human rights entirely.[73]

[69] A Fagan, 'Taking Class Seriously' (2023) 45 *Human Rights Quarterly* 260.
[70] Fagan (n 69) 263–65.
[71] Fagan (n 69) 265.
[72] Fagan (n 69) 273.
[73] Fagan (n 69) 281.

Fagan's analysis has various strengths. Most importantly, it keeps systemic inequality at its centre while emphasising the absence of protections of class in a wide variety of legal sources. Fagan's assessment of the effectiveness of 'human rights law' is strikingly accurate: 'most people are becoming poorer while a tiny constituency of people become exponentially wealthier and more powerful'.[74] His analysis also identifies in clear terms how discriminatory attitudes and beliefs interact with, feed and compound broader structural problems, such as access to healthcare and exposure to the harms of the criminal justice system.

However, Fagan is wrong to argue so strongly against the law developing protections against classism. First, Fagan **oversimplifies the arguments that academics have made.** Referring to scholars such as Shreya Atrey, Sandra Fredman and Geraldine Van Bueren, he characterises their 'existing efforts' as '*almost* entirely concerned with the cause of antidiscrimination'.[75] The word 'almost' does a lot of work here. As I set out in earlier chapters, Atrey recognises the role of poverty in a whole range of discriminatory situations, individual *and* structural. Similarly, Fagan cites an article by Fredman on redistribution and recognition but without explaining how this supports his argument. In that article, Fredman does not argue for class as a protected ground in discrimination law. Even if Fredman had done so, her article nevertheless offers a detailed analysis of how redistribution and recognition should be understood as interacting and intersecting, not as strictly separate from each other.[76]

Throughout Fagan's arguments, he relies too much on certain qualifications. Note his key phrase: '[p]utting *all efforts* into combatting discrimination against the poor will, *by itself*, do little, if anything, to recognize and begin to remedy the systemic inequalities which the poor labor under'.[77] Read closely, Fagan is not actually arguing against protections against classism entirely. In his own qualified terms, he seems to accept that discrimination protections can be a part of the law's broader combatting of classism. In this book, I have repeatedly emphasised that discrimination-related rights only litigated in court disputes will not end classism. For this, we would need at least a framework of new entitlements and duties alongside broader doctrinal developments and abolitions. The proper answer to criticisms like those of Fagan is to use the law to protect against classism, *including by* introducing, developing, using and removing a whole variety of doctrinal tools to ensure that the law can address classism at its most specific and most general – in other words, at its most systemic. Since Fagan seems to accept that introducing class as a new 'protected characteristic' would not by itself address classism effectively, we may not disagree. A range

[74] Fagan (n 69) 268.

[75] Emphasis added.

[76] S Fredman, 'Redistribution and Recognition: Reconciling Inequalities' (2007) 23 *South African Journal of Human Rights* 214.

[77] Fagan (n 69) 273 (emphasis added).

of protections, of different kinds and focuses, is the only way to maximise the prospect of the law doing more good than harm.

Second, Fagan **incorrectly presents classism as if it were distinct or exclusive from systemic inequalities.** Fagan is right to be sceptical of what he calls 'recognition rights', which have symbolic value but little practical or transformative impact.[78] As quoted above, he is right to suggest that putting 'all efforts' into combatting discrimination against lower-class people will 'by itself' do little to address 'systemic inequalities'.[79] However, he falls into error when he assumes that 'discrimination' does little by way of recognition or remedy for systemic inequalities. It is not clear how his reference to recognition here relates to his characterisation of discrimination protections as mere 'recognition rights'. If we agree with Fagan that discrimination protections are 'recognition rights', why should we also accept that they do 'little, if anything, to recognize' systemic inequalities? On this view, isn't recognition the whole point?

That understanding of Fagan's argument might be unfair. Fagan may be suggesting that, though discrimination protections are 'recognition rights', they only recognise discrimination – not 'systemic inequalities'. This is clearly a stronger objection. Indeed, Fagan suggests that 'the main problem the poor are confronted by is the material and fateful condition of being poor in the first place rather than their own and others' attitudes towards the identity of the poor'.[80] Anti-discrimination is 'not the same' as equality.[81] But this is the biggest problem with Fagan's argument. He reduces classism to 'attitudes' and 'identity'. I have spent much of this book suggesting that classism *is* systemic. I argued the same in articles in 2020 and 2021 before Fagan's article was published in 2023. Classism involves attitudes and identity, yes, but it does not stop there. Classism involves layered and severe disadvantage, which is abiding, pervasive and substantial. Fagan's mistake is that he views classism – and, it seems, discrimination overall – as something that is not systemic.

This reading might be unfair to Fagan in another way. He may leave open the question of whether discrimination is systemic. The thrust of his argument may be that *the law relating to discrimination* does little to address systemic inequalities. Here, I agree with him. I have already set out in this book how the current law (concentrating on the UK) needs broader changes to address classism in its specific and general forms. Protections against it must not be confined to slogans on corporate banners or individualistic symbols. While classism can exist in a word or an instance, the law should never reduce the understanding of it to those words or instances alone. But we should still avoid falling into the familiar trap of conceiving classism as merely about attitudes and identities.

[78] Fagan (n 69) 273.
[79] Fagan (n 69) 273.
[80] Fagan (n 69) 273.
[81] Fagan (n 69) 276.

4.2. Harm by Complacency?

A final issue lurks beneath Fagan's arguments. It is the problem of complacency brought by legal protections. Put simply, formal protections against classism in the law might stop the urgency of the more radical solutions we need to end classism (including in its more structural aspects). The concern is that people would become complacent if we were to reform the law to protect against classism, which would do more harm than good to the long-term goal of ending classism. After successful reform to the law, people might assume that the goal has been met. Politicians might gesture towards the Equality Act and other areas of the law and ask: why do we need to make further reforms when we have such protections?

This is a difficult phenomenon to predict. It involves a challenging set of assumptions about the law's relationship with corporate culture and slogans, people's psychologies, politicians' self-advancing strategies and campaigners working in the area of societal inequalities. While these concerns are valid, they rest on precarious assumptions. They risk being simplistic and slightly patronising. For example, to assume that a 'protected characteristic' of class would cause scholars, lawmakers and campaigners to give up on the broader task of ending classism in all its forms rests on little evidence. People have not stopped fighting racism since race became protected by law. The assumption also puts very little faith in anti-classism, and any movement against discrimination, going forward.

Granted, it would be unsurprising if certain groups or organisations were to try to distort the law in this way or were to treat classism as purely an exercise in sloganeering and marketing. I have already accepted the possibilities of misuse and distortion of protections against classism. Yet these possibilities are simply not enough to assume that the law will lead to complacency overall and, therefore, do more harm than good. Their foundations are not solid enough to amount to a persuasive objection to legal reform. What they emphasise is the imperative to meet legal reform with political, cultural, social and economic changes throughout societies, which support the changes in the law and ensure that those changes realise their broadest, most transformative aspirations.

—

Doing more harm than good is a complex issue. It involves a variety of harms and goods, which can be practical and symbolic as well as conceptual. I have argued that there is a real danger of the law doing more harm than good in seeking to protect classism. It would be naïve to suggest otherwise, especially in the light of recent examples of politicians distorting the law. However, by maintaining an accurate understanding of classism and ensuring the best version of other features of the law (such as asymmetrical protection, 'positive action' and judicial scrutiny of supposed justification), we can minimise this danger.

I have repeatedly accepted that the law can only do so much good if it is not accompanied by bigger transformations in societies. Absent those transformations, even the most carefully and intelligently crafted legal system will be confined. This reveals the final topic that a book on classism and the law should address: limits of the law itself.

10

Limits of the Law

The priest: 'I pray for you all.'
The soldier: 'I defend you all.'
The peasant: 'I feed you all.'
The lawyer: 'I eat you all.'[1]

THESE FOUR 'TRUTHS' are translated from a French print made using the woodcut method, dating from 1860. The image of the peasant has him outside, tool in hand. The gowned lawyer (perhaps a prosecutor) stands inside, one hand grasping a pouch presumably made heavy by coins. It is no

[1] J Pellerin, *Les quatre vérités du siècle d'aujourd'hui* (Paris, Pellerin, 1860; copy Bibliothèque Nationale de France via Gallica). This copy has some damage to the lower right-hand side, but the full quartet reads: *je prie pour vous, je vous défends tous, je vous nourris tous, je vous mange tous.*

accident that the peasant and the lawyer make opposite statements. The peasant feeds the people; the lawyer devours them.

The presentation of lawyers as hungry for money – and willing to cannibalise for it – is grim but hardly new. On its surface, the print is just another example of widely held perceptions of the predatory nature of lawyers. Looking deeper, though, the print offers something more revealing for an analysis of classism and the law. The conflict between the activities of the peasant and the lawyer is direct. Lower-class people sustain society while lawyers feast on it. Although these images are stark and simplistic, they make a legitimate criticism about how the law tends to work. In legal systems where disputes often turn on the immense funds of those involved (subject to the crucial, yet precarious, exception of legal aid), classism and wealth seem inseparable from the law. If the law costs lots of money, if it benefits those who already have wealth, all the while being intent on making profit for lawyers, how do we use the law to end a form of discrimination closely connected with those same problems?

The print hints at criticism not only of the role of money in the law, but also of the culture of the law itself. Rather than nourish a society, the law feeds on its conflicts. If we return to the discussion about the restricted paradigm of equality and discrimination law (as in Chapter 7), we come across broadly drawn statutory frameworks that courts and other bodies interpret in limited, granular ways in the light of specific cases of conflict. As a result of those cases, courts and other bodies can offer some guidance for the bigger questions, but their existence relies on a market of conflict. Due to the law's reactionary nature and its individualised mechanisms, like litigation, it may not bring systemic change. All this amounts to a plausible argument that, in truth, the law is unlikely to provide the layered, transformative solutions needed to end classism.

For much of this book, I have argued that the law can be used to address classism. Now is the time to grapple with the law's limits. Drawing inspiration from the French print's presentation of lawyer and peasant, this chapter considers three themes about limits of the law when it comes to classism: (a) the roles that money occupies in the law; (b) the law as a conflict-led and formalistic mode; and (c) the importance of breaking the law.

1. MONEY AND THE LAW

1.1. Moneyed Content

Occasionally, I come across the assumption that the law grows like a tree in an undisturbed wood. That assumption may seem odd to experienced practitioners and academics, but it is a common one to notice in students when they first encounter the question of where law comes from. Despite that assumption, law is something people make. Law exists in complex webs of social, cultural, economic and political beliefs and practices; it did not simply spring from the ground one day.

This should remind us how central people's interests are in the creation and maintenance of *the* law in a society. Most often, powerful groups in society heavily influence the content and operation of the law, including by wielding their weapon of choice: money. The theme of money is one which appears in many forms in the academic literature. Marxist thought tends to criticise the law as a tool for the powerful classes, with one mainstream view holding that the law recognises only 'certain kinds of pressures' to be legitimate (such as threats of physical violence) and depends on 'bourgeois conceptions of rights', which in turn uphold the 'dominant ideology'.[2] Criminologists have observed that the law can be an expression of the interests of powerful, often upper-class, decision-makers.[3] Philosophers and economists have argued how courts, in theory there to protect against the excesses of capitalists, in fact play a part in capitalists' profit-making and markets.[4] Analysing the role of the law in the advent of capitalism, Michael Tigar and Madeleine Levy illustrate the law's ultimate concern with upper-class interests, including changes to the law of real property (replacing feudal ideas of tenure and use with the individualised, fundamental 'right to property'), as well as the difficult integration between the older common law (crafted to benefit the traditional upper class of nobility and aristocracy) and the newer principles from mercantile and maritime jurisdictions.[5] Quoting the US Supreme Court in *Griggs v Duke Power Co* (1971), Noah Zatz observes that it is not uncommon to find discrimination law rationalised in a similar way: the purpose is to remove 'artificial, arbitrary, and unnecessary barriers to employment' in order to make 'qualifications the controlling factor' and discriminatory criteria 'irrelevant'.[6]

A different example of money's influence can be found in the law relating to political elections and campaigns. The US provides a sharp example of the problems. Jacob Rowbottom analyses the role of private funding in US elections in the context of bigger questions of inequalities in wealth and democracy.[7] Rowbottom's central observations, published in 2010, hold true. As Rowbottom puts it, not only is there the general disconnection between the interests of wealthy people and poor people, but there is also a more direct clash when wealthy people use money 'to secure political influence'.[8] Having

[2] H Collins, *Marxism and Law* (Oxford, Oxford University Press, 1984) 50–51. For analysis of the different arguments at different stages of Marx's own work, see P Hirst, 'Marx and Engels on Law, Crime and Morality' in I Taylor, P Walton and J Young (eds), *Critical Criminology* (Abingdon, Routledge, 2012) 228.

[3] See, eg, A Sanders, R Young and M Burton, *Criminal Justice* (Oxford, Oxford University Press, 2010) 1–13.

[4] OO Táíwò, *Elite Capture* (London, Pluto Press, 2022) 57.

[5] ME Tigar and MR Levy, *Law and the Rise of Capitalism* (New York, Monthly Review Press, 2000) 174, 191–92.

[6] *Griggs v Duke Power Co* 401 US 424 (1971); N Zatz, 'Discrimination and Labour Law: Locating the Market in Maldistribution and Subordination' in H Collins, G Lester and V Mantouvalou (eds), *Philosophical Foundations of Labour Law* (Oxford, Oxford University Press, 2018) 156, 160–61.

[7] J Rowbottom, *Democracy Distorted* (Cambridge, Cambridge University Press, 2010).

[8] Rowbottom (n 7) 1.

set out these problems amid a general framework of the principle of political equality and related political freedoms (such as freedoms of expression and association), Rowbottom advances a range of arguments to support the view that using wealth to influence political decision-making and debate undermines the political equality properly viewed as central to democracy.[9] In recent years, high-profile figures have made firm criticisms of this state of affairs. In the words of Bernie Sanders, one of the most recognisable and straightforward critics of wealth in politics both in the US and worldwide, true democracy is 'not about billionaires being able to buy candidates and elections'.[10]

In the law, like in democratic politics, it may be that money, 'like water, has to go somewhere'.[11] On this view, money will always find a way into the law. Attempts to reform the role of money in the law evidently need great care, not least because of consequences we may not anticipate. The problem of money is not specific to classism, though. For example, discussing the rise of 'formal equality' for disabled people in certain states in the early twentieth-century US, Nate Holdren argues that the legal system's creation of greater costs for employers drove the perverse outcome of disabled people becoming 'increasingly excluded from employment', rather than, as had been the case, 'subordinated while included'.[12] The '[n]arrowly economic or financial concerns' combined with 'a new legal distribution of expenses' to create 'incentives to exclude disabled people from employment'. The law became more marketised and less open to other forms of valuation.[13]

While we should recognise the immensity of money's influence on the law, we should resist fatalism. First, as Rowbottom argues in the context of money in democratic politics, the law nevertheless 'has a symbolic role that shows a commitment to equality' and can define 'ethical standards'.[14] Even if upper-class interests seep into the law by the use of wealth, lawmakers can still play a part in disavowing them and promoting anti-discriminatory standards. Second, the inventiveness or pervasiveness of a bad thing does not mean that lawmakers should just give up on minimising it. A legal system that is much less influenced by wealth, but still unduly influenced by it to a degree, would have achieved something that many current legal systems have not. Small restrictions may nevertheless be improvements.

Scholars should bring these issues into focus. One step is simply to talk about them more openly, as people do in relation to democratic politics. It is rare to

[9] Rowbottom (n 7) ch 2, 245–47.

[10] See, eg, B Sanders, 'Post on Twitter' (4 June 2015); Associated Press, 'Sanders Unveils Plan to Overhaul Campaign Financing', *PBS News* (7 October 2019): www.pbs.org/newshour/politics/sanders-unveils-plan-to-overhaul-campaign-financing.

[11] S Issacharoff and P Karlan, 'The Hydraulics of Campaign Finance Reform' (1999) 77 *Texas Law Review* 1705, 1708, cited in Rowbottom (n 7) 6 n 19.

[12] N Holdren, *Injury Impoverished* (Cambridge, Cambridge University Press, 2020) 172.

[13] Holdren (n 12) 173.

[14] Rowbottom (n 7) 6.

hear express scrutiny of legislation purely on the basis that the legislation serves upper-class interests. In the UK Parliament, for example, one way to monitor, and restrict, the extent to which upper-class people use their money to influence the content of the law would be to establish a new parliamentary committee for scrutiny of legislation on that specific basis. There may be other options, such as an independent regulator, which could have express powers on this issue. However, even without 'hard' forms of power, parliamentary committees are one of the few parts of the legislative process in the UK widely regarded as worthwhile, effective in their scrutiny, and expertise-led (rather than simply a partisan mechanism).[15] One option could be a committee of special scrutiny during the legislative process. Its mandate could be targeted to assess proposed legislation with the issue of classist content in mind, tasked with a series of questions for every item:

1. Why has the legislation been introduced, *specifically the extent to which upper-class interest groups have driven it*?
2. What does the legislation seek to achieve, *specifically the extent to which it serves upper-class interests*?
3. How can the legislation be amended to improve it, *specifically by removing or significantly reducing the aspects that serve upper-class interests*?

Granted, the prospect of such a committee seems remote in the current landscape of UK party politics. Even if such a committee could be formed, much would depend on its dedication and effectiveness. Would it end up diluting the issues? Would it have the funding to ensure full and robust scrutiny? Would it retain influence on these contentious topics, particularly without direct powers to amend or quash legislation? Absent a bigger shift in party politics, the answer to those questions is likely to be negative for the time being.

1.2. Moneyed Enforcement

Money does not only influence the content of the law. It also influences the enforcement of the law. Litigation is a prime example. Litigation tends to be expensive. It is often marked by delay and sometimes by publicity. It can be scary for those involved and those close to them. It may require the revelation of material that parties desperately wish to avoid. It comes with a variety of risks. Outcomes are often understood in monetary terms: fines, damages, compensation, legal fees. Given the potential costs, harm to reputation and duties to disclose material, even the threat of litigation can be an effective way to apply pressure and achieve an aim. These steps may be taken for good reasons, such as by giving a warning to a public body that you intend to seek judicial review of its

[15] House of Commons Liaison Committee, *The Effectiveness and Influence of the Select Committee System (Fourth Report of Session 2017–19)* (September 2019) 105.

conduct.[16] They may also be taken for bad reasons, particularly by upper-class groups who have the money and connections to absorb the risks.

This is a familiar problem. Like the Ritz hotel, the law's justice has long been open to all.[17] It is also a growing problem. In recent years, the problem of upper-class misuse of legal actions seems to have become more prominent, at least in the media. Oligarchs and plutocrats have repeatedly used actions in the law of libel and data protection to guard their own interests.[18] Donald Trump's resorts to litigation – and threats of litigation – have been widely regarded as uses of his money and position primarily to intimidate, coerce and silence voices of opposition.[19] After various threats, his lawsuit against the BBC for billions in damages appeared in late 2025.[20] Although Trump is only the latest in a long line of powerful people (usually men) to approach the law in this way, his example as a head of state is perhaps the most egregious.[21] The situation reflects one distinction that Rowbottom draws when discussing democratic politics: wealth and democratic politics interact in terms of policies addressing economic resources (such as taxation) *as well as* in how 'economic resources can shape that political debate and impact on which speakers and arguments are heard'.[22] Framing Rowbottom's distinction in the context of litigation, upper-class interests and the law interact in terms of the content of specific legal doctrines (as discussed) *as well as* in how upper-class people use money to influence the enforcement of the law and how certain people realise entitlements and duties to the detriment of others.

Solving the problem of money through litigation is very difficult, even if you accept the real harm that upper-class people can do by using, or threatening, litigation. As Se-shauna Wheatle observes in the context of a common law constitutional right to access to justice, access to courts and tribunals is seen as crucial.[23] The freedom to litigate or otherwise have resort to the law is vitally important, especially when it guards against the overreaches of the nation state.[24] There may

[16] See, eg, Administrative Court, Pre-Action Protocol for Judicial Review 2021.

[17] R Cranston, *How Law Works: The Machinery and Impact of Civil Justice* (Oxford, Oxford University Press, 2006) 35.

[18] D Hooper, *Buying Silence: How Oligarchs, Corporations and Plutocrats Use the Law to Gag Their Critics* (London, Biteback, 2025) 139. Hooper sets out the idea of 'SLAPPs': strategic lawsuits against public participation.

[19] J Zirin, *Plaintiff in Chief: A Portrait of Donald Trump in 3500 Lawsuits* (New York, All Points Books, 2019) ch 5; R Abel, *How Autocrats Are Held Accountable: Resistance to Trump and Trumpism* (Abingdon, Routledge, 2025) esp ch 6; T Zick, 'Executive Watch: Trump's Weaponization of Civil Lawsuits' (18 March 2025), *Foundation for Individual Rights and Freedoms*; 'Donald Trump and His Long Histroy of Lawsuits against the Media', *Sky News* (15 November 2025): www.news.sky.com/story/donald-trump-and-his-long-history-of-lawsuits-against-the-media-13468501.

[20] C Hayes, A Walsh and I Aikman, 'BBC Says It Will Defend Trump Defamation Lawsuit over Panorama Speech Edit' (16 December 2025): www.bbc.co.uk/news/articles/cpvd81470v1o.

[21] Zirin (n 19) 188, 220; B Bennett, 'Silencing the Critics', *TIME Magazine* (2025) 206(11/12) 13–14.

[22] Rowbottom (n 7) 2. Rowbottom goes on to discuss other priorities given to wealthy people and groups in democratic politics, such as advantages in opportunities for political participation, shaping public opinion and agendas for political debate, and more general influences on people's chances to participate: 4–5.

[23] S Wheatle, 'Access to Justice: From Judicial Empowerment to Public Empowerment' in M Elliott and K Hughes (eds), *Common Law Constitutional Rights* (Oxford, Hart Publishing, 2020) 49, 50.

[24] Wheatle (n 23) 54–57.

be examples of upper-class people harnessing their resources in litigation, or in threatening litigation, in ways we commend. At the same time, like controls on the use of wealth in influencing political debate, controls on wealth in litigation may be needed to enhance people's autonomy as a whole by preventing the powerful from further skewing the legal system in their favour.[25]

On the issue of upper-class people wielding litigation as a weapon, there is unlikely much to be gained from the establishment of a regulator or a parliamentary committee. Plainly, a protective judiciary is essential: actions brought to advance upper-class interests could fall foul of some of the proposals I have outlined, perhaps especially an administrative law protection against classism. This is primarily an issue of a legitimate framework – the ability to seek adjudication, independent and impartial, in relation to disputes – operating within a deeply discriminatory society.

Some argue that the solution to a problem like this – which I understand as upper-class people hindering others' access to, and use of, the law – is to remove the market from the law entirely.[26] The harms of the market to equality, fair distribution and other values have been explored in a variety of contexts, from the media to healthcare.[27] On this view, instead of allowing individuals and organisations to use their own funds to pay for lawyers and fund legal actions, legal services would be publicly funded. This would seriously limit (if not wholly remove) the unfairness resulting from wealthy people litigating or using other legal mechanisms to entrench their power. However, the major problem with this approach is that, unless coupled with the broader removal of the market's influence, it could damage the law in various ways: decline in recruitment of talented candidates who view a career in the law, at least in part, as a way to achieve high salaries and financial stability (rather than the possibility of much lower salaries in publicly funded legal services); and dependence on states to fund services properly, which experience tells us states fail to do. While I support the removal of market forces from the law as a step in ending classism in the enforcement of the law, such a step must come with a wider reckoning of the market in society.

1.3. Moneyed Professions

Alongside the role of money in the law's content and enforcement, there is the role of money in *who* makes up the legal professions. Return to the 'truths' from the French print at the start of this chapter, which draw a series of sharp distinctions. In them, peasant and lawyer have no overlap. Perhaps to be expected in

[25] See, for an argument that controls on wealth may enhance audience autonomy by preventing one-sided debate in democratic politics, Rowbottom (n 7) 58–59, 61.

[26] See, eg, F Wilmot-Smith, *Equal Justice* (Cambridge, Massachusetts, Harvard University Press, 2019).

[27] See, eg, C Sunstein, *Democracy and the Problem of Free Speech* (New York, Free Press, 1993) 71 (on media); A Jani and A Papanikitas, '"More than My Job is Worth": Defensive Medicine and the Marketisation of Healthcare' in T Feiler, J Hordern and A Papanikitas (eds), *Marketisation, Ethics and Healthcare* (Abingdon, Routledge, 2018) 99 (on healthcare).

nineteenth-century France, the print assumes that a peasant cannot be a lawyer. By definition, they are distinct. Throughout this book, I have repeated that some of the reforms proposed would require a significant shift in societies, both in party politics and in more everyday contexts. One such shift concerns the legal professions. For a lawyer, the law is often a means to an end. That end is frequently a lawyer's own living. There is no injustice inherent in lawyers wanting money for their work. However, as with almost any profession in a society driven by the maximisation of production and profit, money is a relentless factor in the culture and structure of the legal professions.

This issue splits into two related topics. The first is more familiar and often understood as **a question of 'access'** to the legal professions. The problem with the legal professions is that they are still unrepresentative, partly because lower-class people struggle to enter them. Lack of access harms the professions overall, not least undermining the credibility of claims that talent rises to the top as well as de-legitimising the professions by indicating that they are elitist and outdated.[28]

Granted, lawyers are not peasants. They may represent lower-class people, but, like many people who act for lower-class people, they become dissociated from them. Lennard Davis's analysis of those who move 'between' classes helps us here.[29] For example, it is common to find classist advantage among judges and barristers. Research under the banner of 'socio-economic background' in 2024 showed that a much higher proportion of barristers attended private school than the general population.[30] It is not so simple as classist advantage fading on entry to traditionally prestigious professions, as Davis notes. Classism remains in the transition from practice to the judiciary. Applicants who did not have a parent with a university degree remained less likely to be recommended for judicial selection in 2025 compared with those who had one or two parents with a degree.[31] Those categorised as 'from a lower socio-economic background' (based on the occupation of the main household earner when the applicant was 14 years old) were also less likely to be recommended compared with those 'with a professional or intermediate socio-economic background'.[32] This information suggests that, even *within* the professions, classism persists. However, even lawyers who grew up lower-class and continue to experience some types of classism will have gained some advantage by virtue of their professional status. In

[28] Panel on Fair Access to the Professions, *Unleashing Aspiration: The Final Report of the Panel on Fair Access to the Professions* (2009) 45; E Holt-White and Others, *A Class Act: Social Mobility and the Creative Industries* (The Sutton Trust, 2024) 15.

[29] L Davis, *Poor Things* (Durham, North Carolina, Duke University Press, 2024) ch 3.

[30] Bar Standards Board, 'Diversity at the Bar 2024: A Summary of the Latest Available Diversity Data for the Bar' (January 2025) 26: www.barstandardsboard.org.uk/about-us/data-and-research/research-and-analysis.html.

[31] Ministry of Justice, 'Diversity of the Judiciary: Legal Professions, New Appointments and Current Post-Holders – 2025 Statistics' (23 July 2025): www.gov.uk/government/statistics/diversity-of-the-judiciary-2025-statistics/diversity-of-the-judiciary-legal-professions-new-appointments-and-current-post-holders-2025-statistics--2#fn:41.

[32] Ministry of Justice, 'Diversity of the Judiciary' (n 31).

some areas of the law, especially in commercial, corporate and chancery work, that advantage will come in the form of substantial economic capital.[33] In other areas of the law, the economic capital will be much less, but it will be enough to put lawyers firmly out of poverty and bring them certain cultural knowledge and social connections.

Although much is still to be done, the legal professions have developed initiatives targeted at improving access and representation. In England and Wales, perhaps the best known are the Kalisher Trust (which offers scholarships and internships to those who could not otherwise afford to become barristers) and Bridging the Bar (committed to 'increasing the equality of access to opportunities in the legal profession across all underrepresented groups').[34] Programmes like these, which have a clear focus on practical consequences, are vital in shifting the make-up of the professions. Beyond the limits of anti-classist reforms to the law, these kinds of programmes remain necessary to change the composition of the legal professions and to ensure that they do not persist as reserves for certain classes.

The second topic is more difficult and likely the cause of greater damage. It is **a question of the function of the professions.** Questions of 'representation' and 'access', while needed, are not enough in themselves to eradicate classism. To have a thoroughly anti-classist legal system, we must detach money from motivation and success. Those within the legal system should understand that their role ought not to be primarily to make money for their clients and themselves. Yet this is not the case. Often, money-chasing is a product of lawyers' self-interest. It can also be a more practical issue. Certain areas of the law – especially commercial and corporate law – are attractive to many. The salaries are high. Largely because of those salaries, the prestige is relatively high. The salaries buy a lifestyle, with its various accessories of status and success. They offer stability. Related to the prospect of future income and stability, many commercial firms offer sponsorship of visas, a fact which makes such a path the only realistic option for students who come from other countries to study in the UK and want to stay. Within the profession itself, the data reflect this. Commercial and chancery practices at the bar were recently estimated to have a median gross annual fee income of over £500,000 for men of 11 to 15 years' call and nearly £1,500,000 for men of King's Counsel. Those barristers fall easily within the top 0.5% of all income taxpayers in the UK.[35] Faced with these kinds of figures, wealth is intimately linked with many lawyers' professional lives. If a significant motivation for lawyers continues to be the

[33] See, eg, Bar Council, 'Gross Earnings by Sex and Practice Area at the Self-Employed Bar' (November 2025) 27: www.barcouncil.org.uk/resource/bar-council-gross-earnings-at-the-self-employed-bar-report-2025.html.

[34] Kalisher Trust, 'About' (undated): www.thekalishertrust.org/about; Bridging the Bar, 'About Us' (undated): https://bridgingthebar.org/about-us.

[35] Estimated by comparing the 2019 figures in Institute for Fiscal Studies (IFS), *IFS Briefing Note BN253* (London, IFS, 2019) with the 2025 data in Bar Council, 'Gross Earnings by Sex and Practice Area' (n 33) 27.

achievement of their own wealth alongside the wealth of others, there will always be a market for wealthy people and organisations to use the law to entrench classism.

The view may appear naïve, but I agree with those who say that lawyers have a duty to use the law to make the world better. There is a healthy tradition of this in the law, not least in the Haldane Society of Socialist Lawyers.[36] However, in the most important sense, anti-classism remains weak among judges, barristers and solicitors. We do not have groups equivalent to those concerned with anti-ableism, anti-racism, anti-misogyny, anti-homophobia and anti-transphobia.[37] The Judicial College's Equal Treatment Bench Book refers to 'social class' in the context of 'sex', and refers to poverty, educational attainment and literacy in the context of 'social exclusion' – but it still lacks any concept of classism.[38] Although we have judicial training and initiatives, we do not have a movement about classism in the professions. Yes, we may disagree on what using the law to make the world 'better' really involves. However, the fact of disagreement does not defeat the overarching point: that the pursuit of what is 'better' is why the law *really* matters. Yes, practitioners and academics should try to realise fair access to the professions, partly to ensure proper representation within them. Nevertheless, if dismantling classist barriers to access and representation simply means lower-class people going into the legal professions to make money for themselves and their clients, the mission of anti-classism flounders and money wins.

Perhaps predictably, then, I also have sympathy for the view that the legal professions should not be driven by money and the market. I am persuaded that free legal representation is much more likely to avoid the damages of marketisation and competitive incentives, which tend to undermine lower-class people's autonomy and worsen asymmetries in the quality of legal representation.[39] This is an especially pressing point in the context of the legal professions of England and Wales. Against the backdrop of Thatcherite marketisation and the further damage to legal aid by Blairite reforms, the professions have lost a significant degree of legitimacy and reputation. Meanwhile, financial support for those wishing to become lawyers remains, as Richard Abel put it over two decades ago, 'most available where least urgent': 'merit scholarships, pupillages and tenancies in prosperous commercial chambers [and] City traineeships'.[40] A presumption in favour of publicly funded legal representation would, in principle, be

[36] See, eg, Haldane Society of Socialist Lawyers, 'Our History' (5 November 2015): www.haldane.org/our-history.

[37] See, eg, the Association of Disabled Lawyers, Black Barristers' Network, the Inns of Court Alliance for Women, Women in the Law UK and FREEBAR.

[38] Judicial College, *Equal Treatment Bench Book* (2025) 105, 183–84.

[39] See, on the topic of the effects of marketisation in criminal legal aid, T Smith and E Johnston, 'Marketisation and Competition in Criminal Legal Aid: Implications for Access to Justice' in K Albertson, M Corcoran and J Phillips (eds), *Marketisation and Privatisation in Criminal Justice* (Bristol, Policy Press, 2020) 133, 140.

[40] R Abel, *English Lawyers between Market and State: The Politics of Professionalism* (Oxford, Oxford University Press, 2004) esp ch 11, 476.

compelling. It is a possible way that, at least according to the four truths of the French print at the start of this chapter, we can attempt to soften the disconnect between lawyer and peasant.

That said, the most effective solution to these professional questions is unlikely to be a 'legal' one, such as a single step of nationalising legal services. Concentrating on ending the asymmetries within the professions and the accumulation of wealth as the primary incentive of many lawyers must form part of the broader transformations that we need to end classism. Proposals to remove the market from legal services can only be effective if they come with more general transformations to end classism. Although the social and cultural factors (which heavily influence awareness of legal remedies and use of high-quality legal representation) will lose some force with the removal of the market from the law, they will persist so long as classism surrounds the legal system. As with the incorrect tendency to use the idea of 'labour' to detach workers from the rest of their lives, we should also take care not to use the law to detach lawyers from theirs.[41] The law always forms part of the society that makes it. The upper class will continue to deploy the law to their advantage, whether that is by lobbying parliamentarians, by bringing actions before courts or by filling the professions with their own. In short, so long as a society makes some people rich and other people poor, the law will not be an effective means to end classism.

2. LAW AS A MODE

2.1. Led by Conflict

While overlapping to a degree with the roles of money in the law, we should consider another limit of the law separately: the features of the law as a mode of reasoning and resolution of disputes. I do not mean the granular properties of the reasoning that judges and lawyers use, such as analogy or deduction.[42] Instead, I mean the features that tend to shape how the law encounters problems in societies and then understands those problems. One such feature is the conflict-led nature of the law.

Unlike some other systems in a society, the legal system thrives on conflict. This may explain why the French print labels the lawyer the devourer of all others. Such an observation is provocative as well as pessimistic. It seems a little unfair. The law, clearly, has some role in finding a better way to run a society (or else this book would have little purpose). Too much conflict may also be the

[41] K Polanyi, *The Great Transformation: The Political and Economic Origins of Our Times* (Boston, Massachusetts, Beacon Press, 2001) 75–76.

[42] See, for a more detailed analysis of the accuracy of understanding legal reasoning in terms of analogy and deduction, L Alexander and E Sherwin, *Demystifying Legal Reasoning* (Cambridge, Cambridge University Press, 2008).

law's undoing: if the law sustains itself on endless conflict, it is likely to become ineffective. People may start to view the law as lacking authority and legitimacy if it is not a reliable means of resolving disputes. However, certainly in common law systems, disputes are at the beating heart of the law. They challenge the parameters of statutes; they occupy national and international headlines; they generate major debates that span doctrinal, moral, political and economic issues. Conflict prompts legal actions, which come before the courts and can develop the law. Even if the law's relationship with conflict is not as simple or as sinister as the metaphor of the cannibalising lawyer suggests, conflict is nevertheless a fundamental part of it. Understood in this way, the lawyer in the print is not eating because of desire or greed. He eats because he knows little else.

My proposals in Chapters 5, 6 and 7 – in relation to classism in the Equality Act 2010, criminal and administrative law – put the issue of conflict before the courts at their centre. Granted, this may be a weakness of my focus. I have chosen to consider in detail protected grounds and principles as part of possible litigation and the development of them through the courts. It is correct that litigation and case law are only parts of any legal system. The law also implements reforms by schemes of primary and secondary legislation and wide-ranging regulatory frameworks, as well as softer forms of influence that shape the policies and programmes of organisations across societies. Traditional views of labour law, for instance, have often emphasised issues of the collective, like industrial action, rather than the individual. It is also correct that case law can bring broader changes and cause democratic bodies to take action, sometimes to undo a court's decision or to resolve a problem that a court has identified.[43]

However, pointing to these different aspects of the law should not obscure the conflict-led nature of much of the law, especially discrimination law. Zatz identifies this theme in the context of discrimination across areas of law, with the law commonly understanding discrimination as a 'personal wrong' and emphasising 'merit-based productivity considerations, not costly deviations from a market baseline'.[44] Given the centrality of conflict in the development of the law, the architecture of legal disputes is deeply influential. Lawyers are often dealing with a limited set of facts, a context that may be ill-suited to the broader questions that ending classism would entail. At its most extreme, the reactionary nature of litigation makes it difficult to imagine litigation leading the way.

[43] See, eg, for illustrations of these patterns across a range of jurisdictions, *Golak Nath v State of Punjab* (1967) 2 SCR 762 (on the role of Parliament of India in relation to the fundamental rights in the Indian Constitution, leading to the passing of the 24th Amendment in 1971); *Barker and Others v Corus (UK) Plc* [2006] UKHL 20 (on employers' contributions to the risk of mesothelioma, leading to the Compensation Act 2006); *Ledbetter v Goodyear Tire & Rubber Co* 550 US 618 (2007) (on discriminatory payment decisions under Title VII, leading to the Lilly Ledbetter Fair Pay Act 2009); *R (Reilly) v Secretary of State for Work and Pensions* [2013] UKSC 68 (on benefit regulations and leading to the Jobseekers (Back to Work Schemes) Act 2013).

[44] Zatz (n 6) 159–61.

Are judges likely to overhaul the rights and duties protecting capitalist ideas of private property, for example?

I will make this more concrete. Take the issue of class and a lack of formal education. Consider an example of a dispute that gets to a tribunal involving an employer and employee. The employer has implemented a policy that prohibits employees from using racist words in the workplace. One employee, who is white and lower-class, uses a racist word which they used throughout their childhood and did not think was racist. The employer dismisses the employee for racism. The employee brings a claim against the employer for indirect discrimination, using the new section 12A of the Equality Act 2010, proposed in Chapter 5 and refined in Chapter 9. The argument put forward is that, for lower-class people, like the employee, who have not had access to the same quality of formal education as their class-advantaged colleagues, the policy puts them at a substantial disadvantage by comparison with upper-class colleagues. The employer argues that no such disadvantage can be traced to lower-class people, pointing to examples of other lower-class employees who have adhered to the policy without issue. The employer argues that, in any event, the policy is justifiable because it is a proportionate means of achieving a legitimate aim.[45]

The tribunal must determine the issue. It is entirely possible for the members of the tribunal's panel to reject the claim because there is no reasonable basis to suppose that lower-class people struggle more than others to adhere to anti-racism policies. It is also possible for them to reject the claim on the basis that, even if it does have such an impact, it is a proportionate means of achieving a legitimate aim, which is stopping discriminatory language in the workplace and advancing equality in that context. However, it is possible to conceive a scenario in which the panel is persuaded by the (valid) points about the lower quality of formal education to which many lower-class people have access. There does also seem to be a plausible foundation in the research on this issue that lower-class people may not have had access to the social and cultural resources in order to know, with ease, what language might be acceptable. Of course, this depends on what lower-class people we mean: if a lower-class black person were to be subject to such a policy, they might be less likely to fall foul of it, perhaps because their experiences of classism and racism intertwine.

Imagine that the panel finds in favour of the employee. Imagine that the employer pursues an appeal and, at the highest levels, the courts uphold the panel's decision. This could lead to guidance issued by a huge range of organisations suggesting that such a policy might need to be removed, or at least amended, so as not to be classist. What effect would this decision have, then, on the law's effectiveness as a recourse for those who suffer racism?

[45] Equality Act 2010, s 19(2)(d).

In addition to raising familiar issues about the law doing more harm than good (considered in Chapter 9), this discussion indicates that the *mode* of litigation has significant restrictions when compared with other modes.[46] For instance, we might consider that issues of the kind raised in the example – such as inequalities of wealth and education – can be adequately addressed by different means. A government-wide consultation, or an inquiry or body dedicated to class issues, might offer a much wider frame, drawing on a variety of perspectives without the confines of the facts of the particular case or the limits of the constitutional role of the judiciary. Rather than being approached as a specific conflict between parties that a court or tribunal must resolve, the issue should perhaps be understood as a systemic one, considered from various perspectives with a range of input from experts and stakeholders. Evidently, litigation needs a place, in some form, in any use of the law to end classism. However, to ensure that the law can also contribute to ending the more structural senses of classism, the law must operate beyond the limits of litigation and in conjunction with other modes, such as political consultations and inquisitorial bodies.

2.2. Forms, Rights and Neatness

In the French print at the start of this chapter, there is smaller text beside the image of the lawyer. Partly obscured in this copy due to damage, a better-preserved copy of the print reveals an exchange between the lawyer and a 'client'. The lawyer offers a range of arguments to fend off criticisms from the client, who sees him as a predator. The lawyer argues that, unlike the soldier who has nothing 'in his own right', a lawyer's 'rights are always yours'. Whatever the self-interestedness of his arguments, the lawyer's speech taps into yet another common association with the law: the language and idea of 'rights'.

Much of legal analysis is formalistic like this. By that, I mean the tendency to frame issues in societies by the means of particular prescribed and accepted forms.[47] The law often talks in terms of specifically definable and enforceable rights and duties (though lawyers tend to use those terms only to refer to a sub-category of cases to which ordinary language applies them).[48] The main benefits of this framework have been thoroughly explored in the literature. 'Rights' appear to be democratic in their linguistic and conceptual individualism. A claim to have a 'right' may be expressive in a political, legal or moral sense ('I have a right to do something', 'we *all* have these rights') and of practical

[46] See, eg, J Clarke, 'A Public Policy Approach to Inequality' in S Atrey and S Fredman (eds), *Exponential Inequalities: Equality Law in Times of Crisis* (Oxford, Oxford University Press, 2023) 161, 169.

[47] I do not mean the strand of jurisprudence that refers to the discovery of legal rules and principles by a certain type of logic, which are then applied consistently to sets of facts, though there is a relationship between this approach and the forms that the law uses.

[48] J Raz, *The Morality of Freedom* (Oxford, Oxford University Press, 1988) 165.

consequence ('I can *enforce* my right against another who is under a related duty').[49]

The main weaknesses have also been dissected, especially in criticism of the individualist and ahistorical paradigm of the law.[50] 'Rights' prioritise abstract individuals in an established framework of entitlements, usually limited to those which a nation state permits. Those individuals are presumed to want certain things that are themselves controversial, rather than structural changes for the collective.[51] In their focus on specific claims, such rights reinforce the dominant ideology, especially when they form part of 'a package' that confines societies to the expansion of international organisations and 'regime change'.[52] The problem of the framing of rights folds into more general criticisms of liberalism, which formalises 'abstract rational identities' and requires 'the dissociation between socio-economic and political realms'.[53] 'Rights' are therefore made worse by the content that liberalism gives them: they present certain behaviour as valuable or even crucial.[54] Marxists have been at the forefront of these criticisms, identifying the law's rights ideology as a way to shape societies in accordance with capitalist objectives.[55]

Related to 'rights' and forms is the law's desire for neatness. A reference to neatness might sound trivial. Is the law really concerned with being tidy? The issue here, though, is more important than mere organisation. It is how legal reasoning tends to simulate aspects of societies. This feature of the law rests on sensible justifications. People should be able to agree on ideas that we use in the law. This is part of the clarity and certainty of the law, which are important to avoid arbitrariness and to enable people to plan their lives.[56] Lawyers should also be able to apply the ideas. Part of the challenge when trying to find a legal definition of class is the tension with the law's desire for neatness. Revisit my argument in Chapter 2 about the concerns around a legal definition of class. To develop a definition, I had to work within the confines of some features that make legal reasoning distinctive when compared with, for example, everyday language or the openness of other fields of scholarship like social theory. While

[49] Raz (n 48) 166–68.

[50] See, eg, A Shafi and I Nagdee, *Race to the Bottom: Reclaiming Antiracism* (London, Pluto Press, 2022) 118–21.

[51] M Sandel, *Liberalism and the Limits of Justice* (Cambridge, Cambridge University Press, 1982); J Lacroix and J Pranchère, *Human Rights on Trial: A Genealogy of the Critique of Human Rights* (Cambridge, Cambridge University Press, 2018) 43.

[52] R D'Souza, *What's Wrong with Rights?* (London, Pluto Press, 2018) 55, 206.

[53] N Dimitrijevic, 'Liberal Rights between Radical Democratic Critique and Liberal Failure' in A Sajó and R Uitz (eds), *Critical Essays on Human Rights Criticism* (The Hague, Eleven International, 2020) 81, 83.

[54] CFREU, Art 17 (on the right to property).

[55] See, for discussion of Marx's related criticism of the values wrapped in the right to (private) property, D Bensaïd and R Nichols, *The Dispossessed: Karl Marx's Debates on Wood Theft and the Right of the Poor* (Minneapolis, Minnesota, University of Minnesota Press, 2021) 10–11.

[56] J Raz, *The Authority of Law: Essays on Law and Morality* (Oxford, Oxford University Press, 1979) 214–17, 219–20.

there are many ideas in the law that are deeply contested and surrounded by vagueness, this is usually not seen as acceptable. Scholars tend to argue for one definition over the others. Although it has its virtues, this tendency is a limit of legal reasoning that may inhibit legal protections against classism. A sizeable portion of this book has been concerned with legal definitions and distinctions. Perhaps, though, the only accurate approach to issues like class, classism and discrimination is not neat but messy. Erik Olin Wright describes the messiness inherent in much of social scientific theory, including in his idea of 'contradictory class locations'.[57] By contrast, for some good reasons like certainty, the law is reluctant to concede that ideas *cannot* be reduced to familiar definitional statements. The law struggles to grapple with untidy, sprawling issues like class and classism.

One clear limit of my doctrinal proposals in this book is my reliance on legal forms such as 'rights' and 'duties'. With this in mind, it is essential to maintain an outward-looking approach. I have tried to do so by considering the more systemic focus of principles in administrative law (moving beyond specific cases of employment claims or criminal prosecutions, for instance) and by repeatedly emphasising broader changes that the law must make. Even critics of rights and the accompanying 'legalism' accept that we should not 'vacate the legal sphere, ignore repressive laws or concede rights to the political right'.[58] Despite the truth of all these limits, there is an opportunity here. Nuanced, pervasive ideas like class and classism remain difficult to fit into the tight formalistic moulds that the law tends to use. Instead of accepting the limits of the law's forms and merely seeking to cram classism into them, the topic of classism should add renewed force to criticisms of those forms and how we might, once more, try to innovate them.

3. THE IMPORTANCE OF BREAKING THE LAW

What if the law *is* the limit and the best way forward is to break it?

In the French print, the question of breaking the law is not expressed in the image or the words of the lawyer. The omission is telling. Much of legal practice and scholarship is limited to interpreting the law, determining where it begins and ends, what constitutes a violation of it, and if there is a (moral, prudential) duty to obey the law even in an unjust society.[59] Once more, this emphasis makes sense. Practitioners are usually seeking to give advice about what their clients should do to adhere to legal frameworks or to minimise the consequences

[57] EO Wright, *Understanding Class* (London, Verso, 2015) 155

[58] Shafi and Nagdee (n 50) 157.

[59] See, eg, RP Wolff, *In Defense of Anarchism* (London, University of California Press, 1998) 25–26; Raz (n 56) ch 12; N Gur, 'Actions, Attitudes, and the Obligation to Obey the Law' (2013) 21(3) *Journal of Political Philosophy* 326.

of violating them, such as by receiving a particular kind of sentence after a conviction or by keeping costs low after the failure of a claim. Scholars are often interested in what the law means and what it should be, such as what a statutory definition of discrimination means and how the law should address discrimination. Especially in the scholarship about discrimination law, it is rare to read about the importance of *breaking* the law. However, there is a strong tradition in the literature on class (especially by Marxists) emphasising not merely the importance of breaking the law, but the need to do so.[60] This is a controversial and important limit of the law that we should address squarely, both in practice and in theory.

3.1. Practical Importance of Breaking the Law

Although ideas of law-breaking, like 'revolutionary disobedience' and 'civil disobedience' are 'essentially contested' concepts, their practical importance is easy to recognise.[61] If the law is unjust, whether in general or in specific aspects, breaking it can be an important and even necessary part of changing it and the society beyond. Law-breaking has long been a tool open to those protesting against a range of injustices. Martin Luther King Jr is often cited for his remarks in 1963 about judging people 'not by the colour of their skin but by the content of their character'. As scholars including Ronald Turner and Erin Pineda argue, little mention tends to be made of the aspects of King's thought in which he calls for people to be prepared 'to go to jail together' in the struggle for freedom.[62] Yet King accepted that, alongside his more general rhetoric about integration, law-breaking would be a necessary part of the process of change.

The practical importance of law-breaking manifests in various ways.[63] It may express the injustice in question. High-profile cases draw attention to the cause. They may apply pressure to lawmakers to change the law in question. Even accumulations of small infractions, which gradually reflect the dissonance between the law and popular practices, can chip away at the authority and legitimacy of the law. After years of such infractions, the law in question may appear outdated and ineffectual, prompting reform. Given all these potential benefits, movements of many kinds (Marxist, anti-racist, trade unionist, feminist, environmentalist) have deployed law-breaking as a central technique to drive change.

[60] See, eg, Collins, *Marxism and the Law* (n 2) ch 6.

[61] W Scheuerman, 'Introduction: Why, Once Again, Civil Disobedience?' in W Scheuerman (ed), *The Cambridge Companion to Civil Disobedience* (Cambridge, Cambridge University Press, 2021) 1, 5, citing WB Gallie, 'Essentially Contested Concepts' (1955–1956) 56(1) *Proceedings of the Aristotelian Society* 167.

[62] R Turner, 'The Dangers of Misappropriation: Misusing Martin Luther King, Jr's Legacy to Prove the Colourblind Thesis' (1996) 2 *Michigan Journal of Race and Law* 101, 126, 129; E Pineda, 'Martin Luther King Jr and the Politics of Disobedient Civility' in Scheuerman (n 61) 56, 68.

[63] See, generally, E Chenoweth and M Stephan, *Why Civil Resistance Works: The Strategic Logic of Nonviolent Conflict* (New York, Columbia University Press, 2011).

There have been some examples of disobedience consistent with anti-classist aims. For instance, Juan Manuel Sánchez Gordillo, the mayor of Marinaleda in southern Spain, oversaw a series of 'raids' on supermarkets in the towns of Cádiz and Seville in 2012, which involved the taking of essential food and drink to give to food banks and lower-class people.[64] This served a practical end (to help people) and an expressive aim (to castigate austerity policies). The example of Sánchez Gordillo also shows that there may be a hazy line between legal and illegal action in some instances: the behaviour violated a number of criminal and civil legal rules, but Sánchez Gordillo was a mayor with immunity from prosecution and the town of Marinaleda had removed its police force.[65] Law-breaking, whether clearly defined or not, is often part of the movement that causes change, including by leading to reform of the law itself. It is not the law that brings this about but rather the symbolic, strategic and political impact of the law-breaking.

Although my analysis hopes that the law can have a positive role *among* broader transformations of societies to end classism, I have accepted that legal reform alone will not achieve this in practice. The topic of disobedience, though, requires me to recognise that the way forward might require law-breaking and not simply law reform. This may be controversial. Yet scholars from as diverse perspectives as Joseph Raz (writing in the tradition of liberal jurisprudence) and Andrew Sabl (writing on political realism) accept that there are moral, political and strategic reasons to choose disobedience over legal means.[66] For classism, the basic point is as follows. Transforming society to tackle classism will require a variety of strategies and assessments of competing risks, including short-term publicity that may undermine long-term goals. Reform through the law is one avenue and, I suggest, a necessary one. However, there is a reasonable argument that even considerable legal reform would be cumbersome, costly, biased towards upper-class interests, and inherently conservative. Actions like those of Sánchez Gordillo may be justifiable and unavoidable. If that is so, the quickest end to classism may come not by making law but by breaking it.

3.2. Theoretical Importance of Breaking the Law

The idea of breaking the law is not just a question of publicity or effectiveness in creating change. It is also a vital question for some theories of class change. To this end, I consider two thorny issues in the theory of breaking the

[64] D Hancox, 'The Spanish Robin Hood', *Guardian* (15 August 2012): www.theguardian.com/world/2012/aug/15/spanish-robin-hood-sanchez-gordillo.

[65] S McAdam, '"We Don't Want Police Here": Land of the Real-Life Robin Hood', *Salon* (25 July 2013): www.salon.com/2013/07/25/we_dont_want_police_here_land_of_the_real_life_robin_hood.

[66] Raz (n 56) 273–75; A Sabl, 'Realist Disobedience' in Scheuerman (n 61) 153, 162, 166.

law: (a) Marxist hostility to the law and the role of revolutionary politics; and (b) liberalism and civil disobedience.

A. *Marxism and Revolutionary Politics*

I have referred to Marxism at points throughout this book. Marxists in the main are cynical of the law, viewing it as an instrument of the dominant classes. Marxists do not typically think that revolution will be achieved, at least substantially, through the law. Without delving into an analysis of the complex relationship between ideas like the economic 'base' and 'superstructure' in Marxism (or the lack of a detailed theory of law in Marx's work), the law tends to be viewed as a corollary of the fundamental economic system that must be overthrown.[67]

The law plainly reflects class antagonisms alongside the interests of what Marx would call the bourgeois and traditionally aristocratic classes. But do not let the existence of limits become pessimism. Even among a range of scholars writing about Marxism, the law is not totally disregarded. Paul O'Connell, for instance, accepts that Marxist analyses should be 'attentive to the contradictions prevailing in given regimes, and the potential within them to advance the immediate interests of working class and other subaltern groups'.[68] I may prefer a Bourdieu-inspired approach to class over a Marxist one, but O'Connell's insight is still instructive. As he argues, the 'legal rhetoric and rules' that protect certain forms of power can also 'become [a] site of struggle for those who would dislodge that very power'.[69] The choice for legal scholarship is not, then, one or the other.

That said, lawyers must be alive to the contradictions and tensions within the law and other systems in societies that, together, serve upper-class interests. I have set out many in this book. That awareness will give academics and practitioners greater chance to craft reforms that help to undo classism, including as it manifests in capitalism, at its most systemic.

B. *Liberalism and Civil Disobedience*

Raz's work is well known in the field of jurisprudence. His writing about the rule of law, the authority of law, and the role of autonomy has influenced scholars in a range of legal and philosophical specialisms. Like most jurists, Raz's work never addresses classism in express terms, though it does explore freedom, equality, discrimination (briefly) and justice.[70] Raz considers one form of

[67] P O'Connell, 'Law, Marxism and Method' (2018) 16(2) *tripleC* 647, 653.
[68] O'Connell (n 67) 653.
[69] O'Connell (n 67) 653, citing A Chase, *Law and History* (New York, The New Press, 1997) 56 (internal quotation marks omitted).
[70] See, eg, Raz (n 48) 217–44.

breaking the law in a chapter in *The Authority of Law* (1979). While Raz accepts that civil disobedience may often be justified in a liberal society, he argues that there is no moral 'right' to it. By contrast, there may be such a right in an illiberal society.[71]

To make these arguments, Raz takes a wide definition of civil disobedience as politically motivated to lead to change in law or policy or to express protest at law or policy. He also takes a malleable definition of a 'liberal state': it is one that adequately recognises and protects in law every person's right to political participation in their society.[72] As liberal states by definition adequately protect this general right, people in such states have no right to break the law in the form of civil disobedience. To claim otherwise would mean that the state does not adequately protect political participation, which would make it an illiberal state. Raz accepts various practical consequences of his view, including that the lack of a right may make people more cautious about disobeying the law in this way.[73] One especially important theoretical consequence of his view is that civil disobedience is 'an exceptional political action' in a liberal state.[74]

An understanding of classism and the law may prompt us to rethink Raz's view. Should we cast civil disobedience as 'exceptional' when classism pervades the law? Analysis of classism reminds us how extensively the law of powerful 'liberal' states – which may well guard the right to political participation – still *needs* disobedience in order to criticise and change that law. In the UK in the twenty-first century, the law still permits, maintains and sometimes even requires a range of classist attitudes and beliefs in labour practices, 'wage fraud', poverty, huge differences in wealth and property, and systems of policing and imprisonment. One way to confront this is to challenge Raz's definition of a liberal state entirely. However, this is likely to be unhelpful: Raz concedes that his working definition is 'technical and narrow'. Those who support Raz's approach could simply reformulate his definition of a 'liberal' state, suggesting that a thoroughly classist state could not be liberal because it would inadequately protect political participation.[75]

The more fruitful challenge concentrates on the assumption that civil disobedience must hold some inherent virtue. In the 'political realist' tradition, Andrew Sabl argues that this assumption is misdirected. Rather than seeking a theory of civil disobedience that is 'self-sacrificing, principled, or public-spirited', theorists should emphasise civil disobedience as 'a form of *countervailing* power' against the power of the state.[76] Sabl uses the examples of racism and misogyny alongside, tellingly, 'wage theft': even if we disagree with each of them in

[71] Raz (n 56) ch 14.
[72] Raz (n 56) 263–64, 272–73.
[73] Raz (n 56) 275.
[74] Raz (n 56) 275.
[75] Raz (n 56) 273.
[76] Sabl (n 66) 162.

principle, that theoretical position tells us little about 'their actual (high) prevalence'.[77]

Sabl is not rejecting the pursuit of theoretical coherence in approaches to civil disobedience or to breaking the law in general. We should want theoretical coherence. But, partly because of his concerns and traditional analytic method, Raz minimises the '[s]trategic reasons' for political action that Sabl emphasises.[78] While Raz leaves open the possibility that civil disobedience can be justified in liberal states (which may have many 'bad' laws), this does not stop him from concluding that it is 'an exceptional action'. Yet the pervasiveness of classism *even in a liberal state* is not consistent with civil disobedience being 'exceptional'. If the law habitually feeds into classist ideology, such as by helping such a small portion of the population that lower-class people never experience systemic change, civil disobedience may need to be frequent and not 'exceptional'. While Raz's concern with the existence of a 'right' to civil disobedience is a valid subject in his abstract form of jurisprudence, it should not have led him to label civil disobedience 'exceptional'. Drawing on Sabl's argument, classism and 'wage theft' may be highly prevalent in a liberal state *even if* scholars like Raz reject them as wrong in principle.

A defender of Raz may suggest he is only using 'exceptional' in a technical sense: that civil disobedience is not covered by a general right to political action. In fact, by casting it as 'exceptional', he may preserve its transformative quality. An attempt 'to routinize it and make it a regular form of political action' may misconceive it.[79] Here, Raz seems to be making a claim about the idea of disobedience *and* a claim about the practice of it. The **first claim** is that civil disobedience is rightly understood as beyond both toleration and the general right to political action. However, putting civil disobedience in this theoretical space stops it from playing a big part in a theory of change in the legal systems of liberal states, whether by pushing at their limits or by contributing to the upending of them. By contrast, prioritising the countervailing power of civil disobedience (which Sabl recognises) keeps it *central* to the theory of change in even liberal societies, rather than leaving it exceptional or even peripheral.

The **second claim** seems to chime with Raz's discussion, earlier in the same chapter, of his view's practical consequences on people's reasoning. Raz accepts that people may be more cautious about civil disobedience if they do not have a 'right' to it, due to concerns about the justification for disobedience and the potential disadvantages of disobedience. These considerations 'should make one very reluctant to engage in it'.[80] Here, Raz's theory meets reality. Casting civil disobedience as 'exceptional', *even in theory*, puts too little emphasis on its potential in the strategy of change in reality. Perhaps because of his focus on the

[77] Sabl (n 66) 162.
[78] Sabl (n 66) 166.
[79] Raz (n 56) 275.
[80] Raz (n 56) 275.

theory of a 'right', Raz does not consider the power of routine civil disobedience from a strategic and anti-discriminatory perspective (as Sabl, for example, does). This is another indication that legal scholarship's tendency to prioritise questions of rights and forms may be misdirecting us. If classism is pervasive, including in the law, we must be open to the possibility that the *only* effective way to address it may be frequent, not 'exceptional', disobedience. In other words, to drive transformation against classism in the law and beyond, in theory and in practice, disobedience may have to be routine.

Struggling against classism may tell us that it is *often* important to break the law. This may seem a controversial conclusion for an academic book about the law. It is a conclusion I need to be careful with. Nevertheless, if the law, at least in some aspects, reflects the values societies endorse and enact, we may have to break the law to ensure the transformation of societies for the better. This process may be *necessary*, rather than merely important or exceptional, in the struggle to end classism in both the practice of change and the theories driving (and mapping) such change.

However, I reject the further suggestion that the necessity and frequency of law-breaking mean that the law has little role to play in fighting classism. Yes, we would need political, moral and social frameworks that are radically different from those that we have now. Yes, the law has its limits – and this chapter has explored three of them. But the law still has a role in a bigger process that, at the same time, may involve frequent law-breaking in order to draw publicity to causes or to challenge societies' norms, including by triggering further legal reform. It is likely that the law will need to be broken and, in the same breath, re-imagined in order to create societies without classism.

—

Read one way, this chapter is a negative way to bring this book to its later stages. Much of the chapter has drawn inspiration from an unpleasant depiction of a cannibalising lawyer in an old French print and suggested that, without thorough transformation of societies, the law can do little to end classism. While that view may seem gloomy, it is honest. There is little point idealising the law or abstracting the law from the societies that make it.

Yet confronting some limits of the law can offer opportunity and hope. Read another way, this chapter has been an attempt at ambition. The law can and should be part of the end of classism. It will only be so if we recognise its limits and push at them. Properly addressing classism must come with a reckoning about what the law does, too. If we fail to do this, lawyers may keep eating us all.

Conclusion: Challenges

According to some people, classism does not even exist. For others, it obscures capitalist structures and pressing systemic issues, distracting us with trivial questions about attitudes and prejudices. For others still, classism exists, but it is solely an economic problem or one too hazy to take practical steps to address. In most legal systems, it is either ignored or understood as separate from the topic of discrimination.

In this book, I have criticised these points of view. I have made various arguments as I have done so. The following are, in my view, the most important:

1. Class has been ignored or misunderstood in many contexts, especially in the law and scholarship concerning discrimination.
2. It is possible to understand class for the purposes of legal analysis, even though class is a contested idea and one often used in different senses.
3. Classism is properly understood as a form of discrimination. It is systemic. It can be personal and structural. Big inequalities relating to class, even if unintentional, are examples of classism.
4. Class should be a protected ground in the law concerning discrimination at work and the conduct of public bodies, as well as in the law concerning hate crime. A principle against classism should also form part of administrative law.
5. The law should be reformed in a variety of other ways to protect against classism, both by using doctrinal features that we already have and by removing some of them.
6. Proposals of reform to the law must, however, be conscious of whether they would do more harm than good to the overall aim of ending classism in societies.
7. Anti-classist work must also recognise limits of the law in market-driven societies and in the mode of legal decision-making. It should preserve the possibility that effective transformation of societies may require frequent breaking of the law, too.

I have explored some of the major issues with classism and how the law might be a way to address them. There are other important possibilities to pursue, such as a new legal framework for property relations. However, rather than continue what would be a more traditional type of conclusion, I want to keep the focus on what remains ahead, even if you accept my arguments about classism. In this book, I have concentrated on classism in doctrinal and theoretical contexts of the law. But the topic is closely connected with problems in our daily lives, politics and intellectual activities. It is worth, then, setting out some of the challenges that I have encountered while writing this book. They are likely to emerge for anyone doing work in this area in the future.

CHALLENGE 1: DISTINGUISHING DISCRIMINATIONS

One challenge is to have distinctive ideas of class and classism while recognising, and drawing insight from, other forms of discrimination. The task is to develop an idea of classism that is meaningful but not isolated. In part, this reflects the usual concern of intersectional analysis: people may fall into many groups and sealing those groups off from each other prioritises the most advantaged members of each group. In part, it reflects a different concern. The aim is to build an approach to class and classism that can stand alone, so that we can identify situations where classism is the only wrong at work. Classism has not yet been subject to the watering down that many corporate programmes and initiatives have inflicted on other forms of discrimination. This is a distortion that may soon come.

Yet classism also reminds us that other forms of discrimination have structural and economic aspects as well. Cloudy categories like 'socio-economic disadvantage' reinforce the perception that misogyny and racism, for instance, do not inherently entail such 'disadvantage'. This is where classism, understood not solely as personal but as systemic, emphasises that all forms of discrimination have these aspects. While class is not gender or race, it weaves into both. The challenge is to tell them apart and, in the same breath, understand how they layer and fuse.

CHALLENGE 2: CLASS ACROSS CONTINENTS

Because I have focused on the UK (with some references to other countries), my analysis is necessarily limited. Some aspects of it will translate well to class systems elsewhere. Some will not. India's caste system has features that remind me of race, class, religion and gender. Speaking of class in that kind of setting might not make sense. In different places across the world, an approach inspired by Bourdieu will lead to different markers and problems of class. That said, the framework in this book offers a basis for anyone who wants to use class and classism in their analysis of the law in any jurisdiction. The answers they get, however, may be very different.

CHALLENGE 3: FADING 'EQUALITY'

Equality is fading. That is both a fact of trends in many countries and a pattern in theory, with equality rejected in favour of 'equity', 'diversity' or 'fairness'. Yet inequality in what we have – the material things, the status indicators – influences people's perceptions of each other and hinders people's capacity to think of each other as equal in moral worth. If the law were somehow to give effect to the reforms I have proposed without broader societal transformations, a firmly anti-classist legal system would remain hindered. For all I have made of the law's potential, it would have limited influence in societies where the main institutions sustain perceptions of certain people as beneath the status of equals. Here, of course, equality should never be confused with sameness: it is the inherent equal worth that people have which is central, that difficult quality of humanity that we share, and not simplistic ideas of treating people the same or of equality (collapsed into sameness) 'versus' equity.

The development of the law against classism offers a challenge to those who call for societies to move away from the idea of equality. Classism, both legal and societal, is inherently unequal. It is unequal in social, cultural and economic terms. While there is inequality in what we have, while some people have immense resources and others do not, we will have classism in our beliefs, attitudes, practices and structures. Inequality and classism cannot be separated in theory or in practice. This argument about 'equality' and 'discrimination' may be a linguistic one, but I suspect that it is a more fundamental argument about our concepts. I have suggested that an anti-classist society would be an equal society because I do not think that there can be discrimination without inequality or inequality without discrimination.

Perhaps I have conflated the two. Perhaps I am completely wrong. Even so, the topic of classism seems to tap into this debate more than any other form of discrimination because of how often questions of class are reduced to questions of the distribution or allocation of resources. If classism indicates one way to show why *any* inequality in resources is always discriminatory, that might be – to use a well-worn word – radical.

CHALLENGE 4: LAW AND CAPITALISM

Michael Tigar summarises the tension between anti capitalism and legal analysis in the introduction to the second edition of his book with Madeleine Levy, *Law and the Rise of Capitalism*:

> I . . . rejected the insistence of many radicals and revolutionaries that 'law doesn't matter'. I thought such a view ahistorical. I noted that there were many ways in which legal ideology could be and was being deployed by dissident groups to advance their own agendas. . . .
>
> [E]ven after a fundamental social change, a new society would need rules and procedures to enhance justice—so that legal ideology was worth thinking about regardless of what you thought was going to happen.
>
> At the same time, I recognized that an alternative to capitalism was not going to be found in law books.[1]

[1] ME Tigar and MR Levy, *Law and the Rise of Capitalism* (New York, Monthly Review Press, 2000) 1.

Like Tigar, I have aimed to look at classism in relation to the law *and* to give a sense of the wider issues. I agree that there must be a rigorous analysis of legal doctrines in order to think about how protections against classism might take shape in the law. However, that analysis should not be for its own sake. It should also enable the law to contribute, as best as it can, to the broader transformations that will bring the end of classism. One of the major wrongs of capitalism is how classist it is. However, I remain of the view that classism can be meaningfully understood both inside capitalism and in other systems (such as feudalism and enslavement economies). If that is right, the end of classism requires – yet, crucially, may not be identical to – the end of capitalism.

CHALLENGE 5: PROCEDURE, COMPARATORS, EVIDENCE, LITIGATION

Another challenge is the detail of my proposals in legal practice. I have not delved into questions of procedure, evidence, comparators, courtroom strategy or funding. As with many reforms, the success of proposals concerning classism will depend on how well people draft them and use them in practice. A bad decision on the issue of a comparator, for example, could spell disaster for claims alleging classism. A judge could be on board with the concept of classism but struggle to make it out based on the evidence available. Litigants may struggle to find helpful statistics. These are all issues that need more time and thought than I have given them in this book. They may be technical, but they could be the most impactful of all.

CHALLENGE 6: NOT DENIGRATING CLASS

I have found one challenge to be not to denigrate class as if those at the top of class hierarchies are better, smarter or happier. Questions about 'capital' can sometimes, as Bourdieu found, suggest that lower-class people's culture is worse or lesser according to some patronising standard. They can also cement feelings of shame associated with lower-class people. This is not the point, though. There are parts of upper-class people's lives that we should never want. Lower-class communities do much better on certain issues than upper-class communities. At the same time, scholarship about classism and the law should recognise that *on the whole* the disadvantage is suffered by lower-class people.

Reconciling these issues is a familiar task for those who write about class. In the words of Jessica Taylor, describing an encounter with a condescending colleague: 'If I was honest with myself, I would say that I had hated my council estate, until that very moment, when all of a sudden, all I wanted to do was defend it.'[2] The challenge is to recognise the harms that people suffer without degrading things associated with being lower-class and without treating class advantage as the ultimate aspiration.

CHALLENGE 7: LANGUAGE

Academic books like this one tend to be written in technical and obscure language. I have tried to avoid too much of it in this book. Despite my efforts, the issues have sometimes been difficult to discuss in simpler ways. When language starts to become complicated, the topic of classism looms large. If part of classism is the denial to many of formal education, and academia is so often technical and communicated accordingly, the way we write about these issues is also a challenge. A lot of the research I have cited is dense. Because it is packed with thoughts, it is written in ways that some people may struggle to unpick. The challenge for those working in this area in the future will be to maintain the intellectual sophistication while never forgetting that, if we are not careful with our language, we will continue to exclude so many.

CHALLENGE 8: PROTECTING CLASS IN POLITICS

My hope is that, by understanding classism as a discriminatory thing, we can use it in politics. I mean this in the sense of political theory, yes, but also in the more practical setting of party politics. In recent years, some figures have noticed the potential connections between class and discrimination. Much has been written about the 'white working class', populism and democratic politics. However, though some well-known politicians have begun to include class in their rhetoric and their proposals, few have realised the importance of the idea of classism.

Recognising classism may help us to rectify some of the conceptual and rhetorical deficits in traditionally 'left-wing' politics. Classism does not accept that our concern with discrimination has been misplaced, as some now try to suggest. It does not bow to those who claim we should move away from anti-discrimination altogether or those who say that watery forms of 'identity politics' and 'politics of privilege' have undermined the political 'left'. Instead, it holds firmly to the importance of anti-discrimination in our approach to the world around us and in solving what is wrong in societies. Understanding classism may help us to fill gaps in popular understandings of discrimination, which have either minimised class or ignored it entirely.

In the law and beyond, we must not allow class to be taken and distorted by those who ultimately wish to preserve discriminatory hierarchies. This point

[2] J Taylor, *Underclass* (London, Constable, 2024) 11.

grows more urgent as some politicians peddle the 'lived, collective myth' of a white working-class history that has been lost.[3] Rooted in disadvantage and prioritising the most vulnerable, a credible understanding of classism is necessary to ensure that this does not happen.

—

As I finish writing this book, the law upholds classism. It does so by helping to sustain class hierarchies, by misunderstanding classism and, crucially, by ignoring it. There is much to be done. However, even with the most radical reforms, the law alone will not end classism. That would require the transformation of aspects of societies beyond the law and, beyond the scope of this book, debate about what exact form the transformation might take. The law may be part of the problem, but the real challenge is how to make it part of the solution.

[3] A Toscano, *Late Fascism* (London, Verso, 2023) 121, ch 5.

Bibliography

WORKS BY THE AUTHOR CITED

Benn A, 'The Big Gap in Discrimination Law: Class and the Equality Act 2010' (2020) 3(1) *Oxford Human Rights Hub Journal* 30

Benn A, 'Classism as Hate Crime: Proposing Class as a Protected Ground in Criminal Law' (2021) 10 *Criminal Law Review* 809

Benn A, 'Besting Monarchy: The Anti-Classism Argument' (2023) 94(3) *The Political Quarterly* 393

OTHER WORKS CITED

Abel R, *English Lawyers between Market and State: The Politics of Professionalism* (Oxford, Oxford University Press, 2004)

Abel R, *How Autocrats Are Held Accountable: Resistance to Trump and Trumpism* (Abingdon, Routledge, 2025)

Accent Bias Britain, *Accent Bias in Britain* (2020)

Advisory, Conciliation and Arbitration Service (Acas), *Equality, Diversity and Inclusion Policy Template* (Acas, 2022)

Akala, *Natives: Race & Class in the Ruins of Empire* (London, Two Roads, 2018)

Alexander L, 'What Makes Wrongful Discrimination Wrong?' (1991) 141(1) *University of Pennsylvania Law Review* 149

Alexander L and Sherwin E, *Demystifying Legal Reasoning* (Cambridge, Cambridge University Press, 2012)

Al-Hakim M, 'Making a Home for the Homeless in Hate Crime Legislation' (2015) 30(10) *Journal of Interpersonal Violence* 1755

Ashworth A, 'The Elasticity of Mens Rea' in P Tapper (ed), *Crime, Proof and Punishment: Essays in Memory of Sir Rupert Cross* (London, Butterworths, 1981)

Associated Press, 'Sanders Unveils Plan to Overhaul Campaign Financing' (PBS News, 7 October 2019)

Atrey S, 'The Intersectional Case of Poverty' (2018) 18(3) *Human Rights Law Review* 411

Atrey S and Fredman S (eds), *Exponential Inequalities: Equality Law in Times of Crisis* (Oxford, Oxford University Press, 2023)

Atrey S and Fredman S, 'Introduction' in S Atrey and S Fredman (eds), *Exponential Inequalities* (Oxford, Oxford University Press, 2023) 1

Bailey S (ed), *Cross on Local Government Law* (London, Sweet & Maxwell, 2025)

Bakalis C, 'The Victims of Hate Crime and the Principles of the Criminal Law' (2017) 37(4) *Legal Studies* 718

Baker T, 'Labour Is "Absolutely Not" Engaged in Class War, Prime Minister Keir Starmer Insists', *Sky News* (19 November 2024)

Ballinger C, *The House of Lords 1911–2011: A Century of Non-Reform* (London, Bloomsbury Publishing, 2014)

Bensaïd D and Nichols R, *The Dispossessed: Karl Marx's Debates on Wood Theft and the Right of the Poor* (Minneapolis, University of Minnesota Press, 2021)

Bar Standards Board (BSB), *Diversity at the Bar 2024: A Summary of the Latest Available Diversity Data for the Bar* (BSB, 2025)

BBC Radio, 'Ten Words that Prove You Aren't Posh', *BBC Radio 4* (undated)
Beaudry J, 'Theoretical Strategies to Define Disability' in A Cureton and D Wasserman (eds), *The Oxford Handbook of Philosophy and Disability* (Oxford, Oxford University Press, 2018) 3
Benito Sanchez JC, 'Towering Grenfell: Reflections around Socioeconomic Disadvantage in Antidiscrimination Law' (2019) 5(2) *Queen Mary Human Rights Review*
Bennett B, 'Silencing the Critics' (2025) 206(11/12) *TIME Magazine* 13
Bjorge E, *Domestic Application of the ECHR: Courts as Faithful Trustees* (Oxford, Oxford University Press, 2015)
Bogg A and Stanton-Ife J, 'Protecting the Vulnerable: Legality, Harm and Theft' (2003) 23(3) *Legal Studies* 402
Bogg A and others (eds), *Criminality at Work* (Oxford, Oxford University Press, 2020)
Boliver V and others, *Admissions in Context* (London, Sutton Trust, 2017)
Bottero W, 'Class Identities and the Identity of Class' (2004) 38(5) *Sociology* 985
Bourdieu P, *Distinction: A Social Critique of the Judgement of Taste* (R Nice trans, Abingdon, Routledge, 2010)
Bowen J, *The Russell Predictions on the Working Class, the National Debt, and the New Poor Law, Dissected* (London, Hatchard & Son, 1850)
Brandon A and Dingwall G, *Minority Ethnic Prisoners and the COVID-19 Lockdown* (Bristol, Bristol University Press, 2022)
British Social Attitudes, *British Social Attitudes 40: Overview* (London, National Centre for Social Research, 2023)
Brook O and others, 'Social Mobility and "Openness" in Creative Occupations since the 1970s' (2022) 57(4) *Sociology*
Brown F, 'Reform Candidate Quits and Backs Tories – as Nigel Farage Says Some BNP Supporters "Gravitate" to His Party', *Sky News* (30 June 2024)
Burke C, 'Bourdieu's Theory of Practice: Maintaining the Role of Capital' in J Thatcher and others (eds), *Bourdieu: The Next Generation* (Abingdon, Routledge, 2018) 8
Butler J, *The Force of Nonviolence: An Ethico-Political Bind* (London, Verso, 2020)
Campbell A, *Independent Review of Hate Crime Legislation in Scotland: Final Report* (Scottish Government, 2018)
Campbell B, 'Women: Not What They Bargained For', *Marxism Today* (1982)
Campbell M, 'Capping Motherhood: Equality-Based Analysis of UK Benefit Cap Cases' in M Davis, M Kjaerum and A Lyons (eds), *Research Handbook on Human Rights and Poverty* (Cheltenham, Edward Elgar Publishing, 2021) 156
Campbell M, 'The Proportionality of Economic Crisis' in S Atrey and S Fredman (eds), *Exponential Inequalities* (Oxford, Oxford University Press, 2023)
Campbell M, *Hanging in the Balance* (Oxford, Hart Publishing, 2025)
Carey H and others, *Getting In and Getting On: Class, Participation and Job Quality in the UK Creative Industries* (London, Creative Industries Policy and Evidence Centre, 2020)
Carey M and Davis MA, *The Meaning of Mariah Carey* (London, Macmillan, 2020)
Carter A and Swinney P, 'The UK Towns and Cities with the Highest and Lowest Wages', *BBC News* (2018)
CBS News, 'Clinton Links Campaign to Middle Class Fight' (12 June 2015)
Chakraborti N and Garland J, 'Reconceptualizing Hate Crime Victimization through the Lens of Vulnerability and "Difference"' (2012) 16(4) *Theoretical Criminology* 499
Chenoweth E and Stephan M, *Why Civil Resistance Works: The Strategic Logic of Nonviolent Conflict* (New York, Columbia University Press, 2011)
Cho S, Crenshaw K and McCall L, 'Toward a Field of Intersectionality Studies: Theory, Applications, and Praxis' (2013) 38(4) *Signs* 765
Clark G and Cummins N, *The Son Also Rises: Surnames and the History of Social Mobility* (Princeton, Princeton University Press, 2014)

Clark TN, 'The Debate over "Are Social Classes Dying?"' in TN Clark and SM Lipset (eds), *The Breakdown of Class Politics: A Debate on Post-Industrial Stratification* (London, Johns Hopkins University Press, 2001)
Clark TN, Lipset SM and Rempel M, 'The Declining Political Significance of Social Class' (1993) 8(3) *International Sociology*
Clark TN, Lipset SM and Rempel M, 'The Declining Political Significance of Social Class' in TN Clark and SM Lipset (eds), *The Breakdown of Class Politics: A Debate on Post-Industrial Stratification* (Baltimore, Maryland, Johns Hopkins University Press, 2001) 77
Clarke J, 'A Public Policy Approach to Inequality' in Atrey and Fredman (eds), *Exponential Inequalities* (Oxford, Oxford University Press, 2023) 161
Cohen J, *Class and Civil Society: The Limits of Marxian Critical Theory* (Amherst, Massachusetts, University of Massachusetts Press, 1982)
Collins H, *Marxism and Law* (Oxford, Oxford University Press, 1984)
Communities and Local Government, *Discrimination Law Review: A Framework for Fairness* (Communities and Local Government, 2007)
Compass Group UK, 'Diversity, Equity & Inclusion Policy' (Compass Group UK, 2024)
Constitution of the Republic of Cyprus, Art 28(2)
Cook M, 'Split Scenes in Leeds' in M Cook and Al Oram, *Queer beyond London* (Manchester, Manchester University Press, 2017) 42
Craig P, *Administrative Law* (London, Sweet & Maxwell, 2021)
Craig-Henderson K and Sloan LR, 'After the Hate: Helping Psychologists Help Victims of Racist Hate Crime' (2003) 10(4) *Clinical Psychology: Science and Practice* 481
Cranston R, *How Law Works: The Machinery and Impact of Civil Justice* (Oxford, Oxford University Press, 2006)
Creative Access, *Class Barriers & Accent Bias Report* (2023)
Crenshaw K, 'Demarginalizing the Intersection of Race and Sex' (1989) 1 *University of Chicago Legal Forum* 139
Crenshaw K, 'Mapping the Margins: Intersectionality, Identity Politics, and Violence against Women of Color' (1993) 43 *Stanford Law Review* 1241
Crompton R, *Class and Stratification* (Cambridge, Polity Press, 2008)
Crossley N, 'Social Class' in M Grenfell (ed), *Pierre Bourdieu: Key Concepts* (Abingdon, Routledge, 2012) 85
Cunneen C, *Defund the Police* (Bristol, Policy Press, 2023)
Curtice J, *British Social Attitudes 40: Overview – Secular or Cyclical?* (National Centre for Social Research, 2023)
D'Souza R, *What's Wrong with Rights?* (London, Pluto Press, 2018)
Daly P, *A Theory of Deference in Administrative Law* (Cambridge, Cambridge University Press, 2012)
Davis AY, *Are Prisons Obsolete?* (New York, Seven Stories Press, 2003)
Davis AY, *Gender, Race and Class* (London, Penguin, 2019)
Davis C, Walsh A and Aikman I, 'BBC Says It Will Defend Trump Defamation Lawsuit over Panorama Speech Edit', *BBC News* (16 December 2025)
Davis L, *Poor Things* (Durham, North Carolina, Duke University Press, 2024)
de Castella T, 'The Evolution of the Middle Class', *BBC News* (16 January 2014)
De Oliveira B, *Austerity* (Abingdon, Routledge, 2025)
Dean A, 'Shake that Class', *Town and Country Magazine* (6 September 2023)
Delaney E, 'Searching for Constitutional Meaning in Institutional Design: the Debate over Judicial Appointments in the United Kingdom' (2016) 14(3) *International Journal of Constitutional Design* 752
Department for Communities and Local Government, *Discrimination Law Review: A Framework for Fairness: Proposals for a Single Equality Bill for Great Britain* (Department for Communities and Local Government, 2007)

Difford D, 'How Do Britons Define Social Class? (YouGov, 12 December 2024)

Diman JL, *The Alienation of the Educated Class from Politics* (Cambridge, Massachusetts, Riverside Press, 1876)

Dimitrijevic N, 'Liberal Rights between Radical Democratic Critique and Liberal Failure' in A Sajó and R Uitz (eds), *Critical Essays on Human Rights Criticism* (The Hague, Eleven International, 2020)

Dokoupil T, 'The Devil Deryl Dedmon', *Irish Examiner* (2012)

Donald A, Leach P and Puddephatt A, *Developing a Bill of Rights in the UK* (Equality and Human Rights Commission, 2010)

Donnelly M and Gamsu S, *Home and Away* (The Sutton Trust, 2018)

Dwyer P, 'The Neurodiversity Approach(es): What Are They and What Do They Mean for Researchers?' (2022) 66(2) *Human Development* 73

Earnshaw S, *The Attitudes of the Working Class Towards Religion* (Sheffield, Leader & Sons, 1870)

Eidelson B, 'Treating People as Individuals' in D Hellman and S Moreau (eds), *Philosophical Foundations of Discrimination Law* (Oxford, Oxford University Press, 2013) 203

Eidelson B, *Discrimination as Disrespect* (Oxford, Oxford University Press, 2015)

Elliott M, 'A "Principle" of Consistency? The Doctrinal Configuration of the Law of Judicial Review' (2018) 77 *Cambridge Law Journal* 444

Elson D and Sharples M, 'Addressing Intersecting Inequalities through Alternative Economic Strategies' in S Atrey and S Fredman (eds), *Exponential Inequalities* (Oxford, Oxford University Press, 2023)

Engels F, *The Condition of the Working-Class in England in 1844* (FK Wischnewetzky trans, London, Penguin, 2009)

Equalities Review, *Fairness and Freedom: The Final Report of the Equalities Review* (Cabinet Office, 2007)

Equality and Human Rights Commission (EHRC), *Guidance: What Equality Law Means for You as an Education Provider – Further and Higher Education* (EHRC, 2014)

Equality and Human Rights Commission (EHRC), *Equality Act 2010 Code of Practice: Employment* (EHRC, 2019)

Eribon D, *Returning to Reims* (M Lucey trans, London, Penguin, 2019)

Evans D, 'Is the Working Class Back?', *New Socialist* (2024)

Evans G, 'Class Voting: From Premature Obituary to Reasoned Appraisal' in G Evans (ed), *The End of Class Politics?* (Oxford, Oxford University Press, 1999)

Evans Peterman D, 'Socioeconomic Status Discrimination' (2018) 104(7) *Virginia Law Review* 1283

Equality Trust, 'Socio-Economic Duty Briefing' (26 June 2025)

Fagan A, 'Taking Class Seriously' (2023) 45 *Human Rights Quarterly* 260

FBI, 'Ten Sentenced in Hate Crime Case' (FBI News, 2015)

Fikfak V, 'Protecting Human Rights in Austerity Claims in the UK' (2016) 8(2) *Hague Journal on the Rule of Law* 205

Forbes, 'Gerald Cavendish Grosvenor & Family – Profile' (2016)

Fordham M, *Judicial Review Handbook* (London, Hart Publishing, 2012)

Fraser N, 'Social Justice in the Age of Identity Politics: Redistribution, Recognition, and Participation' (1996) *The Tanner Lectures on Human Values*

Fredman S, 'Recognition and Redistribution: Reconciling Inequalities' (2007) 23 *South African Journal on Human Rights* 214

Fredman S, 'The Potential and Limits of an Equal Rights Paradigm in Addressing Poverty' (2011) 22 *Stellenbosch Law Review* 566

Fredman S, 'Substantive Equality Revisited' (2016) 14(3) *International Journal of Constitutional Law* 712

Fredman S, 'Direct and Indirect Discrimination: Is There Still a Divide' in H Collins and T Khaitan (eds), *Foundations of Indirect Discrimination Law* (Oxford, Hart Publishing, 2018) 31

Fredman S, *Discrimination Law* (Oxford, Oxford University Press, 2022)

Gallie WB, 'Essentially Contested Concepts' (1955–1956) 56(1) *Proceedings of the Aristotelian Society* 167

Ganty S, 'Poverty as Misrecognition: What Role for Antidiscrimination Law in Europe'? (2021) 21 *Human Rights Law Review* 962

Garcia Rodriguez D, Smith EW and Brawner J, *Evaluating the Socio-Economic Duty in Scotland and Wales* (Equality and Human Rights Commission, 2021)

Gelsthorpe L, 'Working with Women Offenders in the Community: A View from England and Wales' in R Sheehan, G McIvor and C Trotter (eds), *Working with Women in the Community* (Abingdon, Routledge, 2010) 127

Given-Wilson C, *The English Nobility in the Late Middle Ages* (Abingdon, Routledge, 1996)

Goldthorpe J, 'Class and Politics in Advanced Industrial Societies' in TN Clark and SM Lipset (eds), *The Breakdown of Class Politics* (London, Johns Hopkins University Press, 2001)

Goodall K, 'Conceptualising "Racism" in Criminal Law' (2013) 33(2) *Legal Studies* 215

Graham S, 'I'm Just a Mixed-Race Kid from Flats in Kirkby', *BBC News* (15 September 2025)

Green S, 'Wage Theft as a Legal Concept' in A Bogg and others (eds), *Criminality at Work* (Oxford, Oxford University Press, 2020)

Green T, 'The Future of Systemic Disparate Treatment Law' (2011) 32(2) *Berkeley Journal of Employment & Labour Law* 395

Green T, *Discrimination Laundering: The Rise of Organizational Innocence and the Crisis of Equal Opportunity Law* (Cambridge, Cambridge University Press, 2017)

Grenfell M (ed), *Pierre Bourdieu: Key Concepts* (Abingdon, Routledge, 2014)

Grusky D and Weeden K, 'Decomposition without Death: A Research Agenda for a New Class Analysis' (2001) 44(3) *Acta Sociologica*

Grzymala-Busse A, 'Failure of Europe's Mainstream Parties' (2019) 30(4) *Journal of Democracy* 35

Guardian, 'The Guardian View on Class Politics: It Has Faded as Culture Wars Have Risen' (5 February 2025)

Haldane Society of Socialist Lawyers (HSSL), 'Our History' (HSSL, 2015)

Hall S, 'New Ethnicities' in D Morley and K Chen (eds), *Stuart Hall: Critical Dialogues in Cultural Studies* (Abingdon, Routledge, 1996) 442

Halliday J, 'Durham University Withdraws Fresher's Place over "Abhorrent" Online Posts', *Guardian* (2020)

Hancock A, *An Intellectual History of Intersectionality* (Oxford, Oxford University Press, 2016)

Hancox D, 'The Spanish Robin Hood', *Guardian* (2012)

Hare J, *Autism Is Not a Disease* (London, Verso, 2024)

Harris A, 'Race and Essentialism in Feminist Legal Theory' (1990) 42(3) *Stanford Law Review*

Hart HLA, *Law, Liberty and Morality* (Oxford, Oxford University Press, 1963)

Hayes C, Walsh A and Aikman I, 'BBC Says It Will Defend Trump Defamation Lawsuit over Panorama Speech Edit', *BBC News* (2025)

Hayward M, '"Outlandish Superfluities": Luxury and Clothing in Scottish and English Sumptuary Law from the Fourteenth to the Seventeenth Century' in G Riello and U Rublack (eds), *The Right to Dress* (Cambridge, Cambridge University Press, 2019) 96

Hazeldine T, *The Northern Question* (London, Verso, 2021)

Hellman D, *When Is Discrimination Wrong?* (Cambridge MA, Harvard University Press, 2008)

Hellman D, 'Equality and Unconstitutional Discrimination' in D Hellman and S Moreau (eds), *Philosophical Foundations of Discrimination Law* (Oxford, Oxford University Press, 2013) 51

Hepple B, Coussey M and Choudhury T, *Equality: A New Framework* (Oxford, Hart Publishing, 2000)

Hepple B, 'The New Single Equality Act in Britain' (2010) 5 *The Equal Rights Review* 11

Herring J, *Criminal Law: Text, Cases, and Materials* (Oxford, Oxford University Press, 2020)

Hirst P, 'Marx and Engels on Law, Crime and Morality' in I Taylor, P Walton and J Young (eds), *Critical Criminology* (Abingdon, Routledge, 2012)

Hobbs A and Ogden FJ, *A Guide to the Representation of the People Act, 1918* (London, Butterworth & Co, 1918)
Hobsbawm E, 'Identity Politics and the Left' (1996) I/217 *New Left Review*
Holdren N, *Injury Impoverished* (Cambridge, Cambridge University Press, 2020)
Hooper D, *Buying Silence: How Oligarchs, Corporations and Plutocrats Use the Law to Gag Their Critics* (London, Biteback, 2025)
House of Commons Liaison Committee, *The Effectiveness and Influence of the Select Committee System* (London, House of Commons, 2019)
Hout M, Brooks C and Manza J, 'The Persistence of Classes in Post-Industrial Societies' (1993) 8(3) *International Sociology*
IDS Employment Law Handbooks, vol 5 (London, Informa Law, current edn)
Ignatieff M, *The Rights Revolution* (Toronto, Anansi Press, 2000)
Independent Advisory Group on Hate Crime, Prejudice and Community Cohesion, *Report of the Independent Advisory Group on Hate Crime, Prejudice and Community Cohesion* (London, Home Office, 2016)
Independent Schools Council (ISC), *ISC Census and Annual Report 2025* (ISC, 2025)
Institute of Health Equity, *England's Widening Health Gap: Local Places Falling Behind* (Institute of Health Equity, 2024)
Institute of Race Relations, 'BME Statistics on Poverty and Deprivation' (Institute of Race Relations, 2024)
Isaac M and Lopez A, *The Socio-Economic Duty in Action: Case Studies from England and Wales* (Just Fair, 2023)
Isenberg N, *White Trash: The 400-Year Untold History of Class in America* (London, Atlantic Books, 2017)
Issacharoff S and Karlan P, 'The Hydraulics of Campaign Finance Reform' (1999) 77 *Texas Law Review* 1705
Ivanovic M, Byrd D and Morelock J (eds), *The Many Faces of Populism: Perspectives from Critical Theory and Beyond* (Boston, Massachusetts, Brill, 2024)
Jacobs E, 'Class Is the Missing Link in Employers' Diversity Drives', *Financial Times* (2 June 2025)
Jani A and Papanikitas A, '"More Than My Job Is Worth": Defensive Medicine and the Marketisation of Healthcare' in T Feiler, J Hordern and A Papanikitas (eds), *Marketisation, Ethics and Healthcare* (Abingdon, Routledge, 2018)
Jenkins SP, *Changing Fortunes: Income Mobility and Poverty Dynamics in Britain* (Oxford, Oxford University Press, 2011)
Johns N and others, 'When Is Positive Action Not Positive Action? Exploring the Conceptual Meaning and Implications of the Tie-Break Criterion in the UK Equality Act 2010' (2013) 33(1) *Equality, Diversity and Inclusion: An International Journal* 97
Johnson S, *A Dictionary of the English Language* (London, 1773 edn)
Jones N, 'How a Nepo Baby Is Born' (*Vulture*, 2019)
Jones T, Newburn T and Reiner R, 'Policing and the Police' in A Liebling, S Maruna and L McAra (eds), *The Oxford Handbook of Criminology* (Oxford, Oxford University Press, 2017)
Joyce J, *Odd Men Out* (Manchester, Manchester University Press, 2022)
Kalisher Trust, 'About' (London, Kalisher Trust, undated)
Kaplan J, 'Against Economy–Culture Dualism: An Argument from Raced Economies' (2021) 22(3) *Feminist Theory* 381
Keenan R, 'Why Scottish Students at Edinburgh University Want More Support to Counter Classism', *Guardian* (26 December 2024)
Keens O, 'I Will Never Stop Admiring the Ways Posh People Pretend They're Not Posh', *Independent* (3 May 2023)
Kelly J, 'Asbo: The End of an Era', *BBC News* (2012)
Khaitan T, *A Theory of Anti-Discrimination Law* (Oxford, Oxford University Press, 2015)
Krugman P, 'How the "Unforced Error" of Austerity Wrecked Britain', *Guardian* (28 June 2025)

Krutikova S and others, *Intergenerational Mobility in the UK* (London, Institute for Financial Studies, 2023)

Labour Party, *Change: Labour Party Manifesto 2024* (Labour Party, 2024)

Lacey N, 'Responsibility and Modernity in Criminal Law' (2001) 9 *Journal of Political Philosophy* 249

Lacey N and Zedner L, 'Criminalization: Historical, Legal and Criminological Perspectives' in A Liebling, S Maruna and L McAra (eds), *The Oxford Handbook of Criminology* (Oxford, Oxford University Press, 2023)

Lacroix J and Pranchère J, *Human Rights on Trial: A Genealogy of the Critique of Human Rights* (Cambridge, Cambridge University Press, 2018)

Lane J, *Pierre Bourdieu: A Critical Introduction* (London, Pluto Press, 2000)

Lapp A and Lapp D, 'Stigmatizing the Working Class' (2015) *Institute for Family Studies*

Law Commission, *Hate Crime Laws: Consultation Paper No 250* (Law Commission, 2020)

Law Commission, *Hate Crime Laws: Final Report* (Law Commission, 2021)

Lawrence J, *On the Nobility of the British Gentry* (London, 1840)

Lee H, 'Consequentialist Theories of Punishment' in MC Altman (ed), *The Palgrave Handbook on the Philosophy of Punishment* (Basingstoke, Palgrave Macmillan, 2023)

Liebling A, Maruna S and McAra L (eds), *The Oxford Handbook of Criminology* (Oxford, Oxford University Press, 2023)

Lind M, *The New Class War* (London, Penguin, 2020)

Littler J, *Against Meritocracy* (Abingdon, Routledge, 2017)

Lorde A, 'Scratching the Surface: Some Notes on Barriers to Women and Loving' in A Lorde (ed), *Sister Outsider* (London, Penguin, 2007) 35

MacCormack G, 'Dolus, Culpa, Custodia and Diligentia: Criteria of Liability or Content of Obligatio' (1994) 22 *Index* 189

MacKinnon C, 'Substantive Equality Revisited: A Reply to Sandra Fredman' (2016) 14(3) *International Journal of Constitutional Law* 739

Marchesi A, 'Voting Patterns in Western European Countries' (2022) 4 *Frontiers in Political Science* 1

Marx K, *Capital: A Critique of Political Economy, Volume I* (B Fowkes trans, Penguin, 1990)

Marx K, 'The General Formula for Capital' in D McLellan (ed), *Capital: An Abridged Edition* (Oxford, Oxford University Press, 2008) 93

Marx K and Engels F, *The Communist Manifesto* (D McLellan trans, Oxford, Oxford University Press, 2008)

McAdam S, '"We Don't Want Police Here": Land of the Real-Life Robin Hood', *Salon* (2013)

McColgan A, *Discrimination, Equality and the Law* (Oxford, Hart Publishing, 2014)

McGaughey E, *A Casebook on Labour Law* (Oxford, Hart Publishing, 2018)

Meiksins Wood E, *The Origin of Capitalism: A Longer View* (London, Verso, 2017)

Meiksins Wood E, *The Retreat from Class: A New True Socialism* (London, Verso, 1986)

Menendez E, '"Freshers Planned Competition to Have Sex with the Poorest Female They Could Find"', *Metro* (2020)

Meyer S, *Affirmative Action* (New York, Rosen Publishing, 2018)

Ministry of Justice, *Diversity of the Judiciary: Legal Professions, New Appointments and Current Post-Holders – 2025 Statistics* (Ministry of Justice, 2025)

Moore R, 'Capital' in M Grenfell (ed), *Pierre Bourdieu: Key Concepts* (Abingdon, Routledge, 2012) 98

Moreau S, *Faces of Inequality: A Theory of Wrongful Discrimination* (Oxford, Oxford University Press, 2020)

Moyn S, *Not Enough* (Cambridge, Massachusetts, Harvard University Press, 2018)

Muehlenhoff H, *EU Democracy Promotion and Governmentality* (Abingdon, Routledge, 2019)

Nagesh A, 'What Is It Like to Be Repeatedly Asked Where You Are From?', *BBC News* (1 December 2022)

Nairn T, *Enchanted Glass* (London, Verso, 2011)

Nayak A, '"Chavs, Chavettes and Pramface Girls": Teenage Mothers, Marginalised Young Men and the Management of Stigma' (2014) 17(10) *Journal of Youth Studies* 1330

Neiman S, *Left ≠ Woke* (Cambridge, Polity Press, 2023)

O'Cinneide C, 'Equality: A Core Common Law Principle, or "Mere" Rationality?' in M Elliott and K Hughes (eds), *Common Law Constitutional Rights* (Oxford, Hart Publishing, 2020)

O'Connell P, 'Law, Marxism and Method' (2018) 16(2) *tripleC* 647

Ordover N, *American Eugenics* (Minneapolis, University of Minnesota Press, 2003)

Ortner S, 'Identities: The Hidden Life of Class' (1998) 54(1) *Journal of Anthropological Research*

Pakulski J and Waters M, *The Death of Class* (London, Sage, 1996)

Pakulski J and Waters M, 'The Reshaping and Dissolution of Social Class in Advanced Society' (1996) 25(5) *Theory and Society*

Panel on Fair Access to the Professions, *Unleashing Aspiration: The Final Report of the Panel on Fair Access to the Professions* (Cabinet Office, 2009)

Payne G, *The New Social Mobility* (Cambridge, Polity Press, 2017)

Pellerin J, *Les quatre vérités du siècle d'aujourd'hui* (Paris, Pellerin, 1860)

Petersen H, 'The Ambivalence of the "Macpherson Moment": Re-examining the Political Struggles Following the Racist Murder of Stephen Lawrence' (2025) 6 *Ethnic and Racial Studies* 1

Phipps A, 'Rape and Respectability: Ideas about Sexual Violence and Social Class' (2009) 43(4) *Sociology* 667

Piekarska A, 'Challenging the Rule of Law Universalism: Why Marxist Legal Thought Still Matters' (2023) 34 *Law and Critique* 269

Piketty T, *A Brief History of Equality* (Cambridge, Massachusetts, Harvard University Press, 2021)

Pillay A, 'Reinventing Reasonableness: The Adjudication of Social and Economic Rights in South Africa, India and the United Kingdom' (doctoral thesis, University College London, 2011)

Polanyi K, *The Great Transformation: The Political and Economic Origins of Our Times* (Boston, Beacon Press, 2001)

Potter H, *Intersectionality and Criminology* (Abingdon, Routledge, 2015)

Raz J, *The Authority of Law* (Oxford, Oxford University Press, 1979)

Raz J, *The Morality of Freedom* (Oxford, Oxford University Press, 1988)

Red Lion Chambers, 'Equality & Diversity' (undated)

Rise Associates, *Class Ceiling: A Review of Working Class Participation in the Arts Across Greater Manchester* (Rise Associates, January 2026)

Robinson A, Ruebain D and Uppal S (eds), *Blackstone's Guide to the Equality Act 2010* (Oxford, Oxford University Press, 2021)

Robinson C, *Black Marxism* (London, Penguin, 2021)

Rodrigues da Silva R, *The Anglo-Saxon Elite: Northumbrian Society in the Long Eighth Century* (Amsterdam, Amsterdam University Press, 2021)

Roessel J, Schoel C and Stahlberg D, 'Modern Notions of Accent-ism: Findings, Conceptualizations, and Implications for Interventions and Research on Nonnative Accents' (2019) 39(1) *Journal of Language and Social Psychology* 87

Rowbottom J, *Democracy Distorted* (Cambridge, Cambridge University Press, 2010)

Runnymede Trust and Centre for Labour and Social Studies, *We Are Ghosts: Race, Class and Institutional Prejudice* (London, Runnymede Trust, 2019)

Sabl A, 'Realist Disobedience' in W Scheuerman (ed), *The Cambridge Companion to Civil Disobedience* (Cambridge, Cambridge University Press, 2021)

Sandel M, *Liberalism and the Limits of Justice* (Cambridge, Cambridge University Press, 1982)

Sanders A, Young R and Burton M, *Criminal Justice* (Oxford, Oxford University Press, 2010)

Sanders B and Albanese F, *It's No Life at All: Rough Sleepers' Experience of Violence and Abuse on the Streets of England and Wales* (Crisis, 2016)

Savage M, *Social Class in the 21st Century* (London, Pelican, 2015)

Scheuerman W, 'Introduction: Why, Once Again, Civil Disobedience?' in W Scheuerman (ed), *The Cambridge Companion to Civil Disobedience* (Cambridge, Cambridge University Press, 2021) 1

Schweppe J and Haynes A, 'You Can't Have One without the Other: "Gender" in Hate Crime Legislation' (2020) *Criminal Law Review* 148
Scottish Government, *Fairer Scotland Duty: Guidance for Public Bodies* (Scottish Government, 2022)
Sen A, 'Conceptualizing and Measuring Poverty' in DB Grusky and R Kanbur (eds), *Poverty and Inequality* (Stanford, Stanford University Press, 2006)
Shafi A and Nagdee I, *Race to the Bottom: Reclaiming Antiracism* (London, Pluto Press, 2022)
Sheinman H, 'Two Faces of Discrimination' in Hellman and Moreau (eds), *Philosophical Foundations of Discrimination Law* (Oxford, Oxford University Press, 2013) 28
Shin P, 'Is There a Unitary Concept of Discrimination?' in D Hellman and S Moreau (eds), *Philosophical Foundations of Discrimination Law* (Oxford, Oxford University Press, 2013) 164
Shrubsole G, *Who Owns England?* (London, Profile Books, 2019)
Siegel R, 'From Colorblindness to Antibalkanization: An Emerging Ground of Decision in Race Equality Cases' (2011) 120(6) *Yale Law Journal* 1278
Singh H, 'Class, Caste, and Social Stratification in India: Weberian Legacy' in E Hank and others (eds), *The Oxford Handbook of Max Weber* (Oxford, Oxford University Press, 2019) 393
Simon R, *Gramsci's Political Thought* (London, Lawrence & Wishart, 2015)
Smith D, *The Fall and Rise of the English Upper Class* (Manchester, Manchester University Press, 2023)
Smith T and Johnston E, 'Marketisation and Competition in Criminal Legal Aid: Implications for Access to Justice' in K Albertson, M Corcoran and J Phillips (eds), *Marketisation and Privatisation in Criminal Justice* (Bristol, Policy Press, 2020)
Social Mobility Commission, *Innovation Generation: Next Steps for Social Mobility* (Social Mobility Commission, 2024)
Sprague A, Raub A and Heymann J, 'Protecting Workers' Equal Rights during Crisis and Recovery' in S Atrey and S Fredman (eds), *Exponential Inequalities* (Oxford, Oxford University Press, 2023)
Standing G, *The Precariat: The New Dangerous Class* (London, Bloomsbury Publishing, 2011)
Steenson G, *After Marx, Before Lenin* (London, University of Pittsburgh Press, 1991)
Steinbach S, *Understanding the Victorians* (Abingdon, Routledge, 2012)
Sunstein C, *Democracy and the Problem of Free Speech* (New York, Free Press, 1993)
Swinney P and Carter A, 'The UK Towns and Cities Worse Off than 100 Years Ago', *BBC News* (2018)
Symeonidou S, 'Researching Disability Politics: Beyond the Social Model and Back Again' in S Symeonidou and K Beauchamp-Pryor (eds), *Purpose, Process and Future Direction of Disability Research* (Rotterdam, SensePublishers, 2013)
Táíwò OO, *Elite Capture* (London, Pluto Press, 2022)
Taylor J, *Underclass* (London, Constable, 2024)
Thatcher M, 'Don't Undo My Work', *Newsweek* (27 April 1992)
Thompson EP, *The Making of the English Working Class* (London, Penguin, 1968)
Tigar ME and Levy MR, *Law and the Rise of Capitalism* (New York, Monthly Review Press, 2000)
Torche F and Corvalan A, 'Estimating Intergenerational Mobility with Grouped Data: A Critique of Clark's The Son Also Rises' (2018) 47(4) *Sociological Methods & Research* 787
Toscano A, *Late Fascism* (London, Verso, 2023)
Trades Union Congress (TUC), 'Housing, Homelessness and Young LGBT People' (TUC, 2016)
Trades Union Congress (TUC), *Building Working Class Power* (TUC, 2019)
Trades Union Congress (TUC), *Making Work Pay: Call for Evidence on Unpaid Internships* (TUC, 2025)
Turner R, 'The Dangers of Misappropriation: Misusing Martin Luther King Jr's Legacy to Prove the Colourblind Thesis' (1996) 2 *Michigan Journal of Race and Law* 101
Tyler I, '"Chav Mum Chav Scum": Class Disgust in Contemporary Britain' (2008) 8(1) *Feminist Media Studies* 17

UK Government, *New Opportunities: Fair Chances for the Future* (London, HMSO, 2009) Cm 7533
Ulmschneider K, 'Settlement Hierarchy' in D Hinton (ed), *The Oxford Handbook of Anglo-Saxon Archaeology* (Oxford, Oxford University Press, 2011)
UN Administrative Committee on Coordination, *Statement of Commitment for Action to Eradicate Poverty* (New York, United Nations, 1998)
Vitale AS, *The End of Policing* (London, Verso, 2018)
Walby S, Armstrong J and Humphreys L, *Review of Equality Statistics* (Government Equalities Office, 2008)
Walkerdine V, 'What's Class Got to Do with It?' (2020) 42(1) *Discourse: Studies in the Cultural Politics of Education* 60
Wallace D, 'Reading "Race" in Bourdieu? Examining Black Cultural Capital among Black Caribbean Youth in South London' (2016) 51(5) *Sociology*
Walters M, Owusu-Bempah A and Wietlizka S, 'Hate Crime and the "Justice Gap": The Case for Law Reform' (2018) *Criminal Law Review* 961
Weber M, *Economy and Society: An Outline of Interpretive Sociology* (G Roth and C Wittich trans, Berkeley, California, University of California Press, 1978) vol 2
Weldon D, *Two Hundred Years of Muddling Through* (London, Abacus, 2022)
Wenxi Z, *Property and Justice: A Trend towards Marxist Political Philosophy* (Abingdon, Routledge, 2023)
Williams C, *Police Control Systems in Britain, 1775–1975* (Manchester, Manchester University Press, 2014)
Williams G and Baker D, *Treatise of Criminal Law* (London, Sweet & Maxwell, 2021)
Wilmot-Smith F, *Equal Justice* (Cambridge, Harvard University Press, 2019)
Wintemute R, *Sexual Orientation and Human Rights* (Oxford, Oxford University Press, 1993)
Wheatle S, 'Access to Justice: From Judicial Empowerment to Public Empowerment' in M Elliott and K Hughes (eds), *Common Law Constitutional Rights* (Oxford, Hart Publishing, 2020)
Wolf J, *Turning Points: The Memoirs of Lord Wolfenden* (London, Bodley Head, 1976)
Wolf M, *The Crisis of Democratic Capitalism* (London, Penguin Random House, 2023)
Wolff RP, *In Defense of Anarchism* (London, University of California Press, 1998)
Women's Budget Group, *The Female Face of Poverty* (London, Women's Budget Group, 2018)
Woodcock A, 'Angela Rayner: "Basic Instinct" Slur Was Not Only Sexist but Classist', *Independent* (26 April 2022)
Woods EM, *The Origin of Capitalism* (London, Verso, 2020)
Woolf H and others (eds), *De Smith's Judicial Review* (London, Sweet & Maxwell, 2024)
Wray M and Newitz A, 'Introduction' in M Wray and A Newitz (eds), *White Trash: Race and Class in America* (Abingdon, Routledge, 1997) 1
Wright EO, *Understanding Class* (London, Verso, 2015)
Wright EO, *Classes* (London, Verso, 2023)
Yoshino K, *Covering* (New York, Random House, 2006)
Zatz N, 'Discrimination and Labour Law: Locating the Market in Maldistribution and Subordination' in H Collins, G Lester and V Mantouvalou (eds), *Philosophical Foundations of Labour Law* (Oxford, Oxford University Press, 2018)
Zick T, 'Executive Watch: Trump's Weaponization of Civil Lawsuits' (Foundation for Individual Rights and Freedoms, 2025)
Zipursky B, 'Philosophy of Private Law' in J Coleman and S Shapiro (eds), *The Oxford Handbook of Jurisprudence and Philosophy of Law* (Oxford, Oxford University Press, 2004) 623
Zirin J, *Plaintiff in Chief: A Portrait of Donald Trump in 3,500 Lawsuits* (New York, All Points Books, 2019)

Index

www.ingramcontent.com/pod-product-compliance
Ingram Content Group UK Ltd.
Pitfield, Milton Keynes, MK11 3LW, UK
UKHW021619111026
476453UK00009B/176

9 781509 986644